Asian Faces
of Jesus

FAITH AND CULTURES SERIES
An Orbis Series on Contextualizing Gospel and Church
General Editor: Robert J. Schreiter, C.PP.S.

The *Faith and Cultures Series* deals with questions that arise as Christian faith attempts to respond to its new global reality. For centuries Christianity and the church were identified with European cultures. Although the roots of Christian tradition lie deep in Semitic cultures and Africa, and although Asian influences on it are well documented, that original diversity was widely forgotten as the church took shape in the West.

Today, as the churches of the Americas, Asia, and Africa take their place alongside older churches of Mediterranean and North Atlantic cultures, they claim their right to express Christian faith in their own idioms, thought patterns, and cultures. To provide a forum for better understanding this situation, the Orbis *Faith and Cultures Series* publishes books that illuminate the range of questions that arise from this global challenge.

Orbis and the *Faith and Cultures Series* General Editor invite the submission of manuscripts on relevant topics.

Also in the Series

Faces of Jesus in Africa, Robert J. Schreiter, C.PP.S., Editor
Hispanic Devotional Piety, C. Gilbert Romero
African Theology in Its Social Context, Bénézet Bujo
Models of Contextual Theology, Stephen B. Bevans

FAITH AND CULTURES SERIES

Asian Faces of Jesus

Edited by
R. S. Sugirtharajah

ORBIS BOOKS

Maryknoll, New York 10545

Second Printing, January 1995

Acknowledgment is gratefully extended for permission to reprint the following:

"The Crucified Christ Challenges Human Power" from *Your Kingdom Come: Mission Perspectives* by Kosuke Koyama, copyright 1990 and reprinted with permission of the World Council of Churches Publications, Geneva, Switzerland. "Confessing Christ in the Islamic Context" by Alexander J. Malik, "Jesus and People (Minjung)" by Byung Mu Ahn, "The Hope of Liberation Lessens Man's Inhumanity: A Contribution to Dialogue at Village Level" by Michael Rodrigo, and "Jesus Christ in Popular Piety in the Philippines" by Salvador T. Martinez, reprinted with permission of the Christian Conference of Asia, G/F, 2 Jordan Road, Kowloon, Hong Kong from *CTC Bulletin* 7 (1987). "Jesus and Krishna" by Ovey N. Mohammed (© 1990) and "Christ and Buddha" by Seiichi Yagi (© 1991) are reprinted with permission of the *Journal of Ecumenical Studies*, Temple University, Philadelphia PA 19122. "Oh, Jesus, Here with Us!" from *Jesus, the Crucified People*. Copyright © 1990 by C. S. Song. Reprinted by permission of The Crossroad Publishing Company.

Published by Orbis Books, Maryknoll, NY 10545
Published in Britain by SCM Press Ltd, 26-30 Tottenham Road,
London N1 4BZ

Manufactured in the United States of America

Library of Congress Cataloging-in-Publication Data

Asian faces of Jesus / edited by R. S. Sugirtharajah.
    p. cm. — (Faith and cultures series)
    Includes bibliographical references
    ISBN 0-88344-833-5 (pbk.)
    1. Jesus Christ—History of doctrines—20th century. 2. Jesus
Christ—Person and offices. 3. Asia—Religious life and customs.
I. Sugirtharajah, R. S. (Rasiah S.) II. Series.
BT198.A845 1993
232'.095—dc20   93-536
                                                   CIP

Contents

Part One
JESUS AMID OTHER ASIAN WAYS, TRUTHS AND LIGHTS

Part Two
NEWLY EMERGING PROFILES OF JESUS AMID ASIA'S POVERTY AND RELIGIOUS PLURALITY

Acknowledgments

Though at the outset producing a book may seem to be a solitary effort of a single person, in reality it is a corporate work of a number of people. I am deeply grateful to the following for their generous help: Robert Ellsberg, the editor-in-chief of Orbis Books for asking me to edit this collection; Susan Perry, editor, for her invaluable comments and, more important, for her friendship and support; Daniel O'Connor, a former colleague with whom I first discussed the idea of this volume, for the encouragement which enabled me to carry this project through; the Central Library staff at the Selly Oak Colleges — Meline Nielsen, Louise Wilmot, Katrina Youster, Griselda Lartey, Gill Davies and Willemina Morton — who continue to welcome me in spite of my outrageous demands; all the copyright holders of the articles for their kind permission to reprint them; and finally, my wife, Sharada, whose presence persistently reminds me that there are many paths to the Truth.

R. S. Sugirtharajah

Prologue and Perspective

R. S. SUGIRTHARAJAH

I would like to begin by juxtaposing three statements:
"Are you the one who is to come, or should we expect someone else?"
(John the Baptist).
"Where is he?" (the Magi).
"Sir, we wish to see Jesus" (Greek worshipers at Jerusalem).
These three statements from the gospels broadly encapsulate the anxiety, mood and expectations of Asian Christians about Jesus. The first one expresses the misgivings and the ambivalence Asian Christians feel about the images of Jesus that were first introduced to them by foreign missionaries and still dominate their thinking. The other two epitomize the urge and the desire of Asian Christians to discover for themselves the evidence of his presence in their midst and his place among other savior figures of the region. This volume of essays attempts to illustrate the range and diversity of their discoveries in recent times.

Images of Jesus imported to Asia are so wrapped up in various christological configurations that one often overlooks the fact that Jesus came from Asia, or to be precise, west Asia. He was raised up and engaged in brief public activity in and around the villages and cities of Palestine. Early on, there was a strong eastward thrust of the Jesus movement through Persia and Afghanistan, but much of this was disintegrating by the time of the emergence of Islam, leaving only a struggling minority in South India and a church precariously established in China and ultimately disappearing in a welter of civil war. It took nearly fifteen hundred years before the rest of Asia could feel the full impact of Jesus' personality and the significance of his teaching. It was only through the Western missionary irruption beginning in the fifteenth century that the rest of Asia came to know Jesus.

When Jesus made his belated second visit to the eastern part of Asia, he did not come as a Galilean sage showing solidarity with its seers and wisdom teachers. Rather, he came as an alien in his own home territory, and more tellingly, as a clannish god of the *parangis* (a term used by Indians during the salad days of the empire to describe the foreigners) sanctioning the subjugation of the peoples of Asia and their cultures. He was projected and paraded as the totem symbol of the privileged and the powerful.

Since then there have been a number of attempts by Asian Christians to counteract this imperial, supremacist and absolutist understanding of Jesus. The essays assembled here are examples of such an enterprise. These discourses try to re-Asianize and refashion Jesus on Asian terms to meet the contextual needs of Asian peoples.

These discourses were produced under a wide variety of cultural, political, social and ecclesiastical contexts in Asia. They encapsulate the richness and the diversity of the continent and its people. In spite of their divergent situations, one can identify certain common elements highlighted by them.

1. They fiercely resist any attempts to apply well-established and timeless truth about Jesus. For them, all understandings of Jesus arise out of particular contextual needs. They demonstrate that perceptions of Jesus are not validated by their timeless claims or by their dogmatic soundness, but by the appropriateness of the image to a specific context. In other words, Asian Christians continue the hermeneutical tradition created by early Christian writers. Like the producers of early Christian literature, these essayists try to respond to the questions, priorities and needs of their community. For them, christological discourse is not only about the explication of preconceived notions about Jesus or an exercise in the application of time-tested truths, but also about their experience of struggle and survival. Thus they are consciously aware that their understandings of Jesus do not represent a neutral, detached, value-free enterprise. Nor are they subjective sentimentality devoid of any critical reflection. The primary purpose of these Asian faces of Jesus is not only to help people to understand their Christian faith but equally to help them change the desperate inhuman situation in which many of them are placed.

2. Their christological constructions demonstrate that one need not necessarily appeal to precedents or paradigms enshrined in the gospels or in other early Christian works, nor have these constructions necessarily based on or legitimated by canonical writings. As new hermeneutical horizons open, new interpretative resources can be creatively employed to unravel the mystery of Jesus. Thus they weave a wide variety of cultural symbols, philosophical insights and social concerns of Asia into their christological articulations. These understandings of Jesus indicate that as fresh horizons open up, the perceptions of Jesus that emerge may not resemble either in form or content portrayals of him depicted in the Christian scriptures. They also raise the question of why Jewish thought patterns have to be the norm for the christological enterprise of people who are not familiar with their nuances. It is not that Asians are reluctant to learn from or utilize the hermeneutical resources of the Jewish people. The point of the Asian articulations of Jesus is that if the Christian church in the fifth century was successful in delicately maintaining the enigma of Jesus in the language, mood and the spirit of that hellenistic period, why should not Asians draw on their own hermeneutical reservoir to fashion Jesus for their own time and place?

3. These christological formulations arise primarily out of the theological import of Jesus and his message. They are concerned, in consequence, with the contextual relevance and essential significance of Jesus for the Asian masses. They see their task as making sense of Jesus amid the poverty and religious pluralism of Asia. Thus they show little interest in an academic reconstruction of biographical details.

There is at present a new interest among Euro-American interpretative guilds in combing extra-canonical literature to construct the historical figure of Jesus from among apocryphal materials and archeological evidence. However, the academic vigor they show in investigating the historical Jesus recedes when they apply their findings to the concerns of the contemporary world. For instance, E. P. Sanders, in an otherwise remarkable portrayal of Jesus in his own Jewish milieu, refuses to offer any suggestion as to how the Jesus he describes is relevant to Christian faith and practice. He writes in *Jesus and Judaism* that this is a theological problem into which he "is not going to venture."[1] Asian interpreters, on the other hand, see their task as bringing the vision of Jesus to the masses of Asia. For them, the artificial dichotomy imposed by Western academics between historical exegesis and theology—between the brute historical facts and faith formulations—does not exist. The crucial hermeneutical question is not what the historical Jesus looked like but what he means for Asia today.

Contextual demands prompt them to unleash sketches of Jesus intuitively and imaginatively without benefit of the technical skill or sophisticated knowledge displayed by present Jesus researchers. Whereas Euro-American christological reflections insist on logic, internal coherence, and precise theories of knowledge, prefer to discover Jesus in the pages of the written text, and place him in a social, political and religious environment, Asian understandings of Jesus rely on impulses and assortments of ideas and contextual needs; they take him out of his milieu and place him with the peoples of Asia and with other venerated sages like Buddha, Krishna and Confucius. They try to take Jesus out of the study into the dusty streets of Asia and let him mingle with other seers and savior figures.

4. These christological reflections accentuate the hermeneutical emphases of a minority community. Asian Christians live as an insignificant and divided group among domineering and often overpowering neighbors who profess other faith traditions. Thus for them hermeneutical activity is more than knowing about Jesus; it is a way of coping as Christians amid external and internal pressures. Through these christological articulations they try on the one hand to redeem themselves from the Western associations with which they have been tainted, and on the other to resist the easy option to allow themselves to be assimilated into the religious and cultic systems of the larger communities. What these discourses indicate is the confidence with which Asian Christians make use of their own indigenous resources, which they have often been asked to repudiate and disparage. The vigorous and creative use of local resources is an indication that any christological

formulation should not separate them from their neighbors but enable them to cooperate in the struggle for an equitable society and the search for a better tomorrow. In other words, these understandings of Jesus are a way of feeling and contributing toward the struggles for social and spiritual emancipation of all the peoples of Asia.

SELECTION AND ARRANGEMENT

Recently there has been an explosion of new, powerful and bold Asian reflections on Jesus. The materials span many different cultures and countries. It is not an easy task to produce a manageable volume choosing from a vast and ever-expanding amount of material. The essays included in this volume are chosen on the criterion that in their christological articulation they take into account at least one of the following:

a) a particular religio-cultural or socio-political reality of Asia;
b) Asian symbols, sense, impulses and popular and philosophical insights;
c) interreligious enrichment or eradication of class, caste, tribal and gender barriers.

These essays are arranged under two themes, though they obviously overlap. Though this division is not clear cut, it enables one to feel the tension between the religio-cultural and socio-economic realities of Asia. Part One, "Jesus Amid Other Asian Ways, Truths and Lights," as the title suggests, contains some contemporary attempts by Asian Christians to redefine Jesus in a context that brims with founders of religions, teachers of wisdom and proclaimers of truth. Firmly committed to Jesus, these essayists try to reorient Jesus to Hindu, Buddhist, Islamic and Chinese contexts in order to tone down some of the offensiveness and triumphalism of an earlier era; they look for common elements to provide starting points for dialogue with people of other faiths. The last two essays in this section try to offer a theology of religion for a multi-religious context.

Part Two, which is entitled "Newly Emerging Profiles of Jesus Amid Asia's Poverty and Religious Plurality," addresses issues raised by the new departure point for doing theology in Asia—poverty and economic oppression, which is partly the consequence of colonialism and the continuing exploitation by mercantile firms of industrialized nations, and partly of internal origin. The essays' main thrust is to extricate Jesus from abstract, historicist and dogmatic clichés and re-envision him as one who identified with the everyday struggles for survival of Asian people. This section also includes reflective examples from an Asian feminist perspective, which is relatively new to the Asian theological scene. They clearly demonstrate the intrinsic connection between the life of Jesus and the lives of Asian women. At the same time, traditional images of Jesus are radically refashioned in the light of their suffering and praxis.

The last essay in this section illustrates peoples' profiles of Jesus. Understandably, as this selection indicates, ordinary people use their own parameters to profile a Jesus who can empower and sustain them. Whether the religiosity of the Asian masses and the poverty of its teeming millions should together form an inseparable locus for Asian theological reflection, or whether poverty alone should be its proper context, is still an ongoing matter of debate among these Asian Christian thinkers.

These essays germinated out of different contextual concerns and were also produced to meet different publishing styles and formats. They are reproduced here with little editorial touch-up beyond a tidying of the footnotes to bring them to a uniform style. Some contain sexist language. Others continue to use condescending terms like *non-Christians* to describe people of other faiths. Many of them continue to use BC and AD instead of the neutral BCE (Before the Common Era) and CE (Common Era). Christian scriptures are frequently referred to as Old and New Testaments, giving the impression that one is archaic and ancient whereas the other is recent and new. These outmoded terms are all retained as a historical reminder that some of the essays were written at a time when sensitive use of language was not a matter of great concern.

Two final thoughts.

Various terms have been used to describe the plethora of christologies formulated over the years by Christian interpreters—low, high, from above, from below, vertical, horizontal, ascending and descending. In essence, these formulations focus on Jesus and his relation to God. They see Jesus either as coming down from above to fulfill God's predetermined plan or ascending upward while remaining faithful to his human condition. The Asian profiles of Jesus found here seek to perceive Jesus in a different way—from the side. These are the understandings of men and women who are on the periphery, searching for a meaningful life. They do not address the traditional issues, such as two natures and one person, or endeavor to uncover the historical personality of Jesus. Rather, they try to grasp Jesus dynamically as they wrestle with the meaning of their very existence.

No understanding of Jesus is ever completely new. Every fresh perception of Jesus is part of an ongoing critical conversation with earlier or contemporary articulations. These essayists lend their own small but markedly distinct voices to the inexhaustible and ever-growing debate about the significance of Jesus. In raising their distinctive voices they seek emancipation for themselves, but in the process they also seek to liberate Jesus. No one can deny that for the sake of human enhancement and harmony both are needed badly and urgently.

NOTE

1. E. P. Sanders, *Jesus and Judaism* (Philadelphia: Fortress, 1985; and London: SCM Press, 1985), p. 327. See also pp. 333-34.

Part One

JESUS AMID OTHER ASIAN WAYS, TRUTHS AND LIGHTS

It seems that the Christ that has come to us is an Englishman, with English manners and customs about him, and with the temper and spirit of an Englishman in him. . . . Is not Christ's native land nearer to India than England? Are not Jesus and his apostles and immediate followers more akin to Indian nationality than Englishmen? Why should we, then, travel to a distant country like England, in order to gather truths which are to be found much nearer our homes? Go to the rising sun in the East, not to the setting sun in the West, if you wish to see Christ in the plenitude of his glory.

Keshub Chunder Sen (1838-1884)

An Interpretative Foreword

R. S. SUGIRTHARAJAH

THE STORY SO FAR

Interestingly, the first persons to undertake serious theological reflection on Jesus from the perspective of Asia's religious traditions were not Asian Christians but Indian Hindus. It was these Hindus from Calcutta—like Rajah Ram Mohun Roy, Keshub Chunder Sen and P. C. Mozoomdar, who belonged to the Brahmo Samaj, a Hindu reform movement—who pioneered christological discourse in the nineteenth century. It would be true to say that among other faith traditions only Hindus have worked out such elaborate and varied images of Jesus. These articulations of Hindus, though they emanate from different philosophical strands within that tradition, demonstrate personal admiration and affection for Jesus and his teachings. Their reflections have provided a variety of images:

- Jesus as Supreme Guide to human happiness—Rajah Ram Mohun Roy;
- Jesus as true *Yogi* and Divine Humanity—Keshub Chunder Sen;
- Jesus as *Jivanmukta* (one who has attained liberation while alive)—Vivekananda;
- Jesus as the Son of Man, seeking the last, the least and the lost—Rabindranath Tagore;
- Jesus as the Supreme *Satyagrahi* (lover and fighter for truth)—Mahatma Gandhi;
- Jesus as *Advaitin* (one who has realized destiny with Brahman/God)—Swami Akhilananda;
- Mystic Christ—Radhakrishan.

These Hindus enthusiastically incorporated Jesus into the thought world of Hinduism(s) and continued to remain faithful to their own traditions. None felt the urge to renounce the Hindu way of life as the gospel of Jesus did not offer anything dramatically new or different from the teachings of their seers or their own sacred texts. In their view the message of Jesus was simply the reappearance of the eternal truth. Jesus was, in essence, restating anew some of the forgotten and overlooked aspects of the perennial message.

In a curious way it was these Hindu responses that provided the impetus, inspiration and confidence for Indian Christians to develop their own indigenized portrayals of Jesus. At the early stage of missionary expansion there was reluctance among the newly converted to undertake any reflection on Jesus using their own cultural or philosophical resources. Their understanding of Jesus was largely shaped by the denominational and pietistic tendencies of the time. Like the Hindus, Indian Christians were the first among Asian Christians to free themselves from the shackles of Western ecclesiastical images of Jesus and evolve their own sketches. Here are some of their pioneering efforts:

Jesus as *Prajapati* (Lord of creatures) — K. M. Banerjee;

Jesus as *Cit* (Consciousness) — Brahmobandhav Upadhyaya;

Jesus as *Avatara* (Incarnation) — A. J. Appasamy, V. Chakkarai;

Jesus as *Adi Purusha* (the first person) and *Shakti* (power/strength)
    — P. Chenchiah;

Jesus as Eternal *Om* (logos) — S. Jesudasan.

At a time when Western missionaries were using Jesus to expose the deficiencies of Hinduism, these Indian Christians took as their task to show how Hindu philosophical vocabulary can elucidate their experience of Jesus. However, some of the present-day Indian Christian *dalits* and tribals may not view such interpretations as innovative or receive them with much enthusiasm. For them, the Sanskritistic tradition from which these interpreters were trying to derive inspiration was the very system instrumental in their own oppression and marginalization. The *dalits* themselves have yet to develop their own understandings of Jesus in any particularly distinctive way. Yet seen from their context, these early Indian Christians' expositions of Jesus were a bold hermeneutical strategy. By redefining Jesus using Hindu religious concepts, Indian Christians helped to nullify the "Jesus against religion" posture adopted by missionaries of the time, a position that Indian Christians found offensive and degrading to their own rich and ancient traditions.

THE CURRENT STATE OF PLAY

At present Indian Christians, or for that matter Asian Christians as a whole, stand at a new hermeneutical juncture. The old era of competition or even comparison among great religious traditions is slowly coming to an end. The theological mood now is to encounter religions on their own terms rather than to judge them by preset norms. Enormous and meticulous comparative studies of various sacred texts, doctrines and teachings of different savior figures have shown that theologically and doctrinally other religions do not depend on Jesus for their existence or pine for fulfillment in him. There is also a new realization that religious pluralism has to be actively valued and not just passively tolerated. Rather than merely credit other religions with unfulfilled potentialities or latent values, the inherent and autonomous merit that has kept them alive over centuries is now increasingly recognized. The hermeneutical task is to bring the person of Jesus, in conjunction with other religious figures, into a revitalizing and enriching encounter with them and with Christian faith itself. The set of essays in this section seeks to do that.

In the first essay, Ovey N. Mohammed[1] explores the theological resemblance between Jesus and one of the more colorful Hindu savior figures — Krishna. After accentuating the parallels in the lives of these two leading religious personalities, Mohammed goes on to engage in an intratextual exegesis that highlights the similarities in the notion of salvation offered by Krishna in the *Gita* and Jesus in the New Testament. He then proceeds to discuss the implications of such a liberation-based theology of religion.

Hindu philosophical resources have provided a healthy hermeneutical background for numerous audacious sketches of Jesus. The dominant faith among Asians, however, is not Hinduism but Buddhism. While Hinduism and Confucianism are narrowly identified with specific ethnic communities, Buddhism has become a universal Asian phenomenon whose power and presence is felt in the social, cultural and political spheres of several Asian countries.

Unlike the Hindu appropriation of Jesus, which has been pleasant and cordial, Buddhism's encounter with Jesus has been less than hospitable. This was particularly evident in nineteenth-century Sri Lanka (then Ceylon), where the historical context of the time necessitated an anti-Christian posture. Polemics against Jesus involved caricaturing him as a spiritual dwarf in comparison to the Buddha. But in a contemporary hermeneutical context, Japanese theologian Seiichi Yagi evolves a new appreciation of Jesus in the light of the Buddhist claims. Borrowing from another Japanese Christian thinker, Katsumi Takizawa's distinction between first contact (the unconditional fact that God is within each of us) and secondary contact (awakening oneself to this fact — enlightenment according to Buddhism), Seiichi Yagi[2] perceives Jesus as the person who was awakened to this fundamental fact just as Buddha was in his time. Such an understanding of Jesus, Yagi reckons, creates new possibilities for Christians and Buddhists to learn from each other and build bridges, rather than each claiming absolute significance for its respective founder-figure.

In the next essay Sri Lankan theologian Aloysius Pieris[3] further explores the conflicting truth claims made on behalf of the Buddha and the Christ. Unlike Yagi, Pieris goes beyond the complex philosophical nuances and grounds the debate in the concept of human liberation and welfare. Pieris sees this as an effective starting point for sorting out the competing kerygmatic assertions in which Gautama is seen as the Buddha and Jesus is proclaimed as the Christ. After tracing the history of these interpretative claims and the ensuing religious debates, Pieris demonstrates that at the core level of these religions Buddha and Jesus meet at the path of liberation. In Pieris's view, Buddhism's liberative knowledge (gnosis) and Christianity's liberative love (agape) complement each other. Pieris's article was a trail-blazer in advocating liberation as the common ground for a theology of religions. Echoes of such a proposal are evident in Ovey Mohammed's essay.[4]

In the fourth essay Korean theologian Jung Young Lee[5] tries to relate Jesus to the *Yin* and *Yang*, which are characteristic of the Chinese thought world. He perceives in the interaction between *Yin* and *Yang*, a corrective to the either/or way of thinking that dominates the Western way of doing theology with its absolute and exclusive claims. Over against this the interplay between *Yin* and *Yang* offers a middle way of complementariness and a possibility for change and creativity. Jung Young Lee tries to relate Jesus to *Yin* and *Yang*; he perceives Jesus as the way of change and progress. Lee also provides a new understanding of divinity/humanity, death/resurrection and creation/redemption in the light of the Chinese conception of *Yin* and *Yang*—change and relativity.

Unlike the sacred texts of Hinduism and Buddhism, Islam has worked out its discourse about Jesus within its own holy texts. The hermeneutical task in an Islamic context is to promote and clarify Christian understandings of Jesus among Muslims, who already have their own perceptions of him. Alexander Malik,[6] who comes from a predominantly Muslim country, Pakistan, advocates theological engagement with his fellow Muslim neighbors with a view to illuminating each other's perceptions. Such an interaction, he reckons, will highlight areas of christological agreement as well as incompatible differences. His essay also elaborates a Bible-centered christology that addresses the religious, social and cultural demands of the Islamic situation.

Faced with the challenge of religious pluralism to traditional christology, recent theological thinking has broadly identified three positions in defining Christian attitudes to other religions—exclusive, inclusive and pluralist. However unsatisfactory this categorization may be, it does at least try to address the question of how one views Jesus in relation to other faith traditions. Michael Amaladoss,[7] an Indian Christian, seeks a paradigm that would place Jesus between inclusivist and pluralist positions. Like Raimundo Panikkar, he perceives the distinction between the universal Word and the particular manifestation of it in the historical Jesus. There is more to the Word than its historical concretization in Jesus of Nazareth. The Word can appear differently in other faith traditions. Amaladoss likens this to the advaitic concept of the One and the many. Such an understanding, Amaladoss holds, would allow for other historical names and manifestations of the Word, without requiring Christians to give up their personal commitment to Jesus as the Christ or urging others to accept him.

Stanley Samartha,[8] like other Indians, tries to wrestle with the perennial question: how to evolve an image of Jesus which is Indian and at the same time Christian. He sees in India's long acceptance of a sense of Mystery, which is the common possession of all religions, the starting point to work out a God-centered christology. Samartha reckons that a Mystery-centered

Christian faith would avoid any clannish claims upon God or any claim to exclusive understanding and would be helpful in establishing new relations with neighbors of other faiths.

In sum, these essays are a genuine and vigorous attempt to present Jesus without depreciating, renouncing or belittling other religious traditions or savior figures. They consciously acknowledge that Jesus is the paradigm and promise for Christians. This affirmation enables Asian Christians to discover other instances of God's revelation and love in other people and in their spiritual quests.

NOTES

1. Ovey N. Mohammed, *Journal of Ecumenical Studies* 26 (1989): 664-80.

2. Seiichi Yagi, *Journal of Ecumenical Studies* 27 (1990): 306-26.

3. Aloysius Pieris, in *The Myth of Christian Uniqueness: Toward a Pluralistic Theology of Religions*, ed. John Hick and Paul F. Knitter (Maryknoll, N.Y.: Orbis Books, 1987; and London: SCM Press, 1988), pp. 162-77.

4. See, for example, Paul Knitter, "Catholic Theology of Religions at a Crossroads" in *Concilium* 183 (1986): 99-107; idem, "Interreligious Dialogue: What? Why? How?" in *Death or Dialogue? From the Age of Monologue to the Age of Dialogue*, ed. Leonard Swidler, et al. (Philadelphia: Trinity Press International, 1990; and London: SCM Press, 1990), pp. 19-44. For liberation as the theological theme among major religions of Asia such as Hinduism, Buddhism, Sikhism, Islam, etc., see *Religions and Liberation*, ed. Asghar Ali Engineer (Delhi: Ajanta Publications, 1989); idem, *Islam and Liberation* (New Delhi: Sterling Publishers, 1990); Dharam Singh, *Sikh Theology of Liberation* (New Delhi: Harman Publishing House, 1991); Daniel Cohn-Sherbok, ed., *World Religions and Human Liberation* (Maryknoll, N.Y.: Orbis Books, 1992).

5. Jung Young Lee, *The Theology of Change: A Christian Concept of God in an Eastern Perspective* (Maryknoll, N.Y.: Orbis Books, 1979), pp. 86-102.

6. Alexander Malik, *CTC Bulletin* 7 (1987): 37-43.

7. Michael Amaladoss, *Making All Things New: Dialogue, Pluralism and Evangelization in Asia* (Maryknoll, N.Y.: Orbis Books, 1990), pp. 83-99.

8. Stanley Samartha, *One Christ—Many Religions: Toward a Revised Christology* (Maryknoll, N.Y.: Orbis Books, 1991), pp. 76-91.

SOME RELEVANT LITERATURE

Baago, Kaj. *Pioneers of Indigenous Christianity*. Madras: The Christian Literature Society, 1969.

Banawiratma, J. B. "Jesus as Guru: A Christology in the Context of Java (Indonesia)," *Exchange* 8 (1984): 33-57. (An English summary by J. Bastiaens, E. v.d. Peet, and E. Wiegant.)

Boyd, Robin. *An Introduction to Indian Christian Theology*. Madras: The Christian Literature Society, 1969.

de Silva, Lily. "Wisdom and Compassion of the Buddha and Jesus Christ in Their Role as Religious Teachers," *Dialogue* 17 [1-3] (1990): 1-28.

Gandhi, M. K. *The Message of Jesus Christ*. Bombay: Bharatiya Vidya Bhavan, 1964.

Ikuo, Matsunaga. "A New Quest for Christology? A Current Issue for Theology in Japan," *The Japan Christian Quarterly* 52 (1986): 150-66.

Jesudasan, Ignatius. "Gandhi's Way of the Cross," in *Gandhi on Christianity*, edited by Robert Ellsberg, pp. 92-100. Maryknoll, N.Y. : Orbis Books, 1991.

Jesus Christ with People in Asia: Report of a Consultation in Singapore. Singapore: Christian Conference of Asia, n.d.

Koyama, Kosuke. "The Asian Approaches to Jesus," *Missiology* 12 (1984): 435-47.

Lee, Peter, K. H. and Shih Heng-Ching. "Karma and Christ," *Ching Feng* 31 [1] (1988): 24-47.

Panikkar, Raymond. "Confrontation Between Hinduism and Christ," *New Blackfriars* 50 (1968): 197-204. Idem, *Salvation in Christ: Concreteness and Universality, the Supername*. Santa Barbara, 1972.

Pieris, Aloysius. *An Asian Theology of Liberation*. Maryknoll, N.Y.: Orbis Books, 1988; and Edinburgh: T&T Clark, 1988. See pp. 59-65. Idem, *Love Meets Wisdom: A Christian Experience of Buddhism*. Maryknoll, N.Y.: Orbis Books, 1988. See 110-35.

Raju, R. J. "The Gospels with an Indian Face," *Vidyajyoti* 55 [2 and 3] (1991): 61-72 and 121-41.

Samartha, Stanley, J. *The Hindu Response to the Unbound Christ*. The Christian Literature Society: Madras, 1974.

Sen, Keshub Chunder. *Lectures in India*. London: Cassells and Company, 1866.

Sharma, Arvind, ed. *Neo-Hindu Views of Christianity*. Leiden: E. J. Brill, 1988.

Thomas, M. M. *The Acknowledged Christ of the Indian Renaissance*. London: SCM Press, 1969.

Yagi, Dickson Kazuo. "Christ for Asia: Yellow Theology for the East," *Review and Expositor* as [4] (1991): 357-78.

Yagi, Seiichi. " 'I' in the Words of Jesus," in *The Myth of Christian Uniqueness*, pp. 117-34.

———. and Leonard Swidler, eds. *A Bridge to Buddhist-Christian Dialogue*. New York: Paulist Press, 1990, pp. 139-44.

1

Jesus and Krishna

OVEY N. MOHAMMED

At the turn of the century, the childhoods of Krishna and Jesus were much discussed by Western scholars.[1] Since then, however, the comparison between these two savior figures has received little or no serious attention, even though Krishna has become widely known among Christians since the 1960s and there is great interest in interreligious dialogue. To help fill this lacuna, and to foster and promote what Hindus and Christians have in common, this article attempts to highlight similarities between the notion of salvation offered by Krishna in the *Bhagavad Gita* and the notion of salvation offered by Jesus in the New Testament. As each point is examined with respect to Krishna, the New Testament is examined to see if there is a parallel with respect to Jesus. There are concluding observations on the significance of the findings for Hindu-Christian dialogue.

To begin, it may be helpful to sketch briefly the story of Krishna as he is known by Hindus. The earliest reference to him is found in the *Chandogya Upanishad* (sixth century B.C.E.), where he is mentioned as a student of philosophy (III.17.6). In the *Mahabharata* (fifth century B.C.E.) he is portrayed as a tribal hero; in the *Bhagavad Gita* (second century B.C.E.), as God incarnate who instructs Arjuna and, through him, all humankind. Our earliest source of his childhood is the *Harivamsa* (third century C.E.); an enlarged account of his life is found in the *Vishnu Purana* (fifth century C.E.). However, the most complete account of Krishna's life is that given in the *Bhagavata Purana* (ninth century C.E.).

From this vast array of literature covering several centuries emerge three Krishnas, or rather three aspects of the one Krishna of the Hindus: the tribal hero, the God incarnate, and the Krishna of the *Puranas*, which tell of his life in Gokula as the divine child, the young herdsman, and the endearing lover. The three aspects of his character are cumulative, not discrete, for each aspect melts into the others. As a hero he met the wor-

9

shiper's need for a divine father; as a young herdsman, for a divine lover; and as a child, for a son.

The young Krishna's love affairs have been the source of much romantic literature.[2] Invariably, his love for the cowherds' wives is interpreted as symbolic of the love of God for the human soul. The sound of his flute calling the women to leave their husbands' beds and dance with him in the moonlight is more than a melody. It represents the voice of God calling men and women to leave earthly things and turn to the joys of divine love. Likewise have Christians interpreted the Song of Songs.

The story of the child Krishna developed into a cult that appealed to the warm maternity of womanhood, and even today the village women of India worship the divine child. This practice closely resembles devotion to the infant Jesus common among Christians from the earliest centuries.

More intriguing is the fact that the nativity stories of Krishna and Jesus are alike in many ways. Just as Nanda came with Yashoda to Mathura to pay tribute, so Joseph came with Mary to Bethlehem to be taxed (Lk. 2:1-6; *Bhagavata Purana*, X.5; *Vishnu Purana*, V.3, V.6). In both cases a star portends miraculous birth, and that birth comes in the middle of the night as an evil king sleeps (Mt. 1:18-25; Lk. 1:26-38; *Bhagavata Purana*, X.3). The cruel king Kamsa has his parallel in Herod, and in both cases there is a massacre of infants when the king awakens (Mt. 2:14-16; *Bhagavata Purana*, X.4, X.6; *Vishnu Purana*, V.4). As wise men came to see Krishna, so wise men came to see the infant Jesus; heavenly musicians rained down songs of praise, just as Bethlehem's shepherds were startled by the angels' glorias (Mt. 2:9-12; Lk. 2:8-20; *Bhagavata Purana*, X.2, X.3; *Vishnu Purana*, V.2, V.3). The flight to Braj is similar to the flight into Egypt; in Braj, as in Israel, the parents were forewarned to take their child away to a place that lay safely beyond the despot's reach (Mt. 2:13-15; *Bhagavata Purana*, X.3; *Vishnu Purana*, V.1, V.3, V.5). Thus, Krishna's identity was hidden as he began his life in Braj, much as that of Jesus was concealed by the stables of Bethlehem and the carpenters' stalls of Nazareth (Mt. 2:19-23).[3]

Whatever one may conclude about these similarities, it seems certain that there is some historical basis for the story of Krishna, even though the stories of his life are diverse. Moreover, it is through faith in him that Hindus have the conviction of his existence and the truth of his teachings.[4]

The new wave of biblical scholarship points in an analogous direction with respect to Jesus. The story of his life and teachings is found in four Gospels, not to mention the many Epistles written by various authors. It is true that no serious scholar today doubts his existence, yet the Gospels, even conservatives would admit, are documents of faith molded by the needs of the early Christians to interpret the Christ-event rather than efforts to offer a literal, chronological account of what Jesus actually said and did. Understandably, many Christians now put more emphasis on the meaning and spirituality of the Jesus-story than Christians did in the past and as Hindus do with respect to Krishna.

In any event, in attempting a comparison of Krishna and Jesus, it is immaterial whether the Krishna of the *Bhagavad Gita* is a historical figure or not. The essential point is that this scripture articulates the Hindu recognition of Krishna as God. This recognition merits a comparison between him and Jesus in the New Testament.

GOD

In the *Bhagavad Gita* Krishna is God, and God is personal—"the Person eternal and divine, primeval God, unborn and all-pervading Lord" (10:13); the "all-highest Person" who bestows "being on all contingent beings" and "Lord of all the world" (10:15, 13:22); the "Person All-Sublime" who is wholly immanent and wholly transcendent (13:22, 16:16-20). Though God is the origin of all things (10:15), and the world depends on God (9:10), God does not depend on the world (9:4-5). Beyond the visible universe God has another mode of being in the heavenly home (8:20-22). Yet, as "father of the world" (9:17-19; 11:43), God is the source and sustainer of all virtues (10:4-6), the "light of lights" (13:17) who resides in the heart of all (18:61).

In the New Testament, too, God is personal. It is true that God is called the "Most High" (Lk. 6:35), "the Deity" (Acts 17:29), "Power" (Mk. 14:62), "the immortal, invisible, and only God" (1 Tim. 1:17)—affirmations of God's supremacy that do not emphasize God as person. Yet, God is our "father." The Lord's Prayer (Mt. 6:9-13) is a model of reverence and simple trust in a God who is personal. As in the *Gita*, God is both transcendent and immanent, "above all and through all and in all" (Eph. 4:6). Though the creator of all things (Eph. 3:9) and the one who exercises care over all creation (Mt. 6:30, 23:22), God is distinct from the world (Rom. 1:25), for God "dwells in unapproachable light" (1 Tim. 6:16), and heaven is God's throne (Mt. 5:34, 23:22). As our heavenly "father," God is the source of all goodness (Mk. 10:18), the "light that shines in the darkness" (Jn. 1:5; 1 Jn. 1:5), in whom "we live and move and have our being" (Acts 17:28).

THE INCARNATION OF GOD

Although Krishna in the *Gita* is unborn and eternal, he explicitly stated that he incarnates himself in the world "whenever the law of righteousness withers away and lawlessness arises" (4:7). The purpose of his coming into the world from age to age is "for the protection of the good ... and for the setting up of the law of righteousness" (4:8).

Krishna in the *Gita* is, therefore, true God and true human. This is also evident in Krishna's stupendous theophany: Not content with Krishna's account of his "far-flung powers," Arjuna asks to see Krishna's "Self which does not pass away" (11:1-4). Krishna grants Arjuna's request and gives him a "celestial eye" (11:8) with which to behold his transfiguration;

Arjuna, in terrified ecstasy, confesses Krishna as God (11:35-46). Aware that he has been unduly intimate with Krishna in his human form, Arjuna is filled with a sense of unworthiness and sin and appeals for the end of the terrifying vision and the return of Krishna to human forms. We see here that Krishna is no mere teacher of what is right and wrong but God who answers the prayers of God's followers. Arjuna asks for mercy, and Krishna responds, comforting him in his fear, and "once again the great-souled (Krishna) assumed the body of a friend" (11:50). There is no doubt that Krishna has a human body, for he eats, drinks, plays, and sleeps as people do (11:42).

Arjuna's sense of awe before the transfiguration of Krishna recalls Isaiah's reaction before the vision of God in the Hebrew Bible: "Woe is me! For I am undone; ... for my eyes have seen the King, the Lord of Hosts" (Is. 6:5). It also recalls the scene in the New Testament where Peter, James, and John fell on their faces, filled with reverence, at the transfiguration of Jesus (Mt. 17:1-8).

In the New Testament, also, God became human; the purpose of God's coming into the world was for our salvation (Nicene Creed; Mt. 9:12; Mk. 2:17; Lk. 5:32, 19:10; Jn. 3:17). The clearest expression of the incarnation of God is found in the Prologue to the Gospel of John, which states that "the Word became flesh" (Jn. 1:14). That Jesus was true God and true human is also implied here, for we are told that "the Word was God" (Jn. 1:1) and "dwelt among us" (Jn. 1:14). While John expressed the incarnation through the use of the philosophical term "Logos," the other Evangelists expressed a similar faith by setting their narrative in a theological framework and by the use of stories. Thus, Mark placed the work of Jesus against the preparatory mission of John the Baptist. Matthew and Luke started with the birth narrative, giving both the Virgin Birth and the genealogies of Jesus through Joseph to Abraham and Adam.

The Pauline writings also contain teaching on the incarnation in what scholars call the "christological hymns" (found in Phil. 2:6-11; Col. 1:15-20; and 1 Tim. 3:16), which may be Pauline though not written by Paul. Whether or not Paul wrote these hymns is irrelevant here, though it is usually thought that Paul adopted them to explain his exalted view of Jesus. Philippians tells us that Jesus was in the "form" of God but "emptied" himself and took the "form" of a servant. There is a possible docetism in the phrase "being made in the likeness of men," but faith in Jesus' true humanity is asserted in the phrase that he "became obedient unto death." In Colossians Jesus is called "the image of the invisible God" in whom "the fullness of God was pleased to dwell." Here, also, Jesus' humanity is asserted, for peace comes to us "through the blood of the cross." Jesus, then, like Krishna in the *Gita*, is true God and true human.

There is some diversity within the Hindu tradition in interpreting how this is so for Krishna, a diversity akin to that found in the Christian tradition. In the foundational Christian scriptures, one encounters a Jesus who is, above all, God-for-us and human-for-us, but out of this there emerges a later conciliar affirmation of Jesus as God-in-Godself and human-in-self, which gives rise to a variety of interpretations. The similarity of Jesus and Krishna as God and human appears to be more deeply rooted the closer one gets to the origins of both religious faiths, but it perdures even as one moves into later stages of articulation that take place in cultural contexts that differ quite significantly.

The incarnation of God boggles the imagination and overwhelms human thought. Krishna mourns that "fools despise him because he has taken a human body" (9:11). There is a parallel lament in Paul, who regarded it as "a stumbling block to the Jews" and "folly to the Gentiles" (1 Cor. 1:23). Folly or not, Krishna asserts that it is through him that human beings find salvation, "But that highest Person is to be won by love-and-worship directed to none other" (8:22; also 8:7; 9:25, 29, and 30-32; 11:55; 12:6-8 and 30; 13:18; Zaehner, 437-439). That "highest Person" refers, of course, to Krishna. Moreover, Krishna says that to follow him is "to tread the highest way" (32; also 6:45). Those who worship other gods are "anonymous Krishnas": "Whatever form . . . a devotee with faith desires to honor, that very faith do I affirm in him . . . thence he gains his desires, though it is I who am the true dispenser" (7:21-22; also 9:23-24). Krishna's "way" is parallel to the "way" of Jesus: "I am the way, the truth, and the life" (Jn. 14:6); Christians maintain this claim when they say that "there is no other name than Jesus among men whereby we must be saved" (Acts 4:12). Karl Rahner has expressed this theologically with his doctrine of "anonymous Christians."[5]

To reflect on what we have seen so far, we observe that, while Christianity and Hinduism are two great religions that accept the fact that God incarnates Godself as a human being, the question of one or many incarnations highlights a difference between the *Gita* and the New Testament. The difference, however, is not rooted in dogmatics but is ultimately a question of two different visions of time and history. Yet, the difference may not be as great as it first appears to be, for, on the one hand, although Jesus came once for all for this present world era, traditional Christian faith holds that he will come again. On the other hand, while Krishna incarnates himself age after age, the ages are separated by thousands of years so that the incarnation of Krishna made known to us in the *Gita* is for our present age. Moreover, in the *Gita*, there is no suggestion that other incarnations of God are other than that of Krishna. In other words, whether incarnation is one or many, Krishna is the mediator of salvation. Furthermore, the law of *karma* in the *Gita* (3:9, 4:14, 9:28, 18:60) does not work independently of Krishna. By following Krishna, history is no longer the drudgery of *chronos* but the surprise of *kairos*. The time in which we live is a new era. Salvation and freedom from rebirth are, for the first time, available to all (4:9, 8:15, 12:7, 13:25, 14:2, 20, 14:4).

What of *karma* and Christianity? The law of *karma*, the notion that we reap what we sow, is recognized in the New Testament (2 Cor. 9:6; Gal. 6:7). The Christian hope is that we will be ushered into the presence of God, but our achievement of this hope is in some sense linked with our activity during this life. Good actions lead to God, while evil actions have consequences, the living-through of which offers the means of purification. Most of us know about the costliness of love to accept the view that all moral and spiritual progress is likely to be painful. However, many people would agree that a short life is not long enough for achieving perfection. For them the doctrine of purgatory suggests moral and spiritual evolution and resonates with the belief that God wills all to be saved (1 Tim. 2:4). The doctrine of God's universal salvific will expresses the Christian hope that God gives up on no one no matter how evil and alienated he or she has become. At the same time, Christianity, unlike Hinduism, recognizes the possibility of hell, of ultimate nonfulfillment based on the free rejection of God, but it has not declared that any human has been relegated to that state.

Can the law of *karma* and rebirth be brought into harmony with Christianity? Religious language is symbolic. The law of *karma* and rebirth in the *Gita* is an attempt to reconcile the justice and love of God. Rebirth affirms that God's love is so infinite that God gives us the opportunity to grow until we achieve perfection. If some Christians believe that nothing defiled shall see God and recognize that most of us need further purification at death, and if it is this recognition that has prompted the doctrine of purgatory, then the doctrine of rebirth as an opportunity for further purification, for working off our bad *karma*, has its parallel in the doctrine of purgatory. Through the doctrine of purgatory, it is possible for Christians to hope that, because God's nature is one of love, no one finally fails to make the journey to God. From a universalist perspective, then, the law of *karma* and rebirth can be harmonized with the doctrine of purgatory without denying the possibility of hell.

In spite of the issue of one or many incarnations, the teachings of Krishna and Jesus on salvation are similar in many respects, as we shall now see. In the *Gita* Krishna's offer of salvation is made in terms of grace: "Thinking on Me you will surmount all dangers by my grace" (18:58; also 9:30-31, 18:56, 18:62). However, though Krishna is the God of grace, always ready to save those who are devoted to him (9:26ff), we are free to reject his offer if we choose (16:7-20), for the efficacy of grace depends on our faith and love. Faith is trust and commitment, self-abandonment to Krishna. When we respond to Krishna's grace in faith, Krishna gives us salvation, forgiveness, and new life:

> Those who cast off all their works on Me, solely intent on Me, and mediate on Me in spiritual exercise, leaving no room for others, [and so really] do honor Me, these I will lift up on high out of the ocean of recurring birth, and that right soon, for their thoughts are fixed on

Me; thenceforth in very truth in Me you will find your home. (12:6-8; also 9:30)

Further, love should be total. Krishna regards even our humblest offering as a gift of love: "Be it a leaf or flower or fruit that a zealous soul may offer Me with love's devotion, that do I [willingly] accept, for it was love that made the offering" (9:26). Whatever we do we should do for the love of God: "Whatever you do, whatever you eat, whatever you offer in sacrifice or give away in alms, whatever penance you perform, offer it up to Me" (9:27).

In the New Testament Paul also spoke of human salvation in terms of grace: "By grace you have been saved" (Eph. 2:5); three verses later, he added that grace depends on faith (Eph. 2:8). He acknowledged, too, that we can decline God's offer of grace. For example, he wrote in Gal. 2:21 of "nullifying" the grace of God, and in Gal. 5:4 he chided his readers because they had fallen away from grace (see also 2 Cor. 6:1). As in the *Gita*, Paul instructed that we should offer to God in love whatever we do: "Whatever you eat or drink or whatever you do, do all for the glory of God" (1 Cor. 10:31).

REPENTANCE AND FORGIVENESS

In the *Gita* repentance born of love and faith effaces all sin, and no one who comes to God with a humble heart fails to win salvation. Not only the high-caste and the rich can be saved, for Krishna cuts through the sharply drawn lines of caste and sex and opens the way of salvation to all in words reminiscent of Paul that with God there is neither slave nor free, male nor female (Gal. 3:28; also Rom. 10:12-13): "none who worships Me with loyalty-and-love is lost to Me. For whosoever makes Me his haven, base-born though he be, yes, women too and artisans, even serfs, theirs it is to tread the highest way" (9:31-34). Krishna is the Good Herdsman in quest of the worst sinner who has not repented: "However evil a man's livelihood may be, let him but worship Me and serve no other, then he shall be reckoned among the good indeed, for his resolve is right" (9:30).

The New Testament also teaches the forgiveness of sins through repentance. We find it in the preaching of John the Baptist (Mk. 1:4) and in the ministry of Jesus. When Jesus came into Galilee his first message to his hearers was that they should repent (Mk. 1:15). Throughout his ministry, when people came to him in a spirit of humility and sorrow for what they had done, Jesus forgave them. As God incarnate, he claimed that he had the power to forgive sins (Mk. 2:7-12). He said that his mission was not to the righteous but to call sinners to repentance (Lk. 5:32; also Mt. 9:12; Mk. 2:17; Lk. 19:10; Jn. 3:17). There are many examples of the experience of God's forgiveness in the stories of how Jesus said to men and women individually, "Thy sins are forgiven: go and sin no more" (Mt. 9:2; Mk. 2:5;

Jn. 8:2-11). Moreover, from Jesus we learn that God not only forgives the sinner who turns to God in repentance, but God also goes out in search of the sinner who has not repented, as a Good Shepherd goes out in the wilderness to find the one lost sheep (Lk. 15:3-7). In the parable of the prodigal son (Lk. 15:8-32), Jesus said that God's response to the repentant is like the father in the story who comes running out to meet his son and will not even allow him to finish his awkward confession of guilt. God comes to meet us in love and forgiveness, but there must first be true repentance, for God does not wish to forgive those who do not wish to be forgiven. What Jesus taught about the forgiveness of sins is continuous with what Krishna taught in the *Gita*.

GRACE, NOT WORKS

The *Gita* further teaches that we are saved by grace through faith and not by works (6:37-47). In response to Arjuna's inability to relate this teaching to the various duties, ritualistic and ethical, prescribed by the Vedic law and the Hindu tradition as necessary for salvation, Krishna says: "For knowledge of the Veda, for sacrifice, for grim austerities, for gifts of alms a meed of merit is laid down: all this the athlete of the spirit leaves behind" who knows that the law finds fulfillment in him (8:28; also 3:10-16; 11:48 and 53). In words that echo the epistle to the Hebrews, Krishna says that he is the sacrifice that links salvation in this world to the next: "I am the rite, the sacrifice, the offering for the dead, the healing herb; I am the sacred formula, the sacred butter am I: I am the fire and the oblation offered [in the fire]" (9:16). As the *Gita* comes to a close, Krishna again tells Arjuna that he is not to worry about the law but to have faith in Krishna's love and grace: "Give up all things of law, turn to Me, your only refuge, [for] I will deliver you from all evils; have no care" (18:66). That is, salvation is not something that we must try to win by our own means but to accept as a gracious gift from God. In confirmation of this teaching, Arjuna is told that the revelation of God he received was due to grace (11:47), not works (11:48).

As in the *Gita*, the New Testament teaches that we are made right with God through grace, not through works (Rom. 3:20-28). As Paul explained: "If it is by grace, it is no longer on the basis of works; otherwise grace would no longer be grace" (Rom. 11:6). Grace is the antithesis of law (Rom. 6:14). Successful obedience to the Mosaic law was known as works. It is this view that Paul contrasted to grace. Salvation is not our own work but God's gift (Rom. 3:24; Eph. 2:8). Even Paul admitted that the revelation he received was through grace, not works (Gal. 1:15).

This is the heart of the teaching on grace in the *Gita* and the New Testament: God loves us "while we are yet sinners" (Rom. 5:8). It is God who takes the initiative in reconciliation, by becoming incarnate, and it is for us to accept God's free gift that we can never earn. What the *Gita* emphasizes so strongly has its parallel in Paul.

LOVE AND KNOWLEDGE

Reliance on grace in faith and love leads to knowledge of God. When devotion grows, God dwelling in the soul imports to the devotee the light of wisdom. The *Gita* puts it this way: "By love-and-loyalty he comes to know Me as I really am, how great I am and who; and once he knows Me as I am he enters Me forthwith" (18:55). To know the truth is to lift up our hearts to and adore God. The knower is also a devotee and the best of them: "Of these the man of wisdom, ever integrated, who loves-and-worships One alone excels: for to the man of wisdom I am exceeding dear and he is dear to Me" (7:17).

In the New Testament, too, knowledge of God is the fruit of faith and love. The twin notions of knowledge and faith occur together (Jn. 4:16, 6:69), 8:31-32). The same is true of knowledge and love, for knowing is the result of becoming one and being one with God through love: "He who loves is born of God; he who does not love does not know God; for God is love" (1 Jn. 4:7-8).

SIN AND IGNORANCE

In the *Gita* wisdom is the opposite of ignorance, which is the parent of attachment, for the roots of attachment lie in the wrong belief that we are self-sufficient. Ignorance is not theoretical error but spiritual blindness. To know the truth we require conversion of soul. Arjuna could not see the truth with his natural eyes; through grace he was granted the divine light (11:8). After his long struggle to know the will of God, it was through revelation through grace that he finally found peace: "Destroyed is the confusion; and through grace I have regained a proper way of thinking: with doubts dispelled I stand ready to do your bidding" (18:73).

For Paul knowledge was also the opposite of ignorance because ignorance is a factor of human sin (Rom. 1:18). Thus, no matter how keen and bright our intellect may be, natural wisdom is futile (Rom. 1:21), foolish (1 Cor. 3:19), and blind (2 Cor. 4:4). Paul showed this clearly when he contrasted the basic human ability to know God with present human ignorance rooted in a false sense of self-sufficiency: "For although they knew God they did not honor him as God or give thanks to him, but they became futile in their thinking and their senseless minds were darkened. Claiming to be wise, they became fools" (Rom. 1:21-22). On the one hand, sinful persons by "their wickedness suppress the truth" (Rom. 1:18), and, on the other hand, "since they do not see fit to acknowledge God, God gives them up to a base mind" (Rom. 1:28). To have true knowledge we need to be converted to God, for only God is able to lead us to an acceptance of the truth (1 Cor. 2:10-13). Even Paul was unable to know the truth before his conversion; only after his conversion did he come to know God's will (Gal. 1:15).

THE NEED FOR DETACHMENT

In the *Gita* to remove ignorance we must kindle the spiritual vision: "A man of faith, intent on wisdom, his senses [all] restrained, wins wisdom; and wisdom won, he will come right to perfect peace" (4:39). We must cleanse the soul from attachment to the self and the world. It is for this reason that Krishna makes detachment the key to spiritual growth: "I love the man who is the same to friend and foe, the same whether he is respected or despised, the same in heat and cold, in pleasure as in pain, who has put away attachment and remains unmoved by praise or blame" (12:18-19). Such a man holds "profit and loss, victory and defeat to be the same" (2:38), for he is undismayed by sorrow "who rejoices not at whatever good befalls him nor hates the bad that comes his way" (2:56-57). The same to him are clods of earth, stones, and gold (6:8). "Content to take whatever chance may bring his way, surmounting [all] dualities, knowing no envy, the same in success and failure, though working [still] he is not bound" (4:22).

In the New Testament, too, the removal of ignorance calls for spiritual vision, which is the result of unwavering commitment: "If any one of you lacks wisdom, let him ask God . . . and it will be given him. But let him ask in faith, for he who doubts is like a wave of the sea that is driven and tossed by the wind" (Jas. 1:5-6). As in the *Gita*, spiritual vision calls for self-denial. We must put to death what is earthly in us—"immorality, impurity, passion, evil desire and covetousness, which is idolatry" (Col. 3:5; also Rom. 6:12; Titus 2:12; 1 Pet. 2:11, 4:2); mortify the body and crucify the flesh (Rom. 8:13; Gal. 5:24); prefer the good of others before our own (Lk. 3:11; Rom. 14:20-21, 15:1-2; 1 Cor. 10:24 and 33, 13:5; Phil. 2:4); put off our old nature, which belongs to our former manner of life, and put on the new nature, created in the likeness of God in true righteousness and holiness (Eph. 4:22; Col. 3:9); be crucified to the world (Gal. 6:14), and not love the things that are in it (1 Jn. 2:15); and forsake all (Lk. 14:33), even lawful things (1 Cor. 10:23). In both the Gita and the New Testament, then, complete detachment from self leads to complete knowledge of God.

TRUE KNOWLEDGE IS EXPERIENTIAL

In the *Gita* complete knowledge of God is experiential knowledge that we abide in God and God abides in us (11:54 and 55). It is through experiential knowledge that the knower of God is established in God (5:20). It is the great purifier: "For nothing on earth resembles wisdom in its power to purify" (4:38). It has the power to destroy the effects of sin: "Who knows my godly birth and mode of operation thus as they really are, he . . . is never born again; he comes to Me. Many are they who, passion, fear, and anger spent, inhere in Me, making Me their sanctuary; made pure by wisdom and hard penances, they come [to share] in my own mode of being" (4:9-10). It is worth noting in passing that, in this passage, meditation on the birth and incarnate life of God, combined with the stilling of the passions through the discipline of detachment, leads to an experiential knowledge of God, as in the *Spiritual Exercises* of St. Ignatius of Loyola.[6]

In the New Testament true knowledge is also experiential in character. It is the revelation of the mystery of God (1 Cor. 2:6ff), which God gives to those who have faith in God (1 Cor. 2:10-16, 12:8). The believer knows, because God dwells in her or him (Jn. 14:7) and transforms her or him into God's likeness (1 Jn. 3:2). Those who have this knowledge know the truth, and the truth sets them free from sin (Jn. 8:3-32). It is a blessed vision that is the fruit of a perfect life lived in and for God. As the beatitudes state, "Blessed are the pure in heart, for they shall see God" (Mt. 5:8).

KNOWLEDGE AND ACTION

The experience of God is not the final goal of faith and love, for in that case the *Gita* would have ended with Arjuna's tremendous experience of the celestial vision of Krishna (11:9-55). Arjuna cannot forget the thrilling scene he saw, but he has to work it into his life. He has seen the truth, but he has to live it by transmuting his whole nature into the willing acceptance of the Divine. By taking Arjuna beyond the visible universe, Krishna merely broadens his horizon; that is, Krishna makes possible Arjuna's ability to work for the good of others.

To put it more generally, true knowledge expresses itself in action. It must bear fruit in the lives of those who love if it is to be effective in leading people to salvation. Thus, Krishna says that those who reject action are ineffective (3:4), self-deceiving (3:5), hypocritical (3:6), antisocial (3:16, 20), and uninformed (3:27), then sets out ethical requirements for the person he loves:

> None hurting, truthful, free from anger, renouncing [all] begins, free from nagging greed, gentle, modest, never fickle, [a]rdent, patient, enduring, pure, not treacherous nor arrogant—such is the man who is born to [inherit] a godly destiny. (16:2-3; also 12:15-17; 16:4, 6-7)

In the *Gita* the necessity for action becomes clearer when we note that God works for the good of the world: "If I were not to do my work, these worlds would fall to ruin" (3:24; also 4:14 and 9:9). The central event of God's activity in history is the coming of Krishna into the world for the protection of the good and the establishment of righteousness in the world (4:8). Most importantly, he invites all to join him in this enterprise: "Whatever the noblest does, that will others do: the standard that he sets all the world will follow" (3:21). Here the "noblest" refers to Krishna himself. That is, God's activity is the norm and model of all worldly actions. We must imitate God's work without selfish desire and imitate God's concern for the welfare of the world. Action is what Krishna wanted Arjuna to be interested in. Action is unavoidable; hence, the renunciation of action is impossible, but the renunciation of the fruits of action *is* possible (3:5, 33; 18:5-6). In the words of the *Gita*: "To work alone you are entitled, never to its fruit. Neither let the motive be the fruit of action, nor let attachment be to non-action" (2:47).

For the *Gita*, then, the realm of God is not exclusively an interior reality. It enters into the exterior life of the human being in the world. In fact, the very purpose of the dialogue between Krishna and Arjuna is to persuade Arjuna to do his duty to society. Arjuna wanted to flee from the world and save his soul in isolation from the world. He wanted to seek refuge in religious quietism, but Krishna dissuaded him from doing so and asked him to work for the welfare of others: "It is better to do one's own duty, though devoid of merit, than to do another's, however well-performed. By doing the work prescribed by one's own nature, a man meets with no defilement" (18:47). It seems clear, then, that discipleship in the *Gita* has two aspects: a focus on the activity of God in the world, and an emphasis on detachment through which the individual participates in this activity.

In the New Testament, also, experiential knowledge born of love must express itself in action. Thus, in the Gospels, Jesus makes moral demands upon those who would follow him: "If you love me, keep my commandments" (Jn. 14:15); "He who has my commandments and keeps them, he it is who loves me" (Jn. 14:21); "Why do you call me 'Lord, Lord,' and do not do what I tell you?" (Lk. 6:46); "Not everyone who says 'Lord, Lord' shall enter the kingdom of heaven," but the one who does God's will (Mt. 7:21). According to Paul, the love of God makes moral demands on us: "Love is patient and kind; love is not jealous or boastful; it is not arrogant or rude. Love does not insist on its own way; it is not irritable or resentful; it does not rejoice at wrong, but rejoices at the right. Love bears all things, believes all things, hopes all things, endures all things" (1 Cor. 13:4-7).

The necessity for action in the New Testament is also evident, since we are told that God works for the benefit of the world (Mt. 6:25-31; Lk. 12:24-27; Jn. 5:17, 10:25, 14:10-11). At the center of God's activity in the world is God's incarnation in Jesus to inaugurate the divine realm (Mk. 1:15). Like Krishna, Jesus also invites us to become magnanimous co-workers with him in his activity, for the harvest is great and the laborers are few (Mt. 9:36-37). In fact, he repeatedly calls us to labor with him as his disciples (Mt. 5:19, 8:22, 9:9; Mk. 1:17). In the New Testament then, as in the *Gita*, the realm of God is not just an interior reality but enters into the visible reality of the world, for opposed to God's activity in and through Jesus is the growth of evil in the world. Following Jesus liberates one from spiritual captivity. However, the struggle for the realm of God against the powers of darkness demands our faithful cooperation with Jesus through detachment from the self (Mt. 10:38-39; Mk. 8:34; Lk. 17:33; Jn. 12:25). The salvation of the world calls for action, because God's plan for the world is at stake.

THE GOAL OF ACTION

In the *Gita* the twofold end of action is the salvation of the individual and the welfare of humanity (3:25), for when action is performed in view of the welfare of humanity, based on the pure love of God, action and the true knowledge of God are fused, and the double concern of the salvation of the individual and the love of neighbor is achieved. Commitment to action has its basis in the longing to bring about the welfare of all and is based on God's own caring for the world. God works to secure the wealth of all contingent beings (5:5, 12:3-4); it is in doing and being like him that salvation consists (2:71; 10:10; 12:13, 15, 18; 18:53). Love of God has to be expressed in concern for one's neighbor.

In the New Testament the goal of action is also twofold: the salvation and perfection of one's self, and the salvation and perfection of one's neighbor: "You shall love the Lord your God with your whole heart, and with all your soul, and with all your strength, and with all your mind; and your neighbor as yourself . . . do this, and you will live" (Mt. 22:35-40; Mk. 12:18-31; Lk. 10:25-28). Whoever loves God must also love his or her neighbor. When action is performed by the total person in complete union with God, action and the knowledge of God interpenetrate one another to a perfect unity, in which the love of both God and neighbor is achieved. Work done for the sanctification of others is not only the highest expression of the love of neighbor but also of the love of God, insofar as all the work is undertaken for the love of God, as a surrender of one's self entirely to God's plans and wishes in order to cooperate in the divine redemptive mission in the world.

SALVATION

In the *Gita* cooperation with God through action is not only for the welfare of the world; it is also salvific. It is *moksha*, salvation from the world. We work in the world with selfless devotion because we know that our ultimate end is to be united in love with God beyond the world. As Krishna says: "They come to Me, 'they come to my own mode of being'" (4:10); "Do works for Me, make Me your highest goal, be loyal-in-love to Me, cut off all [other] attachments, have no hatred for any being at all: for all who do thus shall come to Me" (11:55; also 7:28; 9:14, 28, 34; 10:10). This is the real message of the *Gita*: salvation is eternal communion with a living God in God's heavenly home. It is only fitting that the book should end by again stating its main theme: "And now again to this my highest Word, of all the most mysterious: 'I love you well.'" Therefore, I will tell you your salvation. Bear Me in mind, love and worship Me, sacrifice, prostrate yourself to Me: so you will come to Me, I promise you truly, for you are dear to me" (18:64-65).

In the New Testament, too, "your homeland is in heaven" (Phil. 3:20); "there is no eternal city in this life but we look for one in the life to come" (Heb. 13:14). Salvation is communion with God forever, as is evident in much of Jesus' teaching about the reign of God that pictures it as a messianic banquet (Mk. 14:25; Lk. 13:28-29; 22:1-14, 18, 29-30), as do the parallels of the mustard seed (Mt. 13:31-34), the tares (Mt. 13:24-30, 36-43), and the dragnet (Mt. 13:47-50). Eternal communion with God is the same good conferred in salvation by the New Testament and the *Gita*.

CONCLUSION

In highlighting the similarities between the notion of salvation offered by Krishna in the *Bhagavad Gita* and the notion of salvation offered by Jesus in the New Testament, we have seen that it is God who takes the initiative in reconciling us to Godself by becoming incarnate; that God's offer of salvation is through grace; that grace leads to repentance and the forgiveness of sin; that grace is a free gift of God and cannot be won by works; that through grace we grow in knowledge of God; that ignorance of God is rooted in our false sense of self-suffering, and knowledge of God involves detachment from the self; that true knowledge is experiential and expresses itself in action out of the pure love of God; that the end of action is twofold: the salvation of one's self and the welfare of humanity; and that our ultimate salvation is eternal communion with God beyond the world. What Krishna taught in the Gita has its parallel with what Jesus taught in the New Testament. Of course, an investigation of differences in the notion of salvation in the two scriptures would complement this study, but that calls for another article.

Nevertheless, it is appropriate to ask what the implications are of the findings of this article for interreligious dialogue between the followers of Krishna and of Jesus. This study both corroborates and refines the recent theocentric approach to Hindu-Christian dialogue. Concretely, we have seen that God takes the initiative in reconciling us to Godself by becoming incarnate in Krishna and Jesus. This theocentric view of salvation allows Christians to continue to affirm that God has really spoken in Jesus, but it does not compel them to say that God has not spoken through Krishna, especially when we recall that the notion of salvation offered by Krishna and Jesus is similar. In other words, in dialogue with Hindus, Christians can be fully committed to Jesus and at the same time can be fully open to Krishna's message in the *Gita*. In the theocentric view, both Krishna and Christ are important for the history of salvation.

Whatever merit a theocentric model of dialogue may have, however, both the *Gita* and the New Testament suggest that a liberation theology of religions may be a more fruitful approach to Hindu-Christian dialogue. According to the method of liberation theology, that which unites Hindus and Christians in common discourse and praxis is not how Christ and Krishna are related to God but to what extent they are engaged in promoting salvation—the welfare of humanity. As the New Testament asserts, it is not they who say "Lord, Lord" of Jesus who will enter the reign of God (Mt. 7:21-23). The *Gita* makes the same point when Krishna says that work for the welfare of others is necessary for salvation (3:4-6). As our discussion of action in the *Gita* and the New Testament has shown, love of God must be verified in concern for one's neighbor. Indeed, the soteriologies of the scriptures would seem to suggest that the liberation of the poor and the disadvantaged is central to the purpose of Hindu-Christian dialogue. This dialogue calls for interreligious sharing and praxis. The result should prove encouraging, since, as we have seen, the goal of salvation in the *Gita* parallels that found in the New Testament.

The emphasis on praxis in a liberation theology of religions may even help theologians of religion to discern not only whether but also how much Krishna and Christ are ways of salvation. All Hindu and Christian claims on behalf of Krishna or Christ will have to grow out of, and be confirmed in, the praxis and lived experience of these claims. Granting that the disciples of Krishna and Christ are those who seek the reign of God and God's justice (Mt. 6:33), by evaluating the fruits of discipleship with respect to Krishna and Christ, theologians may find reason to affirm that it is Jesus and not Krishna who unifies and fulfills all efforts toward a full humanity. Or, they may discover that Krishna offers a means of salvation equal to that of Jesus. At least, as in a theocentric approach to dialogue, they may find that Krishna and Christ are important for the history of salvation.

NOTES

1. George Grierson, "Modern Hinduism and Its Debt to the Nestorians," *Journal of the Royal Asiatic Society* (1907), pp. 311-335; J. Kennedy, "The Child Krishna, Christianity, and the Gujars," ibid. (1907), pp. 951-991; J. Kennedy, "The Child Krishna and His Critics," ibid. (1908), pp. 505-521; Arthur B. Keith, "The Child Krishna," ibid. (1908), pp. 169-175.

2. W. G. Archer, *The Loves of Krishna* (London: George Allen and Unwin, 1957); Deben Bhattachaya, tr. *Love Songs of Chandidas: The Rebel Poet-Priest of Bengal* (New York: Grove Press, 1970).

3. For a fuller comparison of the nativity stories of Krishna and Jesus, see John S. Hawley with Shrivatsa Goswami, *At Play with Krishna: Pilgrimage Dramas from Brindavan* (Princeton, N.J.: Princeton University Press, 1981), pp. 52-59; and S. Radhakrishnan, *Eastern Religions and Western Thought* (London: Oxford University Press, 1969; orig.—1939), p. 182.

4. On the historicity of Krishna, see S. Radhakrishnan, tr. *The Bhagavad Gita* (New York: Harper & Row, 1973; orig.—1948), pp. 28-29. Arthur Llewellyn Bashiam, *The Wonder That Was India: A Survey of the Culture of the Indian Sub-continent*

before the Coming of the Muslims (New York: Grove Press, 1959), pp. 305-306; and Sri Aurobindo, *Essays on the Gita* (Pondicherry: Sri Aurobindo Ashram, 1966), pp. 17-18. On archaeological evidence for the cowherd Krishna as early as the second century B.C.E., see Sukumar Sen, *A History of Brajabuli Literature* (Calcutta: University of Calcutta, 1935), p. 480.

5. Karl Rahner, "Christianity and the Non-Christian Religions," in his *Theological Investigations*, vol. 5 (Baltimore: Helicon Press, 1966), pp. 115-134.

6. On the *Spiritual Exercises* and the *Gita*, see Ovey N. Mohammed, "Ignatian Spirituality and the Bhagavad Gita," *Thought* 62 (December 1987), pp. 423-434.

All quotations from the *Gita* are taken from R. C. Zaehner, tr. *The Bhagavad Gita* (Calcutta: H. C. Dass, 1987).

For the *Harivamsa* citations, see M. N. Dutt, *A Prose Translation of Harivamsa* (Calcutta: H. C. Dass, 1987).

For the *Vishnupuranam* citations, see M. N. Dutt, *A Prose Translation of Vishnupuranam* (Varnasi: Chowkhamba Sanskrit Seris Office, 1972).

For the *Bhagavata Purana* citations, see J. M. Sanyal, tr. *The Srimad-Bhagavatam of Krishna-Dwaipayana Vyassa*, 5 vols. (Calcutta: D. N. Bose, n. d.); also in 2 vols. (New Delhi: Munishiram Maroharlal, 1973).

2

Christ and Buddha

SEIICHI YAGI

SIDDHARTHA GOTAMA AND JESUS OF NAZARETH: WHAT AND HOW THEY TAUGHT

How are Siddhartha Gotama and Jesus of Nazareth, the founders of two great religious traditions, to be compared? This is not solely a problem of the science of religion or of so-called comparative religion. Today this question must be asked in the context of interreligious dialogue with reference to the "absolute uniqueness of Christianity." In the following I would like to demonstrate the possibility of understanding both Gotama and Jesus as great figures who, in each situation and tradition, found and realized religious truth common to all humanity.

First, we will examine the problems young Gotama had. Usually a legend is told of the young Gotama who went out of the four gates of his castle and saw, first, an aged man, then a sick man, then a funeral, and finally a monk and a bird picking an insect. Realizing the pains of life, he left his status as the prince to search for freedom from pain.

Hajime Nakamura and an older tradition have shown us a different picture.[1] Young Gotama left his family, according to Nakamura, not because he found human life full of sufferings. Rather, he was troubled by an irrational self-assertion. All human beings must age or get sick and die. However, silly men and women disdain the inevitable. They are ashamed of suffering and abhor it. "It is also the case with me," thought Gotama, and that was the starting point of his reflections.

If Nakamura's version is correct, then Gotama's problem did not lie in the fact that to live was to suffer. If he had found his problem just in the pain of living, he could have sought a way to ignore or forget his suffering. He could, for instance, practice austerities in order to attain agelessness

25

and immortality. In reality, he found freedom from the pains of life in *nirvana,* where pain no longer exists.

Early Buddhism, Nakamura wrote, saw the cause of the irrational self-assertion as arrogance. Although each human being exists in relation to other beings and is, of necessity, transitory, he or she ignores the fact and is arrogant as if only the ego is changeless. The arrogance arises from the illusion in which the ego separates itself from its relations to other beings and understands itself as a changeless substance. Further, the ego holds itself to be at the center of the world and strives to subordinate other beings to its will. This we call the "absolutization of the estranged ego." We define "absolutization" as positing something apart from its original bond with other beings and holding it to be the highest, the ultimate, or the most central. Being the betrayal of its own nature, the absolutization of the ego thus implies its estrangement from its ground and degeneration (see Sec. II, below).

Young Gotama was already aware, in a sense, that the cause of human delusion lay in the absolutization of the estranged ego. Indeed, in *Vinaya-pitaka* we find Gotama preaching *anatman:* It is illusory to substantialize the nonsubstantial ego or to become attached to it. To find the problem of human life in the pain itself is one thing; to see it in the silly arrogance that causes the pain is another. In the former case we could seek a solution in politico-economic revolution or in medical innovations. In other words, the absolutization of the estranged ego is not necessarily problematic here, but religion, including both Buddhism and Christianity, I believe, sees the cause of the human predicament in this absolutization.

This is clear in the Buddhist doctrine of the so-called four noble truths. The first of them is *Dukkha-satya* (the truth about suffering): To be born, to get ill, to age and to die—that is pain. To meet those whom one hates, to part from those one loves, not to obtain what one wants, that is pain. But, we may say, human life does not consist of incessant pains. To meet those whom one loves and to part from those one hates is pleasure. The lack of burdensome goods is very often bliss. If this is so, pain does not cover the whole of human life.

With the second truth, *Samudya-satya* (the truth about the cause of suffering), however, the cause of the pain is seen in ignorance, *avidya.* The pain of life, therefore, comes from the falsehood of the absolutized ego. The self-attachment of the estranged ego is so unnatural that it necessarily produces perpetual friction with everything it encounters. If we understand the situation of the estranged ego in this way, we can hear even in the pleasures of the happiest human existence the creaking of this friction.

When we shift our focus to Jesus, we must note that in the Christian tradition we have no reliable information about the youth of Jesus. We know nothing of the problems young Jesus tried to solve. New Testament scholars hold few of the words of Jesus in the Gospels to be historically genuine. Still, it is possible to recognize where the Jesus of history—and I am here concentrating on the historical Jesus—saw the problematic of human existence: He saw it in the absolutization of the relative.

First, a very rigid interpretation of the law was absolutized by certain "separatists" of his time. The view of the Jewish law in general corresponded roughly to our notion of law and morality together, though it was by no means restricted to them. The most important characteristic was that God and God's absolute authority were claimed to stand behind this interpretation of the law so that the law in its rigorist interpretation was seen as valid in itself, independent of and prior to the varying circumstances of factual daily life. We can even say that the law thus understood did not take root in daily life; the law was separated from daily life and determined the actions of the people as the supreme standard.

Under this interpretation of the law individuals were held to be justified if they observed the law without error. They could then enter the Reign of God and inherit eternal life in the age to come while being honored by people in this age. It is no wonder that persons under this notion of the law would be interested in their own fate with infinite passion. The ego as the object of such passionate interest factually becomes central; although the ego still holds God as supreme, God virtually becomes that which decides the fate of the ego in this age and in the age to come, and the law is little more than a means of safety. Real interest in one's neighbor is lost.

The result of such an understanding of the law was a lack of "immediate" encounter between persons. The relation between persons was mediated by the law. A person did not respond any longer to the voice of the neighbor because the actions of that person were determined by the law. The law was the reality, was the *real* to the person, for we understand reality as something that, being outside, still relates itself to me and moves me. Consequently, primary reality was not God or the neighbor but the law. The person, as the subject of action, was cut off from the immediate relation to other persons. A person was "posited" by the law and strove, through the observance of the law, to be justified and secured by God and by other people, ignoring his or her own real situation before God. We can say that the absolutized law, cutting the ego off from its real relation to other persons and making the ego the ultimate object of its own interest, absolutized the ego and grounded itself in the arrogance of worldly success. The following story illustrates the point:

> He [Jesus] also told this parable to some who trusted in themselves that they were righteous and regarded others with contempt: "Two men went up to the temple to pray, one a Pharisee and the other a tax collector. The Pharisee, standing by himself, was praying thus, 'God, I thank you that I am not like other people: thieves, rogues, adulterers, or even like this tax collector. I fast twice a week; I give a tenth of all my income.' But the tax collector, standing far off, would not even look up to heaven, but was beating his breast and saying,

'God, be merciful to me, a sinner!' I tell you, this man went down to
his home justified rather than the other; . . ." (Lk. 18:9-14a)

It is no exaggeration to say that interpretation of the law at that time
was like an invisible wall that, separating one person from another, made
real encounter impossible. Every moralism today does the same thing.
Where the morals or standards of action are absolutized, they become the
primary reality to the persons who, on their side, are "posited" by them,
not as "substances," but as the subjects of moral acts, something like nuclei
that stand apart from the real relation to other persons. The "nuclear
subject" is made stable through the observance of the standards, so that
the subject, looking at its own faithful observance, relies upon its successful
results and becomes proud of them. This was abhorrent to Jesus, who held
"arrogance" to be more sinful than any transgression of the law.[2]

Both Gotama and Jesus saw the problematic of human ego. The absolutization of the relative produces arrogance. Of course, they differed in
their view of the nature of arrogance. For Gotama, the result of arrogance
was pain; for Jesus, it was sin. Pain centers in the self; sin is a matter of
personal relations. Both saw the authenticity of human existence in overcoming the absolutization of the relative, especially of the ego. Once this
overcoming has been achieved, one becomes aware of the deeper ground:
dharma (religious truth) in the former; the Reign of God, in the latter.
Here, again, we see meaningful agreement.

However, Jesus and Gotama also disagreed on fundamental issues; this
was expressed in the way they taught. According to Nakamura, we cannot
know with certainty what Gotama taught directly after his enlightenment,
though in early *sutras* his teachings are summarized as the middle path, the
four noble truths, the eightfold noble path, *anatman,* and impermanence.
Although to depict the historical Gotama is just as difficult, if not more so,
as to depict the historical Jesus, it is clear that, as differentiated from Jesus,
Gotama taught "dharma," that is, he taught the goal *nirvana* and the way
to it, in rather theoretical fashion, at least to his elite disciples.

If we look at the religions that surrounded or flowed from these two
teachers and compare the preaching methods of Judaism and Christianity
with those of Buddhism, we find remarkable differences. Buddhism expli-
cates universal truth rather philosophically, while Judaism and Christianity
relate it historically, telling the story of the saving acts of God. Judaism
tells how God selected the people of Israel, liberated them from the oppressive bondage of Egypt, established the covenant with Israel that made them
God's people, gave them the law, and promised them peace and prosperity
on the condition of their observance of the law. Christianity announced
that the salvation of humanity was attained by the historical event of the
death and resurrection of Jesus Christ. It has not preached, at least in its
mainstream, the universal, timeless Logos that anyone in any time can
recognize.

However, Jesus behaved differently from both subsequent Judaism and Christianity. Jesus did not enumerate the saving acts of God in the past in order to justify his teaching. Nor did he refer to the covenant of Israel with God as the guarantee of the salvation of the Israelites. Rather, from his manner of addressing and teaching the people, we conclude that Jesus was convinced of the possibility of anyone's understanding his teaching without specific historical presuppositions.

Jesus taught about ultimate concerns touching every human being in any situation.The sympathy many Buddhists feel for his words confirms this. In this sense the nature of the teaching of Jesus is very different from the message of the primitive Christian church, which did not preach the Reign of God that Jesus taught. It preached Jesus Christ as the object of Christian faith. There are many problems here that must be clarified or solved, but this article is confined to the comparison of Jesus with Gotama.

To be sure, Jesus did not teach philosophical theories. Rather, he often told stories—stories, however, that disclosed the mystery of God and God's Reign in the events, occurrences, and behavior of men and women. For example, to the lawyer's question of who is the neighbor he should love in obedience to the commandment to love one's neighbor, Jesus' reply makes clear not how to *think*, but how to *love*:

"A man was going down from Jerusalem to Jericho, and fell into the hands of robbers, who stripped him, beat him, and went away, leaving him half dead. Now by chance a priest was going down that road; and when he saw him, he passed by on the other side. So likewise a Levite, when he came to the place and saw him, passed by on the other side. But a Samaritan while traveling came near him; and when he saw him, he was moved with pity. He went to him and bandaged his wounds, having poured oil and wine on them. Then he put him on his own animal, brought him to an inn, and took care of him. The next day he took out two denarii, gave them to the innkeeper, and said, 'Take care of him; and when I come back, I will repay you whatever more you spend.' Which of these three, do you think, was a neighbor to the man who fell into the hands of the robbers?" He [the lawyer] said, "The one who showed him mercy." Jesus said to him, "Go and do likewise." (Lk. 10:30-37)

In another story, Jesus sees in nature not the universal Logos but the love of God very concretely at work:

"Therefore I tell you, do not worry about your life, what you will eat or what you will drink, or about your body, what you will wear. Is not life more than food, and the body more than clothing? Look at the birds of the air; they neither sow nor reap nor gather into barns, and yet your heavenly Father feeds them. Are you not of more value than they? And can any of you by worrying add a single hour to your span of life? And why do you worry about clothing? Consider the lilies of the field, how they grow; they neither toil nor spin, yet I tell you, even Solomon in all his glory was not clothed like one of these." (Mt. 6:25-29)

In reality, the teaching methods of Gotama and Jesus were more similar than they appear at first glance. Gotama, discussing theoretically, bore living witness to the existence of *nirvana* and to its meaning to our life. He also showed through his own life the way to attain it. To Gotama, *nirvana* was something to which his disciples should awaken for themselves, not something he could teach or describe discursively. Hence, we can say further that Gotama "told" *nirvana* rather than discussed it. Jesus' stories about the behavior of men and women implies his understanding of the human being before God or under the Reign of God. Of course, differences remain. Buddha spoke more theoretically; Jesus, more concretely, with images taken from daily life. Considering the similarity of the essential message, the question remains: Are these differences significant? One approach to this issue is to ask what differences existed in the audience's experience of the teaching of their masters.

Gotama taught *dharma*. Since his audience—many of them belonged to the intelligentsia—did not initially know what *nirvana* was, they began with belief in his teachings. Once they had attained *nirvana*, they were able to distinguish *dharma* itself from the person of Gotama, even though it was embodied in him. Jesus told and announced, trying to call forth something in his hearers. To whom did he speak? It is important to note that Jesus spoke to those who at that time were held to be excluded from the Reign of God. He spoke to the "people of the earth" or "the sinners," those who could not study and therefore did not know the law and could not meticulously observe it. He spoke as well to those who suffered from certain sicknesses that were widely held to be punishment. They, too, according to a general view at that time, could not enter the Reign of God to inherit eternal life, yet Jesus acted for them. He addressed them with the language used in daily life. He held intercourse with them, regarding them as partners of his existence. He ate and drank with "sinners" (Lk. 15:2; Mt. 9:11). It is important in this context to remember that the disciples whom Jesus "called" to himself also belonged to "the people of the earth."

Here, we cannot separate the word from the man or from the behavior of the man who spoke it. Not only is the content of the word essential but also the fact that he spoke to these people directly. The fact that "The man who represents God helped me, acted for me, who was excluded from the Reign of God" testifies to the salvation of the "sinners." Surely Jesus did that because he held the arrogance of the Pharisees more sinful than the ignorance or the legal transgressions of the "sinners." This shows the difference between the dimension of Judaism that developed as a law-centered religion and the aspect of the Christian tradition that attempted to play down the law.

To the "sinners" at that time, the behavior of Jesus was decisive but not intelligible. They could not see how "sinners" could be justified before God. Possibly some of the "sinners" sought for an explanation that was intelligible to them and found it at last in their own interpretation of the inexplicable death of Jesus as an atonement: He died for sinners so that they could be justified and enter the Reign of God. Not the teaching, but the man, Jesus, was himself decisive to them.

Herein lies a critical distinction. These Christians believed in the person, Jesus Christ. Buddhists rely upon the *dharma,* not upon the person, Gotama. Thus, the difference in the teaching methods and the audiences to whom Jesus or Gotama spoke and the difference in the ways some of the hearers experienced the behavior of their masters seem to anticipate the difference between Buddhism and Christianity.

The matter is complicated. While Jesus was with his disciples, they did not understand their teacher. Still, Jesus spoke with an authority they never heard before. In some interpretations the disciples, consequently, held him as someone divine without understanding his teaching. We find this kind of Jesus-comprehension, the Jesus-picture it produced—numinous understanding—in the Gospel according to Mark. Accordingly, after the death of Jesus, the disciples understood Jesus presumably through their interpretation of his death as atonement. This liberated them from the bond of law-centered religion promoted by some at that time and allowed them to see from whence the word and acts of Jesus had really come. (I have treated this matter elsewhere.[3]) Thus, there are different levels or strata of Jesus-understanding. We will deal with one such stratum—the Jesus-understanding based on "enlightenment"—in the following section, though this understanding is also inseparably connected with the "numinous" understanding of Jesus.

The situation of the disciples of Jesus was different from that of Gotama's disciples. Jesus could teach for only a few years. His disciples were not highly educated. There was presumably no one who really understood Jesus sufficiently to succeed his leadership or teaching directly. All of this was different with Gotama, so in comparing Jesus with Gotama we cannot forget these differences.

"JESUS IS GOD"—"I AM THE FORMLESS"

In the dialogue between Buddhism and Christianity there is, as is well known, a point of disagreement even among those who are ready to recognize fundamental agreement in both religions: the view of God. Buddhists in general do not admit God as creator. This disagreement is, I think, accentuated in the difference between Christology and Buddhology. The difference, somewhat accentuated, may be formulated as follows: Whereas traditional Christianity understands Jesus as God (in the sense of the Second Person of the Holy Trinity), Zen Buddhists hold any "objective" understanding of the ultimate to be an illusion.

In contemporary critical New Testament studies, there is hardly any scholar who describes Jesus as "God walking on the earth." However, the scholar is rare who in his or her theological treatment holds Jesus to be a mere human being. In light of the lack of agreement on Jesus' essential nature, we will examine here the thesis, "Jesus is God," not so much from the point of view of New Testament scholarship but philosophicotheologically.

Before we enter the discussion, we should recall what Shin-ichi Hisamatsu, the great teacher of Professor Masao Abe, said of the Formless, the true Buddha: In our life we are confronted by an absolute contradiction; we find ourselves in the midst of it, namely, in the manifold contradiction of being to nonbeing, of value to valuelessness, of sense to nonsense. This contradiction is not to be solved. In this situation of absolute despair we must die the great death to be resurrected. "The Formless" awakens to itself as the human "Self," as "I," so that "I" can say that "I" am the Formless and the Formless is "I." In other words, the Buddha as "I" or "I" as Buddha is the true Buddha. We cannot find Buddha outside. Any conception of Buddha as something objective is false or, at best, secondary. Is this thesis reconcilable with the other thesis mentioned above, namely, "Jesus is God"?

To examine our problem it is helpful to take into consideration the view of Katsumi Takizawa, for he offered a remarkable Christology that, *mutatis mutandis,* can be the starting point of our examination. In 1964, he wrote *Buddhism and Christianity: Critical Comments on Hisamatsu's Atheism.* In this book he argued as follows: There are two kinds of contact between God and human beings. The primary contact is the primordial fact of Immanuel: God with us. This fact lies unconditionally at the foundation of each human being's existence, whether or not one is a Christian. However, this contact is not always known to the person in question. In virtue of the primary contact, an awakening can take place in which the person becomes aware of the primary fact. This event Takizawa called the secondary contact between God and the human being. Based on this distinction between the primary and the secondary contact, Takizawa criticized Hisamatsu's view of the true Buddha, saying that Hisamatsu did not clearly distinguish the ultimate Buddha (the primary contact) from the Buddha who "I" am (the secondary contact).

It is interesting that it was in this context that Takizawa developed his Christology. According to Takizawa, we should apply his distinction to the analysis of the person of Jesus. Jesus, so argued Takizawa, was a human being who qualitatively was no different from each of us. However, he was a man in whom the secondary contact was realized so perfectly that he can be regarded as the perfect expression of God, namely, as the model of the secondary contact. Nevertheless, Jesus did not bring the primary contact itself into existence. Traditional Christianity in general (including Karl Barth, Takizawa's teacher) made a mistake in this crucial point. In other words, Christianity did not make a clear distinction between the primary and the secondary contact in the person of Jesus. As a result, Christianity was unjustly absolutized. In reality, Gotama Buddha was a man who realized the secondary contact, so that Buddhism as a whole is another form of true religion, parallel to Christianity.

What is the difference between Jesus and Christ for Takizawa? "Jesus" is the proper name, while "Christ" means "Anointed One," so that Jesus Christ means in abbreviated form the confession, "Jesus is Christ." Though in the New Testament "Jesus" and "Christ" are often synonymous, New Testament scholarship has made a distinction between "Jesus" and "Christ." "Jesus" means the historical Jew who preached the "Reign of God," while the primitive Christian church understood him as Christ, the divine Anointed One or Savior. The New Testament, as a whole, is the document that proclaimed the faith of the church. Now the distinction made by Takizawa is not the same as that in New Testament studies. He often said that the primordial fact of Immanuel, God with us, meant "Christ," without, as far as I know, developing this "Christology" in its full scope. To him, Jesus was the man who realized the secondary contact so perfectly. Below, we shall see the relation between the distinction made by Takizawa and that made by modern New Testament scholarship.

Further, for the following discussion, it is important to note that Takizawa believed that the primordial fact of "God with us" was also the primordial "reality" in my sense; it is working at and in every person, even if he or she is ignorant of the fact. We should also note that Takizawa formulated the relation of the primary contact to the secondary as inseparable, unidentifiable, and irreversible, just as he formulated the relation between God and human beings at the primary contact in the same way: inseparable, unidentifiable, and irreversible.

In principle, I approve of the distinction Takizawa makes between the primary and the secondary contact of God with human beings. Naturally, there are many problems with his view, such as what "God" or "the contact" means, how his claims are verified, etc. Since we cannot examine these problems in detail here, in the following, I give only my understanding of his doctrine.

We must first ask whether Takizawa is right when he insists that the primary fact is equally real whether we are aware of it or not. How can we be sure it is real when we are ignorant of it? Apart from the logical question, there is an ontological problem. Natural powers are at work and real whether or not we are aware of them. Apples fell to earth even before Newton found the law of gravity (if the story about how he came to the idea of gravity is true). Gravity did not become real because of its discovery. However, this is not the case in certain ontological areas. For example, the sense of a text written in a language that no one can read is virtually nonexistent, though we can assume that it is there. The text speaks to no one. A historical event of which I am ignorant is virtually nonexistent to me, for it does not move me. A piece of music that I do not understand at all is to me a mere accumulation of sounds. "Music" is virtually nonexistent to me in this case.

Generally speaking, cultural products and historical events are virtually nonexistent or unreal when they are not understood, whereas natural powers are real irrespective of my nonawareness of them. The same is true with the human heart. If I do not understand at all any expression of one who loves me, his or her love is virtually nonexistent to me, for it does not move me. Is this not also true of "religious" matters?

Paul says that he had been in the grace of God even from his mother's womb (cf. Gal. 1:15). However, when he was ignorant of that, he persecuted the early Christian church. Christ had not been real to him until the event of revelation: "God ... called me through his grace, [and] was pleased to reveal his Son to me" (Gal. 1:15- 16a); God "shone in our hearts to give the light of the knowledge of the glory of God in the face of Jesus Christ" (2 Cor. 4:6). Since this event, Paul could even say: "I have been crucified with Christ; and it is no longer I who live, but it is Christ who lives in me" (Gal. 2:19b-20a). Christ was then *the real* that bore his whole existence, and Paul was aware of that.

This shows that "the primary contact" is not real, virtually nonexistent, insofar as one is not aware of it. Even if we had the knowledge of God, the contact is not real. It is potential. Only when "God shines in our heart" does the knowledge of God come into reality. This is the meaning of the words of Paul quoted above. In other words, the secondary contact calls the primary into reality or activates the primary. The matter is somewhat paradoxical. On the one hand, we can and must say that the secondary contact is based on and realized because of the primary contact. On the other hand, the reverse is also true. At the realization of the secondary contact, the primary contact is activated.

This aspect of affairs is reflected in the following paradoxical sayings: On the one hand, it is said that those who receive Christ become children of God, as if the decision of faith or human subjectivity played a decisive role. On the other hand, it is also said that only those whom God gave to Christ can come to him and believe in him, as if the decision of faith or human subjectivity does not play any role (compare Jn. 1:12 with 6:44, 65, and Lk. 15:4 with 15:17-18). Because of the "predestination" of God, one can come to believe in Christ. However, the decision of faith changes the potential relation of human beings to God, their becoming children of God, bringing this relationship to a new level of reality.

For our discussion it is important to remember the same aspect in Buddhism. On the one hand, we can say that based on Buddha-nature one can be awakened to it; on the other hand, the Buddha-nature becomes real in awakening. Dogen (1200-1253, founder of Soto-Zen in Japan) says that Buddha-nature is there, not prior to awakening but after awakening, and that Buddha-nature is simultaneous with it.[4] Hisamatsu agrees. According to him the Formless becomes real at awakening.

If this is so, Takizawa's view is open to criticism. Although it is true that the primary contact itself was not brought into existence by Jesus for the first time, it existed only potentially and, therefore, was virtually nonexistent, before the secondary contact was realized in Jesus. In this sense it is still true that "The law indeed was given through Moses; grace and truth came through Jesus Christ" (Jn. 1:17; in John, truth is the revelation or reality of God). "Truth" had been real nowhere in our historical world before and outside Jesus Christ, of course, as far as the Evangelist knew.

We must modify the view of Takizawa as follows: Jesus was the only human being, at that time and in that place, as far as the writers of the New Testament knew, in whom God was real. In this sense God was real nowhere outside Jesus, or God acted through Jesus and as Jesus. God was real *in* Jesus, or God acted *through* Jesus, for God must be distinguished from Jesus. No one in that time and situation could find the reality of God outside Jesus. In this sense Jesus was God, and God was Jesus (see more on this, below).

We can ask a further question: Who could justifiably make this claim? Not all Jews at his time understood Jesus as the reality of God in the historical world. To some lawyers Jesus was blasphemous (Mk. 2:7). They found even demonic authority in him (Mk. 3:22). There are, as mentioned, various strata of understanding of Jesus. To some, Jesus was something numinous in the sense of Rudolf Otto's *Das Heilige*. In the Gospel according to Mark, Jesus appears as something indefinable, terrible, and astonishing, as if something mysterious had come into this world from the *totaliter aliter* world. However, from the synoptic traditions we can say that some who encountered Jesus experienced the reality of God in the encounter with Jesus—whatever "God" may mean here.

This is also our experience today: Whoever encounters Jesus encounters God. This thesis finds its expression in the Christian doctrine of Jesus: Jesus himself is the Word of God in the primary sense. The Bible that testifies to Jesus is also the word of God in the secondary sense, and the preaching of the Christian church is the word of God in the tertiary sense (Karl Barth). God addresses us through Jesus, through the Bible, and through the preaching of the Christian church (see 2 Cor. 5:20). Thus, to encounter Jesus is to encounter God (see Jn. 14:9). This is the primary meaning of the statement that Jesus is God. We understand Jesus not as "the numinous" but as the realization of "the secondary contact."

At the same time, I agree with Takizawa that Jesus is not the exclusive realization of the secondary contact. If we can say that Jesus is God, we can even say that there are "gods," and this—although somewhat exceptional—is biblical (see Jn. 10:34). Then, for Christians, Jesus is the realization of the secondary contact *par excellence,* as Gotama Buddha is for Buddhists. "Jesus is God" is a cognitive confession, not an expression of the mysterious, non-cognitive feeling of the numinous seen in the Gospel according to Mark. The cognitive confession that Jesus is God takes place in the encounter with Jesus. The locus of this cognition is encounter, not primarily an "awakening" to the deeper Self. Still, we can ask how it is possible for us to know, to cognize the reality of God in Jesus in the encounter with Jesus. What is the condition that enables this cognition?

This cognition is possible when one is aware of the primary contact, namely, when one has realized the secondary contact. Perhaps the cognition is deeper in proportion to the depth of one's cognition. Maybe there are degrees of quality and quantity. Moreover, there is the problem of understanding. We need much training in order to understand historical documents or cultural products in general. However, this is not our question here. In our case, the cognition is essentially a matter of sympathy or consonance, not of objective knowledge or observation. The reality in "me," of which I am aware, resonates with that in "Jesus."

If this is so, the condition in which we, in the encounter with Jesus, can say that Jesus is God is our awareness of the primary contact or, in other words, enlightenment. It is a condition in which one can say, "I am the Formless," not in an encounter with someone else but in relation to myself. "Jesus is God" and "I am the Formless" condition each other.

In the Meiji era, there was in Kyoto a famous Zen-master named Gasan. One day he read the Bible. He began with the first page of the Gospel according to Matthew and, having read the Sermon on the Mount (Mt. 5-7), he said, "These are really the words of a great master." Then he called his disciples and warned them, saying that they should not speak ill of Christianity. The words of Jesus awaken, call forth, and activate in their hearers the reality of the primary contact or, in the case of an awakened master like Gasan, they call forth a consonance so that the hearer can find in the person of Jesus the activated reality of the primary contact. The words coming from reality appeal to the same reality in the hearer or in the reader.

Peter Berger has assumed that there are two models of religious experience: the confrontation model and the interiority model. In the former, one "encounters" the ultimate, as is the case with the Hebrew prophets. In the latter, one becomes aware of the ultimate in oneself, as is the case with mystics. Berger has tested his hypothesis in group work with the result that in many religious personages—for instance, Paul, Francis of Assisi and Shinran—both models are found. The one does not exclude the other.[5] We see why. Both types condition or supplement each other because the cognition of the ultimate in the person encountered is mediated by the awareness of the same reality in the person who encounters. Only in Christianity where the feeling of one's sinfulness is strong is the encounter model dominant (Jesus is God, who, as God, spoke to the sinner showing that the sinner could participate in the truth). In religions in which the awareness of the ultimate reality in the person is more important than the consciousness of one's sinfulness, the model of "interiority" is dominant.

However, it is a matter of comparison, not of mutual exclusion. In the encounter situation, one does not encounter God directly as such but always through some medium, such as Jesus or the Bible. This is the case even in the interiority model. Here, the person is the medium. One does not find "God" as such in the self. Rather, the person as a whole is the medium of such awareness, as is seen in the expression, "I am filled with the Holy Spirit." In this sense one can say that in the interiority model one "encounters" the ultimate "in" oneself, while in the encounter model the ultimate "in" the person who encounters resonates with the ultimate "in" the one encountered. The one who encounters becomes aware of the ultimate "in" oneself. The two models are thus polar and supplementary. I do not think that, for example, Professor Abe, who advocates the interiority model, would deny that he "encountered" the Formless as he encountered his great master Hisamatsu.

In the following section we ask more precisely the meaning of the statements, "Jesus is God" and "To encounter Jesus is to encounter God," as well as the meaning of "I am the Formless." Are they not the apotheosis of the human being? Are they not the absolutization of the relative, which was abhorrent to both Jesus and Gotama? What is the meaning of "Jesus" or "I"?

CHRIST AND BUDDHA-KAYA

In this section we examine more strictly the meaning of the thesis, "To encounter Jesus is to encounter God." What do we see in Jesus in the encounter with him that leads to this cognitive confession? What does it mean to see in Jesus something divine? Naturally, our answer is that we see in Jesus the reality of the primary contact. This thesis is explicated in the following, not as the problem of "Christology" in the exclusive sense, but as a matter of the analysis of human existence in general.

As quoted above, Paul wrote: "I have been crucified with Christ; and it is no longer I who live, but it is Christ who lives in me" (Gal. 2: 19b-20a). Then Paul continued: "And the life I now live in the flesh I live by faith in the Son of God, who loved me and gave himself for me" (Gal. 2:20b). In the former saying Paul and Christ are one, whereas in the latter they are two. We must identify them and distinguish one from the other.

Christ is "the true Self" of Paul, but the ego of Paul, which died once, "having been crucified with Christ," does not disappear. Instead, it is created anew: "So if anyone is in Christ, there is a new creation: everything old has passed away; see, everything has become new!" (2 Cor. 5:17; cf. Gal. 6:14-15). The old ego seemed sovereign in Paul when he, a Pharisee, strove for the complete observance of the law, but in reality it was in slavery.

The fate of Paul hung on his obedience to the law. The more he strove for such obedience, the more the letter of the law became his factual "lord." Paul did not know the reality of God apart from the letter of the law. The real subject of Paul at that time was the mere ego, which did not know the reality of "Christ in me." So, the ego was separate from divine reality and estranged from real life. "When the commandment came [and "I" began to strive to observe it], sin revived and I died" (Rom. 7:9). The very craving of the ego after eternal life brought Paul into the captivity of sin and death. However, as the Son of God was revealed in him (Gal. 1:16), the change of the subject took place. "Christ" became his real subject; his "ego," Christ's organ. In reality the ego came to its own nature. It became "free" because it lived from its own ground.

We make a distinction between the Self and the ego. "Christ in me" is the Self, for it is the true subject of "mine." "Christ in me" and "I" are in this sense identical. Indeed, Paul could say that his entire mission was the act of Christ through Paul (Rom. 15:18). Nevertheless, the ego of Paul was clearly distinguished from Christ, because Christ was his sovereign and the object of his faith. Now "the Son of God" was revealed "in" Paul so that the Son of God "lived in him." We should understand this "in" both in the sense of "to" as well as in the sense of "in": The Son of God was revealed *both* "in" and "to" Paul—that is to say, in and to his ego, for the ego is precisely that which is conscious or aware of anything.

On the one hand, we can understand the "revelation" as the widening of the awareness of the ego. We see that, when Paul says that God "shone in our hearts to give the light of the knowledge of the glory of God in the face of Jesus Christ" (2 Cor. 4:6), the ego is then aware of the Self. On the other hand, the Self (Christ in me) is not identical with the ego. Anyway, we can say that the event of enlightenment or the "revelation of the Son of God" is the event in which the Self is revealed in and to the ego, or it is the event in which the ego becomes aware of the Self that was hidden to it. To speak more strictly, in this event the Self (which was formerly hidden and not actual, potential and nonexistent) becomes "real" not only in itself but also in and to the ego.

This is not merely a matter of cognition. It is a matter of life. The whole person becomes alive. "To me to live is Christ" (Phil. 1:21), said Paul. It is highly interesting that in this statement Christ is neither substance nor person but, so to speak, the Formless. The infinitive of the verb "live" is the subject of this sentence, and "Christ" is the predicate: "that he lives" is "Christ." The reality of his life is the reality of Christ. Here, we have another expression of the matter Paul formulated in Gal. 2:20. In this sense we can compare this saying of Paul with one by Lin-chi (one of the greatest Chinese Zen-masters of the ninth century): The Formless is at work as seeing in the eyes, as hearing in the ears, as smelling in the nose, as talking in the mouth, etc. Lin-chi was aware that his life-activities were borne by the Formless, so that the Formless saw when Lin-chi saw. Further, he said that the True Human of no Rank (the Formless Self) is active in the sensations of which we must become aware.

Christ bears all the life-activities of Paul, and Paul is aware of this fact. In other words, human life comes to its real nature when it is illuminated. This is suggested by the fact that Christ as well as Amida-Buddha[6] is Life and Light at the same time. Life must be illuminated. It wants to make itself manifest to itself, revealing itself in and to the ego. Otherwise, life remains a dark impulse, a "blind" will, and we remain ignorant of its nature.

What is the relation of our distinction between the Self and the ego and the distinction made by Takizawa between the primary and the secondary contact? It is easy to see that "the primary contact" of Takizawa, namely, "God with us" or "Christ," corresponds to "the Self." "The secondary contact," that is, the event of our awakening to the primary contact, corresponds then to the manifestation of the Self to the ego. Perhaps we should make a comment here also: The Self is virtually nonexistent before enlightenment, and it becomes real or actual when the ego awakens to it. Hence, in Christianity it is often said that we "receive" the Holy Spirit when we make the decision of faith. Therefore, we have gained something we would not have if we did not have faith in Christ. It is described "mythologically" with the image of something heavenly descending onto us, or, as Søren Kierkegaard said, we receive then the very condition of the cognition of Truth (Philosophical Fragments). We do not, in "the secondary contact," find or discover what was there but just hidden; rather, something potential becomes actual. "The Son of God was revealed in (and to) me," so that something quite new takes place: "It is no longer I who live, but it is Christ who lives in me."

What is the relation between the distinction made by Takizawa and that made by modern New Testament scholarship? As noted above, in New Testament studies today the historical Jesus is distinguished from the "Christ" of kerygma preached by the primitive Christian church. This distinction is made in the context of the historical process: Jesus, the preacher of the Reign of God, became the preached, the Christ of faith, in primitive Christianity.

This distinction is diachronic. In contrast, the distinction made by Takizawa is synchronic, for he sees the reality of the primary contact. "God with us," or "Christ," is in the person of Jesus. We can say, interpreting Takizawa, that the primitive Christian church named the primary contact that the disciples of Jesus found in them after the death of Jesus "Christ." Takizawa has made this claim at least once, and I concurred in my New Testament studies.[7] After the death of Jesus, his disciples found in themselves the reality of the primary contact, that is, that which had once spoken and lived as "Jesus." Hence, they held that Jesus had been resurrected and that his power was at work in them. People at the time interpreted such an event in just this way. (See Mk. 6:14-16; many held that John the Baptist, who had been killed, was resurrected and that, therefore, his powers worked in Jesus.) In reality, the disciples of Jesus awakened to "the primary contact," which had been real in Jesus as he had been with them. They comprehended the event of Christophany in the same manner as Paul did (see 1 Cor. 15:5-8).

If we identify the "Christ in me" with "the Self," then the Self is something divine and human. It is divine because it is the "Son of God," and it is human because it is "in me," truly my subject. It is the human Self. "The Self" is therefore divine-human or divine humanness. I interpret the primary contact of Takizawa, "Christ" in his sense, in this way. Then "Jesus Christ" means that the ego of Jesus of Nazareth was at one with the Self (Christ), the Self being manifest to him. We can go a step further and make a distinction between "Logos" and "Christ," for "Christ" is divine-human, while the eternal "Logos" of Jn. 1:1-3 is divine. It is, to use the language of the ancient church, the Second Person of the "Trinity" — God as the Son. In other words, "Christ" is the Logos incarnate in the awakened, activated Self, as distinguished from the ego. The word "incarnation" is relevant because, as is often said, it denotes the actualization of the potential, not a mere discovery of the existent. Thus, we make a distinction among Logos, Christ, and Jesus. This threefold distinction is necessary in order to compare Christ with Buddha. I am referring here to the trikaya-theory on the side of Buddhism that there are the three following Buddha-bodies: *dharma-kaya* (the transcendent Buddha-body as the Ultimate), *sambhoga-kaya* (the manifestation of *dharma-kaya,* such as Amida-Buddha, to help suffering beings), and *nirmana-kaya* (the incarnation of Truth, such as Gotama Buddha).

Before we begin that discussion, we must explore the problem of understanding the words of Jesus as the expression of the Self through the ego, his ego being at one with his Self. We do not need a lengthy explanation of the ego as the locus of ego-centeredness or egoism. We note here only the fact that the ego is self-conscious, that it uses ordinary language, and that it works with ordinary logical thinking, which elsewhere I have called the "differentiating intellect."[8]

Jesus asks:

> "Which one of you, having a hundred sheep and losing one of them, does not leave the ninety-nine in the wilderness and go after the one that is lost until he finds it? When he has found it, he lays it on his shoulders and rejoices. And when he comes home, he calls together his friends and neighbors, saying to them, 'Rejoice with me, for I have found my sheep that was lost.' " (Lk. 15:4-16)

It is characteristic of the word of Jesus that it sounds so natural, though it is absurd to the discriminating intellect. This is the case with the Parable of the Lost Sheep. The reader thinks involuntarily, "Really, who does not do so?" Yet, what shepherd would engage in such folly? Ninety-nine sheep are, economically, more valuable than one. Who leaves the ninety-nine sheep without a shepherd in the dangerous wilderness where they can be scattered and where there are dangerous animals or thieves? Jesus shows us what love is. Love knows the moment when it concentrates itself on the one, forgetting all others. It is not rational. It does not calculate or weigh. If calculation is a matter of value, love is above the opposition between the valuable and valueless. Love, Jesus taught, is not love "from above to below," as is often held, for in this parable the point is not that the shepherd searched for the lost one but that he left the ninety-nine in the wilderness. Yet, if we have "natural" sympathy with this story, from whence does it come?

The same question arises with the Parable of the Good Samaritan (Lk. 10:30-35), quoted above. We discuss it again because it is so important for us. It was a Samaritan who rescued the Judaean who lay half dead, even though the Judaean belonged to those who were quite inimical to the Samaritans. However, the Judean's compatriots, a priest and a Levite, having seen the fallen Judaean, ignored him. (Here we see Jesus' irony toward the priesthood.) That the Samaritan was moved to pity when he saw the Judaean (v. 33) sounds quite natural, but is it "natural" to love an enemy? Again, it is absurd to our discriminating intellect. It is quite impossible for the ego to love the enemy. How then does the act of the good Samaritan appear to be natural and appeal to our heart? The words of Jesus, coming from the Self, appeal to our Self, while they are absurd to the ego. If we interpret the words of Jesus as the words of the Self, our distinction between the Self and the ego is confirmed.

We can also compare the Self, "Christ" in our sense, with the activated Buddha-nature, or a *Buddha-kaya,* that is, *upaya-kaya,* the manifestation or activity of Buddhist Truth as the "means" of leading sentient beings to the Truth. (We put aside the problem of the relation between Buddha-nature and *Buddha-kaya.* They are not the same but often seem to be synonymous.) The key to this comparison lies in the relationship of the "Christ in me" with an *upaya-kaya,* for, as is shown below, the Amida-Buddha, who corresponds to Christ, is *upaya-kaya.* How far do or do they not coincide? It is impossible to elucidate this problem here; in the following I can only give some suggestions.

Consider a passage from the writings of a Zen-master, Ryomin Akizuki: "One day Ungan (780?-841), a Chinese Zen-master, made tea. His friend Dogo (769-835) came to him and asked: 'For whom are you making tea?' Ungan answered, 'There is the One who wants tea.' Dogo asked, 'Why do you not let him make tea?' Ungan responded, 'Fortunately I am here.' "

Akizuki continued:

There is an antecedent to this dialogue. When Ungan, who gave this splendid answer to Old Dogo's *Koan* [a "riddle" that novices in Zen monasteries must solve in order to attain enlightenment], was a young

bonze in his study, he visited one of the greatest Zen-masters of that
time, Hyakujo (720-814). Now Hyakujo was famous for his saying: "If
I do not work a day, I do not eat that day." Ungan conversed with
Hyakujo as follows:

Ungan: For whom are you working every day so hard?

Hyakujo: There is the One who needs that.

Ungan: Why do you not let him work?

Hyakujo: He cannot do daily work for himself.

This dialogue is helpful in understanding our first *Koan*. The point lies
in the relation between "the One" and "I." Here is the whole secret of
Zen. We can even say that here is the important secret of Buddhist existence as a whole. It is not too much to say that to understand this, this
alone, is to understand Zen Buddhism.

Zen does not posit God or even "Buddha" besides the One. More accurately, Zen speaks of Buddha, for it is Buddhism; however, it does so only
to show the relation between "the One" and "I." Zen also asserts that the
things of everyday life, such as making tea, drinking tea, etc., are what truly
matter. Now the One cannot make tea. It cannot sweep the garden for
Itself. It cannot do anything alone, but "fortunately" "I" am there, and the
One works through the "I." In this way the One makes tea, drinks tea, and
sweeps the garden. It does everyday work. Zen Buddhists work quite diligently because they feel and perceive the inner needs of the One, and this
One is again no other than Hyakujo, Ungan, the Zen Buddhist himself.

Lin-chi called this One "the True Human." He said: "There is the True
Human of No Rank in the mass of naked flesh, who goes in and out from
your facial gates (i.e., sense organs). Those who have not yet testified (to
the fact), look! look!" The One is evidently at work when you see, hear,
think, and so on. Those who have not yet been aware of It should see It
with their inner eye.

Hisamatsu, the late Zen-master and famous Zen philosopher, called this
"True Human," "the Formless Self." Zen Buddhists testify only to this one
reality. The Zen slogan shows it: "To testify straightforwardly to the mind
of the person, i.e., to become aware of the (Buddha-)nature and to become
a buddha, the awakened."[9]

Evidently, "the One" corresponds to "the Self" and "I" to "the ego" in
our sense. Then enlightenment means that the ego becomes aware of the
Self. Here, again, we have a parallel to the "revelation" of the Son of God
in and to Paul. Indeed, Paul shows a wonderful parallel to the dialogue
above: "For I will not venture to speak of anything except what Christ has
accomplished through me [namely, Paul's mission], to win obedience from
the Gentiles, by word and deed" (Rom. 15:18). Christ wants to speak his
word but cannot do this by himself. "Fortunately," Paul is there, and Christ
does his work through Paul. Now the Self, the True Human of No Rank,
and the Formless Self are all synonymous, and they denote the activated

Buddha-nature. To become aware of the Self means to become aware of the Buddha-nature, because to become a buddha means to become aware of the Buddha-nature. However, as shown above, the Self means "Christ in me." Thus, we can conclude and say that "the Self," "Christ in me," and "activated Buddha-nature" are synonymous. Of course, because of the rich connotations of the words we cannot with ease say that they are completely synonymous. We can say that they are the same, at best, at the level of the matter, not at the level of verbal expressions.

One would ask: Is "the Formless Self" the same as "I," or is "the True Human of No Rank" then *upaya-kaya*? Is it not *"dharma-kaya"*? Is there in Zen really any distinction between "the Formless" and "the Formless Self"? To be frank, I am not sure. Zen Buddhism admits no mythological, objective deity, so the Formless Self alone is real. But, is not "the Formless as I" the manifestation of *dharma-kaya*? What role does *upaya-kaya* play in Zen Buddhism? D.T. Suzuki has written:

> When the seed of an apple is buried in the soil, the vow of Amida-Buddha which is in the seed begins to work. In the world of dependent origination the vow of Amida-Buddha in the seed operates in its right order, so that the seed sprouts and the leaves, then twigs come out, so that after several years it becomes an apple-tree which blooms and bears apples. . . . All these take place in "no Mind" [*Mushin*] and go on just as the vow of Amida-Buddha works.[10]

It is very interesting to compare the passage above with Jesus' parable in Mk. 4:26-29: "The kingdom of God is as if someone would scatter seed on the ground, and would sleep and rise night and day, and the seed would sprout and grow, he does not know how. The earth produces of itself, first the stalk, then the head, then the full grain in the head. But when the grain is ripe, at once he goes in with his sickle, because the harvest has come." The Reign of God is not something merely heavenly. It means that the earth produces a crop of itself. Here we see a New Testament version of "the identity of the absolute contradictory" of Nishida, or "Jinen-Honi" of Shinran: "To become so of itself, for Dharma lets it be so." We also see here the expression of *"Mushin"* (no Mind). Taking the matter one more step, "the vow of Amida-Buddha" is, according to Shinran, *upaya-kaya,* and we can compare "the vow of Amida" in the passage above with "the True Human of No Rank" of Lin-chi or the "Formless Self" in Hisamatsu. Are they not identical?

Shinran says that there are two kinds of *buddha-kaya: dharma-kaya* and *upaya-kaya. Upaya-kaya* comes from *dharma-kaya* and expresses *dharma-kaya (Kyo-gyo-shin-sho, shokan).* Amida-Buddha is *upaya-kaya,* and it is "the corporealized form of *tathata* (as-it-is-ness) or *dharmata* (truth-ness) manifesting itself to help suffering beings" (Japanese-English Buddhist Dictionary). Shinran defines it also as *sambhoga-kaya* and says further that

Amida-Buddha comes from *tathata* and manifests himself not only as *sambhoga-kaya* but also as *nirmana-kaya* and *upaya-kaya*. *Upaya-kayo* or *sambhoga-kaya* is the manifestation of the formless *dharma-kaya*, working for the salvation of sentient beings. The salvation is attained, according to Shinran, by transmission *(Eko)* of the vow of Amida-Buddha. The faith itself is based on it, so the faith is an activity of the vow, that is, Amida-Buddha himself.

It is no wonder that we often find sayings such as the following in the writings of Jodo-Shin-Buddhists: "To call the name of Amida is to encounter Him, to find myself in the light of Amitabha. ... In this moment my former subjectivity falls back and His vow constitutes my subjectivity. ... The True Heart of Tathagata [manifestation of as-it-is-ness] becomes I myself."[11] However, the sinful care for oneself *(bonno)* does not disappear, but "when *bonno* operates as *bonno,* the vow operates as the vow."[12]

From this we see that Jodo-Shin-Buddhism[13] makes the distinction between *dharma-kaya* and *upaya-kaya*. *Amida-Buddha* is *upaya-kaya* or *sambhoga-kaya,* and Amida-Buddha as the Savior stands very close to "Christ" in the New Testament. The story of *Dharmakara,* a manifestation of *dharma-kaya* as a man, corresponds structurally to the Christ-hymn (Phil. 2:6-11). Further, Amida-Buddha and Christ are both, as Life and Light, powers working for the salvation of humanity. They are both "in" the believers as their true subject. At the same time, believers find themselves "in" the saving activities of the Savior. So it is evident that "Christ in me," "the Self" in our sense, corresponds to Amida-Buddha working in the believers as the true subject. Further, when we recall that Amida-Buddha manifests himself as many *nirmana-kaya,* we get the following correspondence, and this is the conclusion of our study:

Comparative Outline of Relationships

In the case of Takizawa:
God _____ the primary contact _____ the secondary contact
                        (the self)   (the activated Self – Ego)

Position of this essay:
Logos (God as the Son) _____ Christ (Logos incarnate) _____ Jesus
                                                        (Logos incarnate – Ego)

In the case of Shinran:
Dharma-kaya sambhoga-kāya or *upāya-kāya* _____ *nirmana-kaya* as Gotama
                        (Amida-Buddha)

In the case of Jesus:
God _____ The Reign of God _____ Jesus as the Son of Man – Ego
        (The Son of Man as its personification)

NOTES

1. Hajime Nakamura, *Gotama Buddha* (Tokyo: Shunjusha, 1969), pp. 63-71.

2. If so, we have good reason to revise traditional atonement theology, because it presupposes that those who observe the law without error are justified (Rom. 2:13; Gal. 3:12). However, Jesus shows that those who observe the laws as the Pharisee in the parable cannot be justified before God. Romans 7:7-24 implies the same, according to the interpretation of modern New Testament scholarship. Atonement theology then loses its fundamental presupposition.

3. *Shinyaku Shisono Seiritzu* [*The Formation of New Testament Thinking*] (Tokyo: Shinkyo Shuppansha, 1963); Kirisototo Iesu [*Christ and Jesus*] (Tokyo: Kodansha, 1969).

4. "Bussho" [*On Buddha-Nature*] in Dogen's major work, *Shobō-Genzō* [*The Quintessence of Right Teaching*]; text: Nippon Shisotaikei 12 (Tokyo: Iwanami, 1970), p. 53.

5. Peter L. Berger, *The Other Side of God: A Polarity in World Religions* (New York: Anchor Press, 1981).

6. According to Pure Land Buddhism, Dharmakara fulfilled his vows, established the Pure Land, and became Amida-Buddha, so that anyone who, believing in him, calls his name will be born after his or her death in the Pure Land and will come to Enlightenment.

7. See Seiichi Yagi, " 'I' in the Words of Jesus," in John Hick and Paul Knitter, eds., *The Myth of Christian Uniqueness* (Maryknoll, N.Y.: Orbis Books, 1987; and London: SCM Press, 1988), pp. 117-134.

8. Cf. Seiichi Yagi and Leonard Swidler, *A Bridge to Buddhist-Christian Dialogue* (New York and Mahwah: Paulist Press, 1990), pp. 107-113.

9. Quoted from Ryomin Akizuki's paper presented at the international conference, "Buddhism and Christianity: Toward the Human Future," August 12, 1987, Berkeley, California. We find almost the same sentences in Ryomin Akizuki, *Zen to Jinsei* [*Zen and Human Life*] (Tokyo: Sekkasha, 1982), pp. 43ff.

10. D. T. Suzuki, *Mushin to yuu koto* [*That Which Is Called "No-Mind"*], Selected Works, vol. 10 (Tokyo: Shunjusha, 1955), pp. 146-147.

11. Master Chien Matsubara, in Tenko Fujinami, ed., *Meishi Sannin Shu* (Kyoto: Nagata Bunshodo, 1960), pp. 116-117.

12. Ibid., p. 119.

13. Pure Land Buddhism in Japan, founded by Honen (1133-1212), is "Jodo Shu"; that founded by his disciple Shinran (11731262) is called "Jodo-Shin-Shu."

3

The Buddha and the Christ: Mediators of Liberation

ALOYSIUS PIERIS

Interreligious dialogue is carried out on three different, but essentially related, levels: the levels of *core-experience, collective memory,* and *interpretation.*

The "core" of any religion is the *liberative* experience that gave birth to that religion and continues to be available to successive generations of humankind. It is this primordial experience that functions as the *core* of a religion, at any time, in any given place, in the sense that it continuously re-creates the *psycho-spiritual mood* proper to that particular religion, imparting at the same time its own peculiar character to the *socio-cultural manifestation* of that religion. It is precisely through recourse to this primordial experience that a religion resolves its recurrent crises and regenerates itself in the face of new challenges. In fact, the vitality of any given religion depends on its capacity to put each successive generation in touch with that core-experience of liberation.

The medium by which the core-experience is made available to successive generations is precisely the "collective memory" of that experience. A religion would die as soon as it is born if it failed to evolve some *means of perpetuating* (the accessibility of) its core-experience. Religious beliefs, practices, traditions, and institutions that grow out of a particular religion go to make up a "communication system" that links its adherents with the originating nucleus — that is, the liberative core of that religion. This is why a religion fades out of history even after centuries of existence when its symbols and institutions lose their capacity to evoke in their followers the distinctive salvific experience that defines the essence of that religion. Did this not happen to the great religions of ancient Egypt, Rome, Greece, and Mesopotamia?

Integral to the functioning of the communication system of the collective memory is "interpretation." In order to be remembered, an experience — in its symbols, beliefs, and rituals — has to be framed in terms of historical and cultural categories. Thus, the core-experience in all religions, insofar as it is remembered, tends also to be interpreted in such diverse ways as to form various philosophical, theological, and exegetical schools.

In Buddhism, the core-experience lends itself to be classed as gnosis or "liberative knowledge"; the corresponding Christian experience falls under the category of agape or "redemptive love." Each is *salvific* in that each is a *self-transcending* event that radically transforms the human person affected by that experience. At the same time, there is an indefinable contrast between them, which largely determines the major differences between the two religions, differences quite obvious even to a casual observer. And yet, it must be recognized that both gnosis and agape are *necessary* precisely because each in itself is *inadequate* as a medium not only for experiencing but also for expressing our intimate moments with the Ultimate Source of liberation. They are, in other words, complementary idioms that need each other to mediate the self-transcending experience called "salvation." Any valid spirituality, Buddhist or Christian, as the history of each religion attests, does retain both poles of religious experience — namely, the gnostic and the agapeic. The movement of the spirit progresses through the dialectical interplay of wisdom and love, or, to put it in Buddhist terms, through the complementarity between *prajna* and *karuna,* and in the Hindu tradition, the sapiential spirituality known as the *jnana-marga* and the affective-active paths called the *bhakti-* and *karma-marga.*

But in order to appreciate and dialogue about both the differences and the complementarity between the core-experiences of Buddhism and Christianity, one must enter into their collective memories. Buddhism and Christianity are both vibrant with vitality today because each has developed its own religious system (of doctrines, rites, and institutions), which can make the original experience available to contemporary society. Hence the conclusion is unavoidable: a Christian who wishes to enter into a core-to-core dialogue with Buddhism must have two qualifications: (1) a preliminary empathic apprehension of the real nature of the other religion's core-experience, and (2) an uninhibited willingness to make use of the religious system that the Buddhist offers to the Christian as the only means of access to that core-experience — in other words, a readiness to enter into a *communicatio in sacris* with Buddhists.

Elsewhere I have gone into greater detail concerning the complementarity between the Buddhist and Christian core-experiences and concerning what a *communicatio in sacris* between the two religions would entail.[1] In this chapter I shall take up the third level of dialogue, that of interpretation (which is ancillary or preparatory to the "real" dialogue that takes place when we so "communicate" that we enter into each others' core-experience). My focus will be on one of the most challenging interpretative difficulties in the Christian-Buddhist encounter, one that motivates the other contributors to this book in their search for a "pluralist theology of religions": the problems that arise when *christology* is confronted with the competing claims of *buddhology*.

As far as Buddhism is concerned, interpretation has reached a high point in the doctrine of the buddhahood — "buddhology," as I shall call it in the following considerations. Similarly, insofar as Christ is the very core of Christianity, christology is both the axis and the acme of all Christian hermeneusis. It should be noted that my emphasis on the essentially hermeneutical character of both buddhology and christology is not intended to deny either the theoretical validity or the historical basis of such interpretations. As already argued, interpretations are a necessary means of communication; and as such they reveal the capacity of a given religion not only to *define* (limit) but also to *redefine* (expand) the boundaries of orthodoxy in the process of allowing its theoretical framework to accommodate the intellectual achievements and historical challenges of a given era.

The focus of Buddhist-Christian dialogue on the level of interpretation is the historical figure of the founders of these two religions, who are believed to play a soteriological role in the lives of their followers. This claim is not made by the adherents of other religions. This is what makes Buddhist-Christian dialogue a dangerous exercise. Far from being a religious conversation about Jesus and Gautama, or a comparative study of their different historical and cultural backgrounds, it can easily explode into a kerygmatic confrontation between Jesus interpreted as *the Christ* and Gautama interpreted as *the Buddha*.

GAUTAMA INTERPRETED AS THE BUDDHA

The Buddhist cultures of Asia project a composite picture of the Buddha. Prof. D. J. Kalupahana, a Buddhist, offers us a slow-motion replay of the process by which the scriptural portrait of the extraordinary human teacher grew, in the minds of his followers, into the Transcendent Being of the Mahayanists.[2] The figure of the human teacher *(sattha)* that Kalupahana draws out of the Pali scriptures was not omniscient; nor was his experience of nirvana thought to be different from that attained by his disciples. Quite unlike Jesus of the New Testament, Gautama of the *Tripitaka* (early Buddhist scriptures) did not seem to have clearly claimed that the Saving Truth or the Liberating Path was identical with his own person. He was only the Pathfinder and Truth-discoverer.

But it would be a grave mistake to think of him as a Socrates or a Plato, a mere founder of a school of thought. The kind of Buddhism that Europe imported in the nineteenth century was a "religionless philosophy" and its founder seemed more of a thinker than a holy man.[3] He came to be presented as an areligious person, beloved of rationalists and agnostics, and noted for the "scepticism of his style."[4] This description disregards the fact that the Buddha had listed "logic, inference, and reasoning" among the means that cannot lead to the Truths[5] and put "skepticism" among the five hindrances on the path to nirvana[6] and as one of the three fetters to be freed from.[7]

Much more perceptive in this regard was Clement of Alexandria who was one of the founding fathers of Christian gnosticism; he sensed that the Buddha was more than a mere teacher of a philosophy. According to Clement, those who observed the Buddha's *Regula* (*Monastica*), "regarded him as divine" (*hos theon tetimekasin*) — that is to say, more than human, on account of his superlative sanctity (*di'hyperbolen semnotetos*).[8] It was his sanctity that the medieval Christians celebrated liturgically when they raised St. Joasaph (= *bodhisattva*) to the altars![9]

This is also the image that emerges clearly from the Buddhist cultures in Asia: a saint recognized as such by his followers and therefore revered as the noblest of beings that has ever set foot on earth, higher than the highest of gods, his sanctity alone being the root of his authority over all things in heaven and on earth.

The *locus classicus* that parallels the "Who do people say that I am?" of Matthew 16:13 is found in the Anguttara Nikaya.[10] "Could you be a god?" asks a Brahmin, and Buddha's answer is "No." "A *gandhabba* (demigod)?" "No." "A ghost?" "No." "A human being?" "No." The questioner pursues: "What, then, could you be?"[11] The answer begins with a reference to the Buddha's perfect purity: like the lotus that sprouts and grows in water but remains unsullied by that water, so is the Buddha born and nurtured in this world but untouched by it, as one who "has overcome the world" (*lokam abhibhuyya*).[12] Then comes the long-awaited answer: "Remember, Brahmin, that I am Buddha"[13] — for what distinguishes him from all other beings is his spotless purity.

The legend that describes the Buddha's mother, Maya, as a virgin both *ante partum* and *post partum* (before and after giving birth) is a symbolic variant of the simile of the lotus, and is iconographically expressed in the form of a white elephant,[14] just as in Christian art the dove represents the Holy Spirit hovering over Mary to make her the virgin mother of Jesus. In the first centuries of Buddhism, no artist dared to paint or build a human figure of the Buddha; he could not be classed under any category of being, all of which he transcended by his infinite purity. Instead, the early Buddhists resorted to symbols: the riderless horse represented his Great Renunciation (i.e., his leaving home for the forest); a tree with no one seated beneath it represented the enlightenment; the wheel symbolized the first sermon, his death was signified by the *stupa*, the funeral mound. But when statues did begin to be made in later centuries, they were frequently of gigantic proportions, suggestive of the superhuman stature of his personality. Even today in Theravada countries, to impersonate the Buddha on the stage or in a film is considered blasphemous.

In the medium of the spoken and written word, as in the case of the plastic arts, there was a struggle to formulate this inexpressible dimension of Buddhahood, a dimension that in no way eclipsed Gautama's humanity but in some way transcended it. Though "docetism" *(lokottaravada)* was rejected as a heresy especially in southern Buddhism, the Mahayanists equated the Buddha with the *Dharma,* the eternal Truth that preexists Gautama,[15] similar to the way that Jesus of Nazareth was recognized as the preexistent *Logos* in the fourth Gospel.

Hence there has been, from very early times, a desperate effort to create buddhological titles from terms judiciously selected from the religious vocabulary of contemporary cultures. A random survey has come up with forty-six such titles used in the Pali scriptures.[16] Some describe the Buddha's "person" as such *(mahapurusa* = Supreme Person; *mahavira* = Great Hero; *purusuttama* and *naruttama* = the Most Exalted of persons; *mahajuti* = the Brilliant, etc.); others indicate his relationship with other humans *(vinayaka* = Leader; *purusa-damma-sarathi* = Trainer of tameable persons; *sarathinam varuttama* = the Most Excellent of guides, etc.); still others point to his supremacy over the whole of creation *(lokanatha* = Lord of the Cosmos), and so on.

As one scholar has observed,[17] the long series of epithets cited in the *Upali Sutta* of the Pali canon[18] recalls the *strotra* (i.e., doxological) literature known as *sata-nama* ("hundred names") so characteristic of Hindu devotionalism. The first impression one gets is that here affective or devotional spirituality *(bhakti-marga)* has replaced the gnostic spirituality *(jnana-marga)* which is proper to Buddhism. The fact, however, is that almost all these epithets refer to the Buddha's gnostic detachment and his internal purity.

Since Buddhahood is conceived as the pleroma of gnosis *(prajna)* and agape *(karuna);* one can therefore easily understand why Pali commentators linked these two buddhological qualities with the two most hallowed buddhological titles—namely, *arahan* (the Worthy One) and *bhagavan* (the Blessed One), respectively. The former implies gnostic disengagement from the world, and the latter connotes his agapeic involvement with the liberation of all beings as well as his sovereignty over the whole of creation.[19] These two epithets occur in the most ancient doxology (used even today at the beginning of any liturgy): "Hail to him, the Blessed One, the Worthy One, the supremely Enlightened One!" The exegetes claim that by gnosis (proper to the *arahan),* Gautama crosses the ocean of *samsara* and reaches the further shore of nirvana, but by agape (proper to the *bhagavan)* he also gets others across.[20]

The convergence and concentration of *prajna* and *karuna* in the Buddha (which explains, respectively, his absolute purity and his soteriological impact on the final destiny of others) has also earned for him such titles as *lokavidu* (Knower of the World) and *lokanatha* (Lord of the Cosmos), already in the canonical writings.[21] Also in the subsequent postcanonical literature, his transcendental status and his cosmic lordship began to be indicated through a long string of buddhological epithets such as "King of Kings," "Self-existent," "Self-luminous," "God above (all other) gods (*devatideva*)."[22]

Some eminent Buddhist scholars (e.g., Kalupahana, quoted above) would question the orthodoxy of this development. Perhaps its scriptural roots should be traced back to what we might call the catechetical method or the pedagogy of the Buddha. The scriptures testify that he changed the god-infested cosmos of his contemporaries into an anthropocentric universe wherein humans who fulfill their innate capacity to realize the metacosmic goal of nirvana were held to reach a state far above the level of gods. Thus he divested the gods of all salvific power; even their cosmic influence was restricted to helping or harming humans in their day-to-day temporal needs. The canonical writers make their point when they portray the highest deity of the Brahmanic religion crouching in reverence before the Buddha and his disciples.[23]

This catechetical procedure of the Buddha was continued as a missiological technique in later times in that missionaries did not uproot the cosmic religiosity of the people whom they converted but gave it a metacosmic orientation not only through the doctrine of nirvana but also by installing the Buddha as the sovereign lord immediately *above* and yet wholly *beyond* the local deities of each culture.

This seems to be the origin of what I alluded to as "the composite portrait" of the Buddha emerging from Buddhist cultures. This certainly is what "Gautama the Buddha" means for millions of Asians today. He is as much the Great Being *(mahasatta)* to be revered and praised, the Lord *(bhagavan)* to be loved and trusted, as he is a human teacher *(satha)* to be followed and a saint *(arahan)* to be emulated.

This portrait was brought out in clearer focus during a buddhological controversy that erupted some years ago in Sri Lanka. A renowned Buddhist layman and writer, a humanist and socialist, Dr. Martin Wickramasingha produced a Sinhalese novel based on the life of the Buddha, eliminating the mythical and the miraculous elements from the scriptural accounts and focusing on Siddhartha's *human* struggle not only for his own nirvanic freedom but also for *social* transformation. This novel provoked a massive public protest on the part of monks and laity. The great monk-scholar, the Venerable Y Pannarama, who spearheaded this protest movement, compiled a two-volume refutation of the buddhological and other inaccuracies said to be contained in the novel.[24]

In his critique of the novel, the venerable monk complains that, among other things, in portraying the character of Siddhartha as a human seeker, the novelist had overlooked the quality specific to Siddhartha's Buddhahood.[25] Yet, lest he be accused of docetism *(lokottaravada)*, the monk insists that his criticism should not be construed as a plea for retaining the mythical and the miraculous elements at the expense of Gautama's true humanity. To prove his orthodoxy, he quotes extensively from one of his devotional poems addressed to the Buddha, indeed a credo in the Buddha's historical humanity:

> Had I sensed thee not to be a human
> Never, never indeed would I find in me
> Any love, regard, or fear for thee!
> My Lord is indeed a Man!
> Man in body and thought
> In virtue and action!
> Yet, going beyond common humanity
> He bore a Splendour Transcendent![26]

Then, presuming himself to be the Buddha's contemporary, he expresses his longing to nurse his aging Master, to touch and massage his limbs, kiss his feet, and wash his ailing body.

It is very clear that for this defender of orthodoxy, Buddhahood implies a *truly transcendent* dimension of a *truly human* being. Both these aspects are proclaimed with as much firmness as the *verus deus* and the *verus homo* are affirmed of Jesus in traditional christology.

There is also a third aspect implicit in this credo: the soteriological role of the Buddha. In the orthodox Theravada stream, the Buddha is never regarded as a savior. His soteriological role is restricted to his discovering and preaching the *dharma* (the eternal salvific Truth that preexists him) and to the forming of the *sangha* (a community that, like him, realizes this Truth and continues to preach and practice the Path that leads to it). But once the *dharma* was equated with the Buddha, and the *sangha* was devalued (as happened in certain Mahayanist schools, e.g., in Amidism), Buddha became the savior who grants the grace of salvation to those who invoke him in faith. An agapeic religiosity using a personalist idiom has become a characteristic of such schools of Buddhism.

The more intricate element in the Buddha's soteriological influence is his *cosmic lordship*, at least as far as popular religiosity is concerned. However, no recognized anthropologist has really shown so far that the masses ever confuse this lordship with the cosmic function of gods and spirits. Yet, the cult of gods—that is, this cosmic religiosity—includes as one of its manifestations the *socio-political* regulation of human life. This is at the root of the "Divine Right Theory of Kingship," which the Buddha categorically rejected in favor of a social contract theory.[27] Yet the feudal societies that hosted Buddhism in Asia continued to be dominated by the older theory. Hence, the socio-political order, even in Buddhist cultures, continued to be associated with cosmic religiosity to which Buddhism imparted a metacosmic orientation by placing the Buddha, the *dharma,* and the *sangha* above and beyond the socio-political order.[28] The kingdom of Thailand continues this tradition.

Nevertheless, the social dimension of Buddhist ethics is being reclaimed from oblivion and reexpressed as the Buddha's vision of a just political order for today,[29] so that social justice is regarded at least as an inevitable by-product of Buddhist soteriology. An extreme example of such reclaiming can be found in *Dalit Sahitya* ("Literature of the Oppressed") produced by the schedule castes of Maharashtra in India. Many of them embraced Buddhism as a doorway to social emancipation. The following poem addressed to the Buddha, the liberator of the oppressed, is a sample of *Dalit Sahitya*:

Siddhartha
Never do I see you
In the Jetavana
Sitting in the lotus position
With your eyes closed
Or in the caves of Ajanta and Werule
With your stony lips touching
Sleeping your final sleep.
I see you
Speaking and walking
Amongst the humble and the weak
Soothing away grief
In the life-threatening darkness
With torch in hand
Going from hovel to hovel.
Today you wrote a new page
of the *Tripitaka*.
You have revealed
the New Meaning of suffering
Which like an epidemic
Swallows life's blood.[30]

This indeed is a new interpretation of the Buddha's soteriological role. The belief in his cosmic lordship is hermeneutically extended to the sociopolitical structures whose radical transformation is believed to be possible under the Buddha's soteriological influence. Undoubtedly, this is "a new page in the *Tripitaka*," as the poet declares.

JESUS THE CHRIST IN THE CONTEXT OF BUDDHOLOGY

The "missionary buddhology" that installed the Buddha as cosmic lord in so many Asian cultures anticipated by centuries the missiology of Paul who did the same with Christ in the Hellenistic cultures that he evangelized. He preached and confessed Jesus to be the Lord of all creation, whom all beings "in heaven, on earth, and in hell" adore in fear and trembling (Phil. 2: 6-11). Far from suppressing the Hellenistic belief in "cosmic elements," Paul acknowledged their existence and their power to enslave human beings

(Gal. 4:3) and cause disobedience (Eph. 2:2). Though they appear to be gigantic powers arrayed against humankind (Eph. 6:12), they have all been decisively domesticated by the risen Jesus (Col. 2:15). Thus by liberating us from this "dominion of darkness" (Col. 1:13), Christ has made himself "the head" of all such cosmic forces (Col. 2:10). In other words, he is at once the metacosmic power and the cosmic mediator because in him the whole of existence—in heaven and on earth, visible and invisible—is recapitulated and reconciled (Col. 1:15-16).[31]

Undoubtedly there is a striking parallelism, though not strictly a similarity, between the two confessional formulas, the buddhological and the christological. No wonder that in some Asian countries, the first Christian encounter with Buddhism was to push the Buddha out and install Christ in his place. The Buddhists replied in kind!

In fact, in the polemical mood of the late nineteenth century, when the anticolonial movements had, by historical necessity, to be anti-Christian, the great Buddhist revivalist, Anagarika Dharmapala, took delight in making odious comparisons between the two founders.[32] The "Nazarene carpenter," as he referred to Jesus with disdain, had no sublime teachings to offer, and understandably so, because his parables not only reveal a limited mind, but they also impart immoral lessons and unpractical ethics![33]

> Jesus as a human personality was an utter failure. He made no impression on the public during the three years of his ministry. No thinker or philosopher took the least notice of his philosophy which helped to create imbeciles. The few illiterate fishermen of Galilee followed him as he promised to make them judges to rule over Israel.[34]

In Dharmapala's speeches and essays, Jesus is reduced to the stature of a spiritual dwarf before Buddha's gigantic personality.

But let us humbly acknowledge that this species of Buddhist revivalism owes its anti-Christian thrust to an initial Christian offensive aimed not only against the doctrine but also against the *person* of the Buddha through the written as well as the spoken word.[35]

The peak of this revivalism, as one sociologist sees it,[36] manifested itself in the proliferation of Buddha statues in the major towns of Sri Lanka's western coast; it was an attempt to reaffirm Buddhism, as a socio-political force, against Christianity. May I add my own explanation: Was it not also an attempt to put the Buddha back where he belonged in the urban culture of the westernized Buddhist elite presumably because in that elitist culture the cosmic lordship of the Buddha, taken for granted in the rural areas, was eclipsed by the colonial impact of Western Christianity?

There is also a less aggressive way of affirming the supremacy of the Buddha over Christ and vice versa. The Hindu theology of religions has pioneered this technique. Hinduism neutralizes the challenge of the other religion by absorbing it into its own theological framework. Brought under the Hindu salvific umbrella, Jesus and Gautama become Hindu avatars (incarnations) whom the Christians and Buddhists can hardly recognize as the Christ and the Buddha, respectively.

This ancient theology of religions prevails today on the frontiers of the mainstream churches. The Buddha is accepted as a precursor of Christ, a "holy pagan" preparing the way for Christ the only Savior, as Daniélou, following Guardini, seems to have maintained.[37] Marco Polo's spontaneous observation about the Buddha ("Had he been a Christian, he would have been a great saint of Jesus Christ") had already anticipated this inclusivist theology of religions. In fact, it was as a saint of Jesus Christ that the medieval church accepted the Buddha in the Joasaph cult, as mentioned earlier. No Buddhist is going to be flattered by this condescension. Yet this theory has deep roots in the New Testament approach to the patriarchs and prophets of Judaism—the same approach that Islam adopts toward Jesus!

In the same way, many a well-meaning Buddhist condescends to give Jesus a niche in the Buddhist *Weltanschauung*. At best, Jesus receives the welcome given to a *Bodhisattva*, being full of compassion but still on the way to Buddhahood! This is about the maximum that Buddhists can concede to the founder of Christianity. If they concede one bit more to Jesus, they would cease to be Buddhist.

We are, therefore, obliged to conclude that both the exclusivist and the inclusivist theories of religions end up asserting the supremacy of the Buddha over the Christ, and vice versa. There seems to be no way of avoiding the exclusivist model. This is the impasse that any "dialogical" theology of religions, even in its most inclusivist form, runs into. Is there no other way of seeing the problem? Or, another *starting point?*

I believe that the *false start,* which leads theologians into blind alleys, is their obsession with the "uniqueness" of Christ. At the risk of anticipating my conclusions, I would suggest that the real debate is about the "uniqueness" of *Jesus* in terms of the "absoluteness" that Christians indicate with titles like *Christ, Son of God,* and the like—the same absoluteness that Buddhists indicate with similar terms: *dharma, tathagata,* and the like. To put it more precisely, the crux of the problem is whether it is Jesus or Gautama who is *unique* in the sense of being the *exclusive medium of salvation for all.* That Jesus is unique is obvious even to Buddhists, just as Christians would hardly question the uniqueness of Gautama. Is not each one of us unique? The issue is whether Jesus' uniqueness consists of his absoluteness as conveyed by certain christological titles, and whether the uniqueness of Gautama should be understood in terms of the absoluteness that the word *dharma* or, as in certain schools, *Buddha* seems to convey.

Note that in this context "the Absolute" has a soteriological connotation. Christians know it as the *mysterium salutis* (mystery of salvation) and have learned to distinguish three dimensions in this mystery: (1) *source* of salvation, *(2) medium* of salvation, and (3) *force* of salvation. This is what the "economic Trinity" is all about. In the scriptures these three aspects are distinguished as *theos, logos,* and *pneuma,* respectively; or, more anthropomorphically, as the Father, the Son, and the Consoler/Advocate, who are conceptually clarified in Chalcedonian christology as three distinct *persons* sharing one divine *nature.*

This tridimensionality of the mystery (and process) of salvation is implicitly acknowledged in the soteriology of practically all major religions, as I have suggested elsewhere.[38] In Buddhism, however, the first dimension is not seen as the source of salvation, but seems to be affirmed as the final metacosmic destiny of an individual's cosmic and human history: *nirvana.* Because there is no primordial source of salvation, there is no doctrine of creation *(ex nihilo),* and consequently no doctrine of eschatological consummation, and no theory of grace.

But Christianity sees the source not only as the Alpha, but also as the Omega point of history. Hence, in its agapeic framework, this world and human life itself appears to be *consummated* (fulfilled, perfected) in the *eschaton.* This species of extrapolation characteristic of Christian theology contrasts neatly with the apophatic language of Buddhist gnosticism that sees nirvana as the utter *cessation* rather than the consummation of all that constitutes reality as we now know and experience it. Furthermore, nirvana is the cessation of the human *individual's* history, whereas the *eschaton* is the consummation also of the *collective* history of humankind.

There is, however, a significant point of convergence. Both religions insist: (1) that a positive human endeavor (an ascesis) is a necessary condition for the arrival of final liberation, and yet (2) that this final liberation (the absolute future or the further shore) is never really the result of human effort, for nirvana is beyond the categories of *phala* and *aphala* — that is to say, it defies all human causation, while similarly the *eschaton* is believed to "break in" from the other side of the human horizon.

Though these distinctions and qualifications are necessary when speaking of the source of salvation, there is a greater agreement when we come to the medium of salvation. Salvation implies a paradox: the inaccessible "beyond" (source) becomes one's salvific "within" (force), and the incomprehensible comes within the grasp of human insight. This is possible only because the Absolute contains within its own bosom a mediatory and revelatory self-expression — that is, an accessible dimension: the *Dharma*/the *Logos.* The transhuman horizon stops receding only because there is a path *(marga/hodos)* leading toward it. For, in the beginning was the WORD by which Absolute Silence came to be *heard* — and the ICON by which the Invisible was brought within our *sight!*

But how could we humans, who have *dust* as our origin and destiny (Gen. 3 :19), ever respond to this medium *(dharma/marga/logos/hodos/*word/icon) unless we are equipped with a "response-apparatus" commensurate with that medium? No wonder that all religions seem to postulate a certain *given* capacity within us to seek and find the Liberating Truth, or (as in theistic

religions), a certain innate *force* by which the Absolute draws us toward
Itself. This "given capacity" appears as the "Spirit" in the Christian's vocabulary.

The Buddhist postulates this capacity in the context of the twofold doctrine: "no soul" and "no God." Because no Primordial Source of liberation
is admitted ("no God"), human beings, who are merely a fluctuating series
of psycho-physical events without any permanent substratum ("no soul"),
have to rely on their own "self" or *citta* for liberation (*atta-sarana*).[39] This
citta is therefore that which is developed toward the full attainment of
Absolute Freedom or nirvana. The idea of a *given* human potentiality for
the realization of liberating truth is the most significant presupposition in
Buddhist soteriology, though it is never explicitly analyzed.

Having thus clarified the three aspects of salvation in Buddhism and
Christianity, I can now proceed, with the aid of a common vocabulary, to
juxtapose buddhology and christology, keeping in mind that both are
expressions of the *interpretative* level of religious consciousness (as explained
at the beginning of this chapter).

Let us note first that there is an "ascending buddhology" and a "descending buddhology," if we may borrow terms from Christian theology. The
former defines Buddhahood in terms of a distinctive way of attaining nirvana not attributed to *arahans*. The term *arahan,* which used to be a buddhological title, is now popularly and frequently used as a synonym for
disciples who attain nirvana in a manner different from the Buddha. The
Buddha is therefore a human being who has reached a state that makes
him a category of his own, as explained above. This buddhology constitutes
the principal orientation in Southeast Asia. But in northern Buddhism the
tendency seems to be to equate the Buddha with the eternal preexistent
Dharma. Gautama, then, would be the human manifestation or incarnation
of this revelatory medium of salvation. All buddhological titles are human
efforts to express the transhuman dimension of the Buddha in the context
of one or the other buddhology. The belief in his cosmic lordship is an
interpretive extension of these two basic affirmations.

Christology interprets Jesus as the exclusive medium of salvation for all,
the *logos,* the image, the word, the path, and so on. But as in buddhology,
so also in christology, it is not the interpretation that saves! What mediates
salvation is the medium itself, in whatever linguistic idiom it may be experienced, recognized, and named. Nor are the titles in themselves salvific.
Such titles as "Christ" are only human categorizations limited to a given
culture. What mediates liberation is the medium to which one culture as
much as another can decide what name to give: Christ, Son of God, and
so forth, or *Dharma, Tathagata,* and so forth—each according to its own
religious idiom.

Not even the acclamation "Jesus is Lord" is in itself salvific. For it is not
anyone who says "Lord, Lord," but the person who does the will of the
Father who is saved (Matt. 7: 21). To say "Jesus is the Word" is not enough;

the Word must be heard and executed for one to be saved. To say "Jesus is the path" is not enough; one must walk the path to reach the end. Moreover, not all who obey the Word or walk the path feel obliged to claim its proper name to be Jesus. For what mediates salvation is not the "name" of Jesus in the Hellenistic sense of the term "name," but the name of Jesus and *as* Jesus in the Hebrew sense of "the reality" (or salvific medium) that was seen to be operative in Jesus, independent of the name or designation we may attach to it. In fact, knowledge of the name or title is not expected by the eschatological Judge, but knowledge of the path is (Matt. 25: 37-39 and 44-46).

This holds good for buddhology too. Buddhists must agree with their Christian partners that liberation is possible only through what they both accept to be the "revelatory medium of salvation" and not the titles one gives to it. The major function of christological and buddhological titles is to equate the names of particular historical persons with the salvific medium. The real parting of ways, therefore, begins when either Gautama or Jesus is identified with that medium by means of these titles. It is at this point that dialogue must once more change directions if it is to avoid a blind alley, for we are dealing here with kerygmatic affirmations.

A kerygma is always a metalogical proclamation that cannot be demonstrated rationally. The only convincing proof it adduces is *martyrion* (witness), for we are dealing with soteriology, not philosophy or mathematics. That is to say, liberation is the only proof of liberation! To say Jesus is the medium of salvation is to show the fruits of such liberation in the person who says it. A christology that remains a speculative hermeneusis fails to be a soteriological proclamation about Jesus. A christology receives its authenticity from a transforming praxis that proves that in the *story of Jesus that continues in his followers,* the medium of salvation is operative, though it is not the total mystery of salvation *(totus Deus, non totum Dei* — "entirely God but not the entirety of God"). In Christian theological vocabulary, this medium is designated by titles like "Christ," "Son of God," and the like, as applied to Jesus because this liberation is believed to take place through Jesus the man (therefore through every man and woman *in* Jesus).

This is the inchoative christology found in Paul and in need of refinement. But in the process of being refined, this christology splits up into at least two incomplete models. (1) The classic (Chalcedonian) model focused too narrowly on the theandric composition of the incarnate *Logos* (Jesus) and on the philosophical problem of "one and many" with respect to the triune mystery of salvation, thus neglecting the whole process of salvation in its cosmic magnitude and in its eschatological dimension. (2) A popular catechetical model stressed the *divine* lordship of Jesus ("Christ the King" reigning in heaven) over a given, unchangeably created cosmos, without defining this lordship in terms of our co-mediation with him in the task of co-creating — that is, transforming this world psycho-spiritually and socio-politically into his kingdom of peace and justice.

Now this co-redemptive role of the corporate Christ, missing in both these partial christologies, is being supplied by the emergent theologies of liberation, which are essentially kerygmatic and critical of the christology of domination—that is, the theology of the colonial Christ, which could not be "good news" either for Buddhists or for Christians!

A liberation christology sees the medium of salvation in the form of *Jesus on the cross,* the symbol of the twofold ascesis that constitutes the salvific path—the *via crucis:* (1) Jesus' renunciation of biological, emotional, and physical ties that bound him to the "world" (Jesus' *struggle to be poor*), and (2) his open denunciation of mammon, which organizes itself into principalities and powers by dividing humankind into the class of Dives and the class of Lazarus (Jesus' *struggle for the poor*).[40]

The first form of Jesus' ascesis focuses on interior liberation, so well symbolized by the Buddha seated under the tree of gnosis. The second involves a ruthless demand for a structural change in human relationships in view of the new order of love or the kingdom of God, a demand that led Jesus to a type of death reserved for terrorists (zealots) on what has now come to be the tree of agape.

The uniqueness of Jesus (I am not concerned here with the *uniqueness* of Christ but with the "absoluteness" that titles such as "Christ" were meant to convey) lies in the fact that his claim to be the absolute medium of salvation is demonstrated on the cross by his double ascesis, which, nevertheless, would not be a convincing proof of his claim but an empty boast of his followers unless this double ascesis continues in them as an ongoing salvific process completing in their bodies what is still unfinished in the ascesis of Jesus (Col. 1:24).

This double ascesis is the nucleus around which an Asian theology of liberation evolves into a christology that does not compete with buddhology but complements it by acknowledging the one path of liberation on which Christians join Buddhists in their *gnostic detachment* (or the practice of voluntary poverty) and Buddhists join Christians in their *agapeic involvement* in the struggle against forced poverty.[41] This complementary cooperation is happening today in some basic *human* communities in Asia. Here, co-pilgrims expound their respective scriptures, retelling the story of Jesus and Gautama in a core-to-core dialogue that makes their hearts burn (Luke 24:32). It is only at the end of the path, as at Emmaus, that the path itself will be recognized by name (Luke 24:31).

NOTES

1. In an address given at the "Fünfte religionstheologische Studientagung" on the general theme of "Dialog aus der Mitte christlicher Theologie" ("Dialogue from the Core of Christian Theology"), held at St. Gabriel, Mödling bei Wien, Austria, April 14, 1986.

2. *Buddhist Philosophy: A Historical Analysis* (Honolulu: Hawaii University Press, 1976), pp. 112-26.

3. I have briefly described these historical circumstances and given the relevant sources in "Western Christianity and Asian Buddhism: A Theological Reading of Historical Encounters," *Dialogue* (Colombo) n.s. 7 (1980): 66-67. See also my "Buddhism as a Challenge for Christians," *Concilium* 183 (1986): 60-65.

4. S. Cromwell Crawford, "American Youth and the Buddha," *World Buddhism* 18/8 (1970) p. 199.

5. Anguttara Nikaya (PTS edition), vol. I, p. 188. All Pali texts quoted henceforward will be from the PTS Editions (Pali Text Society, London).

6. Ibid., p. 161.

7. *Majjhima Nikaya,* I:9.

8. *Stromata,* XV:71.6.

9. For references to sources dealing with the Joasaph cult, see my "Western Christianity and Asian Buddhism, pp. 61-62.

10. *Anguttara Nikaya,* II:38-39.

11. In translating this passage, I. B. Horner (*Gradual Sayings,* PTS, 1952, 11:46) insists that the question, as the Pali original has it, is not about what Gautama *is* but what he *will become,* though the final answer is in the present tense — namely, that he *is* (already) the Buddha. For a different view, see Kalupahana, *Buddhist Philosophy,* p. 112. See also note 13, below.

12. Compare John 16:33.

13. Horner *(Sayings)* translates: "Take it that I am a Buddha." This answer is then summed up in the verse that follows: "Therefore, I *am* Buddha" *(tasma Buddho'smi).*

14. Maya is believed to have conceived Gautama at the moment when a white elephant appeared to her in a dream.

15. The proof text adduced by the adherents of this theory is *Itivuttaka,* p. 91, where "seeing the Buddha" and "seeing the *Dharma*" are equated. As for the (eternal) preexistence of the *Dharma,* see *Samyutta Nikaya,* II:25.

16. See B. G. Gokhale, *"Bhakti* in Early Buddhism," *Journal of Asian and African Studies* 15 (1980): 18.

17. Ibid.

18. *Majjhima Nikaya,* I:386.

19. E.g., *Itivuttak' atthakatha,* I:13, 15-16.

20. Ibid.

21. E.g., *lokavidu* in *Digha Nikaya,* III:76, and *lokanatha* in *Sutta Nipata,* p. 995.

22. See Har Dayal, *The Buddhist Doctrine in Buddhist Sanscrit Literature* (Delhi: Motilal Banarsidas, 1931/1970), p. 24.

23. Cf. *Samyutta Nikaya,* I:235.

24. *Bhavatarana-maga ha Buddha-caritaya,* vol. 1 (1976) and 2 (1978).

25. Ibid., I:20.

26. Ibid., p. 25.

27. Cf. *Agganna Sutta,* which is summarized in my "The Political Vision of the Buddhists," *Dialogue* 11 (1984): 6ff.

28. See the diagram with an explanation of this worldview in my "Toward an Asian Theology of Liberation," *The Month* (May 1979), p. 152.

29. See Piyasena Dissanayake, *The Political Thought of Buddha* (Colombo, 1977).

30. Dayar Powar, "Siddhartha," *Panchasheel,* Oct. 1972, p. 7, translated into English and quoted in J. B. Gokhale-Turner, *"Bhakti* or *Vidroha:* Continuity and Change in *Dalit Sahitya,"* *Journal of African and Asian Studies* 15 (1980): 38.

31. Cf. Elias Mallon, "The Cosmic Powers and Reconciliation," *Centro Pro Unione* (Rome) 6 (1974): 18-22.

32. See *Return to Righteousness* (Collection of Speeches, Essays, and Letters of Anagarika Dharmapala), Ananda Guruge, ed. (Colombo: Government Press, 1965), pp. 447ff.

33. Ibid., pp. 448-49.

34. Ibid., p. 475.

35. This thesis is documented in Kitsiri Malalgoda, *Buddhism in Sinhalese Society* (Berkeley, 1976), pp. 192-255.

36. G. Obeysekere, "Religious Symbolism and Political Change in Ceylon," *Modern Ceylon Studies* (University of Ceylon) 1 (1970): 43-63.

37. Jean Daniélou, *Holy Pagans of the Old Testament (London:* Longmans, 1957), p. 22.

38. Pieris, "Speaking of the Son of God in Non-Christian Cultures, e.g., in Asia," *Concilium* 153 (1982): 65-70.

39. For clarification regarding the "self" that is denied in Buddhism and the (empirical) "self" that is identified with *citta,* see my *"Citta, Atta,* and *Attabhava* in Pali Exegetical Writings," *Buddhist Studies in Honor of Walpola Rahula* (London: Gordon Fraser, 1980), pp. 212-22.

40. See the conclusions in "Buddhism as a Challenge for Christians" (note 3, above) and my "To Be Poor as Jesus Was Poor?," *The Way* (July 1984), pp. 186-97.

41. How this theology spells out what is *unique* to biblico-Christian revelation and liberation is discussed in my "Theology of Liberation in Asian Churches?," *Vidyajyoti* 50/7 (1986): 330-51.

4

The Perfect Realization of Change: Jesus Christ

JUNG YOUNG LEE

Christology has been the subject of theological controversy since the Christian church came into being. The first ecumenical council was called at Nicea in 35 to define the nature of Christ, which necessitates defining the nature of the Trinity. The fundamental issue at Nicea was salvation. Athanasius maintained Christ's divine essence against the Arian heresy as a matter of life and death for the church, because Christ's nature pertains directly to human salvation. The council at Chalcedon in 451 attempted to end the controversy by a formulation designed to answer the problem of salvation. Tillich perceived correctly that "the early Church was well aware that Christology is an existentially necessary, though not a theoretically interesting, work of the Church. Its ultimate criterion, therefore, is existential itself. It is 'soteriological,' i.e., determined by the question of salvation. The greater the things we say about the Christ, the greater the salvation we can expect from him."[1]

In other words, the christological question was directly related to the soteriological need of the church and for that reason acquired enormous theological importance. That is why Christian theology has paid more attention to Christ and his work than to God as creator and has commonly regarded the event of salvation as distinct from, and more important than, the event of creation. In other words, the continuity between God's creative work and his saving work has in the past been largely ignored, the saving work being attributed exclusively to the Christ and the creative work to the Father. Almost all past theology disjoins the doctrine of salvation from that of creation, giving the impression that the creation was a discrete event occurring prior to salvation.

The disjunction between salvation and creation, or between the Christ and his Father, resulted primarily from the Euclidian worldview, according to which discrete events take place in a linear time sequence. According to this worldview, creation was accomplished in a given period of time and salvation came afterward. This tendency to separate creation from redemption was reinforced by the exclusive, or "either-or," way of thinking, according to which God's creative work must *either* precede his redemptive work or follow it. Since, according to this view, creation and redemption must be separate events, then it is right to consider Christ the redeemer separate from God the creator. In reality, however, God the savior and God the creator are one and inseparable. Although they are one, they are not identical; there is a functional difference between them. God as creator is prior to God as savior.

There is much evidence to support the idea that God's creativity is prior to his saving process in the world. If we attribute saving efficacy to the Christ and the creative process to the creator, we see clearly the functional primacy of the latter. Salvation is presupposed in creation, but creation is absolutely necessary to salvation because salvation means a return to the original creation.[2] Moreover Jesus Christ said again and again that he came to the world to fulfill the will of his Father, the creator. Christ's work, the work of salvation, was the extension of his Father's work, the work of creation. If Christ came to do his Father's work, then what Christ did, the work of salvation, was the creator's work. Therefore salvation is contingent on creation, not the other way around. Christ's work as savior must be understood as the extension of the creator's work, that is, as God's continuing work of creation in the world. If Christ as savior did his Father's work out of filial piety, we must not attribute that work to Christ alone, since Christ did it for his Father. If Christ had done the work of salvation independently of his Father, then the work of salvation might be Christ's alone. But the testimony of Testament witnesses makes it almost unthinkable to separate the work of Christ from that of his Father. The role of savior is a subsidiary part of the role of creator.

PROBLEMS OF CHRISTOLOGY

The trinitarian doctrine propounded by the early church is therefore mistaken: Christ is not coequal with his Father who "sent" him to do his work. Emil Brunner, who takes the trinitarian doctrine seriously, believes that the early church, failing to understand the specific and necessary hierarchy, or precedence, of the Father, the Son, and the Holy Spirit, placed them side by side. Thus he says, "The theology of the Early Church, as we shall see, did not, it is true, alter this order, but since it had very little idea that this order 'mattered,' its teaching suggests three 'persons,' side by side; this had a disastrous effect upon the doctrine of God."[3] Nowhere in Scripture is the Son identified with the Father. Christ said, "I and the Father are one" (John 10:30), or "He who has seen me has seen the Father" (John

14:9), but he did *not* say, "I am the Father and the Father is I." The exigencies of salvation doctrine led the early church to make Christ coequal with the creator.

But God as the creator is the source of creativity and the source of all that is and will be, while Christ is only what is manifested of God. To identify the creator with the revealer, the Christ, is to deny the inexhaustible nature of the divine creativity. God as creator is more than what is manifested, and his mystery is not and will not be exhausted. He is more than the One revealed in Christ. God as creator is active where Christ is not. "Thus there are works of God which as such are precisely not works of the Son. This non-identity of God and the Son is based upon the fact that God alone is Creator, but that the Son is called simply and solely the mediator of the Creation."[4] In other words, Christ is subordinate to the creator, and his work as savior and redeemer is one part of the work of God as creator. Salvation is an element toward the consummation of creation. Everything that Jesus Christ has done or has been must be understood as an element of divine creativity. By such an approach we can correct the doctrinal errors brought about by undue emphasis on salvation alone.

CHRIST AS THE WORD

Christ as the foundation of the creative process is clearly expressed in the story of creation, where Christ is identical with the Word coming from the mouth of the Creator. The creation story may be the best place to begin the study of Christology, because "the Word" is more expressive of Christ than any other name. The Word was the basis of creative process: It had the power of creativity. The story of creation in Genesis—not factual but metaphorical—reveals profound truth. At each stage of the creative process God *speaks,* saying, "Let there be ... " God's word, in Genesis, is the power of generation; it is not a static, descriptive attribute of God. In Israel, as in all the ancient Orient, in contrast to classical Greece, God's word of utterance signified dynamic force, the power of change and transformation.[5] As Roman says, "In Israel also the divine word had an express dynamic character and possessed a tremendous power."[6] Jeremiah compares the power of the Word with "a fire, a hammer that shatters the rocks" (Jer. 23:29). And Isaiah likens the power of God's Word directly to the power of generation: "For as the rain and the snow come down from heaven and return not thither but water the earth, making it bring forth and sprout, giving seed to the sower and bread to the eater, so shall my word be that goes forth from my mouth; it shall not return to me empty, but it shall accomplish that which I purpose, and prosper in the thing for which I sent it" (Isa. 55:10-11).

Thus, to the Hebraic mind, Christ as the Word of God was not a form or structure but the dynamic force that changes and produces new life and new possibilities. The Word, which in Greek thought is analogous to Rea-

son, is in the Hebrew mind almost identical with the Deed of God.[7] Moreover, in the Fourth Gospel the Greek word *logos,* while retaining its classical
Greek connotation, has acquired the meaning of the Hebrew word, *dabhar.*
In other words, at the beginning of the Fourth Gospel "the Word" means
primarily the power of creativity rather than a form of structure.

There is a close relationship between the first five verses of the Fourth
Gospel and the first five verses of Genesis. Both are cosmogonies: Both
treat the story of creation, but from different perspectives.[8] Genesis narrates the creation in detail in order to emphasize that God is the creator.
The Fourth Gospel summarizes the process of creation for the purpose of
emphasizing that Christ is the Word. But the Fourth Gospel also explicitly
states that the Word is the basis of God's creativity: "All things were made
through him, and without him was not anything made that was made" (John
1:3). Certainly those words affirm that the Word is the creative power of
God, and the next verse reaffirms it: "In him was life, and the life was the
light of man" (John 1:4). "In him was life" can also be translated as "In
the Word was life."[9] Of course, life and light are the most common metaphors of creative power to be found in nature. In the Old Testament they
are considered the essential forces of creation and preservation: God gives
life (Ezek. 37:1-14; Dan. 12:2), which is the source of light (Ps. 119:130).
Today the formula is reversed: Life is sustained by light, which is the basis
of energy. In either formulation Christ as the Word is to be understood as
the energy that is the basis of creation and re-creation.

The Word that becomes the power of creative process is also the wisdom
of God. In Proverbs 8:22-31 wisdom is personified and becomes God's
instrument and architect in creation, bringing salvation to humankind. This
idea undergoes further elaboration, and wisdom and Torah become one in
the creative process. "It becomes a commonplace of rabbinic Judaism that
Wisdom and Torah were one and the same, and therefore Torah was the
pre-existent instrument of creation, without which nothing was made that
was made; indeed, all that was made was created for the sake of the
Torah."[10] Christ is "the image of the invisible God, the firstborn of all
creation; for in him were all things created. . . . All things have been created
through him and unto him" (Col. 1:117). Here Christ, "the image of the
invisible God," is identified with the rabbinic definition of wisdom: Each is
the focal point of creative process.[11] Thus wisdom (*sophia*), like the word
(*dabhar*), signifies the creative activity of God. The creator, the source of
creation, is the background of wisdom, and wisdom, or the Word, is the
foreground of the creator. They are mutually interdependent in the process
of creation and redemption. A similar idea occurs in the Mahayana Buddhist tradition, especially in *Prajnāpāramitā-Sutra,* in which wisdom, or
prajnā, is united with *sūnyatā,* or nonbeing, as the source of creation. *Prajnā,*
which is often translated as "transcendental wisdom" or "divine wisdom,"
is a counterpart of *sūnyatā,* or "emptiness." Suzuki says, "It is the *Prajnā*
that sees into all implications of Emptiness [non-being]."[12] Like *prajnā,*

Christ as wisdom represents the foreground of divine creativity, that is the light and life of the world.

CHRIST AS THE LIGHT

If we believe not only that Christ as Word or wisdom is "the first-born of all creation" but that "all things are created through him," he must be the basis for every creative process, including light and darkness, life and death. In him nothing is separated, whether good or evil. We notice, however, especially in the Fourth Gospel and in apocalyptic writings, that Christ as the symbol of light and life is in conflict with darkness and death. Even though nothing, including darkness and death, can be separated from God's love that is in Christ, these writings apparently exclude darkness and death from the realm of his redemptive love. But as we have seen, absolute monotheism renders this antithesis incidental and superficial. The conflict between light and darkness or between life and death, like all other conflicts, is not ultimate. It is not essential but existential. To define these conflicts as essential presupposes an erroneous dualism.

Christ as the Word or the core of creative process is the solution to the existential problem, the problem of estrangement or sin. Christ as the Word is God in existence, as differentiated from God in essence. Since Christ is God in existence, that is, God in manifestation, he is conditionally limited. Brunner says, "God [God as creator, or in essence] is present where Jesus Christ is not present with His Light and Life, in the darkness, as the God of wrath. Thus there are works of God which as such are precisely not works of the Son."[13] Brunner is partly right, but we may question his saying that Christ is not present in the darkness. Christ as light cannot be excluded from the darkness, because light cannot exist without darkness nor darkness without light. To exclude Christ from the darkness is in fact to exclude him from light also. Because Christ subjected himself to the condition of existence, the darkness must also be in his light. Conversely, Christ as light enters into our darkness.

The relationship between Christ as light and life and the world as darkness and death can be illustrated by the *Tai chi t'u*, the diagram of the Great Ultimate in the *I ching*. The diagram consists of interlocked but differentiated *yin* (darkness) and *yang* (light). It is important to notice, however, that the *yin* portion of the diagram contains a *yang*, or light, dot, and the *yang* portion contains a *yin* dot. Christ as light, or *yang*, is not entirely exclusive of *yin* or darkness, and the world as *yin*, or darkness, is not entirely exclusive of *yang* or light. The expansion of light (*yang*) in darkness (*yin*) is a metaphor of the process of redemption or the growth of Christ-consciousness in us. Redemption, which is Christ, grows within us just as we grow within Christ's redemptive work, which is part of his creative work. Tillich's definition of Christ as the solution to the problem of existential estrangement, or sin, is valid and useful.

CHRIST AS THE SAVIOR

Redemption, or salvation, presupposes the existential estrangement called sin. However we symbolize the concept of sin, we must remember that it is one of the possible relationships between creator and creature, or between the change and that which changes. The idea of existential estrangement resembles the Buddhist idea of *dukkha*. *Dukkha* is usually translated as "suffering," but the Word is better translated as "existential estrangement." The Pali word *dukkha* refers literally to an axle that is off-center with respect to its wheel or to a bone that has slipped out of its socket.[14] Therefore *dukkha* implies an existential estrangement, an estrangement of relationship. Since life in a state of *dukkha*, or distorted relationship, is in constant motion and process, it expresses itself as pain and suffering, just as a leg whose tibia has slipped out of its socket is painful when it moves. That is why the life of sin is a life of suffering. Moreover, this existential estrangement disrupts the natural process of creativity in the world. When the wheel is out of alignment with its axis, it turns with difficulty or not at all.

By sin, or existential estrangement, the normal activity of God is disrupted and the harmony between creator and creature or between the change and that which changes is upset. Sin is the disruption of changing process and becoming. Sin is nothing but humanity's desire to *be* rather than to *become;* it is our unwillingness to change. This desire to *be* is one of the strongest inclinations of all creatures. It is expressed as nostalgia, which is usually defined as longing for the past but might be more accurately defined as futile unwillingness to change. We have no choice but to change. We are sojourners and pilgrims toward the never attained "not yet." In the never-ending process of change we as creatures are born and die, grow and decay. The desire to *be*—to remain unchanged in the moving stream of life—is the existential estrangement, or sin. To overcome this desire to *be*— this clutch at stasis—is the goal or salvation. Thus the work of salvation is the restoration of normal creativity.

Salvation, then, means to follow the way of change without nostalgia. When Jesus said, "I am the Way," he was referring to the way of change. By calling us to him, Jesus calls us to *be* one with the change, which is the source of all changes. To those who want to be, or to remain, Jesus said, "Follow me," which is the core of his message. "Follow me" is Christ's unconditional command. One cannot look back. One cannot even go back to bury one's father. Jesus said, "Follow me, and leave the dead to bury their own dead" (Matt. 8:22). Jesus is the way of change, which is directed to the new creation. To be in the way of change, that is, in Christ, we must give up trying to establish our security on *being*. We must be ready always to become and to change in the direction that Jesus leads. We must not ask: "Are you running with me, Jesus?" but rather: "Am I running with you, Jesus?" Karl Barth defines Christ as the archetype of a person to become the model of what a person should be. Jesus said, "I am the Way," the way of truth and change, and because he is our way, he calls us to follow. He is *yang* and we are *yin*. It is *yang*'s function to act and initiate and *yin*'s to respond and follow. Christ is creative because of *yang*; we must be receptive because of *yin*. Our only proper action, as *yin*, is to respond.

By our response, however, we become creative, because *yin* becomes *yang* by response and *yang* becomes *yin* by creation. Thus we become active by our inaction, creative by our response, and joyful by our suffering. It is a paradox of Christian experience. As Paul says, "We are treated as impostors, and yet are true; as unknown, and yet well known; as dying, and behold we live; as punished, and yet not killed; as sorrowful, yet always rejoicing; as poor, yet making many rich; as having nothing, and yet possessing everything" (2 Cor. 6:8-10). This idea is also expressed in the *Tao te ching,* the Taoist Scripture, which says, "The Way is gained by daily loss, loss upon loss until at last comes rest. By letting go, it all gets done; the world is won by those who let it go! But when you try and try, the world is then beyond the winning."[15] The way of *yin* is to gain by losing itself, or, in Paul's words, "It is no longer I who live, but Christ who lives in me" (Gal. 2:2). By responding to Christ's call to follow him, we cause him to act in us, as *yang* acts in *yin*. That is how "by letting go, it all gets done." The change changes us. Or, in other words, God rules us.

By letting go, our way becomes his way and his way becomes ours. That is the secret of the way of change, the *tao*. Christ triumphed by loss of self. By enduring total defeat in crucifixion, he gained complete victory in resurrection. To give in full is to receive in full. Certainly receiving is giving and giving is receiving. Lao Tzu says, "The movement of the way is a return; in weakness lies its strength."[16] And Jesus' teaching that the last shall be first and the exalted shall be humbled is identical in meaning. All phenomena, upon reaching their ultimate, must revert toward their antitheses. At noon the day begins to wane; at midnight night begins to lighten and day to dawn. By letting go of our *being*—of what we *are* at some finite moment— we become one with the way of change and transformation, and that is the way of salvation.

To be saved means to be part of the process of change and transformation brought about by the power of the change. Salvation is the harmony between the change and the changing or between the creator and the creature. It is like the harmony of *yin* and *yang*. Christ died not to anguish the world but to reconcile it to its creator. As Paul said, "God was in Christ reconciling the world to himself, not counting their trespasses against them, and entrusting to us the message of reconciliation" (2 Cor. 5:19). Salvation does not mean the subjugation of the world by the divine. Rather it means the harmonization of the world with the way of God's creative process of change. It is the process of reconciliation between creator and creature or between the change and the changing world. It is the harmony of *yin* and *yang* which makes all things in peace. Thus to be saved means to be in harmony with the principle of change, which by the process of creation makes all things.

To be in harmony with changing process means to change. Therefore, as Paul said, "If anyone is in Christ, he is a new creation; the old has passed away, behold the new has come" (2 Cor. 5:17). The new creation Paul speaks of is new to the creature, but to the creator it is simply a renewal of what has already been. The new, or renewed, creation is essentially the same but existentially different from the old creation. The process of divine creativity, then, is a process of constant renewal of what has already been. That is what Ecclesiastes meant by saying, "There is nothing new under the sun." Things new to us are not new to the creator. Divine creativity, which is perfectly manifested in Christ, is the power of renewal through the constant interplay of *yin* and *yang*. This interplay makes renewal possible, and renewal makes creativity possible.

In the Book of Changes there are sixty-four archetypes that are continually renewed to create new existences. They are essentially unchanging, even though they are manifest as many different forms in existence. Thus the change does not create anything really new but renews the old. In this renewing process, that is, the creative process, new existences are born of already existing essences. Creativity, in this sense, is never a progress toward novelty. As the Great Commentary says, "Change and transformation are images of progress and regression."[17] Advance necessarily leads to retrogression. As *yin* grows, *yang* decays; as *yang* grows, *yin* decays. Nothing can progress or develop indefinitely. A belief in infinite progression in history is contrary to the cyclic movement of time described in the *I ching*. In the world of relativity and change we cannot claim that history moves always and only forward.

In fact, salvation history includes both progression and retrogression. The end of time, or *eschaton*, must not be understood as the ultimate termination of history. *Eschaton* is the end of the old as well as the beginning of the new, that is, the renewal of the old. As Jacob says, "Eschatology is a return to the beginning; but with something additional which was absent at the first creation."[18] Every day is the end of time and beginning of renewed time. The end of the world in the New Testament does not mean the absolute end but the end of the old and the beginning of the new world through the power of renewal. It is the coming to an end of a cosmic span of change. Everything has its own span of change. When the span ends it is renewed. That is why we see in the ending of the world the images of a new heaven and a new earth. When the Last Judgment is over, the new heaven and new earth appear. "Then I saw a new heaven and a new earth; for the first heaven and the first earth have passed away, and the sea was no more. And I saw the holy city, the new Jerusalem, coming down out of heaven from God, prepared as a bride adorned for her husband" (Rev. 21:1-2). The new heaven and new earth and the new Jerusalem are symbols of renewal. They are not essentially new but are renewals of the old heaven and earth. Thus, in essence, ending is the beginning of renewal. In this process of renewal, that is, in the process of salvation, the world is in constant change and transformation. Christ shows us the way to be in this process of renewal and becoming, for he is the pioneer of our salvation.

Christ is the pioneer of our salvation, because he is "the first born of all creation." He is the origin of creative process toward which salvation history moves, for salvation is a process of returning to the origin of creation. "He is before all things, and in him all things hold together" (Col. 1:17). In other words, he is the center and origin of all creative processes and of all their manifestations. This center is the seed or origin of all creation.

CHRIST AS THE CENTER OF THE CREATIVE PROCESS

Christ as the center of the cosmic process is analogous to the Indian symbol of the cosmic center, the mythic Mt. Meru, which is also the symbol of Brahman, Hinduism's name for ultimate reality. Here Christ, as the symbol of the cosmic center, is parallel to Brahman, the Hindu notion of the ultimate reality, who also symbolizes the cosmic center. He is the center of every creative process, for the cosmic center includes all macrocosmic as well as microcosmic centers. Therefore the cosmic Christ also represents the center of the human soul and the axis of human life. As St. John of the Cross says, "The center of the soul is God."[19] Just as a wheel's axis is empty, Christ as the center of existence is empty; he is *śūnyatā*, or nonbeing, which is the origin of all creative becoming.

Christ is the divine reality. In him, that is, in the core of every creative process, all distinctions disappear. In Christ object and subject, inner and outer, good and evil become indistinguishable. In the center of the changing process, which is Christ, not only *all* things but all times – past, present, and future – come together. This undifferentiated time is eternity, in which the beginning is also the ending and the ending is also the beginning. Therefore to be in the center of changing process is also to be in eternity. By saying, "I am the Alpha and Omega, the first and the last, the beginning and the end" (Rev. 22:13), Jesus meant that he is eternal. In the primordial center he is one "who is and who was and who is to come" (Rev. 1:8). He is then the symbol of eternal change, which is the perfect manifestation of change itself.

Christ as the symbol of the concentric point of every creative process embraces all dimensions of time and space. To return to this primordial origin is in a way to be in union with the eternal reality. In it humanity is free from the illusion of *māyā* and the bondage of sin. For the individual who has "found" – or understood – the center, the wheel of life stops turning. At the center of existence humanity is totally detached from the phenomenal world, yet totally attached to the real world. Thus to be in Christ means to be simultaneously attached and detached. Paul says that in Christ we are not of the world but in the world. Because Christ occupies the center of creative process, where *māyā* and sin do not exist, salvation is in him.

DIVINITY AND HUMANITY OF CHRIST

As the primordial origin of the creative process, Christ is also both divine and human. In this center the distinction between man and God disappears. This continuum between humanity and divinity is the real meaning of incarnation. Because he occupies the center of the cosmic process, the incarnate Christ becomes the focus of the universal aspiration and goal of the whole world. The existence and destiny of everything in the world, personal or impersonal, has its source in Christ. Christ as the primordial center of the creative process is the perfect incarnation of the infinite in the finite world; he is human and divine in the fullest sense. He is fully divine because he is fully human. He is a perfect man because he is a perfect God. His human perfection is manifested in his friendship and brotherhood to all humankind. As a true brother he shows us the way to the Father, and as a true friend he lays down his life for us. He is a man for others, standing in the place where others must stand but cannot. He is also divine in a perfect sense because he occupies the center of divine creativity. In him the power of the change is manifested perfectly. He is in perfect harmony with the process of the change. Because of this perfect harmony, his will and the will of God are one and inseparable. That is what Jesus meant by saying "Believe in me that I am in the Father and the Father in me" John 1:11).

The relationship between Christ's divinity and humanity is like the relationship between *yin* and *yang.* Just as *yang* cannot exist without *yin* nor *yin* without *yang,* the humanity of Jesus cannot exist without the divinity of Christ nor the divinity of Christ without the humanity of Jesus. "In him God is not separated from man nor man from God. They are in complementary relationship. He is God because of man: He is man because of God."[20] In Jesus as the Christ man and God are in perfect harmony. Jesus' divinity does not preclude his humanity but rather presupposes it, just as *yang* presupposes the existence of *yin.* Furthermore, perfect humility presupposes perfect divinity. In his perfect complementarity of divine and human, or of the change and the changing, he is both perfect man and perfect God. Being the symbol of perfect harmony between the change and the changing, Jesus Christ is the ultimate reality of change and transformation.

As the basis of creativity Christ is also the perfect symbol of the divine nature. He is the perfect symbol of the creator who is the eternal subject, unknown to us. He transcends the division between subject and object and all other categorizations by which we express our understanding of reality. God as creator is the background of all process and becoming. Christ as the primordial origin of creative energy becomes the mediator between God as creator and humanity as creature. Christ as a mediator functions symbolically. "Thus the symbol functions as a mediator which can transform subject to object. However, this does not mean that God is no longer revealing Himself as the Subject. He is the Subject of us always, but He is seen as the object of our knowledge when we see Him through the symbol."[21]

Christ is a perfect symbol, not only because we see God in him perfectly, but because we see ourselves in him perfectly. In him "Very God does indeed energize in Very Man."[22] Because we see ourselves perfectly in him, he also becomes the perfect symbol of humanity. We become subjects of God by participating in this perfect symbol of God and man. As a wheel's axis is empty, Christ's mind is still, reflecting like a mirror every impulse of the change. His heart is unadulterated and his attitude unadorned. He is like the *p'o*, the virgin block of wood untouched by human artifice, which is the Taoist symbol of perfection. He is like the children whom he described as "belonging to the kingdom of heaven." His purity of heart, sincerity of conviction, simplicity of life, and conformability with change are attributes of the perfect symbol of both creator and creature. Christ is present to us as a perfect symbol of the reality of God's creativity and humanity's response to it; he is *yang* to humanity's *yin* and *yin* to the creator's *yang*. Because everything owes its existence and renewal to the continual interaction of *yang* and *yin*, Jesus is the perfect symbol of "both-and," which is the normative description of ultimate reality.

THE CRUCIFIXION AND RESURRECTION OF CHRIST

The most vivid reminders of Christ's living presence as the perfect symbol of change are life and death. The perfect symbol of death is Jesus' crucifixion, because Jesus is the perfect symbol of every process, including death and life. The perfect symbol of life is the renewal of life in Jesus' resurrection. Just as death presupposes life, crucifixion presupposes resurrection. In early Indian scriptures Shiva appeared as the destroyer of life, but later he acquired regenerative powers as well, because renewal presupposes the destruction of the old. Like Shiva, Christ symbolizes both the destruction and the renewal of life. Christ's death is not symbolic of the total annihilation of life but of its existential negation. Thus the essential nature, or archetype, of humanity is not thereby extinguished. Christ's resurrection is then the renewal of the archetype in a form existentially different but essentially the same. Since crucifixion and resurrection act upon the same essence, or archetype, they are existentially not contradictory but ultimately complementary. Christ's resurrection is not the conquest of death but the fulfillment of life, and his crucifixion was necessary for that fulfillment. What is to be renewed must first die. Thus Jesus as the perfect symbol of the change unites both decay and growth or death and resurrection in the process of constant change and transformation.

Crucifixion and resurrection represent the matrices of all changes and transformations in the world. They symbolize winter and spring, evening and morning, rest and motion. Crucifixion and resurrection are *yin* and *yang*, the gateways to all changes, and they occur in all things, because all things change. If crucifixion and resurrection are common to all things, how are Jesus' crucifixion and resurrection unique?

Death on the cross was not uncommon in the Roman world, nor was the belief in resurrection throughout the Near and Middle East.[23] Jesus' followers fully expected to die and be raised again to life as he had been. Jesus' crucifixion and resurrection are unique, not because they happened to him, but because they became the primordial symbol of all changing. They also became the primordial symbols of Christian life. As Paul says, "For if we have been united with him in a death like his, we shall certainly be united with him in a resurrection like his" (Rom. 6:5), and, "The death he died he died to sin, once for all, but the life he lives he lives to God. So you also must consider yourselves dead to sin and alive to God in Christ Jesus" (Rom. 6:11). Jesus' resurrection became the primordial symbol of Christianity's renewing power engendering a saving process that consists in a return to original creativity. As Moltmann says, "Christianity stands or falls with the reality of the raising of Jesus from the dead by God. In the New Testament there is no faith that does not start a priori with the resurrection of Jesus."[24] Jesus' resurrection is distinguished from all other forms of life renewal by its primordial symbolism, through which everyone can experience the renewal of life and enter into the creative process. In it we may take part in the renewing process of change and understand the eternal change in the midst of a changing world.

NOTES

1. Paul Tillich, *Systematic Theology* (Chicago: University of Chicago Press, 1957), vol. 2, Existence and the Christ, p. 146.

2. This concept of salvation as the recapitulation of original creation was originally proposed by Irenaeus and came to be accepted widely, especially by the so-called Lundensian theology.

3. Emil Brunner, *The Christian Doctrine of God*, trans. Olive Wyon (Philadelphia: Westminster Press, 1950), p. 217.

4. Ibid., p. 232.

5. Thorlief Boman, *Hebrew Thought Compared with Greek*, trans. Jules Moreau (New York: Norton, 1970; and London: SCM Press, 1960), p. 58.

6. Ibid., p. 60.

7. Ibid., p. 68.

8. John's prologue, especially his use of a cosmogony as the basis of his message of salvation, is often thought to reflect the Hellenistic ideas as expressed in the *Hermetica*. This does not, however, eliminate the fundamental connection between the Old and New Testament meanings of "the Word."

9. C. K. Barrett, *The Gospel According to St. John: An Introduction with Commentary and Notes on the Greek Text* (Philadelphia: Westminster John Knox, 1978; and London: SPCK, 1960), p. 131.

10. Alan Richardson, *An Introduction to the Theology of the New Testament* (New York: Harper and Row, 1958), p. 156.

11. The phrase "image of God" is used in the Greek Old Testament to refer to the divine wisdom (Wisd. 7:26). See also S. Radhakrishnan, *Religion in a Changing World* (London: George Allen and Unwin, 1967), p. 107.

12. D. T. Suzuki, *Essays in Zen Buddhism,* Third Series (London: Rider and Co., 1958), p. 254.

13. Brunner, *Christian Doctrine of God*, p. 232.

14. See Huston Smith, *The Religions of Man* (New York: Harper and Row, 1958), p. 99.

15. *Tao te ching*, trans. by R. S. Blakney (New York: New American Library, 1955), ch. 48.

16. Ibid., ch. 40.

17. *Ta chuan*, sec. 1, ch. 2.

18. Edmond Jacob, *Theology of the Old Testament* (New York: Harper and Brothers, 1958), p. 12.

19. R. C. Zaehner, *Mysticism Sacred and Profane* (New York and London: Oxford University Press, 1961), p. 137.

20. J. Y. Lee, "The Yin-Yang of Thinking," *International Review of Mission*, July 1971, p. 370.

21. J. Y. Lee, *The I: A Christian Concept of Man* (New York: Philosophical Library, 1971), p. 71.

22. Norman Pittenger, *God in Process* (London: SCM, 1967), p. 70.

23. Osiris in Egypt, Tammuz in Babylon, and Attis in Asia Minor exemplify ancient Near Eastern beliefs in resurrection. Even though the manner of resurrection differs in different traditions, we can say that the idea of resurrection was widely held in the New Testament time. There is some truth in what Moltmann said: "Christianity differs from the Hellenistic view for it participates not in perfect resurrection but in the present or the future hope" (Jürgen Moltmann, *Theology of Hope,* New York: Harper and Row, 1967, p. 161).

24. Jürgen Moltmann, *Theology of Hope*, p. 165.

5

Confessing Christ
in the Islamic Context

ALEXANDER J. MALIK

CHRIST OF THE INDIGENOUS RELIGIOUS MOVEMENTS

I have been asked to present a paper in the form of a testimony on *"Confessing Christ in an Islamic Context"*. The topic does assume that confession of Christ may differ in its modes, methods, expressions. phraseology, etc. from context to context; and this is quite Scriptural. For example, Matthew, writing his Gospel especially for Jews, mostly uses Jewish terminology, and even Jewish Scriptures; whereas John, writing for Hellenistic Jews, uses mostly Greek terminology to express the same Christ. For Matthew, to prove Jesus is the Christ seems to be most important; whereas John expresses the same Christ in more Greek philosophical terms like 'Logos,' 'Life' 'Light' etc. Thus we see that the context has colored the confession of Christ in different contexts. As a matter of fact, St. Paul also adopts the same strategy' if we can use that word, to confess Christ, he says, "for the Jews, I became a Jew. . . ."[1] Therefore the same Christ can be confessed in different terms in Islamic, Hindu, Buddhist, or Marxist contexts. When we talk about 'confessing Christ in an Islamic Context' it is with particular reference to Pakistan. This paper has been divided into two sections; section one deals with the difficulties in confessing Christ in an Islamic context, and section two explores different guidelines on which Christ could be confessed in an Islamic context.

SECTION ONE

While confessing Christ in an Islamic context, a Christian is faced with at least three basic difficulties. One, he is faced with a reductionist form of Christology of the *Qur'an*; second, the authority and authenticity of the Christian Scriptures is minimised by a belief that they have been corrupted and abrogated; and third, that the prophet of Islam has been gradually turned into the 'Muslim Christ'. One can easily see a development of the doctrine of 'Muhamadology' over against 'Christology'. Faced with these basic, and other, difficulties, we have to see how Christians continue to confess Jesus Christ as Lord, God and Saviour, in an Islamic context.

Christ in an Islamic context is not an unknown person. He is known to a Muslim through his scriptures — the *Qur'an*. The *Qur'an* perhaps are the only scriptures which mention Christ besides the Bible. There is no mention of Jesus Christ in Hindu, or Buddhist or Confucian scriptures. Jesus Christ is mentioned 93 times in the *Qur'an*. There is a long Surah about the Annunciation and Birth of Jesus Christ[2]. It gives beautiful names and titles to Jesus which have not been given to any other Prophet in the *Qur'an*. For example, he has been called *'Ibni-Maryam'* (Son of Mary); *'Al-Masih'* (The Messiah); *'Abid, 'Nabi,* and *'Rasul'* (Servant); Prophet, and Apostle; *'Kalimat-Ullah'* (the word of God); and *'Ruh-Kallimat-Ullah'* (The Spirit of God)[3]. It has some Surahs about his teaching, works, and finally his ascension to heaven without having died on the cross[4]. All of these are there in the *Qur'an,* and on the surface there seem similarities with New Testament Christology. But when one looks more closely, the *Qur'an* denies very emphatically the basic characteristics of Christian Christology. All through history, the Church has taught that Jesus Christ was very God, and very man in respect to his person. And as regards his work, the threefold office of prophet, priest and king, has been ascribed to him. None of these are there in the *Qur'an*. Rather these truths are emphatically denied. Therefore, it is not so much what the *Qur'an* asserts about Jesus Christ, but rather what it denies, which is important for confessing Christ in an Islamic context.

The *Qur'an* denies the *Deity* and the Sonship of Jesus Christ. He is a creature like Adam:

"Verily, Jesus is an Adam in the sight of God. He created him of dust. He then said to him 'be' and he was". (Surah 3:52).

Those who assert that Jesus Christ is more than human are infidels:

"The Christians say that the Messiah is the Son of God. God fight them! How they lie!" (Surah 9:30)

Not only is Jesus Christ a mere creature, but he is not essential to God nor to God's plan in the world:

"Who can obtain anything from God, if He chose to destroy the Messiah, the Son of Mary, and his mother, and all who are on the earth together?" (Surah 5:19)

Whenever Muslims talk about Jesus Christ, they begin with an assertion that he was only a man among men:

"Jesus is no more than a servant whom we pardoned, and proposed as an instance of divine power to the children of Israel, and, if we pleased, we could from yourself, bring forth angels to succeed you on earth". (Surah 43: 59)

Christ's Sonship is emphatically denied:

"They say the Merciful has taken to Himself a Son — Ye have brought a monstrous thing! The heavens well nigh burst as under threat, and the earth is risen and the mountains fall down broken, that they attribute to the Merciful a Son. But it becomes not the Merciful to take to Himself a Son". (Surah 19:91-93)

"Praise belongs to God, who has not taken to Himself a Son and has not had a partner in His Kingdom, nor had a patron against such abasement". (Surah 17:112)

Though the *Qur'an* has some very distinguished names and lofty titles for Jesus Christ, his dignity, his sinlessness or his power to work miracles, does not distinguish him in any way, as to his nature, from the other prophets who came before him. The pre-existence of Christ is everywhere denied. Any incarnational notion is abhorrent both to the *Qur'an* and to the Muslim. Similarly, is the case with regard to his work and teaching. His death on the cross is denied[5]. The atoning work of Christ is simply not there in the *Qur'an*. He is only a messenger, a message bearer. He brought the *Injil* which later on has been corrupted by His followers.[6] Thus his person, work and teaching are reduced to insignificance, or at the most, a prophet among many more prophets mentioned in the *Qur'an*: 'We make no distinction between them (between the prophets)' (Surah 2:130. 285), are the famous ones quoted in this regard.

"Say, we believe in God and what He has sent down to us, and what has come down to Abraham and Ishmael and Isaac and Jacob; and what came down to Moses and to Jesus and the prophets from their Lord. We make no distinction between them". (Surah 3.78)

Jesus is sinless like all other prophets are sinless. He wrought great miracles. But all of these do not put him in any superior position over against other prophets. The object of his coming was to announce the coming of Prophet Muhammad and as such his main role was of a fore-runner to Prophet Muhammad:

"And remember when Jesus the Son of Mary said, 'O Children of Israel! Of a truth, I am God's Apostle to you to confirm the law which was given before me, and to announce an apostle that shall come after me, whose name shall be Ahmed'." (Surah 61:6)[7]

Faced with these denials of Christ by the *Qur'an*, a Christian has two options in the confessing of Christ. One is that what he confesses about Christ is according to his own scriptures, the Bible, and he has to confess and believe what his scriptures tell him to believe. Here, a Muslim very conveniently leaves out the first option by saying that the Christian Scriptures have been corrupted and abrogated. Even though the *Qur'an* enjoins every Muslim to believe in the previously revealed scriptures, that is, *Tawrat* (Torah), *Zabur* (Psalms), *Injil* (Gospel)[8], there is a common belief among Muslims that the Christian Scriptures have been corrupted and are unreliable. Modern Muslim scholars take full advantage of the critical approach to the Bible, common in the West, to prove their point of view. Moreover, the *Qur'an* is the final revelation according to the Muslim and as such, it abrogates the previous scriptures.

The second option is to talk to the Muslim on his own terms — that is, on the basis of the *Qur'an*. Thus, a Christian picks up all the references in the *Qur'an* and expresses the Christian point of view. Here he tries his best to prove that what the *Qur'an* denies about the person and work of Jesus Christ has nothing to do with Christian 'Christology'. This has encouraged a whole lot of literature in the form of Christian apologetics. Persons like Pfander, Bevan-Jones, W. Bijifeld, have tried to interpret the *Qur'an* from a Christian point of view. But these interpretations and apologetics have not gone very far, except to give a little confidence to Christians that their religion is not as bad as the Muslim depicts. But the real situation as far as confession of Christ is concerned remains unchanged.

The third difficulty is that even though Muslims condemn Christian Christology on the basis that Christians have turned a human into God, they themselves use such honorific names and titles which have turned the prophet of Islam into some sort of 'divine' person. At least, this is true of the popular Islam in Pakistan. It is believed that Muhammad's words had creative power. Things obey him because he is king and lord over them; His kingdom is in all the universe; being earthly as well as heavenly. His name is written in paradise on all things — trees, on all the doors and even in the eyes of *Huris*.[9] The name Muhammad has miraculous power, recitation of it relieves one from pain and suffering. A point to note in this new trend to venerate the prophet is that it is supported by the means of *Hadith* and not so much from the *Qur'an*. Actually, the *Qur'an* does not support the ascription of supernatural powers to Muhammad. The early biographies leave us in no doubt that he was thoroughly human.

When the person of Muhammad in popular preaching is compared with the person of Christ in Christian doctrine, one can find two different movements in Islam and Christianity. But the result has certain formal similarities. In Islam, it is an upward movement, whereas in Christianity it is a downward movement. In Islam, the prophet Muhammad is exalted, whereas in Christianity, Christ who was in the form of God, empties and humbles himself. In Islam, man becomes increasingly "divine", whereas in Christianity, God becomes man. In Islam, man is exalted and becomes a mediator, whereas in Christianity, God becomes man in Christ Jesus and becomes the Mediator.

Thus the confessing of Christ is hindered and hampered not only to "reductionist *Qur'anic* Christology", but also that Muslims have their own 'Christ' in the person of prophet, Muhammad.

SECTION TWO

Confessing of Christ in an Islamic context means our Christology ought to be developed within an Islamic religio-socio-cultural situation and addressed to it. This does not mean that such a Christology is already developed or formulated, but there is a need to do so. Thus, in this section, we will attempt to underline ideas around which such a 'Christology' can be developed. This does not mean that these ideas are mutually exclusive; they can be inclusive as well.

One of the simplest ideas is to remove all those terms and phrases which offend the Muslims, e.g.: 'Son of God', Divinity of Christ, and death of Christ on the Cross, etc. Why quarrel about Christ? God is important. Let us leave both Christ and Muhammad and talk only about God. There is only one God of Christians and Muslims, and we need to live honest and righteous lives according to our own codes of morality and ethics. After all, the end of all religions is to live decent lives. Of course, such an idea has no room for a Saviour, and salvation is on righteous living. But the question is, is it that simple?

The second idea is that we need to rediscover biblical Christology. That we ourselves do not know the biblical Christ. Most of the creeds which express faith in Christ are the result of centuries of debate on his person. In a way, the real Christ is hidden behind the terms and expressions of Greek philosophy and we have to unveil Christ from these terms and expressions. One could argue that one could not do that as all of this is part of our history and no one can take history back to the first century. This may be true, and yet we have to go back to the Bible to find the real Christ. That means we have to know the Hebraic thought forms expressed in Greek by the early writers of the New Testament. It has to be a Bible-based Christology rather than Greek Fathers or Latin Fathers, or Eastern or Western Christology. This does not mean that their (Fathers) struggle is in vain, rather that we should learn lessons from them. Having discovered the Christ of the Bible, it has to be expressed in the thought form of Islamic religio-socio-culture.

What are the thought forms of Islamic religio-socio-culture? The central thought of Islam is the *"Tawhid"* (Unity) and the Greatness *(Allah-O-Akbar)* of God. God is one and he is the greatest. Confessing of Christ in an Islamic context has to begin with the unity and "greatness" of God.

A Christian has to assure a Muslim that in confessing Christ as divine, he is not confessing another God besides God. He is not committing the sin of *Shirk* (associating other gods with God). And here, there are a number of verses in the Bible to state that very belief[10]. One can also quote the Nicene Creed which begins with the words "I believe in *one* God ... "

If God is one, then how is Christ divine—and here one can show a Muslim that Christ Jesus is divine in the self-revelation of God. Muslims regard the *Qur'an* as revealed by God, and as such, divine. Thus phenomenologically speaking, both Jesus Christ and the *Qur'an* can be compared as 'revelations' of or from God and as such divine—one is personal, and the other is verbal. One can find an interesting parallel of eternal 'relationship' between God and the preserved tablet *(Loho Mahfooz)* in the Muslim *Kalam* (theology); and God and the 'eternal Sonship' of Christ in the Christian theology. If the *Qur'an* is revealed from the preserved tablet *(Loho Mahfooz* how does the preserved tablet stand in 'relation' to God? Is it 'in' God or 'outside' God? If 'outside' of God, then are there two eternals— that is, one God; and second, preserved tablet? Of course, Muslims being strict monotheists, cannot and do not believe in two eternals. The second possibility is that it is 'in' God, and if it is 'in' God, then the 'in' of God has got to be a 'personal' revelation, and as such, divine. It is on these lines that we confess Christ Jesus as the perfect revelation of God, and divine. The author of the Letter to the Hebrews, in part, says. 'God who at sundry times and in diverse manners spoke in time past unto the fathers by the prophets, hath in these last days spoken unto us by His Son, whom He hath appointed heir of all things, by whom also He made the worlds; who being the brightness of His glory, and the express image of His person, and upholding all things by the Word of His power, when he had by himself purged our sins, sat down on the right hand of the Majesty on high (Heb. 1:1-3). St. John, in his prologue, also says the same thing. "In the beginning was the Word, and the Word was with God, and the Word was God. The same was in the beginning with God" (John 1:1-2). In Jesus Christ the 'in' of God has taken a human form—God incarnate, and so, divine.

Another aspect of Christology which has to be confessed is the Sonship' of Christ. By this confession, Muslims think that Christians make Mary God's wife and commit the sin of *Shirk* by associating Christ with God, but this is exactly what a Christian does not believe. Christians neither believe that Mary is God's wife nor that Christ is God besides God. If Mary is not God's wife, how is Christ God's Son? There is ample room here for a Christian to discover how Christ is God's Son. The lines on which the Christian confesses this are, that the word 'Son' does not mean 'generation' in a physical sense. Both in Urdu and Arabic languages the word 'Son' is used metaphorically also which does not mean physical 'generation' e.g.: *"Sher Ka Baccha"* (son of a lion), or *"Ibn-ul-waqat"* (son of time). Now, by 'son of a lion' or by 'son of time' does not mean that either lion or time has 'generated' a person. Another common phrase used in the Islamic circles in Pakistan is *"Farzandan-e-Tawhid"* (Son of Tawhid). This *Tawhid* is commonly referred to as God and it could mean 'Sons of God' or 'Children of God'. The point I am making is that the word 'Son' does not mean 'generation' in the physical sense. Therefore, when Christians confess Jesus Christ as 'Son of God', it does not mean that God has "generated" Him in the physical sense. In this sense the *Qur'an* rejects the title "Son of God" for Jesus Christ.[11] Then how does a Christian believe Jesus Christ to be 'Son of God'? I personally have used the story of Gotama Buddha to explain this to Muslims. That Gotama Buddha left his royal throne and went to a jungle to meditate under the banyan tree. Now, whosoever saw Buddha under a banyan tree in the jungle thought he was a *swami, faqir* or *Sadhu,* but in fact, Buddha was a King. He belonged to a royal family. He had royal blood in his veins. Now "Christ, who was in the form of God ... emptied himself and became a servant and took human form" (Phil. 2:6, 7). When Jesus Christ was in his earthly life, people confessed him as "Son of God" as there was no better word to address him. Otherwise, in his person, he was God—he was divine. *La-Illaha-Illa-Allah (There is no God but God).* God is one and there is no God besides Him. In confessing Jesus Christ as 'Son of God'—God incarnate—Christians do not, in any way, mutilate the Unity (*Tawhid, Wahdat*), of God or even raise another God besides God. Jesus Christ is God in self-revelation. In the New Testament words, "God was in Christ reconciling the world unto Himself".

The second central theme in Islam is the greatness of God (*Allah-O-Akhbar*). God's greatness is revealed in creation, particularly in the creation of man whom He had created as crown of creation. Christian theology expresses this through the fact that man is created in the 'image of God'. What is the exact meaning of God's image? Interpretations may differ, but one main strand in these interpretations would be that there is something 'divine' in man— a divine spark which compels man to have fellowship or right relationship with God. For a Muslim, this right relationship is kept by observing the *Shariah* (Law). Though Muslims may not accept the Christian doctrine of 'original sin', they would readily concede the idea that man has failed miserably in observing the *Shariah* (Law). St. Paul discusses this in the Letter to the Romans—the frustration of keeping the Law (*Shariah*), and how man stands in need of grace. As a matter of fact, man as he is, stands in need of a change of heart and mind, and there is a recurring theme in the *Qur'an* that peoples' hearts are hardened and that is why they do not listen to the Word of God, and follow the *Shariah*. To change this— the hardening of the heart—the "Greatness" of God is to remake, or recreate or regenerate man. For God, this is not impossible because He is

Allah-O-Akhbar— the Greatest. Now the confessing of Christ is very meaningful here, that this recreating or regenerating or new birth is effected in man by faith in Christ. God has inaugurated a sort of new or second creation in the person of Jesus Christ. In fact, Jesus is compared with Adam in the *Qu'ran* (Surah 3:45). Adam and Christ are, then, so to speak, the representatives of two orders of creation: the first creation and the second creation. Adam belongs to the first or old creation, and Jesus Christ belongs to the second or new creation. We may call Adam the first Adam, and Christ Jesus, the second Adam. Actually the New Testament uses the title, second or new Adam, for Christ, though such a title is not used for Christ in the *Qur'an*.

The first Adam was created out of dust and then God's creative word was operative on dust (Surah: 3:9). The Bible says, "Then the Lord God formed man of dust from the ground, and breathed into his nostrils the breath of life; and man became a living being" (Genesis 2:7). The second Adam (Jesus Christ) was created by casting God's Word (the creative command, *Kur*) into Mary and hence Jesus Christ is called the Word of God. (See note 6.) For the first Adam, God's creative word was operative on dust, whereas for the second Adam, God's Word itself took "human flesh" in the person of Jesus Christ: The Messiah, Jesus, Son of Mary, was only the Messenger of God, and His Word that He committed to Mary and a Spirit from Him" (Surah 4:169). In the words of the New Testament, "In the beginning was the Word, and the Word was with God, and the Word was God. And the Word became flesh and dwelt among us . . ." (John 1:1-14). This first Adam was from the earth, a man of dust; the second Adam is from heaven, a Spirit from God *(ruh minhu)*. The first Adam through the creative word of God became a living being: the second Adam (God's word in flesh in the person of Jesus Christ) became the life-giving Spirit. Jesus says, "I have come to you with a sign from your Lord. I will create for you out of clay the likeness of a bird, then I will breathe into it, and it will be a bird, by the leave of God. I will also heal the blind and the leper, and bring to life the dead, by the leave of God" (Surah 3:43).

The first Adam, according to the *Qur'an* was a prophet; the Second Adam (Christ Jesus) was a prophet, a Spirit proceeding from God, a (or the) Word of God. The new creation which God has inaugurated through the birth of Jesus Christ supersedes the old or first creation.

Now we live in two orders of creation; one by our natural birth and the second by our acceptance of Christ Jesus as God's Word in the flesh. In the New Testament, we find the concept of the new or second birth very prominent. "Unless", says Jesus, "one is born anew (or from above), he cannot see the Kingdom of God. . . That which is born of the flesh is flesh, and that which is born of the spirit is spirit" (John 3:3, 6).

Again, says St. John, "To all who receive him (Christ Jesus), who believed in his name, he gave power to become children of God; who were born not of blood nor of the will of the flesh nor of the will of man, but of

God" (John 1:12-13). Christians can rightly proclaim with their Muslim brethren *Allah-O-Akbhar* (God is great), who recreates "fallen" man—man who is unable to observe *Shariah* (Law) in the person of Lord Jesus Christ through the power of the Holy Spirit.

"The greatness of God" is defended to the extent that Christ's death on the cross is denied by the Muslims. Christ's death on the cross would be against the "greatness" of God and His being almighty. How could God allow His servant, Christ, to die such a shameful death? Though one could defend Christ's death on the cross within the *Qur'an* it would not take one very far. Christians should follow the Islamic thought pattern to confess Christ's death and resurrection. Christ's death and resurrection then could be confessed within the "greatness" of God. The *Qur'an* mentions that prophets suffered at the hands of their people[12]. Previous prophets and apostles have been suffering at the hands of the ungodly people. So also, Christ suffered at the hands of His own people—the Jews. And when the opposition culminated in the Cross, He (Christ) did not run away from the Cross, rather He was faithful to God (*Islama, Islam*) in the face of death. In the New Testament words, "He was faithful unto death . . ." (Phil 2:5 ff.). God's Greatness is most convincingly exhibited in not rescuing Christ from the Cross but resurrecting Him from the dead. God allowed Man to do whatever he (Man) could do to His servant Christ. At the most, Man could kill; and this is exactly what He (Man) did with Christ. But God showed His "Greatness", that he raised the same Christ whom the Jews had killed. Thus the death of Christ on the Cross does not nullify the "Greatness" of God, rather it showed Him the "Greatest" by conquering death. In the New Testament words, "Death is swallowed up in victory"[13]. While discussing with a Muslim friend the death of Christ, the writer of this paper was struck by a beautiful sentence uttered by his friend. *"Masih ki maut, maut ki maut hai"* (Christ's death is the death of death).

The fourth idea is that the biblical Christ—Emmanuel, 'God with us'; God-Man—may be a folly to the Greeks (philosophers) and a stumbling block to the Muslims; but he is our Saviour through the power of his resurrection. And here the "greatness" of God in becoming man in the life of Jesus Christ has to be communicated in all circumstances through the *resurrected lives of the believers.* One has to stick to the essentials of the biblical Christology. One should not be ashamed of the Gospel. In the present Islamic world, when there is so much emphasis on revival of *Shariah*. Christology has a real relevance. It is on these lines that we confess and we continue to confess Jesus Christ our Lord, God and Saviour. This confession is to be expressed in the Church's preaching (*Kerygma*), fellowship (*Koinonia*), witness (*Martyria*) and service (*Diakonia*).

NOTES

1. 1 Cor. 9:19ff.
2. Surah 3 and 19.

3. Surah 5:79; Surah 3:40; Surah 4:169; Surah 19:17; Surah 21:91.

4. Surah 3:47-48; Surah 4:155-156; Surah 19:34; Surah 5:117.

5. Surah 3:48.

6. Surah 2:89.

7. In order to supplement this idea, a number of verses are quoted from the Bible, e.g.: John 16:7; Deuteronomy 32:2; Isaiah 21:6; the Parable in Matthew 20 and John 4:21; and 1 John 4:1-3.

8. Surah 5:68; Surah 2:41-44; Surah 5:43, 47.

9. Muhammad Yusuf Aslahi, *Qur'ani Taleemat*, vol. 1 (Lahore: Islamic Publishers Limited, 1968), p. 153.

10. Exodus 20:2, 3 (Mark 12:29; James 2:19).

11. Surah 6:102; Surah 9:30; Surah 112:14.

12. Surah 4:155; Surah 5:170.

13. 1 Cor. 15:54.

6

The Pluralism of Religions and the Significance of Christ

MICHAEL AMALADOSS

A growing positive attitude to the possibility of salvation in and through other religions seems to undermine traditional faith in Christ as the unique and universal savior. If we are helping Hindus and Muslims to grow in their own faith, are we not being disloyal to our mission to proclaim Jesus Christ as their savior? Who is Christ for us? How do we understand him and his role in salvation, particularly in relation to the other religions? We are asking these questions not in the abstract, a priori, but in the context of our experience of other religions in India. We are living in a situation of religious pluralism.[1] There is a wide acceptance today of the idea that people are saved not only in spite of, but in and through their religions, because God has reached out to them in the context of their life, community, and history. This realization is not so much the conclusion of an argument as born out of a living experience of other believers. The question is how we are to reconcile this universal salvific will of God with an individual act of salvation in the death and resurrection of Jesus.

I shall try to answer this question in four stages. I shall, first of all, outline rather schematically and critically the present stage of discussion on the question. Then I shall specify my own method of approach. Thirdly, I shall present some new perspectives that must guide our search for an answer. Finally I shall indicate my response to the question. I shall then point out in the conclusion some implications for action. I am aware that this is a difficult question and I do not claim to have found *the* answer to it. I will be satisfied if I have clarified the question a little more and localized more precisely the mystery.

SEARCH FOR A NEW PARADIGM

Authors who have studied this problem in recent times are accustomed to speak of three broad paradigms that classify the answers usually given by theologians: exclusivism, inclusivism and pluralism. As there are many excellent surveys of these trends,[2] it is enough for me here to present them schematically in order to provide a context for our reflection. We should, however, keep in mind that such schemes tend to ignore nuances in particular theoretical positions.

The *exclusivists* say that no one will be saved unless that person confesses explicit faith in Jesus Christ as the savior. Other religions may have many good things in them as the best fruits of human reflection and effort. But they do not mediate salvation. The Church is the only way to salvation.

The *inclusivists* accept that there may be grace and revelation in other religions, so that they may mediate salvation to those who believe in them. But the salvation they mediate is salvation in Jesus Christ. Even if the other believers may not be aware of the fact, they are "anonymous" Christians, related to the Church in some hidden way. Jesus Christ and the Church are then considered the fulfillment of the other religions, and Jesus Christ is the center of the history of salvation.

The *pluralists* find this inclusive attitude a patronizing one. They prefer to say that all religions are ways to the Ultimate, each in its own manner. As Christ is the way for the Christians, so is Buddha the way for Buddhists and Krishna or Rama for Hindus. They opt for a "theocentric," as opposed to a "christocentric," perspective of history.

I find all three paradigms unsatisfactory. The exclusivists are simply negative to all other religions and they ignore the broad Christian tradition that has accepted the possibility of salvation for people outside the Church—even though this may have been explained in various ways. After the Second Vatican Council and the event of Assisi, October 1986, when the Pope came together with the members of other religions, to pray for peace, no Catholic can be an exclusivist.

The inclusivist position is the one most common today. In the context of other religions, its ecclesiocentrism is a problem. To say that someone is an anonymous Christian when one explicitly rejects membership either in the Church or belief in Jesus Christ as unique savior seems presumptuous. Other religions, while they are respected by inclusivists, are placed in a relation with Christianity as "partial" to "full" or as "unconscious" to "conscious." This is an improperly a priori Christian solution to the problem.

The pluralists, on the other hand, do not take the "otherness" of other religions seriously. Real differences, even contradictions, among the religions are played down, while the search for an underlying unity ends up with a lowest-common-denominator rubric such as liberation or human development or the unity of the human race proposed as common to all religious traditions. One could, of course, develop a theology of religions that is soteriocentric because all religions seek to lead to liberation and salvation is a more unifying element than even God. The problem, though, is not to find a point of agreement among religions, but to prove that they are different ways to the same goal. Specificity of faith commitments is not considered. For example, Christ can be considered simply one among many ways only if he can be reduced to being a mere man. For those to whom Christian uniqueness is a myth, the God-incarnate is also a myth.[3] Just as Christians will not recognize the Christ of faith in the pluralists' presentation, neither will Buddhists find their Buddha, nor Hindus their Krishna. Paradoxically, pluralism itself becomes a form of nominalism reducing radically different expressions of religiosity to the same reality or experience. Such a rational conceptual approach looks on religions as systems of doctrine or practice that one can compare from some imaginary vantage point outside all religions and thus ends in simplistic abstractions.[4]

A METHODOLOGICAL FRAMEWORK

The context of our discussion is a community of people living and working together, sharing a common culture and socio-political structures, but belonging to different religions. The role of religion is to be a prophetic, interpretive force in the life of the people. Where there are many religions they have to play this prophetic role in dialogue. We favor neither a secular society without religion, nor fundamentalistic communalism where religions become a political force. Even at the religious level our task is not only to witness actively[5] to our faith (as some evangelicals do), but also treat other believers with respect and tolerance and collaborate with them in common socio-cultural and political tasks like the promotion of peace and development, freedom and human rights. We have not only a mission to witness to our faith, but also a responsibility as members of a human community. A school, for instance, is not a propaganda institution, but should render public service to the community and has responsibilities that a parish church may not have.

Our approach will not be an a priori one. I do not start from a self-understanding as a Christian and beliefs about means of salvation, from this point of view judging from the outside other religions and their role in the history of salvation. Our approach here will be dialogical. We listen to the other believers, and are challenged by their faith and life. Even if we do not actually dialogue with them, we have to be present to them in mind and imagination as we reflect on the meaning—for our faith—of this multireligious situation. It is in the context of this relationship that we seek to rediscover our identity.

The horizon of our search for understanding is our own faith perspective. We are not engaged in a historical or phenomenological study. We are not studying religions objectively as systems of doctrines or behavior. We do not pretend to adopt a neutral, suprareligious perspective. Since our horizon is our faith and we are dialoguing with other peoples of faith, our approach is not rational or scientific in the normal sense. Searching as believers we cannot escape the "hermeneutical circle." We have to explore a vision to which we are committed in faith; and we cannot look at it from outside this horizon.

We are not searching for an abstract universal scheme that will somehow unify all religions. We are not engaged in an evaluative, comparative study. We are searching to make place for other believers in the perspective of our own faith, while respecting the identities of the others without somehow reducing them to or interpreting them in terms of our own. This is the reason why an approach in faith is not opposed to an attitude of dialogue. Neither accepting that we are simply different, nor trying to reduce the other's identity to one's own, we seek to make space for the other in the context of our own faith, leaving to the activity of dialogue the discovery of the concrete articulations of the interrelationships, because we believe that God is one and has a single plan for the universe which includes all these various manifestations. These methodological elements will become clearer as we proceed with our reflection.

ELEMENTS OF A NEW PARADIGM

RELATIONSHIP AND STRUCTURE

If we take a merely phenomenological approach we see religion as a system of doctrines, rituals, and rules for behavior. But religion is more basically a saving relationship between God and the human person. In the context of human life in community, God calls and the human person responds. Conscience and freedom have an essential role in this process. There is an interplay of two freedoms which is a source of pluralism. For instance, God for Christians is Parent, Son, and Spirit. However this plurality in God may be understood, it guarantees a plurality of personal relationships with God. Since the affirmation of God as Parent, Son, and Spirit is not an a priori declaration, but the expression of the pluralistic experience of God in the history of salvation, this possibility of pluralism is of more importance than an abstract unity of the Godhead or of the Ultimate. While it is legitimate to talk of unity in pluralism, any attempt to reduce pluralism to an abstract unity is a rational temptation.[6]

The saving relationship between God and the human person is lived in the context of a culture and of a history. These will certainly influence the concrete forms in which the relationship finds expression. The concrete forms of expression not only symbolically mediate the relationship, but also give visibility to it and in some way constitute it. These forms of expression in scriptures, rituals and organizational structures constitute a tradition.

The experience of relationship is lived through them even if it transcends them. When I love a person, it is not simply an abstract feeling—I give it symbolic expression. I live my love in and through this expression—even if my love is not reduced to this expression. This expression is not simply a medium of communication nor an instrument. It is rather my love in act. While, on the one hand, I can live the intensity of my love even in inadequate expressions of it, on the other hand, I will have to confess that my expression is inevitably limited by culture, history and my own personal inadequacies. In addition, my response may not be all pure and true—there may be such factors operative as mixed motives and hesitations.

In this network of relationship and expression that is the core of religion, one can point to a pair of dialectical poles that constitute a field within which the relationship is lived—namely, the *Absolute* and the *relative*. The personal relationship as commitment in faith has a unique and absolute character about it, particularly because it is a relationship to the Absolute. The symbolic expression of it is culturally, historically and humanly conditioned and therefore relative. The Absolute and the relative are not two different things, but two poles of one relationship—like the spirit and the body intrinsically linked in human personality. I am not talking here of the obvious pair—the Absolute (God) and the relative (the human person). I am, rather, talking of the absoluteness of faith as commitment to the Ultimate and the relativity of its expression in religion. Human fault and error contribute further to the relativity. It is in and through the relative that the absolute relationship is lived. Even when God becomes human in Jesus, God cannot but become part of the cultural context of the Jewish tradition and language and in the historical context of the time in which Jesus lived. But the relative expression does not relativize the absolute relationship. In an earlier paper I distinguished between faith as experience, faith as celebration and faith as reflection.[7] Aloysius Pieris distinguishes between core-experience, collective memory and interpretation.[8] Panikkar speaks of Christianness, Christianity and Christendom.[9] The poles I am talking of here will be experience on the one hand and the other two aspects taken together on the other.

If we look at various religions as structures of expression, we may speak about the more or less developed; the tribal and the great; the popular and the elite; the mystical and the prophetic religions. These classifications are meaningful at a certain level. But we cannot legitimately thus compare religions as simply relative to one another because they have no meaning in themselves apart from concrete relations between members of the respective traditions. Each religion is capable, in its own historico-cultural situation, of giving expression to an absolute relationship. Therefore religions are relative to this absolute relationship and not to one another. Authentic dialogue is not between religions, which are seen as complementing one another, but between persons, who may mutually enrich themselves. Conversion is not the result of a choice of the best that follows a comparative study of religions but the response to the manifestation and call of God in and through a particular tradition. Sinful or imperfect elements in a religion are always to be judged in terms of the Absolute which it mediates in its expression.

At a phenomenological level, concepts like revelation, scripture and prophet, may have a certain basic common denotation. But it would not be proper to make that the sole basis for a comparison, since they are fully meaningful only within a tradition, not in the abstract. In the context of the ongoing relationship between God and a community, a particular person may be given by God a prophetic role; the community may recognize that person as a prophet; other believers in dialogue within that community may recognize this prophetic role in that community. Nevertheless such recognition does not automatically imply an affirmation that prophets have the same role for *every* community. We could say the same thing about the scriptures and the foundational symbols of a community. Many people reading the Bible may recognize Jesus as a great man whose teaching and example have universal relevance. But only a Christian in his faith confesses him as the incarnate Word.

If we take the dialectical relationship between the absolute and the relative poles of religion seriously, then to say that all religions are only different expressions of the same experience is not correct. It is also a fashion to affirm that at the mystical level one is beyond name and form, and that mystical experience is the same in all religions. It is true that at the root of any authentic religious experience there is the same God. But to conclude from this that it is the same experience is to ignore, on the one hand, the various ways in which God can manifest Godself and, on the other, the various cultural and symbolic ways in which the human person lives such an experience. Given the spirit-in-body nature of the human person, one cannot question the possibility of an experience of the Absolute beyond name and form as much as the possibility of the experience itself being beyond name or form or identification of it as the same experience as those common in another tradition.

The main point I wish to make here is that we are not interested in a comparison of religions as systems which can be objectively analyzed, but in a dialogue between believers who are able to make an absolute commitment of faith in and through their religions to the God who is manifested in various ways.

IT IS GOD WHO SAVES

We are accustomed to speak of the salvific value of religions. This is obviously inaccurate. It is always God who saves, not religions. People may be saved *in* and *through* a religion, but not *by* it. Religions are but mediations that do not substitute for but only make present God's saving love. Some would say that it is faith which saves, not religion. But such a distinction is questionable in the light of what we have seen in the previous section about the two poles of religion. This ever present action of God in salvation is sometimes obscured by the way we speak. For example, the Latin church has always had an anxiety to affirm its legitimacy in ontological terms. One speaks of the Church as a sacrament and sacraments are described as causes. The priest is said to be acting "in persona Christi." Active statements like "I absolve you," and "I baptize you," are preferred. Such a manner of speaking may obscure a presence of the Spirit and of Christ in sacramental celebrations in which the role of the church is only ministerial and not representative. The Orthodox tradition is much more sensitive to the continuing action of God through his Spirit which the Church prays for. The difference is seen clearly in the famous dispute concerning the key moment of the eucharistic prayer — the institution narrative or the epiclesis. This overall orientation may tempt the Latin church to reduce God's action to the Church's action and to make the Church's mediation essential, while the Orthodox tradition makes place for God's continuing action not only in, but also outside the sacramental and ecclesial system. This is the principle of "economy."

Speaking of the primacy of God's action in salvation will also help us not to isolate God's action in Jesus, but to set it in the context of the totality of God's action in the world seeking to communicate Godself to human beings which embraces the whole process of history from creation through redemption to its ultimate consummation. We see in the Old Testament how the people starting from their experience of liberation from Egypt through an intervention of God move to recognizing Yahweh both as the creator in the beginning and as the re-creator of the world in the last times. We see the same process in the New Testament, particularly in John and Paul. The experience of Jesus leads them to the discovery of the Word (John 1:1–14) and of the Cosmic Christ and the Spirit (Eph. 1:3–13; Rom. 8). Such a total perspective will dissuade us from opposing creation to redemption as natural to supernatural. A global view will also discourage us both from a dichotomous approach to the religions as Church and non-Church (exclusivism) and from an easy irenicism that sees religions as different human efforts towards the one God (superficial pluralism). We would better respect the pluralism of religions in history and seek for their articulation into a unity according to the plan of the one God. A historical perspective would also make us see this unity not as a system that is already given, but as a unification that has to be achieved, built up, realized both by the Spirit and by us, precisely through dialogue and mission.

Speaking of God's action in salvation is a reminder to us that in the realm of religion nothing is purely human. God is always present and active in creation and in history.[10] This is the meaning of the universal salvific will of God. This presence is articulated in various manifestations that are ordained to a unity. This does not mean that all manifestations are the same or of the same value. It does not mean either that the human response is not conditioned by sin and imperfection, or even by refusal. But it does mean that we must always have a global perspective. God manifests Godself in various ways to various persons and groups in sovereign freedom. Such manifestations are not arbitrary, but ordained to the global plan of God for humankind. A particular manifestation may be more or less important to God's plan. This can be discovered only through revelation and a posteriori in history. There is no problem in recognizing the differences between tribal, folk, and great religions. But even such religious development need not be seen as the result of purely human efforts.

While every divine manifestation is a personal or community experience, some of them, if not all, may also have a social implication. For everyone, the manner in which God reaches out to that person is adequate for that person's salvation.[11] But God's manifestations, as God's gifts and charisms (see 1 Cor. 12:4–11), may have a significance for the human community. Such a gift gives the person or the community a particular mission (role) in history. Such a role and the gifts ordained to it are a call and a responsibility; they are not titles for honor or for a feeling of superiority. No religion is closed in on itself. It is always called to be an open structure. Ultimately one is judged by the depth and the generosity of one's response to the call of God and not by the special gifts one is given for the sake of the community. A Christian is not more favored than a follower of a tribal religion at this level, but the Christian *is* aware of a connection to God's mission of which the tribal is not aware.

JESUS IS THE CHRIST

One of the problems that we face when we speak of Jesus as the Christ in the context of other religions is reductionism. In the past, the Catholic tradition — in spite of the Chalcedonian definition that Jesus Christ is true God and true human being and that these two aspects should neither be confused nor separated — tended to focus on his divine aspect, even when it spoke of the sufferings of Jesus. Today there is a move to rediscover and emphasize his true humanity. It is obviously difficult to hold these two aspects of the mystery in tension. In the New Testament we see the first disciples experiencing the man Jesus and, through reflection on his life and action, especially his death and resurrection, growing in their understanding of his divine aspect. The complexity of this personality of Jesus is expressed in various ways in the New Testament and later. Today we might need to find new ways of expressing this mystery. But if we simply reduce Jesus to being a human person, however extraordinary, then the questions of theological uniqueness and eschatological universality do not arise.

The first question that we have to ask when we talk about Jesus Christ is: Who is Christ *for us*? Are we talking of the *Word* in whom everything was created and who was at the beginning enlightening every one coming into the world (John 1:3–5, 9) or of *Jesus*, the Word incarnate, who emptied himself and took the form of a servant and died on the cross (Phil. 2:6–11) or the *risen Christ* who is transhistorical, no longer bound by space and time, present and active among us but whose action in the Spirit we cannot limit to our own little efforts (Acts 10), or the *Christ at the end of time*, the pleroma, in whom all fullness will dwell (Eph. 1:23)? It is the same person, but a person who is in the process of history while simultaneously transcending it. We should not forget this dynamic complexity of the person of Christ or that part of the complexity is the diversity of the relationships he displays in virtue of that complexity. The divine and the historical human poles of this complexity are sometimes specified with the terms "Christ" and "Jesus." Jesus is the Christ, but the Christ is not only Jesus.[12] The Jesus of history is limited by his humanity, culture, and history. This was his choice. But it was in this Jesus that the action of God—Parent, Son, and Spirit—becomes manifest. The Christ will reach fullness only on the last day when all things will be reconciled.

When we speak of the historical Jesus, distinguishing him from the Christ, we refer to the historical, not the risen Jesus. After the resurrection, Jesus becomes transhistorical or cosmic. He is no longer in time and in history. But we—the Church—experience this risen Jesus who lived and died in history in and through the memory that has been handed down to us—in the community of disciples, in the scriptures, and in other ways. Already the resurrection is a transhistorical event. This memory that we have of Jesus that leads us in faith to experience the mystery of his person is humanly, historically, and culturally limited and conditioned. It is in and through this historical memory that we experience Jesus. But at the same time we are aware that the risen Christ and his paschal mystery is present wherever God's saving grace is present. This presence does not obviously pass only through this particular historical memory that we celebrate. This is what we mean by saying that the Christ is more than Jesus. But to be complete, we must at once specify that here we are speaking of the Jesus of history, and not of the risen Jesus. We need not speculate about the precise nature of the risen humanity of Jesus, but we can talk about his humanity in history. That is why it will be helpful if we talk about the historical Jesus or the Jesus of history and not simply about Jesus or the humanity of the Word. Distinction between the historical and transhistorical stages of Jesus' humanity does not mean separation. We do not mean to say that Jesus in history was a mere human person who becomes divine in his resurrection. We are, instead, before two manifestations of the same person. But the process that leads dynamically from the one to the other—the life, death, and resurrection of Jesus—is a real process and not just "play acting." The risen humanity is what it is because of the historical life and death of Jesus. At the same time, however, the distinction between the historical and the risen manifestations of Jesus helps us to understand the specificity and limitations of the Church-community, whose tradition goes back to the memory of the historical Jesus. The paschal mystery itself is made present to the community in and through the symbol of the Last Supper. In the past, when we spoke of Jesus or of the Church as the sacrament, we referred to the *real* experience of God that they mediated. Now we should become aware that this mediation is primarily *symbolic*, though no less real, and refers directly to a historical memory in and through which we reach out to and experience the mystery. By not identifying the memory and the mystery, in whatever way we may understand the special connection between them we make space for other possible symbolic mediations. We know this is possible even within our own tradition—we may encounter Christ in the poor as much as in the eucharist, though not in the same way. The former encounter may be even more crucial to our Christian life.

When we speak of the theological universality of the Christ we have to take into account the whole cosmic breadth of the action of Christ and not limit it to its manifestation in the historical Jesus. It is true that we should not separate the two poles of the same person. But the relationship between the two will be discovered, not by universalizing the particularity of the historical Jesus but by setting it in the context of the universal action of the Word. The disciples intuit the divine dimension of the personality of Jesus precisely by realizing the universal significance of his salvific act in his death and resurrection. We can say that it is insofar as he is divine that the historical actions of Jesus acquire a universal significance.[13] But this universal significance cannot be fully understood if we do not place it in the context of the universal action of the Word.[14]

This universal action of Christ cannot be localized in a point of time in history, because it will not be complete till the last day when Christ will be all in all. The universality of Christ, therefore, includes all God's manifestations in history. While we Christians see a special, even unique place and role in this history for God's action in Jesus we cannot simply universalize this.

Our perspective here will depend on how we see history in relation to eternity. Eternity is transcendentally contemporaneous with time. When we speak of the divine we cannot speak of before and after. It is *tota simul*— everything at the same time—as the scholastics used to say. Yet when the divine enters history this same divine action has to take place in history— in temporal succession. But when we speak we often confuse the two levels. At the divine/eternal level, the phrase "Christ saves" has universal resonance. The action transcends time, there is no before and after. And yet in time, at the human/historical level, there is a succession and a dynamic progression. The term "eschatological" sometimes indicates this with its dynamic of "already" and "not yet." We cannot separate eternity and history. Yet eternity embraces and transcends history and must not be identified with one particular event however central it may be in the historical process. Correspondingly, history *concretizes* the eternal, without historically particularizing it.[15]

This eternal versus historical dynamic is true of all divine actions, but is particularly so of God's action in Jesus. If we are not careful we will be talking in two registers in a confused manner. Thus talk about universality is meaningful at the divine/eternal level. When we talk about the Word/ Christ we are talking at this level. This universal action of God in Christ is realized in time through a history—in a dynamic progression of actions that constitute a unified structure. These concrete actions have a universal significance and relevance as parts of this structure. But affirming this is different from universalizing the historical/particular, making it historically universal. To come back to our earlier formulation—Jesus is the Christ, but the Christ is more than Jesus. The mystery of Christ includes all the other manifestations of God in history. Therefore we cannot reduce it to its manifestation in the historical Jesus. Much of our talk about Jesus as Christ keeps on playing simultaneously on two registers about the strength of the unity of the personhood of Jesus Christ—eternal/historical, divine/ human—without a clear differentiation. I am trying to point to the differentiation between the divine and the human/historical in that person and to the implications, not only for the way we speak, but also for the way we understand God's action in history.

Our faith affirmation—though it has its foundation in the historical— transcends history. Our encounter with other religions, for instance, is at the historical level of experience. But our theology of religions—while it takes account of this historical experience—is an affirmation of faith "from below," and not "from above." We can also look at the problem from a slightly different point of view. We often tend to talk at an objective, ontological level without taking into account the historical, personal level in which we live and act. It is not helpful to affirm the objective universality of Christ and draw a priori historical conclusions from it without trying to understand the concrete manner in which people actually reach salvation outside the Church which confesses faith in Jesus as the Christ.

A similar differentiation, to which we are accustomed, is between the economic and the immanent Trinity. The Triune God is identical, whether immanent or economic. But there is a story of God's manifestation in history through Word and Spirit that leads us to understand and articulate relationships within the Trinity. It would not always be helpful to speak simply of God or Trinity acting without differentiating the actual person involved in a particular manifestation. It is the Word that becomes flesh. It is the Spirit that descends on Jesus at his baptism in the Jordan.

Starting from this articulation of the economic Trinity, many theologians speak about the differentiation between the manifestations of God in Christ and in the Spirit and see in this differentiation the possibility of understanding the universality of the mystery of Christ. Christ is universal because the Spirit is universal.[16] He is present and active everywhere even when Christ is not acknowledged. Some would even speak of the "absence" of Jesus in the economy of the Holy Spirit.[17] Some, saying that the Spirit is the Spirit of Jesus Christ, seek to reduce the action of the Spirit to that of Jesus Christ. It is the risen Christ that sends the Spirit. The link is certainly there. But the Spirit is not Jesus Christ. Its mediations are real and need not lead to faith in Jesus Christ in the context of history. Here we have another opening to other religions from a Christian perspective. While this articulation between Christ and the Spirit is valid and instructive, I have chosen in this paper to focus on the articulations in the person of Jesus Christ himself.

How do we see God's action in Jesus? The image that seems most helpful to understand the event of Jesus is the biblical one of the covenant. For a Christian what is special about Jesus is that in his paschal mystery has been manifested God's loving self-communication to all peoples. The passion and death of Jesus show that this relationship is not something natural, automatic or physical, simply because Jesus is God-human, but a human transformation that everyone has to undergo in freedom through dying and rising. In raising Jesus to new life God has made a commitment to—an enduring covenant with—humanity. This does not mean that the other manifestations of God in history become useless. They lead people—in their respective cultures—to their personal commitments. As in marriage the formal, public commitment does not take away the value of, but valorizes the expressions and communications of love both before and after the formal covenant, God's covenant in Jesus valorizes all his other manifestations. The covenant in Jesus has a cosmic significance precisely because of the divine (Christ) in him. The whole of salvation history is held together by the cosmic aspect of the mystery.[18]

Sometimes we speak of Christ as the final Word, as the norm by which to judge everything else. There is certainly truth in this claim. But the question is which Christ we are talking about. It is true only if we think of the divine aspect of Christ. The Word is the norm. On the last day Christ will be the pleroma, the fullness. But the historical Jesus is Christ's kenotic form. Jesus promises to send the Spirit who will lead his disciples into all truth (see John 16:13). The fullness of Christ is in the future when God will gather together in him all the riches that he has communicated to the world. Therefore such statements must be understood, not historically, but eschatologically—in a dialectic of already/not yet. Only such a vision will enable us to understand that, in a real sense, Jesus *becomes the Christ in fullness in the process of salvation history*, and thus it is also our task to promote this becoming through mission and dialogue.

The church is the witness and the servant of the mystery. It lives the mystery through the memory of the tradition it has received from its manifestation in the history of Jesus. But it should also be sensitive to other manifestations of Mystery in the history of humanity. Its mission is to proclaim and promote the mystery of the kingdom in its fullness and not itself. The Church's preferred manner of mediating this message must be, following Jesus, *kenotic*.

A SERVANT CHURCH

Part of the problem that we face when we discuss questions concerning the universality of Christ is the image of the Church with which we operate. The church is a visible institution with a creed, rituals, and organization. In this sense we can see it as one religion among others. But sometimes we also think of the Church as a mystery, the Mystical Body of Christ, that includes all who are saved. Whatever be the justification of such language, it is not helpful to think of the Church in this manner in the context of other religions and of history. If we consider the Church as a religion, then we cannot attribute to it the uniqueness and universality that we attribute to Christ. While people attain to salvation outside the Church, the Church itself is a pilgrim, limited by culture and history.[19] It confesses Christ who is the Truth. But it does not possess him and its own understanding of him is limited by the historical memory it has received. The gospels speak to us about Jesus, but do not claim to offer an adequate expression of him despite their multiple attempts.

We often have an image of salvation history as the growth of the Church till the whole world becomes the Church. I do not know where this image comes from. The Bible rather speaks of the remnant, a community that is persecuted which looks forward in hope for the Lord's coming.[20] I think that the image of the Church as the servant, proclaiming the mystery of the Reign of God, ready to offer its life as witness, may be more authentic than the one of a triumphalistic army conquering all before it. Its service is precisely that of helping the unification of all humankind by promoting a human community of dialogue and collaboration. Its task is to proclaim Jesus and his mystery, more in action than in words, so that others too are challenged by him and turn to God — "converted." Some may be called to join the community of his disciples. Others may undergo real change while remaining in their own religions. The concrete way in which the transformation and unification will take place is a mystery that is known to God alone. All we can do is to be faithful witnesses in action, not only to the mystery of God's love, but to its self-sacrificing manifestation in Jesus.

A person, ideally, ought to become a member of the Church not merely to be saved, but because the believer feels called to participate in the mission of the disciples of Jesus. It is a call to a service, a particular role in history — not an honor or a reason to feel superior. One is not saved "more" or "quicker" because one is Christian. The measure of salvation is the freedom and generosity of God. We may recall the parable of the workers sent to the vineyard at various hours of the day (Mt. 20:1–15).

A VISION OF HISTORY

One traditional view of salvation history sees it as a progressive narrowing down from creation to the Mosaic covenant to Jesus after whom it opens up again through the growth of the church. It is a linear view of history, stressing the discontinuity between nature and grace, and between before and after Christ—and envisages other religions as distinct from the divinely authorized history of salvation. This vision is narrow and unsatisfactory. It does not take into account the fact that God is the Father and Mother of all. God's election of a people or of a person is not exclusive, but sacramental and symbolic. The cosmic activity of the Word and the Spirit are affirmed by the Old and the New Testaments precisely on the basis of the particular experiences of God's saving action in a person's or people's life.

An alternate vision affirms a saving plan of God that embraces the whole world and all peoples. It is not cosmic in the sense that it is simply identified with nature and history but because it includes the whole cosmos and history, while taking into account the key element in history—human freedom. It is an interplay between the freedoms of God and of human persons, between call and response. In a sense it is very personal. But it is also communitarian. Election, representation, solidarity, and mission are creative and structural elements of this history. The covenants between God and the human person are played out in the context of cultures and traditions. Both freedom (of God and of the human person) and cultures are factors of pluralism. But this pluralism is integrated within the one plan that God has for the world. The unity of the plan of God is a unity of relationships, neither of identity nor of simple plurality. Relationship implies a plurality of roles and functions within a totality.

A role that one may be called to play in a community is a service; it is not a personal title for honor. In the community itself, a role is ordained to the functioning and the building up of the community; one is not superior to or better than another—all are necessary. From a rational perspective we cannot think of relationships except in terms of a structure whose elements are somehow related as more or less, as superior or inferior. We are accustomed to think that priests are superior to the people or that religious are following a more perfect way of life. We used to think that "objectively" virginity was superior to marriage. Today we are struggling to overcome such stereotypes. To a person who is married, marriage is the best way of life. Priesthood is a role of service in the church, just as the lay people have their role. In the religious sphere the model for pluralism is the Trinity, which is a totality of relationships and not a structure of more or less. The ideal of the Church as a communion of persons and communities is also struggling against older hierarchical or structural models.

God's plan for the world is a network of relationships. We are aware of how God has been manifested to us and what mission God has given us in the world. We are not aware of how God may have been manifested to the others. Nor do we comprehend, much less do we dominate, the plan of God for the world. What Christians can do in this situation is to affirm and live their own identity, witness it in word and deed, and enter into a relationship of dialogue with others. It is in listening to others and in discerning together that we may progressively discover the plan of God as it unfolds in the course of history.

In faith we Christians affirm that God's saving action reaches out to all peoples in ways unknown to us. We confess in Jesus, the Christ, the universal savior. We experience in our dialogue with others that God has also been active in them. We look forward to the transformation and unification of all things in heaven and on earth when God will be all in all (1 Cor. 15:28). With this hope we enter into relationships to contribute to the building of a new heaven and a new earth. Dialogue is the manner in which we witness to what has been revealed to us of Mystery while we respect the ineffable transcendence of Mystery.

THE SIGNIFICANCE OF CHRIST

In the light of our reflections above, the profound meaning of affirming that the Christ is the universal savior is that God is really the savior of all peoples. He is not the God of a particular people. God's action is not limited to a particular historical and cultural tradition. Christ has broken down such walls that divide. Once we have recognized Christ in Jesus, we see with the New Testament, particularly with John and Paul, that Christ and his Spirit are active everywhere. Our task is not to carry Christ where he is not present, but rather to discover him where he is, sometimes in mysterious ways unknown to us. The process of this quest is not a material-scientific study of culture and history, but a listening in dialogue to the people in whom we perceive the salvific dialogue between God and the human person taking place. As we listen to the experience of others, it is also our privilege to actively witness to our own experience of the mystery of Christ in Jesus and its relevance to the contemporary world. We feel that we are sent as witnesses on a mission. However we must not be astonished to find that others, too, may claim such a mission.

We must resist the temptation to reduce the universality of Christ to the universality of the visible, institutional Church. We witness to a mystery with which we cannot simply identify ourselves. We often speak about the link that the Church has with the Reign of God. We do not often reflect on the distance that separates the Church from the Reign. One reason is that we tend to think too juridically in terms of power and representation, and not in terms of freedom and relationship—that is, in personal terms. It would be helpful to reread in this context St. Paul's reflection on the Jews in relation to the mystery of salvation (Rom. 10–11). One could say that the limitations of the Church in culture and history make place for the other religions in the plan of God for the world—just as the going away of Jesus seems to make place for the Spirit in history in the reflection of John (John 16:7).

I spoke in the beginning of three paradigms in contemporary theology of religions — namely exclusivism, inclusivism and pluralism. The paradigm I am trying to evolve will find a place between inclusivism and pluralism. It is inclusivist insofar as it reflects in the perspective of the Christian faith in the mysteries of the Trinity and of the Incarnation and their ongoing action in history. But because of the differentiations I have made between the Word and the Spirit, between the Jesus of history and Christ, and between Christ and the Church, the inclusion is only at the level of the mystery of God and Christ whose universality we affirm in faith. It is pluralist, not merely at a historical, phenomenological level of the religions, but also at the level of the plural manifestations of God in history, through the Word eternal and also incarnate and through the Spirit. Therefore the pluralism is already at the level of religion as experience. In faith I affirm that this pluralism is structured into a unity. All believers, because they believe that God is one, will have to affirm this. But this unity is eschatological, and both the concrete shape and the actual realization of this unity transcend history.

I would like to present this as an *advaitic* perspective that seeks a mediation between the one and the many, not denying either, but making them the poles of one complex reality.

The goal of mission is to make our own contribution to the realization of the plan of God for the world. This requires listening to the others, reading the signs of the times, building up community, promoting freedom, fellowship and justice and witnessing to the hope that is in us (1 Peter 3:15). To proclaim the universal salvific will of God in Christ means not just to talk about it, but to make it happen. We must also proclaim — realize — the Good News of Jesus. This means that it is not enough to talk in general about the values of the Reign, about justice and development, and about peace and freedom. Jesus was involved with the life of the poor. He particularly opted for the poor and the oppressed. He chose the way of the cross, of total self-giving, even unto death. He sought solidarity with people, particularly in suffering. He lived the reality of communion symbolized in the sharing of food as his own very being. It is significant that this aspect of the suffering Christ, who identifies himself with suffering humanity, seems to attract people like Gandhi and many Indian artists who are the pioneers of Christian art in India, though they do not belong to the Church.[21] To narrow down such a broad and rich mission to increasing membership in the church seems a pity. Even such "conversion" is God's work, not ours. A Church open to the world and to God's mystery will have open frontiers and be less worried about its identity and propagation than about the Reign of God.

CONCLUSION

People are afraid that to affirm pluralism is somehow to fall into relativism — that is, to see all religions as the same and to condone pure relativism. If we look at pluralism not in the abstract or in material terms but in personal terms of freedom and relationship, then we will see its richness on the one hand and on the other the need to affirm and witness to one's own identity. I am happy to be a Christian. God has called me to be one. I have discovered the mystery of God's universal salvific will in Christ through Jesus. Jesus has shown me the way to promote this mystery in the world in the particular way of being on the side of the poor, ready to give and to share even unto death. I proclaim this message as more than ever relevant to today's world. But I also respect the mystery of God's free relationship with other free human beings. Other religions do not exist apart from other believers. I respect pluralism as the manifestation of the freedom and personhood of God and of the others. I am not anxious to somehow structure them into a system. As a matter of fact, at the level of religions as institutions, pluralism often becomes a problem.

Respect should find expression in various ways according to the context. If I am simply a member of a multireligious community, I can be satisfied with dialogue and witness. But if I run a hospital, just as I would claim the right for the Christians to be ministered to by their chaplain, I should at least be open to allow others the appropriate means to find support in their own religions in a critical period of their lives. Similarly, if I manage a school, I have a responsibility to provide every one an opportunity for an integral education. The school is not merely, or even primarily, a religious institution; it is a service to the community. One may see it as a good occasion to witness to one's faith and to contribute to the building up of the Reign, but one has also a responsibility to see to the faith education of the members of other religions, especially if reflecting on their faith can have a purifying and prophetic effect for them. This responsibility seems even more obvious and acceptable if we properly understand the universal saving act of God in Christ.

NOTES

1. See M. Amaladoss, S.J., "Theological Bases for Religious Pluralism," in S. Arulsamy, ed., *Communalism in India* (Bangalore: Claretian Publications, 1988), pp. 115-138.

2. See Paul F. Knitter, *No Other Name?* (Maryknoll, N.Y.: Orbis Books, 1985; and London: SCM Press, 1985); Alan Race, *Christians and Religious Pluralism* (Maryknoll, N.Y.: Orbis Books, 1982; and London: SCM Press, 1983); Gavin D'Costa, *Theology and Religious Pluralism* (Oxford: Basil Blackwell, 1986).

3. See, for instance, the use of the term "myth" in two books that John Hick has edited: *The Myth of God Incarnate* (London: SCM, 1977); with Paul F. Knitter, *The Myth of Christian Uniqueness* (Maryknoll, N.Y.: Orbis Books, 1987; and London: SCM Press, 1988). It is true that the word "myth" may be used to mean a symbol that affirms a deeper truth. Yet for Christians God Incarnate is not a "myth" in the same way as the creation narratives in the Book of Genesis.

4. See Leonard Swidler, ed., *Toward a Universal Theology of Religion* (Maryknoll,

N.Y.: Orbis, 1987), especially the strong critique of the idea of rationalist approaches by R. Panikkar, pp. 118-153. See also Wilfred Cantwell Smith, *Towards a World Theology* (Maryknoll, N.Y.: Orbis Books, 1990; and London: Macmillan, 1990).

5. I use the word "witness" not in a passive sense as weaker than proclamation, but in the full biblical sense of "martyrion."

6. In the context of dialogue with Buddhism, it may be problematic to speak constantly about God as I am doing in this paper. Nevertheless, I speak in a Christian context to Christians and so I use a Christian language.

7. See M. Amaladoss, *Education in the Faith in a Multi-Religious Context* (New Delhi: Jesuit Educational Association, 1988), pp. 3-4.

8. See A. Pieris, "The Buddha and the Christ: Mediators of Liberation," in Hick and Knitter, *The Myth of Christian Uniqueness*, p. 162.

9. See R. Panikkar, "The Jordan, the Tiber and the Ganges," in Hick and Knitter, *The Myth of Christian Uniqueness*, p. 104.

10. This occurs through the action of the Word (Wisdom) and the Spirit. See John Paul II, *Redemptor Hominis* 6, 11; and *Dominum et Vivificantem*, 53. See also *Ad Gentes*, 4 and *Gaudium et Spes*, 22.

11. In the middle ages, St. Thomas Aquinas held that even non-Christians were justified at the time of their first moral judgment, if they chose the "Good." Cf. *Summa Theologiae* I-II, q. 89, a. 6.

12. Cf. R. Panikkar, "Un presente senza catture," *Rocca* (October 1, 1987): 54-59. See also Panikkar's "The Jordan, the Tiber, and the Ganges," in *The Myth of Christian Uniqueness*, pp. 89-116; Edward Schillebeeckx, *Jesus in Our Western Culture* (London: SCM, 1987), pp. 2-3; Christian Duquoc, "Appartenance ecclésiale et identification chrétienne," *Concilium* 216 (1988): 141-152. The words of Jacques Dupuis are also suggestive: "It is true to say that, while Jesus is the Christ, the Christ is more than Jesus. To deny this would amount to denying the real transformation, emphatically affirmed by the entire New Testament, of Jesus' manhood as he is raised by the Father. The meta-historical Christ, or cosmic Christ is universally present and active in human history." This citation is taken from Dupuis' unpublished manuscript "Theology of Religions, Christian or Universal." A similar distinction between the two poles in the personality of Jesus is made by K. Rahner in *Foundations of the Christian Faith* (New York: Seabury, 1978), p. 290; and by Wilhem Thusing, in W. Thusing and K. Rahner, *A New Christology* (New York: Crossroad, 1980; and London: Burns and Oates, 1980), p. 180. C. Duquoc in A. Ngindu Mushete, ed., *Bulletin de Théologie Africaine* (1985), p. 294, underlines the necessity "maintenir un écart, non une opposition, entre Jesus et Christ, Christ est le nom de l'ouverture universelle de Jesus, Christ donne l'Esprit au Père. Jesus est celui qui a designé dans une particularité jamais absolutise cette ouverture."

13. See Gerald O'Collins, *Interpreting Jesus* (Mahwah, N.J.: Paulist Press, 1983; and London: Geoffrey Chapman, 1983), p. 167: "If it was Jesus' humanity that made his dying and rising possible, it was his divinity that gave that dying and rising a cosmic value."

14. See Walter Kasper, *Jesus the Christ* (London: Burns and Oates, 1976), pp. 188-189.

15. See the reflection of R. Panikkar on the difference between the "concrete" and the "particular" and the "universal" and the "general" in "The Jordan," in Hick and Knitter, *Myth of Christian Uniqueness*, p. 107.

16. See John O'Donnell, "In Him and Over Him: The Holy Spirit in the Life of Jesus," *Gregorianum* 70 (1989): 24-45: "Pneumatology offers us the key to grasp the universality of God's saving purposes without dissolving the uniqueness of the Incarnation" (p. 45).

17. See John 16:5-15. K. Rahner in *Theological Investigations*, vol. 17 (New York: Crossroad, 1981), p. 43, says: "Christ is present and efficacious in the non-Christian believer (and therefore in the non-Christian religions) through his Spirit." Walter Kasper in *Jesus the Christ* says something similar: "The Spirit who is operative in Christ in his fullness, is at work in varying degrees everywhere in the history of mankind" (p. 268). Cf. also C. Duquoc, "Christianity and Its Claim to Universality," *Concilium* 135 (1986): 64.

18. See O'Collins, *Interpreting Jesus,* p. 167.

19. Cf. Duquoc, *Provisional Churches* (Philadephia: Trinity Press, Int., 1983; and London: SCM, 1986).

20. Cf. Mt. 10:16-25 and parallels; John 15:18-21. K. Rahner speaks of the "Church of the Little Flock" in *The Shape of the Church to Come* (London: SPCK, 1974).

21. Cf. Matthew Lederle, *Christian Painting in India* (Bombay: Heras Institute, 1987), pp. 65-66.

7

The Cross and the Rainbow: Christ in a Multireligious Culture

STANLEY J. SAMARTHA

I

Although most Christians today are unwilling to take a totally negative attitude toward neighbors of other faiths, there seems to be a good deal of hesitation on the part of many to reexamine the basis of their exclusive claims on behalf of Christ. The place of Christ in a multireligious society becomes, therefore, an important issue in the search for a new theology of religions.

Theological claims have political consequences. This is particularly true in contemporary India where the exclusive claims made by any one particular community of faith affect its relationships with members of other communities of faith. Such claims make it difficult, if not impossible, for persons belonging to different religious traditions to live together in harmony and to cooperate for common purposes in society. Such claims, open or hidden, also raise basic theological questions concerning God's relationship to the whole of humanity, not just to one stream of it. Thus both historical pressures and theological imperatives demand a reexamination of all exclusivist claims.

Through the incarnation in Jesus Christ, God has relativized God's self in history. Christian theologians should therefore ask themselves whether they are justified in absolutizing in doctrine him whom God has relativized in history. Today's questions regarding the relationship of Jesus Christ to God are very different from those asked in earlier centuries. In many ways, they are new questions that need new solutions. These new solutions, however, must be theologically credible, spiritually satisfying, and pastorally helpful.

A process of rejecting exclusive claims and seeking new ways of understanding the relationship of Jesus Christ to God and humanity is already underway. From what may be described as "normative exclusivism," Christians are moving toward a position of "relational distinctiveness" of Christ, *relational* because Christ does not remain unrelated to neighbors of other faiths, and *distinctive* because, without recognizing the distinctiveness of the great religious traditions as different responses to the Mystery of God, no mutual enrichment is possible.

Such efforts toward a new Christian theology are taking place in India. Christian theological reflection in India obviously cannot be carried on in isolation and must take into account what is happening in different parts of the world church, but at the same time Indian theologians cannot go on as if, in the long centuries of religious life in India, there had been no theological reflection whatsoever on issues of interreligious relationships. More precisely, the Hindu response to religious pluralism should become a part of Indian Christian theological reflection. Thus, the interplay of these two factors—the ferment within the world church and the experience of religious life lived pluralistically in India—provides the context for the following reflections.

II

During the last two decades significant changes have taken place officially in Christian attitudes toward neighbors of other faiths. The well-known declaration of the Second Vatican Council, *Nostra Aetate* (1965), is regarded as "the first truly positive statement" of the Catholic Church about other religions.[1] Founded in 1948, the World Council of Churches moved rather slowly and somewhat reluctantly on this issue until, in 1971, it accepted an "interim" policy statement on other faiths. After nearly a decade of hard work, often marked by controversy, the WCC accepted in 1979 a theological statement and adopted a set of *Guidelines on Dialogue,* "welcoming the degree of agreement and mutual understanding represented by it among those who held different theological views." With regard to neighbors of other faiths, the statement said: "We feel able with integrity to assure our partners in dialogue that we come not as manipulators but as fellow-pilgrims."[2]

These attitudes are indeed strikingly different from those the Christian church persistently held during previous centuries. It is precisely at this point, however, that there now seems to be considerable hesitation as to what steps the church should take next in a continuously pluralistic world. It looks as if, having opened the door slightly, Christians are afraid that the strangers, long kept outside, might indeed turn out to be fellow pilgrims after all. What if the forbidden frontier turns out to be a welcoming threshold?

Since the mid-1960s there have indeed been many developments both in the Catholic Church and in the churches affiliated with the World Council of Churches. But many internal tensions have also developed. There are Catholic scholars who feel that the tensions regarding other religions are rooted within the official magisterium:

> The failure adequately to explain what Vatican II means, and to square it either with Scripture or with the strong theological tradition that has seen other religions as idolatrous is serious. Unless the magisterium can do so convincingly, it will be under fire.[3]

Catholic scholars in India also feel that there is now a stalemate in interreligious dialogue, with participants repeating the same alternatives in various combinations, unwilling to move ahead.[4] Pope John Paul II convoked an extraordinary Synod of Bishops "to relive in some way the extraordinary atmosphere of the ecclesial communion during the Council [Vatican II]" and "to foster a further deepening and acceptance of Vatican II in the life of the church, especially in the light of new demands."[5] Inasmuch as some of the new demands are precisely in the area of relationship with neighbors of other faiths, one would hope for a more decisive turn in the attitude of the Catholic Church.

Within the World Council of Churches, given the variety and complexity of its membership and the very different theological positions represented within its wide spectrum of opinions, the tensions are even stronger, though not always openly articulated. With the many Evangelicals represented within the fellowship of the World Council of Churches, there is an unavoidable tension between mission and dialogue; yet the problem is even more complex than it appears, for there are tensions *within* the perceptions of mission itself and of dialogue itself. "Though it might *seem* that the tension between 'mission' and 'dialogue' has been resolved," writes Allan R. Brockway, "the real tension remains."[6] The massive studies now underway in ecumenical and evangelical circles on "Gospel and Culture" are important, but they can also become a way of avoiding the challenge and invitation of other religions by diverting resources toward a topic on which a great deal has already been said.[7] What is the substance of *culture,* particularly in Asian societies, without its *religious* dimensions? An essay on the elephant without reference to its ivory is incomplete, and can even be positively dangerous. Even though the theological issues have already been identified and questions for the study of other faiths formulated, there seems to be great reluctance to move ahead.[8]

With regard to conservative Evangelicals, it is difficult to talk about *next* steps when even the first steps have not been taken. One cannot ask a door to be opened wider when it is already latched from within, and chained. Given the evangelical assumption of the inerrancy of the Bible, it is hardly likely that any positive approach toward neighbors of other faiths will emerge in the coming years. Evangelicals' recent talk about "dialogue" with its *seeming* openness to members of other faiths is misleading. Dialogue is understood by them as a means to communicate the message. "The dialogic method is necessary if those who witness to Christ are to engage the minds of their listeners."[9] In "true" dialogue and encounter, it is claimed, "we seek both to disclose the inadequacies and falsities of non-Christian religions and to demonstrate the adequacy and truth, the absoluteness and finality of the Lord Jesus Christ."[10] It is the *instrumental* use of dialogue rather than its *intrinsic* worth as a living way of seeking new relationship in the household of God that is emphasized.

There are many reasons why, in this matter of interreligious encounter, Christians are unwilling to move beyond the positions they have already taken. Sometimes political and economic factors influence the attitude of one religious community toward others. Quite often, unexamined ideological assumptions prevent Christians from critically examining their traditional positions. But the major reason for the present impasse is the unresolved theological tension within the consciousness of the church about other religions.

To ask theological questions about this matter is to go to the very roots of our pluralistic existence today. To truly confront these questions, the study of religions has to be shifted from a *missiological* to a *theological* framework, particularly in our theological colleges and seminaries. The question is not *what* to do with so many other religions that claim the loyalty and devotion of millions of followers in the world, but why are they so persistently present providing meaning and direction to the lives of millions of our neighbors. What does this mean theologically—that is, for our understanding of God and God's relationship to the whole created *oikoumene,* of which Christians are not the only citizens? Can it be that plurality belongs to the very structure of reality? Or can it be that it is the will of God that many religions should continue in the world?

These are difficult questions indeed, and it may take a long time for the church to arrive at clear and unambiguous answers to them. The Western church took quite some time to come to terms with Copernicus and Darwin, with Freud and Jung, with science and technology, and is still struggling with Marx and Mao. The challenge and invitation of other religions may take even longer to elicit firm and clear answers. But beginnings have to be made lest the church look like a fortress to be defended rather than the household of God where strangers and sojourners can become fellow citizens.

III

In contemporary India a radical change in the Christian stance toward neighbors of other faiths is both an existential demand and a theological necessity. It is desperately needed when the unity and integrity of the country are in danger of being torn apart by forces of separation that are often influenced by the claims and counterclaims of diverse religions. And yet the search for new relationships between different religious communities is not just a matter of political adjustments or a redistribution of economic resources. Deep down, it is a theological question seeking to relate different responses to the Mystery of Truth.

By blaming the highly visible religious communities for the political and social ills of the country, one avoids a serious discussion about the spiritual and theological resources available within religions for the critical renewal of community life. No one would deny that religions have exploited persons and have contributed to much of the social injustice in India (as well as in other countries). In the struggle for a just society, established religions have often been on the side of the rich and the powerful, not that of the poor and the oppressed. Religions have been unable to tame political passions and, quite often, have added religious fuel to political conflagrations. Yet recent studies on communal clashes between Hindus and Sikhs (after the assassination of Mrs. Indira Gandhi) have brought out the point that religion "is not the *causative* factor but the *instrumental* factor in such clashes . . . it is made to appear as the causative factor."[11]

A secular "emptying" of religions in light of the role of religion in the real or imaginary ills of society would lead to a tremendous loss of creative power. It is very necessary to accept "the normative plurality" of India's life, and to provide space for dialogue between religious, linguistic, and ethnic groups. The contemporary contribution of India as a civilization to the meaning and content of democracy could be in the way India tolerates this initial babel of multicultural encounters that can lead to the creation of new communities, myths, and languages. The acceptance of plurality can well be an answer to fascism.[12]

Through long centuries of pluralistic existence India has developed a particular attitude toward religious dissent. A systematic and sympathetic study of this mood of "tolerance" is yet to be made.[13] But a few "moments" in India's long history can be profitably noted.

Already in the Vedic period about 1,500 B.C.E., Brahmanism tried to solve the clash between the One and the many by suggesting that while *Sat* (Truth, Being) is One, sages call it by different names. It was not by eliminating the gods or by conquering them but by relating them to the One, and therefore to each other, that they were held together in a structure of difference rather than similarity. The One was greater than any of the gods or even the sum total of the gods. And even when the distinctiveness and legitimacy of different gods were recognized within an existential relationship, the ontological substance remained above and beyond the gods. Without recognizing and accepting this Mysterious Center (the *Satyasya Satyam* — The Truth of the Truth), genuine plurality is impossible.[14]

It took many centuries for Brahmanism, and later on for Hinduism, to "overcome" the challenge of the Buddha who rejected the authority of the Vedas, the superiority of the Brahmins, and the necessity of the sacrificial ritual. Now, however, the Buddha is "co-opted" into the Hindu structure of the *avataras*.[15] Later on, the *sampradayas* (traditions connected with Vishnu, Siva, and Sakti) within Hinduism were held together in a larger framework, despite the tensions caused by different kings who followed different *sampradayas*.[16]

If one takes a leap across the centuries, one encounters moments when Islam, and later on Christianity, armed with their exclusive claims and allied with military, political, and economic power, rudely intruded into India's delicate balance of relationships. This created deep disturbances within Indian consciousness, the consequences of which are with us even to this day. The Hindu arguments against any claim of "uniqueness," "finality," or "once-for-allness" for one particular way are well known. Westerners, together with Indian Christians, are familiar with the English works of Ram Mohan Roy (1772-1833) and S. Radhakrishnan (1888-1975) on this subject.[17] The "Neo-Hindu" emphasis on the equality of all religions *(sarva dharma samonvaya tattva)* was probably more a *political affirmation* of the relationships between different religious communities at a time when political tensions were developing in the country rather than a *theological statement* on the relationships between religions. Perhaps, therefore, one should not attach too much theological significance to this emphasis. On the other hand, there is a body of writings in Sanskrit and other Indian languages that reflects more strongly the tolerant mood and feelings of the people in general; these writings remain a closed book to those who restrict themselves to the English language.[18]

It is worthwhile to note these orthodox Hindu arguments because they are influential even to this day. Basing themselves on two principles — *mataikya,* the unity of all religions, and *matavirodha,* their noncontradictoriness — the pandits advanced three arguments against the claim of Christian superiority. First, the plurality of religions is "intrinsic and purposeful" because of *dharma*. The basic differences in humankind make it natural and inevitable that there should be plurality, not singularity, in religion. In other words, plurality is rooted in the diversity of human nature itself. Secondly, there is the principle of *adhikara* which may be translated aptitude, competence, eligibility, which makes plurality necessary. Birth is never accidental. It is the result of *karmic* repercussions. Therefore one is born in a particular religion because of the *sadhana* (discipline) possible for that particular person. Thirdly, this *adhikarabheda* (differences in aptitude or competence) is not a matter of choice but is a "given" element, even the will of God, and it allows persons to choose different *margas* (paths or ways). God defines one's *adhikara* by the attraction (*ruci*) one feels toward a certain *marga*. Hindus are Hindus rather than Christians because they have aptitude and eligibility only for their *dharma* and not for Christianity. Therefore the question of superiority or "uniqueness" of any one *dharma* over others does not arise. Criticism of one religion based on criteria derived from another is unwarranted. Conversions are unnecessary. The

Hindus are not asking Christians to give up *their* commitment to God in Christ. Rather, they are pleading with Christians not to ask Hindus to give up *their* commitment. One should note that these arguments, so different from the later "neo-Hindu" affirmation of the equality of all religions, are *echoed* even to this day and have a *pervasive* influence on general Hindu consciousness.

Perhaps it is worthwhile to recall an even more recent moment in the history of India just after the nation's political independence (1947). Despite fresh memories of how their country was divided on religious grounds and torn by massive human sufferings, Hindus as the majority community were generous toward their minority neighbors — Muslims and Christians. In the Constituent Assembly, working on a Constitution for the Republic of India, Loknath Mishra introduced an amendment that would delete the words "to propagate" from the Article on Fundamental Rights: "to profess, practice and propagate" one's religion (Article 25:1). During the debate, such well-known leaders as Pandit Lakshmikant Maitra, T. T. Krishnamachari, K. M. Munshi (vice-chancellor of the Bhavan University), and several others argued for retaining the words "to propagate" as a recognition of a fundamental right of minority communities. Without the support of Hindu leaders, the clause would have never passed. Soli Sorabji, a distinguished jurist, remarks, "One cannot but be struck by the broad-mindedness and the spirit of tolerance and accommodation displayed by the founding fathers of the majority community towards their Christian brethren."[19] In no other country, therefore, does the claim for the "uniqueness" of one particular religious tradition or the assertion of the "normativeness" of one particular faith over others sound so rude, out of place, and theologically arrogant as in India. Such assertions contradict India's whole ethos and tear at the fabric of interreligious relationships so carefully woven during centuries of conflict, tension, and massive sufferings by the people.[20]

IV

In this context of ongoing life in India where Christians live and work together with neighbors of other faiths, where a deep-seated *theological* tolerance coexists with *social* intolerance and is sometimes mixed with outbursts of *political* intolerance, can a christology be developed that is free from the burdens of the past but is unmistakably Christian and recognizably Indian?

Any attempt to formulate such a christology should take into account at least two factors that have emerged out of India's long history of multireligious life. One is the acceptance of a sense of Mystery and the other the rejection of an exclusive attitude where ultimate matters are concerned. Mystery is not something to be used to fill the gaps in rational knowledge. Mystery provides the ontological basis for tolerance, which would otherwise run the risk of becoming uncritical friendliness. This Mystery, the Truth of the Truth *(Satyasya Satyam), is* the transcendent Center that remains always beyond and greater than apprehensions of it or even the sum total of those apprehensions. It is beyond cognitive knowledge *(tarka)* but it is open to vision *(dristi)* and intuition *(anubhava).* It is near yet far, knowable yet unknowable, intimate yet ultimate and, according to one particular Hindu view, cannot even be described as "one." It is "not-two" *(advaita),* indicating thereby that diversity is within the heart of Being itself and therefore may be intrinsic to human nature as well.

This emphasis on Mystery is not meant as an escape from the need for rational inquiry, but it does insist that the rational is not the only way to do theology; the mystical and the esthetic also have their necessary contributions to theology. Mystery lies beyond the theistic/nontheistic debate. Mystery is an ontological status to be accepted, not an epistemological problem to be solved. Without a sense of Mystery, *Theos* cannot remain *Theos,* nor *Sat* remain *Sat,* nor can Ultimate Reality remain ultimate.

In religious life, Mystery and meaning are related. Without a disclosure of meaning at particular points in history or in human consciousness, there can be no human response to Mystery. The history of religions shows that these responses are many and are different, sometimes even within a particular religious tradition. Quite often these differences are due to cultural and historical factors. Although each response to Mystery has a normative claim on the followers of that particular tradition, the criteria derived from one response cannot be made the norm to judge the responses of other traditions.

One strand of Hinduism, for example, has described this Mystery as *sat-cit-ananda* (truth-consciousness-bliss). This is one way of responding to Mystery in a particular cultural setting that is very different from that of the early Christian centuries. Christians believe that in Jesus Christ the meaning of this Mystery is revealed in such a way as to constitute a revelation of God and to provide a way of salvation for all human beings. The doctrine of the Trinity, which describes God as Father, Son, and Holy Spirit, is an attempt to make sense of this Mystery through the meaning disclosed in Jesus of Nazareth, identified with Christ, and using categories from Greek thought alien to the Indian context.

Both the terms "Brahman" and "God" are culture-conditioned. One could as well use the term Mystery, which may be more acceptable. In this case the two statements—namely, that "Brahman is *sat-cit-ananda*" and "God is triune, Father, Son, and Holy Spirit"—could be regarded as two responses to the same Mystery in two cultural settings. One cannot be used as a norm to judge the other. The limitations of language are obvious here. Feminist theologians have already objected to the "maleness" of the trinitarian formula; if cultural obstacles could be overcome, they might be persuaded to accept the Hindu notion, which avoids this problem. In any case, neither *sat-cit-ananda* nor Trinity could, in linguistic terms, adequately describe the inner ontological working of Mystery. One could ask, therefore, on what grounds can it be claimed that the trinitarian formula offers a "truer" insight into the nature of Mystery than does *sat-cit-ananda?* At best, the two formulations can only be symbolic, pointing to the Mystery, affirming the meaning disclosed, but retaining the residual depth.

No one could have anticipated in advance the presence of God in the life and death of Jesus of Nazareth. There is an incomprehensible dimension to it. That Jesus is the Christ of God is a confession of faith by the Christian community. It does indeed remain normative to Christians everywhere, but to make it "absolutely singular" and to maintain that the meaning of the Mystery is disclosed *only* in one particular person at one particular point, and nowhere else, is to ignore one's neighbors of other faiths who have other points of reference. To make exclusive claims for our particular tradition is not the best way to love our neighbors as ourselves.

If, then, human responses to the *revolution* of Mystery are plural and are articulated in different ways, the same observation applies to the experience of *salvation* as well, and to the manner in which it is articulated by followers of different religious traditions.

In multi-religious situations such as in India, the notions of "salvation" and of what we are saved from are understood differently. This is to be expected. The question here is not whether there *may be* plural ways of salvation. In multireligious situations the fact is that there *are* plural ways of salvation, experienced and articulated in different ways. Both the context and expression of salvation are different. When the questions asked about the human predicament are different, the answers are bound to be different. How can it be otherwise? Already in the New Testament salvation through Jesus Christ was experienced and interpreted differently by the Aramaic-speaking Jewish Christians, the Hellenic Jews of the diaspora who were much more open to other peoples among whom they lived, and the non-Jewish Christians such as the Greeks, Syrians, and Romans who had no part in the Jewish "history of salvation." And yet, there was no doubt about the root of this experience of salvation in Jesus Christ.

Whereas Christians use the term "sin" to describe the human predicament, Hindus might use *avidya* (ignorance) and Buddhists *dukkha* (sorrow) as the condition from which deliverance is sought. The notions of *moksha* and *nirvana* as the ultimate goals of deliverance are conceived differently, as also the *sadhanas,* the ways of discipline, advocated as necessary to attain these goals. In addition, today one must also take into account the desperate desire of millions of human beings for salvation of a different kind— namely, liberation from oppression, exploitation, and injustice. In this context, many feminist Christian theologians decline to accept as normative the notion of a revelation and salvation through a male person that excludes more than half of humanity.

Where alternative ways of salvation have provided meaning and purpose for millions of persons in other cultures for more than two or three thousand years, to claim that the Judeo-Christian-Western tradition has the *only* answer to all problems in all places and for all persons in the world is presumptuous, if not incredible. This is not to deny the *validity* of the Christian experience of salvation in Jesus Christ, but it is to question the *exclusive* claims made for it by Christians, claims that are unsupported by any evidence in history, or in the institutional life of the church, or in the lives of many Christians who make such claims. If salvation comes *from God* – and for Christians it cannot be otherwise – then possibilities should be left open to recognize the validity of other experiences of salvation.

The nature of Mystery is such that any claim on the part of one religious community to have exclusive or unique or final knowledge becomes inadmissible. Exclusiveness puts fences around the Mystery. It creates dichotomies between the divine and the human, between humanity and nature, and between different religious communities. It leaves little room for the nonrational elements in religious life – the mystical and the esthetic, rituals and symbols, prayer, worship, and meditation. It is not surprising that very often Christian theologians ready to discuss religious "ideas" with others feel extremely uneasy when it comes to matters of "worship" or art in interreligious meetings *(satsang* – fellowship of truth). Further, those who make open or hidden claims of exclusiveness find it impossible to live together with neighbors of other faiths except on very superficial social levels. A one-way, exclusivistic "proclamation" is like a stone hurled into a flowing stream. It makes a little splash, and then remains submerged, and makes no difference whatsoever to the waters flowing past it. Someone might even pick it up and hurl it back to where it came from.

Very often, claims for the normativeness of Christ are based on the authority of the Bible. Exclusive texts are hurled back and forth as if just by uttering texts from scriptures the problem is settled. The authority of the Bible is indeed important for Christians. In the multireligious situations, where there are other scriptures whose authority is accepted by neighbors of other religious traditions, how can the claims based on one particular scripture become the norm, or authority for all? Here, too, the plurality of scriptures is a fact to be accepted, not a notion to be discussed.

But there are even more important factors to be recognized. For example, what does one make of the fact, hardly recognized by Christian theologians, that none of the revelations on which Christians theologize today took place in a West European context or were written down in a West European language? Recent studies in the ontology of language point out how precarious it is to depend on texts and translations when it comes to the question of authority in matters of faith.[21]

Even notions of "authority" are different when it comes to interpreting holy scriptures. To the Hindu and the Buddhist, the authority of the scriptures does not depend on the *writtenness* of the text, but on *hearing* and *seeing* the word *(Sabda)*. Texts are indeed important. But a Hindu or Buddhist would reject the notion that through the study of texts one can encounter the truth behind them, or that merely by quoting texts one can encounter the truth within them, or that merely by quoting texts truth is communicated to hearers. Knowledge of God is not something to be *discovered* through the study of written texts. It is to be *recovered* through *hearing.* The holiness of words is intrinsic. One participates in it not through understanding but through reciting and hearing it.

The Western notion of editing an *original* text is an intrusion into Eastern situations. One has to go behind the written texts to the *sound* of the Word, recited and heard over long periods of time by the community, in order to see how words have functioned religiously in matters of faith. This question of hermeneutics in multireligious situations needs careful study. In India, around 35-32 B.C.E., Buddhists were the first to commit their sacred oral texts to writing. Attempts are now being made by Indian Christian biblical scholars to study Hindu and Buddhist hermeneutical theory as it has developed over the centuries, and to work out the implications of Eastern hermeneutics for the Indian Christian theological enterprise.[22]

If the great religious traditions of humanity are indeed different responses to the Mystery of God or *Sat* or the Transcendent or Ultimate Reality, then the *distinctiveness* of each response, in this instance the Christian, should be stated in such a way that a mutually critical and enriching *relationship* between different responses becomes naturally possible. Exclusiveness regards universality as the extension of its own particularity and seeks to conquer other faiths. Inclusiveness, though seeming generous, actually co-opts other faiths without their leave. Both exclusiveness and its patronizing cousin inclusiveness may even be forms of theological violence against neighbors of other faiths and, when combined with economic, political, and military power, as has often happened in history, become dangerous to communal harmony and world peace. It is not without significance that only after the second world war (1945), when, with the dismantling of colonialism, new nations emerged on the stage of history and asserted their identity through their own religions and cultures, that both the Vatican and the World Council of Churches began to articulate a more positive attitude toward peoples of other religious traditions, although both church bodies remained reluctant to recognize the *theological* significance of these other faiths.

In moving beyond exclusiveness and inclusiveness, Christians must come to a clearer grasp of the uniqueness of Jesus. The distinctiveness of Jesus Christ does not lie in claiming that "Jesus Christ is God." This amounts to saying that Jesus Christ is the tribal god of Christians over against the gods of other peoples. Elevating Jesus to the status of God or limiting Christ to Jesus of Nazareth are both temptations to be avoided. The former runs the risk of an impoverished "Jesusology" and the latter of becoming a narrow "Christomonism." A theocentric christology avoids these dangers and becomes more helpful in establishing new relationships with neighbors of other faiths.

A theocentric (or Mystery-centered) christology is not a new fashion. The Bible continually emphasizes the priority of God, and Jesus himself was theocentric. In recent years, within the Indian and the broader world church, discussion of this question has begun. The issues were earlier hinted at or articulated by certain Christian theologians in different parts of the world. Both in the Catholic Church and in the churches affiliated with the World Council of Churches, new dimensions of this christologico-ecumenical issue are taking shape. On one level, the discussions seem to be within a parochial Christian ecumenical framework, seeking to accommodate different Christian viewpoints. On another level, however, the implications of these new christological insights go far beyond the narrow confines of Christians to the deeper and larger ecumenism that embraces the whole of humanity. In discussions in different parts of the world, a new hermeneutics is developing, a hermeneutics willing to read and hear biblical texts about Jesus in ways quite different from those of the West.

In the West, the International Theological Commission appointed by the pope admits no distinction between christology and theology. And yet it states that "confusion between christology and theology results if one supposes that the name of God is totally unknown outside of Jesus Christ and that there exists no other theology than that which arises from the Christian revelation." The commission thus opens the possibility of recognizing theologies other than Christian. The statement goes on to call the church to cooperate with others in order "to participate in building a civilization of love."[23]

Also in the World Council of Churches, fresh discussions have started on "the inner core" of its basic credal affirmation that "the Lord Jesus Christ is God and Savior." Throughout the council's history, questions have been raised about the adequacy of this formulation. On the one hand, New Testament scholars have pointed out that the statement identifying Jesus Christ with God goes beyond the witness of the New Testament. On the other, Catholic and Orthodox theologians have felt that the statement is narrowly "christomonistic" and needs a full-fledged trinitarian emphasis. More recently, additions have been made to the original phrasing.[24] In the present discussion, two factors have become important: the christological question is being raised against the background of renewed dialogue with adherents of other faiths and of cooperation with persons of secular convictions who are struggling against the forces of death and destruction. The ontological equation of Jesus Christ with God would scarcely allow any serious discussion with neighbors of other faiths or with secular humanists.[25]

Throughout the Bible the priority of God is taken for granted. The affirmation that God is the creator of all life and of all humanity puts Christians and their neighbors of other faiths together at the very source of life. God breathes life into humanity (Gen. 2:7) and in doing so entrusts to it responsibility for all created life (Gen. 2:15). God lets men and women share in the divine power to create life (Gen. 4:1). Life is God's gift, and human beings have the duty and responsibility to cherish and guard it.

This belief in the ontological priority of God is also taken for granted by Jesus Christ and his hearers in the New Testament. He started his ministry by declaring that "the time is fulfilled, and the kingdom of God is at hand" (Mark 1:14). New Testament writers emphasize God's initiative over and over again. "God so loved the world that he gave his only begotten son" (John 3 :16). "God was in Christ reconciling the world to himself" (2 Cor. 5:19). God set forth in Christ "a plan for the fullness of time, to unite all things in him" (Eph. 1:10). "And when all things are subjected to him, then the son also will be subjected to him who put all things under him that God may be all in all" (1 Cor. 15:28). This acknowledgment that God is the Creator and Redeemer of all life enables the entire world, the whole of humanity, to be included in the struggle for life and to feel responsible for its preservation and its continuation. God, in the sense of *Sat* or Mystery or the Transcendent or Ultimate Reality, is the ultimate horizon over the ocean of life. God's covenant with all humanity, of which the rainbow is a timeless symbol, has never been abrogated.[26]

A theocentric christology provides more theological space for Christians to live together with neighbors of other faiths. "Christomonism" does not do full justice to the total evidence of the New Testament, nor does it give sufficient emphasis to the trinitarian dimension of the Christian faith. It tends to minimize the work of the Holy Spirit in the lives of others. The Orthodox rejection of the *filioque* clause in the description of the procession of the Holy Spirit in the Nicene Creed—that is, its insistence that the Spirit proceeds from the Father and *not* from the Son—has far-reaching ecumenical significance. To draw attention to these points is not to minimize the centrality of Jesus Christ in Christian faith, but to put him more clearly into the structure of trinitarian faith. New insights contributed by biblical studies and research on the great christological councils of the church (Nicea 325 C.E. and Chalcedon 451 C.E.) help us better understand how God is in Jesus Christ and how Jesus Christ is related to God. Christocentrism without theocentrism leads to idolatry.

A theocentric christology provides a basis for retaining the Mystery of God while acknowledging the *distinctiveness* of Jesus Christ. It makes commitment to God in Jesus Christ possible without taking a negative attitude toward neighbors of other faiths, and at the same time it offers a more comprehensive conceptual framework for dialogue with these neighbors. Removing the *threat* implicit in one-way proclamations, it offers an *invitation* to all to share in the abundant riches of God. It makes dialogue a normal way of relationship between persons of different faiths instead of artificially contriving to make it a mode of communication. It helps to shift the emphasis from a *normative* to a *relational* attitude toward neighbors of other faiths. New relationships may have to be sought through recognizing differences rather than through seeking *similarities*. It helps avoid the dichotomies between "we" and "they" or those on "the inside" and those on "the outside."

The theocentric circle includes the christocentric circle. It makes it possible to recognize the theological significance of other revelations and other experiences of salvation, a point that for many Christian theologians is frightfully difficult even to admit. Theocentrism allows for an evolving quest for the meaning of Jesus Christ in which neighbors of other faiths can also participate, as in fact they already do, thus opening for Christians undreamt-of possibilities of enriching others and being enriched by them. Further, theocentrism grounds cooperation not on expediency, but on *theology*, providing a vision of participating with all human beings in God's continuing mission in the world, seeking to heal the brokenness of humanity, overcoming the fragmentation of life, and bridging the rift between nature, humanity, and God.

V

Exclusive claims isolate the community of faith from neighbors of other faiths, creating tensions and disturbing relationships within the larger community. But when the *distinctiveness* of a particular faith is stated in a manner that avoids open or hidden exclusiveness, then meaningful *relationships* between different communities become possible. This has been happening throughout the history of different religions in the multireligious life of India. It is unfortunate that Christian theologians, including Indians, have failed to recognize the significance of such relationships for the shaping of an emerging theology of religions.

Perhaps one reason for this failure is the stranglehold of propositional theology and its methodology on the minds of most Christian theologians. This is not to minimize the need for and the importance of serious, rational theological work; rather, it points out that to exclude the cultural, the mystical, and the esthetic from the experience of interreligious relationships is to seriously impoverish theology. Such a claim is based on an understanding of theology as critical reflection on God's relationship to humanity and nature, history and the cosmos.

Nowhere else than in India, perhaps, is the importance of the esthetic more manifest, for here we find that the distinctiveness of Jesus Christ is expressed through art by persons who do not necessarily belong to the visible Christian community. India might well be the only place where persons of other faiths, without crossing over the visible boundaries that separate them from Christians, have related themselves to Jesus Christ through art, thus breaking down the walls of exclusiveness. These artists, standing outside the confines of institutional Christianity, make evident that it is not the dogmas and doctrines about Christ or the institutions of the church that have touched the heart and mind of India, but the life and teachings of Jesus of Nazareth, his death and resurrection, the illumination he has

brought into the Mystery of God, and the transforming power he has introduced into human life, as he invites all persons to move from self-centered-
ness to God-centeredness. He is indeed *jivanmukta,* one who is truly
liberated in life, and therefore able to liberate others.

Visitors to India are often struck by the responses that followers of other
faiths have made to Jesus Christ through the religious dimensions of art —
literature, poetry, and drama in the different languages of India (including
English), as well as painting, movies, and television. Jesus Christ seems to
move beyond the structures of the church, with its dogmas and doctrines
about his person, in order to establish new relationships with adherents of
other faiths. There seems to be an "unbaptized *koinonia*" outside the gates,
which the church is most reluctant to recognize or even talk about. One
must indeed be careful not to exaggerate such phenomena. But neither
should their importance be minimized nor their theological significance for
developing new relationships with neighbors of other faiths be rejected
rudely and hastily.

Over the centuries there have been many examples of this influence of
Christ beyond the confines of the church. Among the more recent ones is
Manjeshwar Govinda Pai, a noted Hindu poet who won the national award
for literature some years ago. His well-known and lengthy poem *Golgotha*
is marked by literary beauty, depth of religious perception, and a sensitive
understanding of the crucifixion of Jesus Christ.[27] Muliya Keshavayya, a
Hindu lawyer, wrote a drama on the life of Christ with the title *Maha
Chetana* ("Great Energy"), bringing out the compassion of Christ toward
the poor, and the power of his cross and resurrection.[28] Gopal Singh, a
well-known Sikh scholar and diplomat, wrote a poem entitled *The Man
Who Never Died.*[29] The poet has the risen Christ speak these lines:

> But, he said unto those that believe
> that nothing dies in the realm of God —
> neither seed, nor drop, nor dust, nor man.
> Only the past dies or the present,
> but the future lives for ever.
> And I am the future of man.
> To me, being and non-being were always one.
> I always was and never was![30]

Many Hindu and Muslim artists have been inspired by themes in the life
of Jesus Christ, particularly his sufferings, death, and resurrection. According to Jyoti Sahi, a noted Christian artist, Indian Christian art was initiated
not by Christian, but by Hindu artists. For example, there is the well-known
painting of the Last Supper by Jamini Roy of Calcutta. More recently, well-
known Hindu and Muslim artists like Hebbar, Panikker, Hussain, Khanna
and others have painted many themes from the life of Christ.[31] All this
might well be regarded as "signs" of the increasing "traffic across the bor-

ders," helping to develop new relationships between persons of different religious communities and bringing out new meanings in christology.

There can be no exclusiveness in art. By evoking feelings of reference and joy and gratefulness, it transforms human feelings and gives to those who participate in it a sense of inner peace, *shanti*. It liberates persons from feelings of possessiveness. Some of these examples, and there are many more, make it clear that although Christianity belongs to Christ, Christ does not belong to Christianity. This kind of art by Hindu or Sikh or Muslim neighbors mediates the mystery of Christ to Christians in new ways, different from those of the West, and builds deeper relationships between members of different faiths. This form of art should be regarded as at least one of the new ways of bringing out the relational distinctiveness of Jesus Christ, the theological implications of which have yet to be worked out. To ignore it would be disastrous to future interreligious relationships.

When theological debates end in sterile apologetics, when social relationships between different religious communities become superficial or degenerate into sullen coexistence, when economic sharing becomes a matter of profit and loss, and when political cooperation in the life of a nation becomes difficult, if not impossible, because of narrow communal interests, quite often it is esthetic experience that provides the bridge for deeper relationships between persons of different faiths. It does not always happen, and when it does indeed happen, it is mostly by the few on behalf of the many. Nevertheless, art combines truth and grace and, in generosity of spirit, through color and sound and symbol and image, it mediates Mystery to a broken humanity. Through participation in art focused on Christ and the experience of enjoying it, the walls of exclusiveness are broken down and new relationships established between persons of different faiths in the larger community.

NOTES

1. Karl Rahner, "Basic Theological Interpretations of the Second Vatican Council," in *Concern for the Church* (New York: Crossroad, 1981), pp. 81-82.

2. *Guidelines on Dialogue* (Geneva: World Council of Churches, 1982), pp. iv, 11.

3. William R. Burrows, "Tensions within the Catholic Magisterium about Mission and Other Religions," *The International Bulletin of Missionary Research* 9 (1985): 3. The same point is made by other Catholic scholars. Paul Knitter remarks that "Christians should seriously consider whether this opening has been toward more abundant life or has now arrived at dead ends" ("Roman Catholic Approaches to Other Religions: Developments and Tensions," *International Bulletin of Missionary Research* 8 [1984]: 53).

4. See *Jeevadhara*, vol. 9, no. 65, September-October 1981 (Theology Centre, Kottayam, India). The whole issue is on "Inter-Religious Dialogue Today." See also John B. Chethimattam, "Christian Theology and Other Religions," *Jeevadhara* 8 (1978): 352-66.

5. Quoted in "The Extraordinary Synod" (editorial), *Vidyajyoti* 49 (1985): 106.

6. "Questions after Vancouver," *Ecumenical Review* 36 (1984): 184, emphasis added.

7. See *International Review of Mission*, vol. 74, no. 294, April 1984. The entire issue is on the theme "Gospel and Culture."

8. See *Guidelines on Dialogue*, pp. 12-13, for a list of concerns and study questions. It must be pointed out, however, that the WCC Working Group on Dialogue, in its March 1985 meeting, decided to launch a substantial study extending over a period of four to five years on the theological significance of other faiths.

9. Arthur F. Glasser, "A Paradigm Shift? Evangelicals and Inter-Religious Dialogue," in *Contemporary Theologies of Mission*, Arthur F. Glasser and Donald A. MacGavran, eds. (Grand Rapids: Baker Book House, 1983), p. 206.

10. John Stott, "Dialogue, Encounter, Even Confrontation," in *Faith Meets Faith: Mission Trends No. 5*, Gerald H. Anderson and Thomas F. Stransky, eds. (New York: Paulist Press, 1981), p. 168.

11. Asghar Ali Engineer, "Bombay—Bhiwandi Riots in National Political Perspective," *Economic and Political Weekly* 19 (1984): 1134ff. "Communalism is a modern phenomenon with medieval trappings to enhance its national appeal. The use of medieval symbolism ensures a relative autonomy to it ... and creates the illusion in the minds of common people about the causative efficacy of religion in the whole conflict" (p. 1136). Muslim, Hindu, Sikh, and Christian writers, political scientists, sociologists, and theologians have emphasized this point, which should not be forgotten lest religions be blamed for all the ills of Indian society. See also Kishan Swarup Thapar, "Genesis of Partition," *Mainstream* (New Delhi), August 18, 1984, pp. 10ff.; S. Tasmin Ahmed, "Second Thoughts on Secular Democracy," ibid., pp. 15ff.; Nirmal Srinivasan, "Majority Communalism versus Minority Communalism: Is It a Threat to Indian Secularism?," *Religion and Society* 30 (1983): 138 46 (Christian Institute for the Study of Religion and Society, Bangalore). Bipan Chandra in a major study clarifies "the misconception of religion as the sole determinant of communalism" in *Communalism in Modern India* (New Delhi: Vikas Publishing House, 1984), p. 165. "Communalism was the false consciousness of the historical process of the last 150 years because, objectively, no real conflict between the interests of Hindus and Muslims existed. ... Seeing religion as the main inner contradiction in social, economic, and political life was certainly an aspect of false consciousness" (ibid., p. 167).

12. Rajni Kothari and Shiv Vishwanath, "Moving out of 1984: A Critical Review of Major Events," *Mainstream Annual: India, 1984* (New Delhi), January 1985, no. 305, p. 31.

13. See the long footnote by Wilfred Cantwell Smith in *Faith and Belief* (Princeton University Press, 1979): "The famed 'religious tolerance' of Hindus, their acceptance in principle of pluralism as something not merely inescapable but right and proper, has become explicit as a formulated affirmation only gradually and especially perhaps in relatively recent times. ... The spirit of recognizing religious life as polymorphic is, however, ancient in India" (p. 215). See also Hajime Nakamura, *Ways of Thinking of Eastern Peoples*, Philip Wiener, ed. (Honolulu: East-West Center Press, 1978), p. 170: "Generally speaking *we cannot find in any Indian religion the conception of the 'heretic'* in the sense of Western usage."

14. In its original context it was a problem that arose within the Brahmanic consciousness, although even to this day this solution is suggested as a way out of

tensions between different religions. The full text reads: "They call him *(Sat)* Indra, Mitra, Varuna, Agni, or the heavenly sun-bird Garutmat. / The seers call in many ways that which is One; / they speak of Agni, Yama, Matarisvan" *(Rig Veda,* 1, 164, 46). In another well-known verse, when the sage Yajnavalkya was asked: "How many gods are there, O Yajvalkya?," the long answer leads the student through the many to just the One—and yet, not just the One, but the One without a second *(Ekam Evadvitiyam. Brihad,* III, 9, 1-9, and *Chandogya, VI,* 2, *1-3.* See *Sources of Indian Tradition,* Theodore de Bary, ed. (New York: Columbia University Press, 1958), pp. 5ff.

15. See Lal Mani Joshi, *Studies in the Buddhist Culture of India* (Delhi: Motilal Banarsidas, 1977), pp. 177-78. There are others who maintain that the ideas of Buddhism are not original but are dependent on Hinduism, e.g., T.M.P. Mahadevan, *Gaudapada: A Study in Early Advaita* (Madras: Madras University Press, 1960), pp. 84, 226. Radhakrishnan argues that what the Buddha did was "to democratize the lofty teachings of the Upanishads" (S. Radhakrishnan, *Indian Philosophy,* vol. 1, [London: Allen and Unwin, 1931, 2nd ed.], p. 471). Although it is extremely difficult to reconstruct past relationships between different religious communities, and one should be careful not to exaggerate the "tolerance" of Hindus, it remains true that when two Chinese travelers, Fa-Hein (5th century C.E.) and Hieuen-Tsang (7th century C.E.) traveled in India they reported that Buddhism was flourishing in northern India with several kings as its patrons. In spite of continuing tensions, "Mutual toleration of prevailing faiths was the general rule of the country during the Gupta period" (7th century C.E.) *(History and Culture of the Indian People,* vol. 3, R.C. Majumadar, ed., Bombay: Bharatiya Vidya Bhavan, 19641, p. 397).

16. The *Bhagavad Gita,* faced with the possibility of many *margas* (paths to God), suggested that those who worship other gods, in reality worship Krishna alone, but *not properly* (IXX:23) or worship him but *unknowingly* (IX:24). Does not this remind one of certain Christian attitudes today? The *Gita* goes even further. Krishna says, "Whatever form any devotee wishes to worship, I make that faith of his steady" (VII:21). Also, "in whatever way persons approach Me, in the same way do I accept them" (IV: 11). If Christians can speak of the "unknown Christ of Hinduism," the Hindus too can talk of the "unknown Krishna of Christianity." See Daya Krishna, "Religion and the Critical Consciousness," *New Quest* (Bombay), July-August, 1978, p. 144.

17. Perhaps one has to reassess the lasting effect of the movement led by Ram Mohan Roy in this last regard. Mulk Raj Anand, the noted novelist, remarks that the Samaj movements led by Ram Mohan Roy, "passed over the ocean of Hinduism and produced some ripples but no deep currents" (quoted by Guru Dutt in an article entitled "Will Hinduism Survive?," in *Bulletin* [Institute of World Culture] [Bangalore] 5 [1985]: 1ff.).

18. In recent years, much valuable research of Sanskrit works has been done. See, e.g., the excellent work by Richard Fox Young, *Resistant Hinduism: Sanskrit Sources on Anti-Christian Apologetics in Early Nineteenth Century India* (Leiden: Brill, 1981). In the year 1839 John Muir, a servant of the East India Company, published a volume in Sanskrit entitled *Matapariksa.* It consisted of 379 terse lines in the form of a dialogue between a guru and a *sishya* to prove the superiority of Christianity as the only way. Three conservative Hindu pandits took up the challenge and published their answers, also in Sanskrit, because at that time Sanskrit was still the

language of scholarship and theological discourse. These were *Matapariksasiksa* (1839), by Somanatha (Subaji Bapu); *Matapariksottara* (1840) by Harachandra Tarkapancanana; and *Sastratattvavinirnaya* (1844-1845) by Nilankanta Goreh. This exchange was a genuinely theological and philosophical debate reflecting a serious attempt to come to grips with the central claims of Christianity and the mood of Hinduism. It was probably far more influential on the minds of people than the English controversy between Ram Mohan Roy and the Serampore missionaries.

19. In an article entitled "Politics" in the *Illustrated Weekly of India,* January 27-February 2, 1946, p. 34. The Constituent Assembly was formed on December 9, 1946. The draft constitution, prepared by the committee headed by Dr. B. R. Ambedkar, was submitted to the Assembly on February 21, 1948. The amendment to delete the word "propagate" was forcefully pressed by Loknath Mishra on the ground that "religious propagation had been responsible for the unfortunate division of the country into India and Pakistan and that its incorporation as a fundamental right would not therefore be proper" (ibid., p. 34).

20. Lest this be misunderstood as an uncritical exaggeration of Hindu "tolerance," it should be pointed out that there are Hindu organizations that indeed manifest a decidedly "intolerant" attitude toward other religions. The Arya Samaj, the Ramakrishna Mission, Rashtriya Svayam Sevak Sangh, the Vishwa Hindu Parishad, and many others are not particularly tolerant of Muslim and Christian efforts to convert Hindus. Earlier, Hindu violence was directed at Jains, particularly in the eighth century C.E. See Burton Stein, *Peasant State and Society in Medieval South India* (Delhi: Oxford University Press, 1980), p. 80; Romila Thapar, "Syndicated Moksha?," *Seminar: The Hindus and Their Isms* (New Delhi), no. 313, September. 1985, pp. 14-22. There has indeed been violent and intolerant resistance to Islam and Christianity, but these were often defensive reactions against both the religious and political implications of conversions. I have drawn pointed attention to these movements in some of my writings, such as "Indian Realities and the Wholeness of Christ," *Missiology* 10 (1982): 301-17; "Dialogue and the Politicization of Religions in India," *International Bulletin of Missionary Research* 8 (1984): 104ff.; "Dialog statt Kreuzzug," *Evangelische Kommentar,* February 1985, pp. 75-77.

21. See Charles H. Craft and Tom N. Wisely, eds., *Readings in Dynamic Indigeneity* (Pasadena: Wm. Carey Library, 1979), pp. 259f.; Jacques Derrida, *Writings and Differences*, tr. Alan Bass (University of Chicago Press, 1978), pp. 280ff., Paul Ricoeur, *Essays in Biblical Interpretation* (Philadelphia: Fortress Press, 1980), p. 4.

22. See *Seminar on Non-Biblical Scriptures*, D. S. Amalorpavadass, ed. (Bangalore: National Biblical-Catechetical-Liturgical Centre, 1974), p. 707. I have just completed a manuscript on "The Search for New Hermeneutics in Asian Christian Theology" (59 pp.), drawing attention to the attempts being made in different countries in Asia to shake off dependence on Western hermeneutics and work toward a more relevant Asian Christian hermeneutics. See also Gopinath Kaviraj, *Aspects of Indian Thought* (Burdwan: University of Burdwan, 1967), pp. 41 ff.; G. Kashikar, *Preface to Rigveda Samhita* (with the commentary of Sayana), N. S. Sontakka and G. Kashikar, eds., vol. 4 (Poona: Poona Vaidika Samsadhan Mandala, 1946); Thomas B. Coburn, "Scriptures in India: Towards a Typology of the Word in Hindu Life," *Journal of the American Academy of Religion, 52 (*1984): 435ff.

23. The International Theological Commission appointed by the pope in 1969 has brought out two volumes on this matter: *Select Questions of Christology* (1980), and *Theology, Christology, Anthropology* (1983), both published by the Publications

Office, United States Catholic Conference, Washington, D.C. The quotations given above are from *Theology, Christology, Anthropology,* pp. 3 and 11.

24. The full text now reads: "The World Council of Churches is a fellowship of churches which confess the Lord Jesus Christ as God and Savior according to the Scriptures and therefore seek to fulfil together their common calling to the glory of God, Father, Son and Holy Spirit." See "Ecumenical Foundations: A Look at the WCC Basis," *One World* (Geneva), no. 107, July 1985, p. 11.

25. Vol. 37, no. 2 of *Ecumenical Review,* April 1985, is devoted to a discussion of the WCC basis. Two writers, Konrad Raiser and Werner Loeser, S.J., draw pointed attention to the need to take into account the dialogue with persons of other faiths in this connection. Raiser describes this as one of the two "crucial challenges" (p. 18) and Loeser observes that the most central question here is "that of the picture of God" (p. 237). Thomas Stransky goes even further in calling for "a basis beyond the basis." He repeatedly refers to Jesus Christ as "Lord and Savior" rather than "God and Savior" (p. 21).

26. A far more careful and systematic exegesis of related texts within a new hermeneutical framework is called for here. New Testament scholars identify five texts in this connection: Titus 2:13; John 1:18; John 5:20; Romans 9:5; and 2 Peter 1:1. In the text from Titus the use of a single word in the original Greek alters the meaning: "the appearing of the glory of *our* great God and Savior Jesus Christ." The alternative reading, equally justified on the basis of the Greek text, would be: *"our* great God and *our* Savior Jesus Christ." Even Paul with his radical christo-centrism is extremely careful in his christocentric statements. He reminds the Corin-thians, "You belong to Christ, Christ belongs to God" (1 Cor. 3:23). "The total Christian faith, as reflected in the New Testament, is essentially and primarily theistic, that is to say monotheistic, and secondarily Christological" (F. C. Grant, *Ancient Judaism and the New Testament* [New York: Macmillan, 1959], p. 130). For a fuller discussion, see A. W. Martin, " 'Well Done, Good and Faithful Servant?' Once More the W.C.C. Basis," *Journal of Ecumenical Studies* 18 (1981): 251-66. Referring to "the continued use of a seemingly heretical formula," Martin asks: "Is it time to retire the formula with the judgement of more or less 'well done'?" (p. 266).

27. Manjeshwar Govinda Pai, *Golgotha* (Mangalore: Baliga and Sons, 1948). It was written in Kannada, the language of Karnataka, one of the southern states, spoken by about thirty-six million persons.

28. Muliya Keshavayya, *Maha Chetana: A Drama on the Life of Christ* (Mangalore: Kodialbail Press, 1976).

29. Gopal Singh, *The Man Who Never Died* (London: Macmillan, 1969). The poem has also been published in German translation.

30. Ibid., p. 77.

31. Jyoti Sahi, "Trends of Indigenization and Social Justice in Indian Christian Art," *Indian Journal of Theology* 31 (1982): 89-95. See also Masao Takenaka, "Christian Art in Asia: Signs of Renewal," in *Asian Christian Theology,* Douglas J. Elwood, ed. (Philadelphia: Westminster Press, 1980, rev. ed.), p. 169.

Part Two

NEWLY EMERGING PROFILES OF JESUS AMID ASIA'S POVERTY AND RELIGIOUS PLURALITY

"He understands the hearts of the wretched, because His entire life was wretched. He knows the agonies of those who die a miserable death, because He died in misery. He was not in the least powerful. He was not beautiful."

"But look at the Church. Look at the city of Rome," Nishi countered. *"The cathedrals we saw were all like golden palaces, and not even the people of Mexico City could imagine the grandeur of the mansion where the Pope lives."*

"Do you think that is what He would have wished?" The man shook his head angrily. *"Do you think He is to be found within those garish cathedrals? He does not dwell there. He lives . . . not within such buildings. I think he lives in wretched homes of these Indians."*

"Why?"

"That is how He spent His life," replied the renegade monk in a voice filled with assurance, then he lowered his eyes to the ground and repeated the same words to himself. *"This is how He lived His life. He never visited the houses of those who were puffed up or contented. He sought out only the ugly, the wretched, the miserable and the sorrowful."*

from Shusaku Endo's *Samurai*

125

An Interpretative Foreword

R. S. SUGIRTHARAJAH

During the 1970s Asian Christians' reflections on Jesus took on a new shape. As the foregoing pages indicate, Asian christological constructions hitherto were largely confined to reorienting Jesus to the various religious traditions of the continent. But a change in theological perspective gradually emerged in Asian thinking during this period.

Disheartened by the failure of massive development programs to alleviate the poverty of the Asian masses, disenchanted with the failure of ancient Asian religions to address the everyday needs of the people, and enthused by the insights of Latin American liberation theology, some Asian Christians pressed for a different starting point to do theology — the staggering poverty of the Asian people. To put it in simple terms, it meant that the crux of the theological problem in Asia was the millions of empty stomachs, and serious reflection on Jesus would have to address this vexing issue. Amid existential poverty, some Asian Christians reckoned the presence of religions irrelevant or even a hindrance to progress. Hence they advocated that poverty and oppression should be at the heart of the hermeneutical process. But not all Asian Christians hold this view. There are notable exceptions. Prominent among them is the Sri Lankan theologian Aloysius Pieris. While conceding that poverty is a common factor between Asia and other third-world countries, Pieris contends that what distinguishes Asia is its multiple religious traditions. Hence, for him, religious pluralism and poverty are inseparable as the reality which constitutes the one source of any theologizing in Asia. In his view, Asian Christian theology must address both these issues together — religiousness and poverty. This is an ongoing debate which needs considerable attention. A comprehensive christology should address these two foci together as both arise out of the same need — to make sense of Jesus. They need not contradict each other.

Articles assembled in this section wrestle with these issues. A common concern runs through the first four essays; namely, to liberate Jesus from the dogmatic, cultic and institutional formulations in which he is enveloped and to place him alongside the peoples of Asia. In other words, it is a concern to seek a socially conscious Jesus who can make sense of Asia's history filled with tragedy and misery; this is necessary because the tradi-

tional profiles of Jesus propagated by the churches alienate him from his
own continent and his own people.

The first four essayists present four different ways of recovering and
rescuing a Jesus who can be identified with the Asian masses.

Taiwanese theologian C. S. Song[1] seeks Jesus not in mass-produced statues, or in cathedral windows or in church traditions but in the passion of
his pain. It is in his pain that the pain of Asian people is mingled and their
hopes are realized for a qualitatively different society.

Kosuke Koyama,[2] who comes from Japan, finds Jesus in the periphery
of life. The "blond Jesus" of Western theology, which has occupied the
center stage in theology and mission according to Koyama, has provided
years of painful irrelevance for Asians. Koyama's contention is that Jesus
is the center, always in motion toward the periphery; he thus reveals the
mind of God, who is concerned about people on the periphery.

Byung Mu Ahn,[3] a Korean biblical scholar, tries to counterbalance the
kerygmatic Christ and the doctrine-oriented Christ that predominate in
Korean thinking by recovering the Galilean Jesus in the pages of the gospels, the Jesus who mingles with and accepts the *minjung*[4] of his time. Such
a Jesus, in Byung Mu Ahn's view, not only comes nearer to the intentions
of the historical Jesus but also offers sustenance to the oppressed peoples
of Asia.

Sebastian Kappen,[5] an Indian theologian, faced with a de-prophetized
and tradition-bound official Christianity and the ritualistic religiosity of
Hinduism, detects a prophetic religiosity in Jesus. Kappen tries to relate
Jesus to the dissenters and protesters of the sub-continent, who from the
time of Buddha onward have initiated a humanizing and creative religiosity.
He also suggests a proleptic aspect to Jesus, and argues for the need to
learn from the Indian tradition the yogic ideal of detachment, and its aesthetic and mystical approach to the earth to complement and enrich the
Jesus tradition.

The next article emanates from Sri Lanka, which is predominantly a
Buddhist country. It is a story of theological discovery and martyrdom.
Personal presence and immersion in a Buddhist village enabled Michael
Rodrigo,[6] a Roman Catholic priest, to discover the meaning of Jesus. Rod-
rigo's involvement with the villagers helped him to learn from the praxis of
Buddha and, more revealingly, helped him to understand his own faith in
God, and in Jesus and in Jesus' praxis, which finally ended in Rodrigo's
brutal killing.

Christological discourses from the perspective of Asian women are a
relatively new enterprise. Utilizing their own experience of triple marginalization — as Third World, women, and Christian — and moving beyond the
concerns of Euro-American feminists, Asian women are trying to create
images of Jesus that will be liberating and empowering for them. The essays
of Virginia Fabella[7] and Chung Hyun Kyung[8] are two such examples. Unlike
their Euro-American counterparts, Asian women do not see the maleness

of Jesus as a vexing issue. Both essays show how Asian women regard Jesus affectionately because of who he is, and how, out of their experience of ordeal and hardship, they invest new meanings in the traditional images of Jesus. They discover in him a new lover, helper, collaborator and companion. In their re-envisioning, he is no more a dominator or the one who lords it over their lives. Instead, he is the one who empowers, affirms and transforms their personality.

Down through the ages ordinary people have in their own ways creatively profiled a range of images of Jesus. Salvador T. Martinez[9] narrates how poor and rural Filipinos who have had no formal education use considerable freedom and eclecticism in appropriating Jesus for their needs. Their articulation demonstrates how they select Christian impulses that resonate with their indigenous beliefs and practice. Their profiles of Jesus indicate that people are not necessarily passive recipients of teachings imposed upon them, but that they can shape and mold their faith on their own terms.

In sum, these construals of Jesus try to reverse some of the traditional images that emphasize his individuality, focusing on his will, his consciousness and his ability to act on his own. Instead, we see the emergence of a social "Jesusology" in which the life and work of Jesus is illuminated by his association with women, children, the poor and the displaced, and he in turn illuminates their lives. These profiles of Jesus are an indication that no christology is genuine for the Asian masses unless it is articulated from the perspective of their struggle for survival and takes due account of their religious history. Asians long for a Jesus who will sustain their battered bodies and enhance their bruised spirits and restore their broken personalities. In these emerging Asian faces of Jesus, the features growing ever clearer, this longing is finding fulfillment.

NOTES

1. C. S. Song, *Jesus, The Crucified People* (New York: Crossroad, 1990), pp. 1-14.

2. Kosuke Koyama, *Your Kingdom Come: Mission Perspectives*. Report on the World Conference on Mission and Evangelism (Geneva: World Council of Churches, 1980), pp. 157-70.

3. Byung Mu Ahn, *CTC Bulletin* 7 (1987): 6-13.

4. *Minjung* is a Korean word referring to people who are poor, oppressed and socially marginalized.

5. This forms a chapter in his book, *Jesus and Cultural Revolution: An Asian Perspective* (Bombay: The Bombay Industrial league for Development, 1983), pp. 52-71.

6. Michael Rodrigo, *CTC Bulletin* 7 (1987): 14-31. (Michael Rodrigo was assassinated on October 11, 1987—Ed.)

7. Virginia Fabella and Sun Ai Lee Park, eds., *We Dare to Dream: Doing Theology as Asian Women* (Hong Kong: Asian Women's Resource Centre for Culture and Theology, 1989), pp. 3-13.

8. Chung Hyun Kyung, *Struggle To Be the Sun Again: Introducing Asian Women's Theology* (Maryknoll, N.Y.: Orbis Books, 1990; and London: SCM Press, 1991), pp. 54-73.

9. Salvator T. Martinez, *CTC Bulletin* 7 (1987): 44-52.

SOME RELEVANT LITERATURE

Amjad Ali, Charles. "Towards a Christology of Rehabilitation: A Look at Two Miracle Narratives in Mark 3.1-16 & 9.14-29." *Focus* 7 (2) 1987: 116-31.

"Asian Face of Jesus," *Logos* 17 (1978).

Beltran, Benigno P. *The Christology of the Inarticulate: An Inquiry into the Filipino Understanding of Jesus the Christ.* Manila: Divine World Publications, 1987.

Balasuriya, Tissa. "Humanity's Fall and Jesus the Saviour," *Voices from the Third World* 11 (1988):40-75.

————. "Christ and the World Religions: An Asian Perspective." In *Future of Liberation Theology: Essays in Honor of Gustavo Gutiérrez,* edited by Marc H. Ellis and Otto Maduro, 337-45. Maryknoll, N.Y.: Orbis Books, 1989.

Byung Mu Ahn. "The Korean Church's Understanding of Jesus: A Historical View." *Voices from the Third World* 8 (1985):49-58.

"Christology in the Making." *Jeevadhara* 21 (1991)—a special issue on peoples' understanding of Jesus, edited by Samuel Rayan.

David, Kwang-Sun Suh. "Jesus and Messianic Theology." *Voices from the Third World* 8 (1985): 86-87.

Delotavo, Allan J. "A Reflection on the Images of Christ in Filipino Culture." *Asian Journal of Theology* 3 (1989): 524-31.

Dingayan, L. Luna. "Towards a Christology of Struggle: A Proposal for Understanding the Christ," *CTC Bulletin* 10 (1991): 14-34.

Endo Shusako. *A Life of Jesus.* New York: Paulist Press, 1973.

Kappen, Sebastian. *Jesus and Freedom.* Maryknoll, N.Y.: Orbis Books, 1977.

Kim Chi Ha. *The Gold Crowned Jesus and Other Writings.* Maryknoll, N.Y.: Orbis Books, 1978.

Pieris, Aloysius. "Christology in Asia." *Voices from the Third World* 11 (1988): 155-72.

Robinson, Gnana. "Jesus Christ, The Open Way and the Fellow Struggler." *Asian Journal of Theology* 3 (1989):403-13.

Soares-Prabhu, George. "The Jesus of Faith," *Voices from the Third World* 15 (1992):46-89.

Sugirtharajah, R. S. "Wisdom, Q, and a Proposal for a Christology." *The Expository Times* 102 (1990):42-45.

8

Oh, Jesus, Here with Us!

C. S. SONG

The Gold-Crowned Jesus is a play by the Korean Christian poet Kim Chi Ha. In the words of Daniel Berrigan, Kim Chi Ha is "a recidivist, seized and tortured again and again, tried and tried again, always charged with the same crimes—crimes of the tongue, misuse of the pen."[1] As the curtain rises on the play, a Christ-pietà figure can be seen in silhouette and a song accompanied by guitar music is heard in the background.

> That frozen sky
> That frozen field
> Even the sun has lost its light
> Oh, that poor, dark, dark street
> Where did you come from
> People with emaciated faces. . . ?
> Running around in search of what?
> Those eyes
> Those emaciated hands
>
> There is no native earth
> There is no place to rest your tired bodies
> There is no place even for a grave
> In the heart of winter
> I have been abandoned
> I have been abandoned . . .
>
> Where can it be?
> Where is the heavenly kingdom?
> Over on the other side of death?

Green forest of the four seasons?
Can it be there? . . .

Endless winter
Darkness of the abyss that I cannot bear
This tragic time and tide
This endless, endless poverty
This empty, cold world
I cannot bear it any longer

Where can he be?
Where can he be?
Where is Jesus?
That frozen sky
That frozen field
Even the sun has lost its light
That dark, dark, poor street
Where can he be?
Where can he be?
He who could save us
Where can he be?
Oh, Jesus
Now here with us
Oh, Jesus, with us . . . [2]

What a world! What a life! The world in the powerful grip of darkness and life tormented by the cruel winter and sapped of its vitality! Is this the world created by a poetic fantasy chained to the prison wall? Or is this the world of chaos God had to contend with at the beginning of time — and at all times? Is this the life painted in despair by the conscience tortured in the police interrogation room? Or is this the life of pain and suffering God must endure and save in the midst of history and at the end of time? It must be both. In this world and in this life God and humanity become engaged in the search for meaning, fulfillment and destiny. This is the huge operation called salvation. But who is the saviour? Where is Jesus, the one who saves the world? Where is the Christ, the one anointed to redeem humanity?

WHERE IS JESUS?

The frozen sky. The dark, dark, poor street. And people with emaciated faces. Where can Jesus be, the Christ who comes to save and redeem? All the power of the pen released in *The Gold-Crowned Jesus* is devoted to probing the question. And of all people, it is Beggar and Leper, the two wretched souls, the scum of society, and not theologians who teach Christian doctrines, not Christians who know their catechisms by heart who ask the question. When a theologian raises it, it becomes a theological question to be settled with massive knowledge of biblical interpretation and church teaching. When a sophisticated Christian asks it, the question turns into the defence of the Christian faith against other faiths. But when a beggar turns to the question, it is not his head or his faith that turns to it. It is the stomach, his empty stomach!

The one who saves must save his stomach first, must fill his empty stomach first. And when a leper asks the question, his immediate concern is not the defence of faith and correct doctrine. What is at stake is his humanity — his humanity eaten away by the horrible disease and himself excluded from human community. Leper and Beggar do not have in the question "Who is Jesus?" a theological axe to grind. For them it is a question of life and death, the question of whether love is strong enough to fill an empty stomach, to restore a disfigured humanity, to create life in the midst of death.

Leper seeks Jesus from his troubled humanity. This is where the search for the saviour must begin, not only for Leper, but for us all. We have studied the history of Israel hard and long to discover the traces of the saviour. We have pored intently over the scriptures of the Old Testament to hear the footsteps of a messiah. We have made great efforts to recapture the image of Jesus from the witnesses of the early Christian community. We have also searched diligently through that strange Book of Revelation to envision the coming of Christ in power and glory. But most of the time we are afraid to look into our own selves, nagged by deep anxiety, unable to make theological sense of Asia, populated by millions of hungry stomachs and disfigured human beings; we are uncomfortable among those longing souls looking for salvation in their gods and lords. Our Jesus Christ is still to be linked up with the life of the vast Asian world.

But Leper sees differently. He sees with his tormented self and not with an abstract ideal humanity. He perceives with the broken world of injustice and not with a heavenly kingdom of harmony. He shivers in the cold winter where the ethical idealism of the Christian community does not apply. He knows something must be wrong, terribly wrong. He bursts out:

When your house gets torn down, "Stay silent, don't fight, turn the other cheek, obey the masters, the gentlemen, the police," they tell you. "Obey them, for these are the true believers." This is what the people who wear luxurious clothes, eat rich food, and prove their high station by displaying their wealth like to say to us. They manipulate and sweet-talk us, deny us our souls, tame us into dumb unquestioning dull-heads, well-trained pups, while they enjoy their glory, their power. Isn't it true, Jesus? Tell me if I lie. Tell me I say this because I am stupid, because I know no better.[3]

These are desperate words. But they are charged with moral force demanding an answer, a response.

What would Jesus' response be, the Jesus who said: "If someone slaps you on the right cheek, turn and offer him your left. If a man wants to sue you for your shirt, let him have your coat as well. If a man in authority makes you go one mile, go with him two" (Matt. 5:39-40). Perhaps Jesus had in mind the situations where someone still has the other cheek to turn, a coat to give, the energy to walk the second mile. But Leper has no other cheek to turn, no coat to give, and no energy to walk the second mile. What would Jesus say to him?

Asia is a huge mass of such lepers. The Aborigines in Australia are such lepers. They have lived in their own land for more than 30,000 years. But since 1770 the British "claimed Australia and began to send settlers. They used it first as a penal colony, then encouraged the development of the sheep industry and agriculture, and eventually expanded into additional areas with the discovery of gold and mineral resources . . . ; [they] negotiated no treaties, made no purchases of land, and paid no compensation. As the invaders covered the land with sheep, cattle and crops, the Aborigines were pushed aside, their food supply destroyed, their sacred sites violated. Individuals and whole groups were massacred. By 1933, the Aboriginal population, which had been 300,000 in 1788, was reduced to 60,000."[4] A heart-breaking story. Listen to what they say about their land taken away from them and alienated from them:

> The land is our Mother. It is the source of our existence, our religion, our identity.
> To us land is a living thing. We are part of it, and it is part of us.
> For many, many years Aboriginal people have been losing a little bit of themselves. We are determined we will not lose anything.
> Until our land rights are recognized, we cannot be free and equal citizens with white Australians.[5]

How can this not touch the heart of each one of us? It shakes the roots of our life. It makes us ponder deeply what life means within God's creation.

"The land is our Mother," it says. When one thinks of life, one thinks of mother. When one speaks of life, one speaks of mother. Life begins within the mother. It grows in her. It receives flesh and blood from her. It moves within her. It breathes with her. It is securely, tenderly, lovingly, embraced in that mysterious womb of hers filled with creativity, vitality and expectation. It is there that life takes shape, forms personality and acquires identity. This is much, much more than a mere biological process. A life growing in the mother's womb is a matter of the spirit, an event of faith, an act of religion. Essentially, religion has to do with life. Is it then not natural that it basically has "the mother-character," the feminine vitality?

There is how Christian faith begins. In Luke's Gospel we are told that the angel Gabriel announced to the startled Mary: " . . . God has been gracious to you; you shall conceive and bear a son, and you shall give him the name Jesus" (Lk. 1:30). In Mary's womb Jesus, the one who saves, is conceived, grows and matures. God's salvation takes form in Mary's womb as the life of one who saves. Is this conception of life, this growth of life, this birth of life in the mother's womb not itself God's saving activity? One has only to recall that famous prophecy of Isaiah when the armies of the Syro-Ephraimite alliance were marching on Jerusalem (735-34 B.C.). Ahab, King of Judah, and the people of Jerusalem were terrified; they "were shaken like forest trees in the wind" (7:2). To them Isaiah came with the message of hope and deliverance. "A young woman is with child, and she will bear a son, and will call him Immanuel" (7:14). In that critical time of the nation, Isaiah did not point to the fortification, to the armaments, to the troops, but to a pregnant woman (or pregnant women) as the sign of God's deliverance. The life in the mother's womb is Immanuel—God-with-us. That life is the power of hope, the key to the future, the pledge of salvation.

Life is an act of faith. To live is to believe. And to believe is to hope. That is why we can look for light in the midst of darkness. That is why we must strive for freedom when bound in bondage. That is also why we believe in the victory of love over hate, life over death. Here is a poem published on the Democracy Wall in Peking at the height of struggle for human rights in China after the fall of "The Gang of Four":

> While I am imprisoned in a cage of pitch darkness
> Still able to endure the pain from torture,
> I will struggle to rise, bite open my fingers,
> And with my blood write on the wall: Believe in Life!
>
> After I have gone through all hardships of life,
> Dying at dawn surrounded by my posterity,
> I will summon my last breath with all my strength,
> Crying as loudly and as clearly as I can: Believe in
>   Life! . . .
>
> If the earth goes round and round without ceasing,
> If History has a new journey to make,
> If my children and grandchildren go on living,
> Then I believe in the future! Believe in Life![6]

What a powerful ode to life! What a strong faith in tomorrow despite the bitter disappointment of yesterday and today! And what a magnificent faith in the power of life reaching into eternity! This is the ode of the people. This is their faith and hope. Do we not hear in this people's ode Jesus' ode? Do we not recognize in this people's faith the faith of Jesus? Do we not believe in this people's hope the hope of Jesus?

When Australian Aborigines say, "Land is my Mother," it means that there is something sacred about their land. It is deeply human. It is profoundly religious. In the land they reach to the root of their life. There they are in tune with the rhythms of life. There they are in communion with God. When they work the land, they are engaged in the sacred act of bringing life into being. And when they return to land at the end of their life's journey, they return to the womb of mother-earth, not to die, but to live. To rob them of their land amounts to robbing them of their life. To rape their land is to rape their Mother. To destroy their land is to destroy their eternity. Land is their right to life, power and eternity. "Land is my Mother!" Jesus would say amen to this. He would never say to the Australian Aborigines: "Give up your rights to the land."

ISN'T IT TRUE, JESUS?

"Isn't this true, Jesus?" asks Leper. But Jesus does not reply—the Jesus pietà encased in cement with a gold crown on its head. That Jesus looks rigid and static; he cannot move. He is not a bit like Mary's son who walked the length and breadth of Palestine. He is silent. He cannot talk. He has lost the power of speech. He bears no resemblance to that workman who used to talk a lot to the crowds that came to him. And the eyes of that Jesus! These eyes do not shine with light, wisdom and love. They are cold, without emulation and passion. They are not the eyes of that man from Nazareth who relentlessly exposed the thoughts of religious leaders and looked at lepers, beggars, prostitutes, with compassion. The only thing in that Jesus pietà that shines, moves, talks, and impresses is that gold crown on its head. It shines with golden splendor in the cold wintry night. It moves with arrogance among the people who worship gold. It talks with authority in the world where everything that glitters counts. It impresses vain bishops, autocratic rulers, greedy company presidents. And it defeats lepers, beggars, prostitutes. The motionless and emotionless Jesus wearing a dazzlingly brilliant gold crown—what a grotesque spectacle! What a cruel invention of religious piety gone astray.

"Isn't it true, Jesus?" Leper asks the Jesus statue in a beseeching voice. If only Jesus would say yes, or just nod his head in sympathy and agreement! But from that gold crown Leper perceives something different. It seems to be saying to him: "Stay silent, don't fight, turn the other cheek, obey the masters, give your land rights away, forget your human rights, obey your military authorities." Is this what Jesus really means? Is this what he wants us to do?

Leper cannot believe that this is true. He does not want to believe this is what Jesus wants. For he remembers that Jesus began his work with a powerful proclamation in the synagogue of Nazareth, his native town:

The Spirit of the Lord is upon me because he has anointed me:
He has sent me to announce good news to the poor,

to proclaim release for prisoners and recovery of sight for the blind;
to let the broken victims go free,
to proclaim the year of the Lord's favor. (Lk. 4:17-19)

This is a strong advocacy for social change. This is a loud protest against corrupt political systems and authoritarian rule. This is a powerful call to repentance, to change of heart, as a sign of God's rule in the world. This is the good news that has been making a lot of difference in Asia in recent years.

The plight of the Korean people in Japan, for example, is well known. Although they have tried to assimilate into Japanese society, they have never been accepted as part of it. Their agony and suffering in the land of their adoption is endless. Here is a story of an old Korean widow who struggled to survive in an inhospitable land:

> The eldest son was fourth in his class at Ikuno Senior High but, while there, he fell in love with a Japanese classmate, and dropped out. The relationship broke up, and now they don't know where the son is. The mother says it is not likely that he has any settled job. The second son was seventeen and at one of the best Senior Highs in Osaka, but lost all desire to study when he ran into harsh discrimination ... As if they did not have enough troubles, fifteen years ago they paid 8,000,000 yen to purchase a small house, but were soon thrown out by the Japanese owner who said "No Koreans." He didn't return the money. Yang San (the widow) says, "Why on earth did we come to Japan anyway? There is no end to our trouble. But sometimes it seems just too much. What kind of happy memories, you ask? None at all."

The gold-crowned Jesus would have said to the Korean mother: resign to your fate! That same Jesus would have warned the Japanese Christian who told the story: Stay silent! But it was not the gold-crowned Jesus, but Jesus who proclaimed the release of broken victims, that was heard by the Japanese Christian. He was very disturbed. In his own words:

> Hearing that, I felt it was like walking along a hot road dragging heavy feet ... I first set foot in the community of Ikano, where Yang San lives, some five years ago. At that time, I had a hunch that this in the end would clarify the problem of the Japanese themselves, myself included. And that hunch was right on the mark in all its hopelessness. In all truth, I could no longer refuse to face the burden which as a Japanese I must bear.[7]

Here in the old Korean widow is the broken victim Jesus mentioned. But perhaps it is more than that. In her, in that prisoner of human discrimination, Jesus is seen and heard. That Japanese friend started a literacy programme for Korean mothers. The purpose "is not just to have the mothers learn to read and write Japanese, but also to bring a release of the humanity of the people."[8] The meeting with Jesus of Nazareth took place there.

Isn't it true, Jesus? Leper continues to ask, for it is still his lot to suffer. This world of Asia is a prison of suffering. No matter where you turn, you are confronted with human tragedies, personal, national, and regional, staggering you and making your heart sink. There is nothing to boast about suffering. Suffering is the pain one feels in one's flesh and bones. There is nothing virtuous about suffering. It is an evil thing which, like sulfuric acid, destroys the beauty and grace of humanity. And suffering is an evil force mobilized by a satanical power to stop the flow of time, to deprive the world of a future, and to take away hope from human beings. As such, suffering is no monopoly of Asian peoples. It strikes men, women and children, in the East and in the West, in the South and in the North. The entire world, even the whole creation, lies exposed to the assault of the destructive power of suffering. As St. Paul so poignantly puts it: "Up to the present, we know, the whole created universe groans in all its parts as if in the pangs of childbirth" (Rom. 8:22). He could not have been more right.

But suffering in Asia has a particularly sinister and ugly face. "More Asians are hungry, homeless, unemployed and illiterate," it is reported, "than all the rest of the world put together. More men and women are despised, humiliated, cheated; more suffer the tyranny of governments and oppressive elites, and the fear and shame that tyranny brings, than all the rest of the world combined."[9] This is the Asia betrayed by the prosperous Hong Kong, the orderly Singapore, the industrialized Japan, and by pseudo-democracy in most Asian countries. This is our Mother-Asia.

But our Mother-Asia has not lain prostrate before the tyranny of suffering. Suffering has given the peoples of Asia their history. True, it is the history of suffering and pain. But it is history. We remember the history of our own nation by the suffering our forebears went through. We feel history in our own person through the pain that disfigures the face of Asia today. We entrust our history to future generations, knowing that suffering and pain will fall upon them also. Suffering makes our history really historical. It makes our history truly contextual. It exhibits the saddest and ugliest in humanity, but it also calls forth the best and the strongest in us to create room in the space of pain and to strive for a new time of joy within the old time of mourning. History is not just dates and places. History is people. History is the story of how people live and die, love and hate, suffer and hope. If this is history, Asia has abundant history, as abundant as the enormous number of its inhabitants.

Here is a Thai song that tells us what the history of the people in Asia can be like:

At dawn I rise
Look at the earth, gaze
at the sky.
A farmer in the wind, I
eat off the land.
Unnumbered seasons pass.
The fields
crawl with our children.
Ages that fade into each
other
undisturbed, now end.
From cities come
the men who think they're
God —
They scrape, they gouge
and suck me out —
my buffalo, my ox,
the piece of earth I stand on;
a landless beast that sells its sweat
and gets just half of what it makes.
Numbed, sick at heart I am
a man no different from an ox.
I wait for my luck to turn.
I wait for fate to change.
I starve and wait for earth
and wait
for heaven —
fields overgrown with debts.[10]

History happens when people's luck refuses to turn, when their fate shows no sign of change, and when their fields are overgrown with debts. History is not created by an ideology to change society. It is not forged by the messianic pretensions of religious and political leaders. History is hatched in people's suffering. It grows in their instinctive will to live and die as human beings and not as beasts. And it bursts into the world through people's power to hope.

Is this not true, Jesus? Leper looks up at the Jesus pietà anticipating a yes answer. But that Jesus stays silent. His mouth is shut tight. His eyes see not. His ears do not seem to catch the question. Leper feels a little embarrassed. Am I asking a stupid question? he wonders aloud. But the silence puzzles him. If only Jesus would break the silence and talk! Then his own suffering would be somehow bearable.

If all this talk about history does not move the gold-crowned Jesus, then what about culture? History is not separable from suffering. Culture, even more, cannot be separated from it. Culture is not just monuments commemorating national glory. Culture is not merely clean streets replacing dusty roads and high-rise buildings that have pushed slums out of tourists' reach. Nor is culture to be identified solely with accepted social behaviors and conventions. *Culture is people, just as history is people.* Culture is what people do, say, sing, paint and write, to express their humanity, to release the emotions hidden in the depths of their hearts, to unburden the pain they carry in their souls, and to seek the meaning of the sufferings inflicted on their bodies.

Suffering is the soul of the culture of people. Culture is suffering and people wedded into union in a poem, in a painting, in a melody. Culture is people in suffering expressed in plastic art. Culture is the suffering of people portrayed in plays, dramas, puppet shows, and mask dances. And culture is people who turn suffering into the power to change their fate, to create their future, and to anticipate their destiny. There must then be culture in slums as well as in palaces, in a humble farmhouse as well as in a museum, in a roadside makeshift theatre as well as in an ornate opera house. There must be culture in protests against nuclear armaments, in demonstrations for human rights, in the fight for freedom and democracy. And there must also be culture in a revolution that struggles against the tyrannical power of social and political oppression. Culture, in a word, is the spirit of people crying out to be human, authentic and true. Culture is the image of God in humanity reaching for redemption, through symbols, words, imageries and actions.

There is a painting called "Prodigal Son" by an Indian artist, T. Chelladurai.[11] It depicts the moment when the father embraces his son. The painting shows the son in rags with an emaciated body and a bald head accentuated by a back revealing the ribs and by an elongated body from which all vitality seems to have gone. This is an appalling image of human suffering. The father, embracing this son, is almost over-shadowed by the enormity of the suffering. His face is completely buried in his son's shoulder. One cannot see it, but it must be streaming with tears. One of the arms however is on the son's back firmly pressing his son to himself. In contrast to the thin and bony back of the son, the father's arm is strong and powerful. It supports the son's frail body, affirming him, loving him, taking him into his heart and soul. What an arm! It is an arm of power, love, and life. And what an eloquent arm! It is an arm that creates the world and recreates it. It is an arm that gives birth to life and sustains it. It is an arm that will create life again and again and redeem it again and again till the end of time. Here is a culture that bursts out of the depth of the conflicts between God and humanity, out of struggles between human beings, and out of inner tensions that gnaw at our hearts and conscience. Culture, in whatever form, is the embodiment of such conflicts, struggles and tensions. That arm of power, love and life that embraces the prodigal son must have been the arm that embraced the dying Jesus on the cross. It must also be the arm that embraces men, women and children suffering from the inhumanity of war, the exploitation of body and soul, the humiliation of human persons through economic injustice and political oppression. That arm is the arm of God. Culture must be a confession of faith in that arm of God.

Is this not true, Jesus? Leper again asks. But he does not see in the gold-crowned Jesus this arm of God. What he sees is a gold crown making mockery of his misery, despising him for his poverty, repelled by the bad odor coming from his diseased body. The Jesus pietà with a golden crown represents a totally different culture. It is a culture without a soul. It is a heartless culture ridiculing human suffering and offering opium to distressed humanity. It is a culture without God. It is not the culture of people.

Suffering then is the cradle of history; it is the matrix of culture. In this kind of history and in this kind of culture people meet God and God meets people — God in people and people in God, touching life at its deepest level and grasping life in its most spiritual dimension. Is it not true that faith is born out of the embrace of God and humanity in suffering? Suffering contains in itself the seed of religious faith. And it is in Buddhism among Asian faiths and religions that this seed grows into the religious culture of the overwhelming number of people in Asia.

At the height of the Vietnam war the world was horrified at the sight of Buddhist monks burning themselves to death in Saigon streets. Most Christians did not understand this act of self-immolation. Even Martin Luther King, leader of the civil rights movements in the United States, did not seem to understand it. In a letter addressed to him, Nhat Hanh, a Vietnamese monk, said:

> The self-burning of Vietnamese Buddhist monks in 1963 is somehow difficult for the Western Christian conscience to understand.... What the monks said in the letters they left before burning themselves aimed only at alarming, at moving the hearts of the oppressors and at calling the attention of the world to the suffering endured then by the Vietnamese.... There is nothing more painful than burning oneself. To say something while experiencing this kind of pain is to say it with utmost courage, frankness, determination and sincerity. During the ceremony of ordination, as practiced in the Mahayana tradition, the monk candidate is required to burn one, or more, small spots on his body in taking the vow to observe the 250 rules of a *bhikshu,* to live the life of a monk, to attain enlightenment and to devote his life to the salvation of all beings.[12]

Self-immolation is not suicide, says the Vietnamese monk. It is not even a protest. It is an act done out of the deeply religious perception of life and the world as suffering and also out of the equally deeply religious commitment to work for the salvation of all suffering beings. Is this so difficult for us Christians to understand? It should not be. For at the heart of the cross in our faith is the suffering of him who laid down his life for suffering humanity.

At ordination a Buddhist monk undergoes the ceremony by burning— some spots on his body are burned. This is a symbolic act with profound meaning. The pain caused by the burning reminds the monk that life is suffering, that the world is pain. *Through the act the pain of humanity penetrates him.* The Buddhist ceremony of ordination is a *sacrament of pain.* The monk takes up the pain of the world and bears it on his body. It is said in the seventh-century Buddhist scripture:

> All creatures are in pain, all suffer from bad and hindering karma . . . so that they cannot see the Buddhas or hear the law of Righteousness or know the Order . . . All that mass of pain and evil karma I take in my own body . . . I take upon myself the burden of sorrow; I resolve to do so; I endure it all. I do not turn back or run away, I do not tremble . . . I am not afraid . . . nor do I despair. Assuredly I must bear the burdens of all beings . . . I must set them all free . . . [13]

This is Buddhist faith at its most sublime. There is a tremendous spirituality crying out of the depths of Asian suffering here. That spirituality comes from the confrontation of the Asian soul with the brutal reality of pain. To set human beings free from the bondage of such pain and suffering—this is the vow a Buddhist monk must take at the ordination. The distinction between salvation by faith and salvation by works does not really matter. The power of the human spirit to become free from pain and suffering is the divine power translated into the human power. The divine power to save gets expressed in the human power to endure. The divine compassion for the suffering multitudes becomes actualized in the human compassion to bear the burdens of karma for others. At this deepest level the Asian spirit that gives glimmers of light through, for example, Buddhist faith can and must move the heart of Jesus who bore the pain and suffering of the world and died on the cross.

WHO IS THE REAL JESUS?

But the gold-crowned Jesus does not seem interested in the Buddhist monks going through the painful ceremony of ordination. That Jesus bears no resemblance to Jesus crucified on the cross. Is he an imposter? Is he a pretender? Is he a fake? If he is an imposter who does not see why God has much to do with the history of Asia, then where is the real Jesus? If he is a pretender who stands for a God aloof from the culture of Asian peoples, then where can the real Jesus be? And if he is a fake incapable of the suffering spirituality of men and women in Asia, where must the real Jesus be found?

It at last begins to dawn on Leper that that gold-crowned Jesus is not the real Jesus. For him this is a very important discovery. He must bring Beggar, his fellow sufferer, to realize this. He puts a question to the latter: Who is Jesus? Beggar takes the question in jest. But even in jest the earnestness of the question becomes very poignant:

BEGGAR: Your stomach has been empty for so long your head's become empty as well. Jesus is the one standing over there with open hands (points to statue). Now do you understand? See, that guy over there (points to the Jesus statue again).

LEPER: That's Jesus! You talk like the biggest fool in a village of fools. That's cement made to look like Jesus. That's not what I mean. I mean the real Jesus.

BEGGAR: Real Jesus. Who is the real Jesus?

LEPER: Do you know or don't you?

BEGGAR: Hell, if I knew, would I be squatting here with you, living like this in this shit? Do you have to act as a leftover cowhead?[14]

Who is the real Jesus? Beggar wants to know. If that cement Jesus with a gold crown is not the real Jesus, then who is?

This search for the real Jesus is soon to take an astonishing turn. Both Beggar and Leper must feel dumfounded when told that they must do something in order that Jesus can be the real Jesus! Of course that cement Jesus with a gold crown is not the real Jesus. That is the false Jesus adulterated by the riches of the world. That is the psuedo-Jesus venerated through pompous liturgy. That is the doctrinaire Jesus encased in a system of rigid doctrines. This Jesus has no taste for Asian culture. This Jesus cannot understand the meaning of Asian spirituality in suffering and in hope. This Jesus cannot make sense of Asian history filled with human tragedies and with divine compassion. In short, this Jesus is remote from history as people, culture as men, women and children, and religion as human persons.

The real Jesus and the people in suffering. The real Jesus and men and women striving for freedom, justice and democracy. The real Jesus and human persons longing for life, for eternal life. Here is the clue to the question of the real Jesus. Here is the secret of the historical Jesus. And here is an entry into the mystery of the Messiah who enables people to have faith in the God of love. Ordinary people like you and me, like Leper and Beggar, are part of this clue and this secret. This is the most exciting part of the quest for the real Jesus. The dramatic moment of the disclosure of this fresh insight arrives when the cement Jesus at long last opens his mouth and speaks to Leper:

I have been closed up in this stone for a long, long time, . . . entombed in this dark, lonely, suffocating prison. I have longed to talk with you,

the kind and poor people like yourself, and share your suffering. I
can't begin to tell you how long I have waited for this day, . . . this
day when I would be freed from my prison, this day of liberation when
I would live and burn again as a flame inside you, inside the very
depths of your misery. But now you have finally come. And because
you have come close to me I can speak now. You are my rescuer.[15]

At last the real Jesus has spoken. The gold crown has vanished from his
head. He now wears a crown of thorns. His emaciated face seems no longer
able to hold back the passion of his pain. And his words are those of the
dying Jesus on the cross, mustering the last drop of his strength, beseeching
God for help: "My God, my God, why have you forsaken me?"

A very strange thing happens here — too strange for many of us to grasp,
and so strange that those who know Jesus only as prophet, priest and king
cannot comprehend. But the change is decisive. People must explain who
Jesus is. People are to reveal where Jesus is. Jesus does not tell people why
they suffer; it is the people who tell Jesus why he has to suffer. And people
must liberate Jesus before Jesus can "burn again as a flame inside them."
The people who are determined to tell who Jesus is, to disclose where he
is, and the people who struggle to liberate Jesus — Jesus calls them blessed:

How blessed are you who are in need; the kingdom of God is yours.
How blessed are you who now go hungry; your hunger shall be
    satisfied.
How blessed are you who weep now; you shall laugh. (Lk. 6:20-21)

God's kingdom is people who are no longer dehumanized by poverty. It
is people who are not victimized by hunger any more. It is people who can
now laugh because their human rights are restored, their political dissension is no longer a crime or sedition, and the voice of their conscience is
heard as a voice from the soul of the nation.

"Because you have come close to me," Jesus said to Leper, "I can speak
now." People come so close to Jesus that Jesus speaks the truth. Do you
remember the story of the Roman centurion who had his servant cured by
Jesus? As Matthew tells it (Matt. 8:5-13), the centurion came to Jesus,
urgently requesting him to heal his servant. Jesus at once offered to go to
his house with him. We would expect the centurion to accept Jesus' offer
without a moment's hesitation. Jesus was his last hope. On Jesus the life
of his servant depended. We can almost see him running, dragging Jesus
along with him. That is what you and I would do. But the centurion did
what was totally unexpected. He said to Jesus: "Sir, who am I to have you
under my roof? You need only say the word and the boy will be cured. I
know, for I am myself under orders, with soldiers under me. I say to one,
'Go,' and he goes; to another 'Come here,' and he comes; and to my servant,
'Do this,' and he does it." These words must have taken even Jesus by

surprise. Here was a complete foreigner—a Roman soldier—telling him what he had never heard before. Jesus was in constant touch with his own people with a long tradition of strong faith. That faith came from Abraham, Isaac and Jacob, their most venerable ancestors. But he never heard them speak in this way. Jesus debated and argued with learned theologians and religious leaders who could speak glowingly about how Moses, their national leader par excellence, led the Operation Exodus out of Egypt. But they did not impress him with their faith.

What the Roman soldier was telling Jesus in all sincerity was something new and astonishing. It could not be understood within the framework of Jesus' own religious tradition. It could not be explained by the faith handed down from Abraham, Isaac and Jacob. And it could not have come directly from the historical experience of the Exodus. But Jesus was above Abraham. He was greater than Moses. And he towered over his own religious tradition. To the deeply sincere words of the Roman centurion Jesus responded with equally deeply sincere words of admiration and affirmation: "I tell you this: nowhere, even in Israel, have I found such faith!" "Not even in Israel!" Jesus must have said this with a profound sense of wonder. Here in that foreigner he touched the humanity in the grip of God with whom Jesus identified himself. That Roman soldier must have reflected, however imperfectly, the kind of Christ, Messiah, to be imaged and to be acted out by Jesus.

Jesus constantly reaches into the hearts of the people and the people also come into touch with Jesus' heart. In the story of the death of Lazarus (Jn. 11:1-44), to give another example, this reaching and this touching develop into reaching and touching the love of God, the source and power of life. Lazarus is dead. Jesus was told. The death of Lazarus and the extreme sorrow of his sisters must have confronted Jesus with the pain of emptiness and the horror of meaninglessness. Death makes a person into a thing. It turns the living life into dead memory. It marks the victory of decay over growth. It puts an end to hope and future; with death, hope vanishes and future ceases to exist. In the death of Lazarus Jesus stared at the abyss of void and darkness.

Four expressions in the story describe how deeply Jesus was touched by the death of Lazarus. He "sighed heavily" and "was deeply moved" when he heard the weeping of Mary and her companions (Jn. 11:33); he "wept" when they confirmed Lazarus' death by offering to take him to the grave (11:34); and he "sighed deeply" when he went to the tomb (11:38). How could death destroy life? How could it render life so powerless? Jesus sighed heavily and deeply, the power of death to create fear and sorrow among the living and to make the world colorless and without joy—Jesus was deeply moved by that power. And standing in front of the tomb where life ceases and death reigns, Jesus wept. Death is the world where God is absent. Death is the power that vanquishes life. Death is the eternal pause and silence of life born in the midst of hope and excitement.

Facing such death, was Jesus hearing an echo of his own cry of God-forsakenness on the cross? Was he muttering to himself: "It is finished," his last words before the moment of his death? The death of Lazarus, the death of human beings, his own death, death of the creation, and death of God—for a moment Jesus must have felt a sinking into the abyss of death. All movement came to a standstill. All creation ceased to whisper, speak and sing through trees, birds, insects, mountains, rivers and human beings. Even God seemed to have fallen into deep silence. The only thing audible was the tomb—the tomb was heard in the weeping of the bereaved, in the sighing of the friends, in the solemn faces of the spectators. Death reigns through its tomb.

This must also be the death that deeply moved Gautama Sakyamuni, the Buddha to be, and made him sigh heavily and perhaps weep too. And this is also the death that moves each one of us profoundly, makes us sigh deeply and weep in bitterness and resignation. But Jesus finally broke the silence ruled by death. From his mouth these words rang out: "I am the resurrection and I am life" (Jn. 11:25). Life is pronounced out of the world seized by death. Resurrection is declared from the very place of death. Jesus' message of life did not come from a paradise which does not know death. It came from Jesus who in his own death experienced the death of people. The Messiah of life sums up the will of people to life, and to live eternally.

The messianic contour of Jesus becomes sharpened as he absorbs more and more the struggle of people to live in faith, hope and love. God is the story of Jesus. And Jesus is the story of people. "Who is the real Jesus?" Beggar asked Leper. The real Jesus is not that cement Jesus pietà with a gold crown. The ready-made Jesus encased in a statue, enshrined in a cathedral, endorsed by church traditions and doctrines, is not the real Jesus. Jesus is the love of God that creates the miracle of life in the world. Jesus is the pain of God mingled with the pain of humanity. Jesus is the hope of God that people show in the midst of despair. Jesus is the eternal life of God which people live in the midst of death. Jesus is, lives, becomes real *when God and people reach for each other to bring about a new world out of the ruins of the old world.* Jesus is the event that takes place between God and humanity. Jesus is the light of God's salvation men and women kindle in the darkness of hell. And Jesus is that power of God's truth that more and more men and women in Asia manifest in front of the power of lies wielded by autocratic rulers.

Do you know a poem called "This Old Man" by Tere Tuakana of the South Pacific? It goes like this:

> Surrounding an evening fire
> A group of children listen,
> They listen and listen to the words,
> The words of an old man.

This old man he draws a story
A story from the ashes,
Together with the flickering fire.

This old man he weaves a story,
A story from the fire,
Together with the rising smoke

This old man he plants a story,
A story of the past,
And he plants it calmly.

The story rises with the smoke
To plant itself in
Minds that are green.[16]

The calm and plain tone of this poem is deceptive. The story of "This Old Man" tells stories drawn from the ashes of the people killed on battlefields and destroyed in slums. It contains stories of men and women woven from the fire that consumes them. And it anticipates the stories of the children constructed on hope and not on despair, on humanity and not on brutality, on life and not on death, on resurrection and not on the cross. Is the story of "This Old Man" not our own story? And is it not in these stories of ours in Asia, stories of our past, our present and our future, that we meet the real Jesus?

In *Samurai* (Warrior), another major historical novel, after *Silence (Chinmoku)*, Shusaku Endo, a Japanese Catholic novelist, continues his search for a god who breaks the silence and speaks, and for a Jesus not alien to the life of people. He takes his readers back to the beginning of the seventeenth century when Japan made one of those sporadic attempts to test the waters of the world outside her. Samurai and his companions, accompanied by a Spanish Catholic priest as interpreter, set out on a long and futile journey across the seas to negotiate trade with Spain. With their efforts completely frustrated, they reached Mexico on their voyage home. There in a small village in Mexico they met again the secularized Japanese Catholic priest they had accidentally come into contact with a few years back on their outbound voyage. Old, weak and sick, that Japanese ex-priest appeared to be completely at home among the poor Indians with whom he had lived for years. He confided to the tired and dispirited warrior friends: "These Indians have stayed in this swampy place on account of me. Otherwise I would perhaps have left here and moved to a faraway place. In these Indians I catch the sight of Jesus from time to time."[17] The Jesus that former Japanese priest caught sight of in the Indians was the real Jesus. Those Indians showed him where Jesus was and who Jesus was.

The song sung at the beginning of the play "The Gold-Crowned Jesus" ended, if you remember, with these words:

> Oh Jesus
> Now here with us
> Oh Jesus, with us.

This is a prayer. This is a plea. And this is also a confession of faith. The real Jesus is a matter of prayer and not a matter of dogma. The real Jesus evokes a plea and not an idea. And the real Jesus, when caught sight of, is the confession of faith, confessing that Jesus is Immanuel, God-with-us, in our brothers and sisters, however humble, here in Asia. In this sense and in this sense alone Christians can claim that Jesus Christ is the life of the world.

NOTES

1. See back cover, Kim Chi Ha, *The Gold-Crowned Jesus and Other Writings,* (Maryknoll, N.Y.: Orbis Books, 1978).

2. Ibid., pp. 85-87.

3. Ibid., p. 119.

4. See *No Place in the Inn, Voices of Minority Peoples in Asia* (Hong Kong: Christian Conference of Asia-Urban Rural Mission, 1979), pp. 32-33.

5. Ibid., p. 15.

6. Kuo Lu-Seng, "Believe in Life" in *Peking Spring and Other Selected Poems,* Wei Chin-Sheng, ed. (Hong Kong: P'ing Ming Publishing House, 1980), pp. 293-95 (translation from the Chinese original—CSS).

7. See *Struggling with People is Living with Christ* (Christian Conference of Asia–Urban Rural Mission, 1981), pp. 97-98.

8. Ibid., p. 99.

9. T. K. Thomas, ed., *Testimony Amid Asian Suffering* (Singapore: Christian Conference of Asia, 1977), p. 19.

10. This song was printed in *Bangkok Post,* August 23, 1981, and reproduced in *In Clenched Fists of Struggle,* Report of the Workshop on the Impact of TNC's in Asia (Hong Kong: Christian Conference of Asia–Urban Rural Mission, 1981), p. 91.

11. See Masao Takenaka, *Christian Art in Asia* (Tokyo: Kyo Bun Kwan, 1975), Plate 54.

12. Thich Nhat Hanh, *Vietnam, the Lotus in the Sea of Fire* (London: SCM Press Ltd., 1967), pp. 117-18.

13. Quoted from the Instructions of Akshayamati and the Sutra of Vajradhvaja. See *The Buddhist Tradition in India, China and Japan,* William Theodore de Bary, ed. (New York: Vintage Books, 1972), p. 84.

14. Kim Chi Ha, *The Gold-Crowned Jesus,* p. 107.

15. Ibid., pp. 121-22.

16. See "Song of the Pacific," *Risk* 12 (1976), p. 16.

17. Shusaku Endo, *Samurai* (Tokyo: Shinchosha, 1980), pp. 279-80 (translation from the Japanese original—CSS).

9

The Crucified Christ Challenges Human Power

KOSUKE KOYAMA

Behold, the Lamb of God who takes away the sin of the world!
(John 1:29)

With his mutilated hands he builds his world community; he challenges the power of efficiency-mindedness towards neighbors.

HE EXPOSES HUMAN DECEPTION

The crucified Christ exposes the deception of those who "have healed the wound of the people lightly, saying 'Peace, peace' when there is no peace" (Jer. 6:14). He exposes human deception, not from the luxury of an armchair, but by abandoning himself to human dominance, even to crucifixion. What a painful and inefficient way to expose human deception. This inefficient way is the secret of his power that confronts human power. It is the secret of his love.

No one now can mutilate him, because he is already mutilated. No one can crucify him. He is already crucified. No one can add or subtract anything from him. Jesus Christ is not "Yes and No" (2 Cor. 1:19). Because he—the crucified Christ—is the ultimate sincerity (*emeth*, "steadfastness"). In the crucified Christ we are confronted by the ultimate sincerity of God.

The sincerity of the crucified Christ was expressed in the taunting words of the people who were passing by the cross: "He saved others. He cannot save himself." Perhaps only taunts can reveal the depth of such sincerity! Normal avenues of theology are closed. All the world *becomes* silent and all human powers *are* challenged by the profound sincerity of the crucified Christ.

It is true that he saved others. He commanded the lame to walk. He gave sight to the blind. He cast out demons from the demon-possessed. He was, let me expand the Apostles Creed by four words, "born of the Virgin Mary, *cast out the demons*, suffered under Pontius Pilate." The demons were cast out. The reign of God came. ". . . If it is by the finger of God that I cast out demons then the kingdom of God has come upon you" (Luke 11:20). He shared his life with the poor and the needy, giving them hope. He was an other-oriented person. His sincerity was identical with this orientation. But this amazing power of healing rooted in the other-oriented sincerity he did not apply to himself. He saved others from humiliation. He himself went to the depths of humiliation. He saved others through not saving himself. He affirmed his lordship by giving it up. By healing others and not himself, he established his authority.

THE MUTILATED HANDS OF CHRIST AND
TECHNOLOGY-BUREAUCRACY

The mutilated hands of Christ represent the sincerity of God towards all humanity. Today hands are a symbol of technology. Are not our hands reaching the moon and beyond by our science and technology? Are not our hands changing our living environment to suit our liking? Do not powerful engines obey the signals we give by our fingers? Are they not capable of sending lethal bombs to destroy our enemies? Our hands are powerful. Ours are not mutilated at all.

Look at the disfigured and mutilated hands of Christ!

Technology is an efficient arrangement to "duplicate" things. By the printing press, newspapers can be duplicated by the thousands. By motors, distance can be rapidly duplicated under the rotation of the wheel. The ability to duplicate is today dangerously divorced from the discussion of the meaning of such ability. Efficiency is suffocating meaning. The good is impoverishing the best. The fertility god Baal is becoming stronger than the Covenant God Yahweh. Meaning is subordinated to efficiency. When meaning is subordinated to efficiency the attractive hands appear. The attractive hands often direct our minds to the fascination of idolatry. Who will make an idol out of the mutilated hands?

We appreciate technology. How could we do so many good things in the sight of the God of the Bible today without the help of technology? Technology may be permitted to duplicate anything, but not human beings. The machine must be switched off when it begins to duplicate the image of God in humans. It must not desacralize the holy in people. The world of efficiency—the world of attractive hands—must be watched by the world of *meaning—the world of mutilated hands*. What does it mean to duplicate human beings? Today perhaps one could speak of the duplication of the human in the sense of biological science. But I am thinking at this moment of the surrendering of human space and human time to the efficient technological space and technological time. When the human environment is thus technologized, the uniqueness of the person will eventually suffer, and there may appear a faceless mass of people. The crucified Christ challenges such a technologically efficient way of dealing with people. Technology must serve the maintenance and development of human values, the values of sincerity and reliability in the human community. The lifestyle of the Atlantic world is not the standard for all humanity. It must be judged together with other lifestyles under the light of the crucified Lord.

Bureaucracy is a world of filing cabinets and endless classification. It can reduce a living person into the set of numbers one sees on his or her passport. Information is stored in the cabinet alphabetically. The infinite amount of information about people can be used for the welfare of the people. Then bureaucracy is practicing the mind of the reign of God. But it can also use the information in order to destroy people. Both the Nazi and the Japanese bureaucracies operated with remarkable efficiency to destroy the lives of the peoples of Asia and Europe. Without bureaucratic systems both militarism and racism cannot work.

We appreciate bureaucracy. But it must be in the hands of the responsible king (*melek*) and not in the hands of the irresponsible king (*molek*) who seeks human sacrifice (Jer. 32:35). Bureaucracy must be judged in the light of the sincerity of the crucified Christ. Both technology and bureaucracy are subject to the danger of efficiency which suffocates meaning. The most extreme example of the triumph of meaning over the idolatry of efficiency is the crucifixion of Christ. There Christ demonstrates the depth of his sincerity in the most painful and "inefficient" way. It takes suffering to expose idolatry. Technology and bureaucracy tell us today "peace, peace." Is there peace? Have they not become the tools of militarism and racism?

WHO SAYS IT TO WHOM?

The sincerity and reliability of the crucified Lord exposes human deception. If someone, quoting from the Bible, says "Blessed are you poor, for yours is the kingdom of God" (Luke 6:20), let us ask, who is this person who is saying this, and to whom? Is a wealthy man saying this to a famished man? The rich to the poor? Literate person to the illiterate? Well-fed to the starved? If someone, quoting from the Bible, says "Man does not live by bread alone, but by everything that proceeds out of the mouth of the Lord," let us ask again who is saying it and to whom? I am not saying that no rich man can say, "Blessed are you poor, for yours is the kingdom of God." Indeed, he may say this *to himself.* Then it will become an extremely embarrassing and painful thought. It will become a call to surrender wealth to God and to work towards a more just society. The passage, "Man does not live by bread alone, but by everything that proceeds out of the mouth of the Lord," does not idealize poverty. It plainly tells us that humanity needs both bread *and* the word of God. It does not say that the word of

God is more important than bread, or vice versa. We cannot live by bread alone. We cannot live by the word of God alone. We need both. This must be the charter of the Christian commitment towards a more just society. Often, however, the well-fed tend to preach to the hungry people that all they need is the word of God.

The hungry do not recognize sincerity in these words of the well-fed people. It is, therefore, difficult for the missionaries sent by the rich and mighty nations to preach the word of God in the poor and starved nations. Not impossible, but difficult. Poverty and hunger are not something the God of the Bible is happy about. They must be eliminated. Poverty-stricken people cannot and do not idealize poverty. The rich can afford to idealize it.

If a rich man says to the poor, "Blessed are you poor, for yours is the kingdom of God," he is gossiping. Gossip is irresponsible talk. It does not heal. It causes a dangerous inflation in human spirituality, which makes us believe that this gossip is the word of God. Idealization of poverty by the rich is just such an arrogant bit of gossip, and not theology. Behind such gossip there must be a "duplication" and "filing cabinet" way of looking at people. The poor are quickly classified and labelled. But when living persons are reduced to sets of numbers, someone begins to have demonic power over them. Such a destructive force ignores the living context in which we all find ourselves. "Blessed are you poor, for yours is the kingdom of God"—even this becomes a detached, classified statement which can be applied, and is indeed applied, in order to enhance the prestige of those who are technologically and bureaucratically in power.

There is a difference between gossip and theology. The presence of the "contrite heart" (Ps. 51:17) makes the distinction between gossip and theology. Contrite heart? Yes. It is the heart shaken by the sincerity and reliability of the crucified Lord. When the one who "saved others but cannot save himself" touches us, the necessity of repentance comes to us. The crucified Christ judges our technological and bureaucratic gossips. With his mutilated hands he disapproves of our gossips. A theology which is not rooted in the contrite heart is gossip. It is irresponsible talk. It may be an impressive theological system with tremendous intellectual cohesion and abundant relevant information. Yet, it may be a gossip and not a theology. Our world conferences of Christian churches are impressive, yet it is possible that what is said there may be a gossip and not a theology.

One of the prevalent gossips is a talk of ascribing all good things to us Christians and bad things to others. "Behold, I send you out as sheep in the midst of wolves . . ." (Matt. 10:16). Immediately we think that we are sheep and the other people are wolves. We seldom stop and think that we can be rapacious wolves eating up sheep. Do we know how the Christians destroyed the Jewish people, for instance, through the centuries? Have you thought how the Christians looked down on the people of other great faiths? When we look down on something, we will soon find ourselves planning to destroy it.

Will not action save us from gossip? Yes, if it is action which is touched by the crucified Christ. When his mutilated hands hold us, we are delivered from the deception.

Then we begin to see the difference between *"he saved others* – he cannot save himself" and *"he saves himself*–he cannot save others." Deception takes place when we think we are other-oriented, while in truth we are self-oriented. The mutilated hands of Christ are sincere and reliable. "For the foolishness of God is wiser than men, and the weakness of God is stronger than men" (1 Cor. 1:25).

Is the church performing the mission and evangelism of God with the mutilated hands? Are the resources of the church managed by attractive hands or by mutilated hands? Are we free from "teachers' complex?" Do we have a crusading mind or a crucified mind? Are not the mutilated hands themselves the resource that is given to the church by her head, the crucified Lord?

Beware lest you say in your heart, "My power and the might of my hand have gotten me this wealth, you shall remember the Lord your God for it is he who gives you power to get wealth; that he may confirm his covenant which he swore to your fathers, as at this day" (Deut. 8:17, 18).

The crucified Christ who is the center is always in motion towards the periphery; he challenges the power of religious and political idolatry.

"MY GOD, MY GOD, WHY HAST THOU FORSAKEN ME?"

"Center" is a fascinating subject to think about. Many cities have their centers. The palace sits at the center of Tokyo. I can make the same observation of Bangkok. I have difficulty, however, to find the center in New York. It is in that sense that New York is a psychologically unsettling city in which to live. I lived in a small university city in New Zealand for five years. The city is located near the southern tip of the South Island. In this end-of-the-world city there is a beautiful center area called the Octagon. The Octagon is the center of the whole city and of the countryside beyond. There one finds shopping complexes, post office, court, city hall, church and so on. To make contact with the center is to come into contact with salvation. The center is the point of salvation. It is there that the confusing reality of life finds a point of integration and meaning.

The church believes that Jesus Christ is the center of all peoples and all things. "He was in the beginning with God; all things were made through him, and without him was not anything made that was made" (John 1:2, 3). But he is the center who is always in motion towards the periphery. In this he reveals the mind of God who is concerned about the people on the periphery.

"When you make your neighbor a loan of any sort, you shall not go into his house to fetch his pledge. You shall stand outside, and the man to whom you make the loan shall bring the pledge out to you. And if he is a poor man, you shall not sleep in his pledge; when the sun goes down, you shall restore to him the pledge that he may sleep in his cloak and bless you; and it shall be righteousness to you before the Lord your God" (Deut. 24:10-13).

Jesus was the center person laid in a manger "because there was no place for them in the inn" (Luke 2:7). He "came not to call the righteous [respectable] but sinners [outcasts]" (Mark 2:17). Jesus Christ is the center becoming periphery. He affirms his centrality by giving it up. That is what this designation "crucified Lord" means. The Lord is supposed to be at the center. But he is now affirming his lordship by being crucified! "Jesus also suffered outside the gate" (Heb. 13:12).

His life moves towards the periphery. He expresses his centrality in the periphery by reaching the extreme periphery. Finally on the cross, he stops this movement. There he cannot move. He is nailed down. This is the point of ultimate periphery. "My God, my God, why hast thou forsaken me?" (Mark 15:34). He is the crucified Lord. "Though he was in the form of God, he did not count equality with God a thing to be grasped, but emptied himself" (Phil. 2:6-7). From this uttermost point of periphery he establishes his authority. This movement towards the periphery is called the love of God in Christ. In the periphery his authority and love meet. They are one. His authority is substantiated by love. His love is authoritative. In the periphery this has taken place, as in the periphery the sincerity and reliability of Christ were demonstrated.

In the sixth century B.C. the people of Judah were threatened by the invading army of Babylonia. This pagan army, the people thought, could not touch the holy city of God. In this center city is the temple of God, the sacred center of all the traditions of Israel. Jerusalem is, therefore, safe; it is the divinely protected center; it is the seat of "religion" and the kings. "This is the temple of the Lord, the temple of the Lord, the temple of the Lord." "Do not trust these deceptive words" says Jeremiah. Jerusalem was destroyed in 587 B.C. The people of Tokyo in the *twentieth century* recited "This is the palace of the sacred emperor, the palace of the sacred emperor, the palace of the sacred emperor" in the face of the powerful American army. "Do not trust in these deceptive words." Tokyo was destroyed in 1945.

The altar and the throne have been related to each other far more intimately than we may admit. Common to both of them is the feature of centrality. In the map of religion an altar stands at the center. In the map of politics the throne occupies the center point of power. From these centers both exercise power and authority. But the mere recitation of the power of the altar and the throne is, according to Jeremiah, a deception. In religion we say that the altar will automatically protect us. In politics we say that the throne will automatically protect us. They do not! Look at Jerusalem of B.C. 587 and Tokyo of A.D. 1945!

Until 1945 the imperial throne was called "the throne coeternal with the universe." In what is termed the "Treaty," promulgated on August 22, 1910, on Japan's relationship with Korea, Article 1 has this to say: "His Majesty the Emperor of Korea makes the complete and permanent cession to His Majesty the Emperor of Japan of all rights of sovereignty over the whole of Korea."

By the time this "complete and permanent cession" came to an end in 1945(!), the fanatic Japanese emperor worship cult had become the center of the Japanese people's life. This cult placed the emperor at the center of the whole universe and asked that all who are on the periphery bow before this central personage of the imperial glory. For the sake of the glory of the center it demanded sacrifice from the periphery. The 35 years of colonial history of Korea under Japan were marked by brutal exploitation and destruction. In this politics of the emperor worship, the periphery was there only to be sacrificed. The center maintained its centrality by affirming centrality and staying at the center. The center engaged in self-idolatry. The Japanese emperor up to 1945 was thought to be the highest person in both religious (he was a god manifest) and political (he had absolute power) worlds. This imperial centrism is in rapid resurgence today!

Over against such destructive centrism in the world of religion and politics, the crucified Christ affirms his centrality by giving it up for the sake of the periphery. This is his way to *shalom*. Jesus Christ is not "imperial." His kingdom does not work in the way that the Japanese empire worked and destroyed itself. "My kingship is not from the world" (John 18:36).

THEOLOGICAL EDUCATION

Jesus Christ moves towards the periphery. He thus bestows his authority *upon the periphery*. With the presence of the center at the periphery the periphery becomes dynamic. Our thoughts on mission, evangelism and theological education must be examined in the light of the periphery-oriented authority of Jesus Christ. Historically the West has been the center of theological education, mission and evangelism. Jesus Christ has been mostly presented to the wider world in the mould of the mind of the West. Languages, such as Spanish, French, English and German, are the center languages in this Christian enterprise. Cultural and religious zones which are outside of these languages have been asked to adjust themselves to the image of Jesus Christ presented in these languages. These "center-theologies" (of the "blond Jesus") have had more than one hundred years of painful irrelevance to the world outside of the West, and most likely to the West itself. Even today most of the world's Christians, including their theologians, believe that somehow Jesus Christ is more present in America than in Bangladesh, and therefore, America is the center and Bangladesh is a periphery. By thus thinking, they unwittingly entertain the idea that in all our Christian mission, evangelism and theological education, America is the standard for all. Such center-complex, coupled with teacher-complex, must be judged in the light of the periphery-oriented authority of Jesus Christ. Christians have only one center. He is Jesus Christ, who affirmed his centrality by giving it up! It is he who stands at the center of our obedience and worship. As we worship him, we are taken into his centrality which he gave up.

There is an important stream of Christian literature coming from the innumerable competent theologians today. But the authors of these important works are doing their best to discourage *people* from reading them. These books are replete with the most difficult words and concepts. It takes a Ph.D. in theology to digest them. The theme of the periphery is discussed with the full-blown center-language. In general, the sin of theologians is that they write books for fellow theologians and thus they build up a special circle in which they admire each other. So, too, far too many students from the world outside of the West come to the West to receive their theological education. But the majority of theological schools in the West are still dreaming a happy dream of center-complex. Such a dream is not innocent. It is harmful to the living reality of the Church Universal. It is idolatrous because it is elevating the tribal to the universal. The crucified Lord is as much present in Jakarta as in Jerusalem, in Rangoon as in London. The dynamism of the periphery judges our center-complex.

In the light of the periphery-oriented authority of the crucified Lord, how do we see the people who are living in the prosperous sections of this world today?

"PEOPLE ARE WASTED"

Affluence and an inhuman level of poverty are coexisting side by side in this world. One section of humanity is dying from overeating and the other from starvation. This global tragedy is reflected often within the nations. The Philippines have a tiny minority of Filipinos who are enjoying enormous wealth while the absolute majority of the people are struggling in despairing poverty. In Thailand, Thai people exploit most brutally their fellow Thais, exhibiting a kind of internal exploitation which came to be known as "Herodianism," as some Filipinos have named it. These exploitative systems are all supported by the guns of the military. Even in so-called democratic countries there exists an impoverished class "colonized" by the affluent.

The Sixth Assembly of the Christian Conference of Asia, in June 1977, describes "The Asian Situation":

The dominant reality of Asian suffering is that people are wasted: wasted by hunger, torture, deprivation of rights; wasted by economic exploitation, racial and ethnic discrimination, sexual suppression; wasted by loneliness, nonrelation, noncommunity.

The conference focused its attention on the people. All other kinds of wastes in this world contribute to this chilling result: *the people are wasted.* That "people are wasted" is, according to this Asian conference, the fundamental pain of Asia. There are multiple reasons for the wasting of people. All these reasons point to the economic exploitation which is going on in our world on both the local and international levels. There is no doubt that those who are starved because of poverty are persons wasted. The conference report continues to say, "In this situation we begin by stating that people are not to be wasted, people are valuable, made in God's image . . ." If a person is starved, the living image of God is wasted. There is a difference between a hungry dog and a hungry man. The hungry man feels an assault upon his human dignity; the dog does not. For the human person, physical humiliation means spiritual humiliation. The empty stomach means an insult to the image of God.

After this fundamental observation, we are invited to take a second look at the focus point of the Asian conference: "People are wasted." There are people who, in their own economic zone, are neither poor nor rich. They have something to eat, somewhere to sleep and something to wear, and they may have more in addition to these. But it is obviously possible that their lives also can be wasted. They are not starved. But they can be wasted. Physical comfort does not necessarily mean spiritual fulfillment. Then there are those who are rich. Ordinarily we think that the lives of rich people are not wasted. But this point cannot be made so easily. Wealth enslaves man and woman. I am not prepared to say that the enslavement by wealth and enslavement by poverty are identical. They are not. We all desire to be enslaved by wealth but we do not want to be enslaved by poverty. The former is a sweet enslavement; the latter is a bitter enslavement. But enslavement is enslavement. The image of God suffers for different reasons. The people who are poor must be emancipated from their grinding poverty. The people who are neither poor nor rich must be emancipated from their "wasting life." The people who are rich must be emancipated from their enslavement to wealth. Life must not be wasted.

Behold, Lord, the half of my goods I give to the poor; and if I have defrauded anyone of anything, I restore it fourfold. And Jesus said to him, "Today salvation has come to this house" (Luke 19:9).

People who are wasted are on the periphery. The poor are periphery. Jesus moves towards them. People who are not poor can be at the periphery if their lives are wasted. Jesus moves towards them. But often people who are not poor do not think that they are at the periphery. Then the irony of Mark 2:17 is applied:

Those who are well have no need of a physician, but those who are sick; I came not to call the righteous, but sinners.

INDISCRIMINATE GOD

Jesus Christ, who has travelled to the extreme periphery, has authority
to speak to and heal those who are "wasting their lives" under many types
of enslavement. "The Word became flesh and dwelt among us" (John 1:14)
to show the supreme importance of people in the mind of God. The name
of Jesus Christ represents more than an economic analysis of society by
Karl Marx. "The Word became flesh and dwelt among us" does not specify
that he dwelt among the poor, or among those who are neither poor nor
rich, or among the rich. He dwelt among *people* to save them from wasting
life. When we say that God has opted for the poor—he has taken the side
of the poor—in Jesus Christ, we must not mean that all others have become
the enemies of God. "The Word dwelt among us" points to the mysterious
dimension of the "indiscriminateness" of the mercy of God for all. "For
God has consigned all men to disobedience, that he may have mercy upon
all" (Rom. 11:32). "All men" ("all humanity" in nonsexist language) here
I understand to be indiscriminately the poor, those who are neither poor
nor rich, and the rich. Here is the depth of God's mercy. It is so deep. It
goes beyond any calculation and prudence. It touches upon a risky quality
of indiscriminateness. "He makes his sun rise on the evil and on the good,
and sends rain on the just and on the unjust" (Matt. 5:45). He shows his
mercy upon all, the rich and the poor. God moves towards the poor; he is
concerned about their empty stomach and cold nights. God must tell us
who is "in his view" his enemy. There are millions of "pious Christians"
throughout the world who benefit from their status quo of the repressive
regimes and merciless exploitation. All American educational systems,
including theological seminaries, are entrapped in the capitalistic system
by receiving capitalist interest for their endowment funds. Shall we just call
military juntas, capitalists and exploiters "enemies" of God? How about
other millions who accept the fruits of such unjust social systems? What
kind of money is it that brought us to Melbourne from the four corners of
the world? Pure uncontaminated money? Is there such money in this world
today? The overwhelming majority of "good Christians" are busy living a
kind of Christian spirituality which does not demand social justice. Isn't it
true that Christians are, in fact, supporting the oppressive regimes? "For
the time has come for judgment to begin with the household of God" (1
Pet. 4:17).

Even the most careful theological language about the poor is paternalistic. Paternalism often breeds idolatry. When the poor are elevated to the
height of history, when all humanity is centered by the presence of the
poor, when the poor are the only mediators through whom we can come
to God in Christ, a new idolatry has been created of which the poor themselves are unaware. Then humanity is divided into two faceless sections:
the rich and the poor. Faceless divisions are highly dangerous. One side is

"absolutized" against the other. "The Word became flesh and dwelt among us" means that the coming of Jesus Christ eliminates this facelessness. He creates community rather than mass. He is against "wasting life" in *all* life contexts. In the parable of the Pharisee and the publican in the temple (Luke 18:9-14) it is possible that the religious Pharisee is far poorer than the secular businessman tax-collector who said, "God, be merciful to me, a sinner."

Jesus, in this particular parable, does not touch on the economic background of these two spiritually contrasting people. Again, in the parable of the Good Samaritan (Luke 10:25-37) one can imagine—and certainly it is possible—that the Samaritan who was able to pay medical expenses for the man beaten on the highway is perhaps economically a little stronger than the religious persons who passed by. Our world is full of confusing and complex social situations, and it is here "the Word became flesh and dwelt among us."

"The Word became flesh and dwelt among us." He "pitched his tent" among us. He did not live in the "big house" (*pharaoh* means "the great house"). He lived his life as a "periphery man." As the periphery man he challenged the idolatry in religion and politics and confirmed the deeper tradition of "God, be merciful to me, a sinner" in the life of the synagogue and the church. When these words are said by someone, whether he or she, rich or poor, they can challenge the existing unjust social order, because such souls are free from idolatry. They do not try to be peaceful when there is no peace. They are "broken souls" (Psalms 51:17). The broken souls can become community-minded souls. They are equipped with keen perception on the whereabouts and works of social injustice. We must not understand these words of humble cry to God only as personalistic, spiritual words which do not have much to do with the world's reality. These words of the tax-collector can challenge human religious and political power. The idolatry-free dynamism of periphery is at work in these words. They point to the authority of Jesus Christ.

In the crucified Christ the reign of God has come: the *scars of Jesus* challenge the power of the good that suffocates the best.

THE SCARS OF JESUS

The Apostle Paul concludes his Letter to the Galatians with these words: "For neither circumcision counts for anything, nor uncircumcision, but a new creation . . . Henceforth let no man trouble me; for I bear on my body the marks of Jesus" (Gal. 6:15, 17).

"The marks" (*stigmata*) mean brands stamped on slaves. It must mean the scars Paul received from beatings as narrated in 2 Corinthians 11:23-28. "Five times I have received at the hands of the Jews the forty lashes less one. Three times I have been beaten with rods; once I was stoned." These scars he carried on his body were a symbol of communion between

Paul and the crucified Christ. It was as if they were the scars of "a new creation." With these scars he was freed from the need for circumcision or uncircumcision. He speaks then unusual words about this most honored institution of all, circumcision. Not scars of circumcision but scars of Jesus are now the central reality for him.

The Christian church is an institution. Life is never free from institution. Vitality which rejects institutional form is a wild vitality. Where there is life there is institution. Then the question is, what kind of institution is it that expresses the power of life and the imagination of life? Creative institution? Destructive institution? Lively one? Petrified one? In the face of the approaching army of Babylonia, the people of Judah recited the name of the most sacred institution, the temple of the Lord. Jerusalem could not be destroyed by the pagan army, they thought, because it had the most sacred institution in it. But it was destroyed. Jeremiah gave the reason for the destruction of Jerusalem:

> If you truly execute justice one with another, if you do not oppress the alien, the fatherless or the widow, or shed innocent blood in this place, and if you do not go after other gods to your own hurt, then I will let you dwell in this place, in the land that I gave of old to your fathers for ever (Jer. 7:6-7).

Even the most sacred institution cannot protect the nation if the life that began the institution is not faithfully demonstrated. In other words, the temple of the Lord will protect the population if they practice the inner message of the institution: "Execute justice one with another." Institutional power is rooted in the ethical responsibility of that institution. "Do not oppress the alien, the fatherless or the widow." Then the institution of the temple of God becomes meaningful to the people of Judah. Jesus stands in this tradition.

COME TO THE ALTAR TWICE

> So if you are offering your gift at the altar, and there remember that your brother has something against you, leave your gift there before the altar and go; first be reconciled to your brother, and then come and offer your gift (Matt. 5:23-24).

You must come to the altar "twice." The first time you come, the living spirit for which the altar is an institutional expression will make you aware of what this "coming to the altar" means. There you will remember that "your brother has something against you," not that you have something against your brother, because the altar stands for the judgment upon ego-centric perspective. Then you must take a side trip, as it were. "First be reconciled to your brother." Then come back and continue your act of offering your gift at the altar. Practice what the altar stands for. Practice what the temple of the Lord stands for. If the scars of Jesus, and not the circumcision, are the fundamental symbol for the Church, the Church must express the meaning of those scars in the way it exists and acts. The Church must show this original quality through its institutional life. Bad institution is that which muffles the meaning of the temple of the Lord. Good institution is then the opposite of this, namely, that in which the original intention of the temple of the Lord will come out clearly to the hearing and seeing of the people.

Where there is life there is institution. But the Church is a strange institution created by the crucified Lord. It is this image of the crucified Lord that must come out through the life of the institutional church. It is the life that accepts humiliation in order to save others from humiliation. That life must be seen in the life of the institutional church. The crucified Christ cannot be easily institutionalized. He cannot be tamed so easily. He is always able to crucify the institution built in his name. He visits his Church as the crucified Lord. He asks his Church to have a crucified mind rather than a crusading mind. The crucified mind is not a neurotic mind. It is a mind ready to accept humiliation in order to save others from humiliation. It is a strongly community-directed mind. It is a healthy mind. The Church is inspired to come to the people with the crucified mind, not with the crusading mind. It is asked to follow the crucified Lord instead of running ahead of him.

But the power of the crucified Christ expresses itself in its own way of "crusading." It is a "crusade" deeply rooted in the crucified Lord. Such a "crusade" is different from the ordinary crusade. It is a crusade staged by the mind that accepts humiliation in order to save others from humiliation! It does not bulldoze others. It takes the way of suffering. "Your kingdom come!" has a history of suffering.

In our world today, "good Christian people" are those who distance themselves from the suffering of the world. They talk about the suffering and give some charity to alleviate inhuman conditions of life. They are upright, honest, hard-working and church-going. They are good people. But it is these "good people" who innocently support the oppressive global system of exploitation. They live in "cruel innocence," as Michael Harrington says. They are concerned about their Christian spirituality. They live a "rich internal life" with Jesus Christ. But their goodness is that of the bystanders. Millions of times the prayer "Your kingdom come!" is said by these good people who live in "cruel innocence." This is perhaps one of the greatest visible and invisible institutions of Christianity. These good Christians are bulldozing others!

This prayer, "Your kingdom come!," does not originate in the Christian Church. The Church inherited it from Israel. The Jews prayed, "Your kingdom come." They prayed this prayer through the catastrophe of the holocaust in recent history. It was not a cheap prayer. Today when we pray this prayer we must know that we are saying it after Auschwitz and the Cambodian genocide. The world is replete with hideous lethal weapons. It is in this world that we pray this prayer. We must know the tragic brokenness of the world when we say this prayer. With the scars of Jesus that heal the wounds of the world, we say, "Your kingdom come."

10

Jesus and People (Minjung)

BYUNG MU AHN

Chi-Ha Kim, a Korean poet, wrote a play titled *The Gold-Crowned Jesus.* The scene plays in front of a Catholic church, where a statue of Jesus, made of cement, is to be found. On his head he is wearing a golden crown. Below the statue there are beggars lying around. The time is early morning on a cold winter's day.

As time passes, first a pot-bellied priest and then a fat man, looking like the boss of a company, walk by. The beggars ask for alms again and again, but are refused with contempt and scorn. Eventually a policeman is seen on the scene. Far from wanting to help them he immediately tries to drive them out of the place and demands a fine from them in return for his connivance.

After all of them are gone, one of the beggars starts to lament: "I have neither home, nor grave to rest from all the exhaustion. I am abandoned in the midst of the cold winter, abandoned in an endless cold, in a bottomless darkness. I cannot endure it any longer, this miserable time. . . . It is unbearable, really unbearable. But where shall I go, where can I leave for, where, where?" As he so laments to himself in despair, his eyes, filled with tears, meet the cement statue of Jesus. For a moment a vague expectation flickers in his mind. Yet, pulling himself together he — with a critical glance at the statue — grumbles in his mind: "This Jesus might well be a saviour to those who have enough to eat, who have a home and a family. But what has he to do with a beggar like me?" And then he says in a loud voice: "Hey! How on earth can Jesus speak without a mouth? Can a lump of cement speak? Even though he were alive, he couldn't open his cemented mouth. So what kind of relationship could there be between that lump of cement and me? — Hey, listen! They choose cement or concrete or bronze or gold to have a statue of Jesus made, so solid as to last for 1000 or 10,000 years."

Crying out loudly, the beggar, overwhelmed with grief, begins to weep. Right at that moment he feels something wet, like small drops falling on his head. Is it raining? No! — When he look up he finds the cement Jesus weeping and dropping tears. The tears are falling right on him. "How strange a thing! Really, there are tears dropping down from his eyes! I could never have imagined a thing like this. Could it be that this cement is made of some strange material?"

He watches Jesus intently, and only then does he realize that Jesus is wearing a golden crown. He begins to touch and feel the crown with his hands. Having found that it is real gold, the idea crosses his mind that if he sold the crown, he would have enough to eat and something to live on. Following an irresistible impulse he grasps the crown and takes it off.

At this very moment he hears a voice: "Take it, please! For too long a time have I been imprisoned in this cement. Feeling choked in this dark and lonely prison of cement, I wish to talk with poor people like you and share your suffering. How eagerly I have been waiting for this day to come — the day of my liberation when I could once again flare up like a candle and bring light to your misery. Eventually you have come and made me open my mouth. It's you who saved me." These are the words spoken by the gold-crowned Jesus.

"Who put Jesus into prison?" the startled and frightened beggar asks. "Who were they?" The Jesus made of cement answers: "People like the Pharisees did it, because they wanted to separate him from the poor in order to possess him exclusively." Then the beggar asks: "Lord, what is it that has to be done for you to be released, for you to live again and stay with us?" Jesus answers: "It is impossible to do so by my own strength. If you are not going to liberate me, I will never become free again. Only people like you, that means the poor, the miserable, the persecuted, but kind-hearted people, will be able to do it. You opened my mouth! Right at that moment when you took the crown off my head, my mouth opened. It is you who liberated me! Now come near to me, come very close! Like you made me open my mouth, you may now make my body become free. Remove the cement from my body. And remove the golden crown too. For my head, a crown of thorns will just be enough. I do not need gold. You need it much more. Take the gold and share it with your friends." But at that very moment the pot-bellied priest, the fat boss of the company, and the policeman reappear on the scene. Immediately they snatch the crown from the beggar's hands and put it back on the head of the Jesus-statue. The beggar is arrested by the policeman and, charged with larceny, taken to the police station. And the Jesus, made of cement, returns to his former state — a blank, expressionless statue, dumb, nothing more than a lump of cement.

Chi-Ha Kim is a lay Catholic. However, he is not a so-called enthusiastic believer. He is unable to submit to the teachings of the Church, for he not only realizes that there is too wide a gap between those teachings and the realities he lives in, but sees the so-called dogma (doctrines) as a barrier that has sealed off our eyes from the realities.

The very thing that makes Jesus turn into cement is the Christology made by the Church. The golden crown on his head is the ideology of the established Church, which was forced on Jesus in order to make him support the Church institution. Today, the Korean Church boasts of the 200th anniversary of the Catholic Church and the 100th anniversary of the Protestant Church. But actually, both churches have only presented the petrified image of Jesus created by the dogma formed in Europe throughout the long history of the Western Church. And accordingly, the Jesus who wants to share the agony and the suffering of the Minjung of this land has long been imprisoned in the cement made by them.

The cries of the Minjung, however, who have been groaning under the military dictatorship during the decade of the 1970s took off the crown of Jesus. So we, for the first time, came to hear his voice and see his tears. That is to say, we experienced that Jesus, confined in the cement, could be liberated only by the Minjung. But now the Church, just like the priest, the boss, and the policeman, is trying hard to re-capture the crown in order to put it back on the head of Jesus. Becoming aware of the existence and realities of the Minjung in the Gospels, we theologians started to see them coinciding with what we experienced in our own situation. To our eyes, the Jesus seen through the lens of traditional Christology was the very Jesus imprisoned in the cement. To liberate or save Jesus from this state of imprisonment was recognized and accepted by some of our biblical scholars as an immediate task. But this task cannot be fulfilled by the intellectual analysis of the Bible only. It needs the help of the Minjung as well.

THE CHRIST OF THE KERYGMA AND THE HISTORICAL JESUS

Even up to the present time the New Testament scholars of the West are giving preference to the Christ of the Kerygma in comparison with the historical Jesus. They stress that it is the Christ of the Kerygma who gives the foundation to the Gospels. On this promise they even say that it is an attitude of disbelief to inquire beyond the Kerygma, and accordingly they block the way to the historical Jesus. Some objections to this opinion, being based on the historicity, are only roaming around skepticism so far as the historical Jesus is concerned. It is true that the Christ of the Kerygma is dominant in the New Testament. And this fact serves as the basis for the Christology and the doctrine of salvation. However, although the existence of the historical Jesus is assumed (presupposed) in the Christology and the doctrine of salvation, it is almost entirely overshadowed. In other words, Christology plays the role of confining the living Jesus to the cement. This fact can be ascertained in all of the Gospels, not to speak of the Epistles of Paul.

It is a well-known fact that Paul, when he formulated his Christology, did not refer to the historical Jesus. He even had no interest in him (2 Cor. 5:16). In his Christology the Jesus who lived in Palestine doesn't exist, only the Christ as an object of worship. The Jesus who cannot speak and cannot move under the weight of the golden crown—he is the Christ of the Kerygma. The Kerygma, too, refers to the death on the cross, yet it actually dehistorised that event, in spite of its historical reality. The same can be said about the historical event of the resurrection of Jesus, which was dehistorised by the Kerygma as well. We do know that this phenomenon of dehistorisation began in 1 Cor. 15:3-8 and Phil. 2:6-11; the so-called Christ-hymn, for example, was formulated by the Christian community before Paul. It is clear that these are confessions on the suffering and the resurrection of Jesus, but the actual substance was dehistorised long before. That is, the historical facts of "when, where, by whom, how and why" Jesus was executed were entirely concealed in the Kerygma. The *Christology in this Kerygma has greatly served as an ideology to preserve the Church, but at the cost of silencing Jesus.* Who took the leading role in the formation of the Christ-Kerygma? It was the leaders of the early Church. They, in an apologetic effort to preserve the Church, endeavoured to formulate the Kerygma. But this effort only resulted in the abstraction of the Jesus-event.

But besides the Kerygma, the stories about Jesus were transmitted as well. Jesus in those stories is entirely different from the Christ in the Kerygma. He is not the gold-crowned Jesus who rules, but the Jesus who wants to associate with people, uses the same language, and shares their joy and their sorrow. It was the author of the Gospel of Mark who handed down to us these Jesus-stories. But even in the Gospel of Mark the Christ of the Kerygma is given as a premise (presupposition). However, the author did by no means conceal the features of the living Jesus before he became the Christ.

The Jesus stories describe the *living* Jesus—the Jesus who returned to Galilee as soon as he heard the news about the arrest of John the Baptist; the Jesus who was rejected by his native town; the Jesus who lived with the poor, the sick and the women, healing them, feeding them, and defending them in their resistance against the ruling class who persecuted, oppressed and alienated them; and the Jesus who finally was killed by the hands of the political authorities.

It is clear that "non-Christ-Kerygma" elements are predominant in the Jesus-stories. But who then were the transmitters of those stories? It is obvious that they belonged to quite a different class than those who formed the Kerygma. In my point of view it was Minjung who transmitted the stories about Jesus. They must have circulated the stories about the event of Jesus' execution by the Roman authorities continuously. Jesus was the victim of political violence, and because of this situation, the stories about the Jesus-event could not, but must, have been handed down secretly in the form of "rumor." The stories had been overshadowed by the Kerygma until the time when the author of the Gospel of Mark accepted and transformed the rumors of the Minjung into a manuscript. We owe it to the editor of the Gospel of Mark that the living feature of Jesus was preserved and handed down to us! Otherwise it might have been lost forever.

The Jesus who was imprisoned in the cement and could not help keeping silent under the weight of the golden crown was liberated by the Minjung. Freed from the heavy crown and the prison of cement, he speaks and works among us.

JESUS AND THE MINJUNG

Because we have been enslaved by the Christology of the Kerygma, even when we read the synoptics, we focused our attention on Jesus as the Christ and considered him to be the center of the Gospel. In this way we used to identify Jesus with the Christ and were quite content with this identification. However, as we began to read the synoptics again with more skeptical eyes, the features of Jesus turned out to be quite different.

First, we found out that Jesus is in incessant action. Unlike the Christ of the Kerygma, Jesus is not holding fast to his unshakable seat (throne) within the Church. By no means is he ruling as an original perfect being, but acts freely without being bound to religious norms. This image of Jesus is quite different from such images as the Son of God, the Messiah, the pre-existent Being, the exalted Christ sitting on a throne, and the coming Christ who will be the Judge on the last day, etc.

Secondly, Jesus associates and lives with the Minjung. On no account is he an aloof, lofty person, but instead he eats and drinks with the Minjung, sometimes asking favors from them or vice versa, granting their requests. So we can say: "Where there is Jesus, there is the Minjung. And where there is the Minjung, there is Jesus."

The Gospel of Mark from its very beginning (1:22) points to the crowd who is gathering around Jesus and reports that the anonymous crowd is always in company with him. By so doing, the author of the Gospel attracts our attention to the anonymous crowd and finally makes it clear that this crowd is in fact *ochlos* (2:4) itself. And afterwards it continues to report that Jesus is surrounded by and living together with this *ochlos* all through his life.

The term *ochlos* occurs 38 times in the Gospel of Mark, is used 49 times by Matthew and 41 times by Luke. Now our question is this: Why did the authors of the Gospels prefer to use this term when describing the characteristics of the crowd who lived together with Jesus? The Septuaguint uses the term *laos*—meaning God's people—instead of *ochlos* when it reports about the crowd. Mark also knew the term *laos*, but he used it only twice and then only when quoting. It is, therefore, evident that Mark deliberately used the term *ochlos* for the characterization of the crowd who gathered around Jesus, because he recognized that the characteristics of *ochlos* exactly corresponded to those of the crowd around Jesus.

According to the Gospels, numerous *ochlos* associated with and shared the activities of Jesus. According to the Feeding Story in the Gospel of Mark, for example, the number amounts to 5,000 (6:44). This number, however, must be regarded as a symbolic figure to show how big a crowd of *ochlos* gathered around Jesus. It was an anonymous force. Mark described *ochlos* in detail.

First, there are the sick. According to the redaction-order of Mark there is a man with an unclean spirit (1:21ff. 34), a leper (1:40 ff), a paralysed man (2:1 ff), a man with a withered hand (3:1 ff), and so on. And in the healing stories that follow, Mark shows that the sick persons held an important position among the *ochlos* of Jesus. And especially when he frequently refers to the many people who were possessed by unclean spirits, he describes Jesus as an "exorcist" who liberated them from the evil spirits.

Second, there are the tax-collectors and the sinners. They are the ones who concretely reflect the character of the Minjung. For example, in the beginning of Mark's Gospel we find the story about the calling of Levi. The following passage deserves our attention: "And as he passed on, he saw Levi the son of Alphaeus sitting at the tax office, and he said to him, 'Follow me.' And he rose and followed him. And as he sat at table in his house, many tax collectors and sinners were sitting with Jesus and his disciples; for there were many who followed him" (2:14, 15).

There is a parallel to this passage in the Q-source (Mt 11:19; Lk 15:1). When Matthew refers to the tax-collectors and the prostitutes side by side (Mt 21:31), he wants to emphasize that he regards the tax-collectors specially to be the members of Jesus' Minjung. Here Minjung clearly means those who are socially alienated.

The tax-collectors, the sinners, and the prostitutes — all of them belong to the alienated class. Thirdly, the Minjung of Jesus were the poor. *Hoi ptōchoi* are the poor people in the materialistic sense of the word. Therefore, we can never think of Jesus without taking into consideration this "ethos of poverty."

It is a well-known fact that in Luke especially, Jesus' words about the poor stand out in bold relief, and the poor are characterized by the contrast between them and the rich. Fourthly, what we must point out, in particular, is the appearance of women on the scene. In the Gospels women appear here and there as patients or poor persons, but what is most important is that they are referred to as those who observed Jesus' suffering right to the end and became eyewitnesses to the empty tomb. This tells us something about the importance of the women's position among the Minjung who followed Jesus.

The question we have to raise here in connection with the Christology is that about the relation between Jesus and *ochlos*.

Traditional Christology has been consistent in its explanation of seeing Jesus' role within the frame of God's drama. That is to say, Jesus is the true Messiah in the sense that he obeyed and fulfilled God's will. In the

Gospels, of course, similar ideas can be found. In the Passion-history, for example, Jesus' agony at Gethsemane and his cry on the cross reflect such an image of Jesus. But we do have another tradition, which conveys an absolutely different image of Jesus, who identifies himself with the cries and wishes of the suffering Minjung. It is particularly the healing-stories that expose this image of Jesus. The Jesus who heals the sick people is by no means described as someone who fulfills a pre-established program. Jesus never seeks for the sick persons voluntarily, nor does he follow an earlier intention (plan) for helping them. On the contrary, the request always comes from the Minjung's side first. And accordingly, Jesus' healing activities appear as him being obedient to the wishes of the patients. In other words, it is the sick who take the initiative for such events to happen. Jesus' healing power, which has a functional relation to the suffering of the Minjung, can be realized only when it is met by the will of the Minjung. It is from this aspect that Mark reports, without hesitation, that Jesus could do no mighty works in his native town, because they did not believe in him (6:5).

Jesus, sharing the living realities of the sick, the poor, the alienated, and the women, speaks to God on behalf of the Minjung, as if he was their spokesman.

To distinguish this point from traditional Christology, let's take the parable of the Good Samaritan in the Gospel of Luke as an example. The allegorical interpretation of this parable—which has been traditional interpretation—identifies the good Samaritan with Jesus. We can for the moment accept this interpretation, but it overlooks one important point: the central figure in the event of this parable is not the good Samaritan, but it is the man who fell among the robbers. The deed of the good Samaritan is the response to the cry of the suffering man. However, the priest and the Levite who were also confronted with this cry for help did not open themselves, but passed quickly by instead. The one who did open himself to the cry was the good Samaritan. Consequently, in order to correctly interpret Jesus as the Christ, we must endow *ochlos* in the Gospels with the proper esteem with regard to their relationship with Jesus. *This Jesus is not the Christ who is facing man from God's side, but the Christ who is facing God from man's side.* So in this case it means that *man* is not an abstract being but the concrete Minjung who are suffering. Therefore, the Jesus who is one with the Minjung, facing God from their direction—HE IS CHRIST. He identifies himself with the Minjung. He exists for no other than for the Minjung (cf. Mk 2:17).

Now, is Jesus as the Christ the Saviour of mankind? If so, salvation is not a manufactured product given to man from heaven to possess. On the contrary, it means the salvation that Jesus realized in the action of transforming himself, by listening to and responding to the cry of Minjung.

This understanding of salvation is to be found in the Gospel of Luke when he speaks about poverty or the poor. It seems to me that Luke's understanding of the Minjung lies in its emphasis on the poor. Luké pictures the poor in relief on the one hand, and casts severe criticism upon the rich on the other hand. This, however, does not mean that Luke puts the emphasis on the class struggle that the communists advocate. We must notice that the audience was most of the time the rich people, whether his passages deal with the rich or with the poor. This means that the purpose of Jesus' preaching was not simply to curse the rich and to proclaim a blessing to the poor, but to pronounce the "paradox" — that the way to salvation of the rich can only be found through the poor As a matter of fact, Jesus himself was one of the poor (Mt 8:20; Lk 9:58), and therefore we can meet him only among the poor. Luke emphasizes this point.

This is the very aspect from which we should understand the relationship between Jesus and the Minjung. And this also means that we should not understand Jesus as an "individual" as the Western scholars do. Such a Western point of view cannot but turn into a metaphysical Christology. No, we should rather understand the Jesus of the Gospels as a "collective" being. That is to say, we must grasp Jesus as the Minjung itself. In the Gospel of Mark, when Jesus was looking around on those *ochlos* who sat around him, he proclaimed, "These are my mother and my brothers"! (Mk 3:31ff). This clearly presents Jesus as being part of the Minjung itself. From this point of view. the meaning of the Passion-history appears different too.

JESUS' SUFFERING AS THE CORE OF THE CHRISTOLOGY

1) Even though the cross of Jesus is undoubtedly a historical event, in the so-called Kerygma it became dehistorised and was consequently reduced to a religious symbol which, in the end, became the object of worship. Those who gave first priority to the Christ-Kerygma were interested in the meaning of the cross only. The emphasis on the soteriological meaning is one such case. Just as Paul did in 1 Cor. 15:3ff, they understand the event of the cross in terms of the fulfillment of God's will (according to the "scriptures"), or in terms of a sacrificial offering for the sin of mankind. It is these two meanings, which are the keynotes in Paul's Christology, that we are soaked with. And this Christology has been ruling over us as the dogma supported by Church authority. Yet, even in Paul's writings, expressions which go beyond the meaning of "he died for our sins" can be found. That is to say, Paul does not simply mention Jesus' death, but expresses it in terms of the death on the cross. But if this cross was the means for the execution, then it is not a symbol for death, but serves as an evidence to the killing or the case of murder. Consequently, to emphasize the cross, instead of simply mentioning his death, presents evidence to the historical event that took place. Then, why on earth does Paul keep silent on the historical questions of "when? where? by whom? how?" It might be said that the social situation of his days made him do so.

The cross, which has been put up by the church as its symbol, has no meaning except that of playing the role of a religious symbol. And traditional Christology, up to the present, kept repeating such an ecclesiastical understanding of Jesus' death.

Luther conceptualized the event of Jesus' suffering as the so-called apostolic Gospel (*apostolisches Evangelium*). But because of this it was rather reduced to merely the criterion by which to judge the doctrine of the cross. In the same way the cross became the backbone of the doctrine of the Kerygmatic Christology. As a result, the event of the cross lost its relationship with the reality of today's suffering, and accordingly the cross without such relationship began to reign on the throne of the Church. In other words the cross of Jesus has been turned into cement. *This petrified cross does no longer associate with the suffering people, but does serve as a dogma to interrogate and judge the sinners.*

2) What about Mark's description of the Passion-history?

First of all, we must admit that the Christ-kerygmatic elements can be found in that history in the respect that Mark describes Jesus' suffering as the necessary stage to pass through "in order to fulfil God's will". The prayer in Gethsemane, the trial of Jesus and the last cry on the cross — all of these are described as if God, not the Roman authorities, nor the Jewish ruling class, put Jesus to death. These elements, of course, make only a small part of the Gospel, though.

Bultmann assumes that the story about the suffering of Jesus was formed by being based on the so-called Passion-announcements. This assumption reveals that his standpoint advocates the predominance of the Kerygma over the Jesus-event. But this opinion does not correspond to the facts with regard to the two following points:

First, the announcement says that Jesus will be rejected by the elders and the chief priests and the scribes, and be killed. But the Passion-history reports that not only the Jewish ruling class but also the Roman authorities executed him. Therefore, it is a stern reality that he was killed as a political prisoner by the Roman power. Moreover, the great crowd in Jerusalem and even his disciples turned their back on him.

Second, what is most important to be aware of is that there is not a single hint about an immediate resurrection anywhere in the Passion-histories, while in the Passion-announcements the prediction that he will rise after three days is a major presupposition. The Passion-history reveals the naked reality of the darkness that prevailed under the rule of the unjust power. And even God seemed to have turned away and did not intervene in the event of the execution of Jesus. The severe reality in fact was the reality of God's absence.

Besides, the Passion stories do not contain any hint as to the existence of a "superman". Jesus appears as nothing more than a weak person who has the same physiological limitations as common people do, and he, just like the powerless Minjung today, was cruelly killed by the strong power of the structural evil of the world. The Passion-history by no means indicates the justification of man's sin in general (if we set aside the scene of "The Last Supper"). On the contrary, it exposes—through the reports of the event of Jesus' crucifixion—the immorality and sin of the offenders.

3) To come to a conclusion, we must deal with the question as to how this story about the suffering of Jesus could be passed on. Most of all I would like to insist on the presupposition that the Passion-history was based on historical facts. Without the recognition of the historical reality, we cannot imagine the feature of the Jesus of Galilee who was persecuted and eventually killed on the cross. This does not mean that I deny the fact that the theological thinking had some effect on the process of documentation of the Passion-history. But strictly speaking, the Kerygmatic theology did not exist first, but was preceded by the testimony of the eye-witnesses to the event of Jesus' death on the cross. If not so, the description of the procedure of the suffering cannot be seen as the non-religious and human tragedy that it actually was. This very feature of Jesus, who so humanly suffers, tears the Kerygmatic Christology to pieces. Who then was interested in this feeble and human Jesus and transmitted the facts about how he was helplessly killed on the cross by the power of the authorities?

If the transmitters had been members of the leading class in the church, who wanted to preserve the Kerygmatic doctrine—"Jesus is the Christ, Jesus is the Son of God, He is the Saviour who conquered the world"—the Passion-history could never have been described in the way it was. At the same time, the Passion-history in its original form reflects none of these elements whatsoever. On the contrary, it was about people whose lives were so full of suffering and misery that they could not even stop at pondering about Church order, its doctrines, and the like. They could not afford to have apologetic interests. Therefore, we can conclude that it was not the leading class of the Church who transmitted the Passion-history, but the nameless, weak and suffering people—the Minjung. They saw their own existential life situation coincide with the story of Jesus' suffering. Therefore they told the story about the Jesus-event not as his story, but as their own story. And as they mourned Jesus' death, they mourned their own death at the same time. By doing so, they exposed the evil and unjust power and resisted it.

The author of the Gospel of Mark seems to have pursued two goals when he documentized Minjung testimony: on the one hand he challenged the Kerygmatic Christology, which had already been generally accepted, and on the other hand he, with some conciliatory attitude, tried to harmonize their testimony with that of the Kerygmatic Christology.

For these various aspects we can see that it is the Minjung of Jesus who open the way to liberate Jesus, still imprisoned in the cement of the dogma, and make him return to the very place where the Minjung today are living.

11

Jesus and Transculturation

SEBASTIAN KAPPEN

Investigations thus far show that the counter-culture Jesus started has much in common with protest movements of our own past. It is also clear that his natural allies in contemporary India are those social and political forces that seek to supersede both casteist and capitalist culture. I shall now try to define the contribution his life and message can make to the creation of a new liberating culture. But first let me briefly state why I speak of Jesus and not of Indian Christianity.

THE CHRISTIAN AMBIVALENCE

Indian Christianity has, by and large, retained its imported character. The Christ of theology and popular devotion still bears the marks of his origin in the West. So too the church that made him. Her dogmas and forms of worship took shape in the context of the Graeco-Roman world. No less foreign is the canon law regulating her internal life. The spirituality of resignation and wordly prudence she instills in the faithful derives less from the Gospels than from Neo-Platonism and Stoicism. Still worse, ever new spurious theologies and spiritualities continue to pour in from the West. Small wonder that neither the Christ of the church nor the church of Christ has made any profound impact on the Indian people.

Christianity has also erred in the opposite direction. It has, in more than one respect, identified itself with the culture of the ruling classes in India. The ethos prevailing in its religious institutions is, on the whole, one of blind obedience, personal dependence, patronage and privileges, while its secular institutions (schools, colleges, hospitals) tend to reflect the values of bourgeois society. Even the caste system has found its way into the ranks of Christians. Politically, Indian Christianity has always sided with whoever happened to be at the helm of affairs. Nor could it have done otherwise.

Only by allying itself with the powers that be could it safeguard its economic interests, especially the free inflow of foreign money. Further, the type of religiosity it represents dovetails, in the main, with that of popular Hinduism. Both religions hold fast the distinction between the pure and the impure, cultic priesthood, the veneration of images, and pietistic devotions. The figure of Christ, who had already taken on the features of a Hellenistic God, became further assimilated to the gods of Hinduism. He has lost much of his uniqueness and has, consequently, little new to give to India.

The root of this ambivalence lies in Christianity's failure to radically criticize its own self-understanding as well as its understanding of non-Christian religions. To substantiate my point, let me make a brief assessment of the current Catholic position in this regard.

From the Catholic point of view it is asked, How can the church use the wealth of Indian culture for the fulfillment of her mission? The answer is given in *Gaudium et Spes* as follows: "The Church, living in varied circumstances in the course of centuries, has made use of various cultures in order to spread and explain Christ's message in her preaching to all nations, to examine and understand it more thoroughly, and to express it more aptly in her liturgical celebrations and in the life of the diverse communities of the faithful."[1] On the surface, the statement is beyond criticism, but, in reality, it is riddled with ambiguities. First, the focus is not on the kingdom of God and its justice but on the church. Non-Christian cultures are seen as but a means to explain her message and express her life. Universal history is thus subordinated to the history of the church. It is also implied there is a hard core of liturgy and doctrine that is eternal and immutable, valid for all peoples and ages. There is no recognition of the fact that what is usually taken for the hard core contains much that is the product of the western cultural history.

This whole approach is based on the belief in the lordship of Christ. The "Decree on the Missionary Activity of the Church" says: "Thus, in imitation of the plan of the Incarnation, the young churches, rooted in Christ and built up on the foundation of the Apostles, take to themselves in a wonderful exchange all the riches of the nations which were given to Christ as an inheritance."[2] Now, the lordship of Christ is not a notion that forms part of the self-awareness of the historical Jesus. It is rather the product of early Christianity's search for compensation in the face of the non-advent of the Kingdom. It, in turn, provided theoretical justification for a missiology of conquest. If the wealth of the whole world belongs to Christ by right, what is wrong with the church, his bride, taking de facto possession of it? How very different was the perspective of Jesus who admitted no lordship other than that of the one God! The message of the reign of God would be welcomed by all men and women. Not so the lordship of Christ, as it implies the superiority of Christians over the rest of mankind. The average Hindu would reckon it an affront and an act of theological aggression were he told that the culture his forebears produced belongs to Jesus Christ, just as any Christian would if he were told one fine morning that all the wealth of the Christian tradition belongs to Siva or Vishnu by right.

No less problematic is the attempt to define the meaning of non-Christian cultures in the light of the so-called theology of incarnation referred to in the passage cited above. The idea of a pre-existing spiritual Logos who "eventually" became incarnate is to be traced to the impact of Greek philosophy on early Christian reflection. It has little to do with Jesus' authentic teaching. For Jesus, as for the prophets before him, God is in a sense eternally incarnate as he is encountered always and only in history. Besides, what does incarnation mean in respect of cultures? If it means that Jesus' message of the new age must assume the idiom and language of the people, none would disagree. If, further, it means that the church herself must become enfleshed in the culture of India, many problems crop up. Is not the church already incarnate in the alien culture of the West? If so, how can she take on the body of yet another culture? Again, what is that culture in which she is to become incarnate? Is it the culture of the ruling classes or that of the ruled? How can a church that has already come to terms with the culture of the status quo identify herself with the culture of protest and dissent?

Nor may we overvalue the church's role of redeeming cultures. Such a role is implicit in the official pronouncements of the church. One such pronouncement reads, "The good tidings of Christ constantly renews the life and culture of fallen man; it combats and eliminates the errors and evils resulting from the ever threatening allurements of sin."[3] Again, "Particular traditions, together with the individual patrimony of each family of nations, can be illumined by the light of the Gospel and then be taken up into Catholic unity."[4] Of course, nothing is said here directly of the redeeming role of the church. But in so far as the church is the official interpreter and vehicle of the tidings of Christ, the church too may be said to be entrusted with the task of purifying and illumining cultures. No doubt the message of Jesus can inspire various peoples to initiate a critique of their respective cultures, as has happened, to a degree, in our own country. But there arises the embarrassing question, "How is it that the same message has failed to purge the church of beliefs and practices that are not in harmony with it?" Might it not be because the *purifying, illumining* power of the Gospel has been neutralized by the concrete reality of the church? If that is the case, the more urgent task confronting her today is to engage in an anguishing self-assessment and self-renewal. Else the non-Christian could well retort, Physician, heal thyself.

It follows that in order to be a subversive-creative force in Indian society, Christianity must, on the one hand, radically revise its traditional self-understanding and repudiate all complicity with the culture of the ruling castes and classes. What this calls for is nothing less than a revolution of consciousness within the churches. Until that happens, the question as to what contribution Christianity can make to the creation of a truly socialist culture will remain a merely academic one. Hence our option to focus on the historical Jesus.

THE INDIAN PRESENCE OF JESUS

The historical Jesus did not land on the Indian soil directly from some heaven above. Paradoxically, his life and message was mediated by the same churches that had thrown a veil over him. Neither dogma nor cult nor institutions could totally smother his message of freedom and love. The light he was radiated, as it were, through the pores of the organized church: through a witness of service to the sick, the disabled, and the unwanted, and through teaching the Bible as literature. And with Jesus a new humanism entered the mainstream of Indian history, a humanism that proclaimed the equality of all men and women irrespective of race, caste or color. So also a new religiosity indissolubly bound up with concern for one's fellow human beings.

Unlike the Christ of dogma, the Jesus of history had an impact that reached far beyond the confines of the Christian community. He has left an imprint on the consciousness of large sections of the intelligentsia. Gandhi was deeply influenced by the Sermon on the Mount.[5] His disciple, Vinoba Bhave, was a devout student of the Gospels. The pilgrimages he made on foot were modelled on Jesus' sending out the disciples on their mission. The Ramakrishna Mission was founded on the Christmas eve of 1886 after its founder, Swami Vivekananda, told his followers the story of Jesus and exhorted them "to become Christs in their turn."[6] Nehru spoke of Jesus as a "great rebel" against the existing social order.[7] Ram Manohar Lohia wrote: "Christ is undoubtedly a figure of love and suffering, than which there has been no other figure in history. Buddha and Socrates are probably greater in wisdom or even in the fine feeling, but are they greater in love?"[8] For M. N. Roy, original Christianity represented the revolt of man against the tyranny of the Jewish God and the despotism of imperial Rome, and the Sermon on the Mount contained the highest moral ideals ever conceived by human imagination.[9] Ambedkar, the author of the Indian constitution, spoke of the Buddha and Jesus as the two personalities that captivated him most.[10] Not even Indian Communists have anything but praise for Jesus of Nazareth. One of their great leaders spoke of him as a prophet whose ideals and values conformed to the needs and desires of millions of men in their time and for centuries afterwards.[11] The figure of Jesus has had an irresistible fascination for modern literary writers. Authors of repute have written dramas, poems, and novels on Gospel themes.[12] Symbols, similes and metaphors of biblical origin have found their way into the language of the people.

The impact of Jesus, however, was too diffuse and vague and, perhaps, too confined to the educated classes to be a significantly creative force in India. It could not become collective praxis. How could it, considering the conservative preaching and practice of the churches? As far as the Catholic Church is concerned, the situation changed for the better with the Second Vatican Council. In its wake there has been a renewed interest in the Bible and in the historical origins of Christianity. The perception has dawned on many thinking Christians, and the Jesus of the Gospels is more relevant for their life than much that official Christianity has to offer, that theology and tradition had served to obscure his visage and soften down his message. The encounter with the historical Jesus has inspired them to join popular struggles for justice. It is in this context that we pose the question what contribution the Jesus tradition can make to the revolution of consciousness India needs.

WHAT THE JESUS TRADITION CAN GIVE TO INDIA

We should first rid ourselves of the illusion that the Gospels contain the answer to every problem our people are facing. Jesus was no social theorist, no authority on the strategy of social change. But as a prophet whose life changed the very course of history, he can, as will be shown in the pages that follow, help energize the positive forces in Indian society that seek to transcend what is obsolescent in our worldview, religiosity and ethos and to initiate a humanizing praxis.

FROM THE CYCLE TO THE DIALOGICAL VIEW OF HISTORY

For the average Indian, life follows the pattern of the ever rotating wheel. This is because his view of history has been formed on the basis of cosmic processes. In nature everything follows the rhythm of emergence, decay, and re-emergence. Plants spring up from the earth, grow, and decay, thus returning to where they came from but only to sprout once again in a fresh spurt of life. The seasons too follow a pattern of birth, death, and rebirth. The Indian mind has always thought of man as part of this cosmic process and consequently subject to the law of cyclic return. It sees history as "a perpetual creation, perpetual preservation and perpetual destruction."[13] The world emanates from Brahman into which it is reabsorbed at the end of every world period (*kalpa*) and where it remains in a state of pure potency until it emanates again, thus initiating a new cycle. The world periods and the periods of repose that follow form, consecutively, the days and nights of Brahman.[14]

Inherent in this view of time is the principle of inevitable deterioration. Each cosmic aeon unfolds itself in a sequence of progressive deterioration. At one end is the age of perfection (*Kritayuga*) and at the other a period of universal misery, evil and untruth (*Kaliyuga*). The present human race has been living in *Kaliyuga* for the last 5,063 years and will have to live through another 420,000 years before it will see the end of this age of ever-increasing decadence.

The cyclic understanding of time has serious implications for man's attitude to life. It may lead him to either indifference towards the past or glorification of it. To indifference, because the unending creation and destruction of the universe makes the achievements of the past devoid of any real meaning; to the glorification of the past, because the principle of progressive deterioration involves belief in the golden age. It is the latter attitude which has characterized the Indian mind to the present day. There is much truth in the oft-repeated saying that India is a country where nothing is forgotten. The tenacity with which people cling to age-old practices points to a certain nostalgia for the bygone. But an uncritical affirmation of the past is not a properly historical attitude and is characteristic of people who have not come of age. Maturity requires that one opposes oneself to the past in order to transcend it, without, however, sacrificing the genuine values realized in it.

The cyclic conception of time has also prevented the birth of a vision of the future that does justice to true human aspirations. In a repetitive pattern of world cycles there is no scope for progress and maturation. The values of the present are not carried over into the future but are doomed to eventual destruction. All that man creates, therefore, is stamped with the sign of death. Nor is the new creation that follows the night of Brahman any richer for the achievements of earlier ages. The end being nothing more than a mere return to the beginning, nothing new, nothing original, ever appears in history. Such a perspective is apt to beget a sense of futility and boredom.

The past is no more; the future is yet to be. The present alone is given to man, to redeem the past and father the future. It is in the present that he is called upon to fulfill the task of self-creation. In the cyclic view of things the now pales into insignificance. It is emptied of its unique, irreplaceable quality as one's present life is but a link in the endless chain of existences. Moreover, since the past is not assumed by the present, and the present will not find a home in the future, man is condemned to live in the oppressive solitude of the now. The now contains no other invitation but to flee from it.

In order to mobilize her potential for self-creation and world-creation, India will have to leave behind the cyclic notion of *time*. The challenge is not anything unique to her, as though resulting from the very mental constitution of her people. Other nations have had to face the same challenge and have done so successfully. The early Hebrews had a cyclic conception of time. So also the Greeks, even of the time of Plato and Aristotle. But all of them were able to get free of the cosmic wheel and step out into the open space of history. We, on our part, for long got stuck at the cyclic phase. Only in recent centuries were we able to make a breakthrough, thanks to the impact of western civilization and the advance made in science and technology. But the most decisive factor hastening the process has been the day-to-day struggles of the exploited classes, following closely upon the struggle against colonialism. It is, above all, through organized action that the masses are learning that they are not mere cogs in the ever rotating cosmic wheel but creators of their own future. In reinforcing this trend the Jesus tradition can play a significant role.

Jesus did not propound any view of history but lived the dialectic of negativity—which is the mainspring of historical growth—to its last consequences. He was born into a tradition charged with the power of a historic negation, the defiant refusal of the Hebrews to slavery under the Pharaoh of Egypt. This negation had for its reverse side an affirmation of freedom crystallized into a project of hope, the hope of settling down in the land of Canaan flowing with milk and honey. The same dialectic of negation and affirmation, of protest and hope, later found powerful expression in the prophets—in their critique of social injustice and political corruption, on the one hand, and in their project of a future of justice and peace, on the other. And Jesus stands out as the one great prophet in whose word, deed and death the dialectic of negativity worked itself out to the full. His no to injustice, religious bondage, and political domination at once sums up and radicalizes all previous prophetic protest and project. And the Cross becomes the most telling symbol of man's refusal to be enslaved and of his resolve to march forward to fuller life. The dialectic of negativity governing universal history finds its concrete, concentrated expression in the personal life and death of Jesus of Nazareth. With him world history enters a new phase.

From where did Moses, the prophets, and Jesus receive this world-transforming power of negating and creating? Undoubtedly from their experience of God. And here we touch upon what is most specific to the Judaeo-Christian religious experience. The prophets experienced God, above all, as an unconditional challenge to break loose from all fetters and set out on the road to freedom which He himself is. To encounter God in this fashion was to take into one's own heart the absolute negation that the divine is, the negation of all that cripples and debases the human. It was like swallowing a flame, which, in turn, consumes the world. So that whoever met God was bound to exclaim, "Can any of us live with a devouring fire? Can any live in endless burning?"[15] Such a person became himself a power that creates the world anew. Hence, the relevance of Jesus' prophetic experience for the millions in India who long to see the birth of a new social order in which every man will be brother to his neighbor.

FROM ESCAPE TO TRANSCENSION

Consistent with its cyclic understanding of human existence, the Indian mind conceives liberation (*mukti*) as release from history itself. The goal of life is to realize freedom from death,[16] mortality,[17] and the womb,[18] from phenomenal existence,[19] and unreality,[20] from sin and the "knots of the heart,"[21] from good and evil,[22] from darkness,[23] from material nature,[24] from

180 SEBASTIAN KAPPEN

the bondage of works,[25] from desire,[26] from suffering and pain,[27] and from illness.[28] The object of the human quest, however, is not merely freedom *from* but also freedom *for*, freedom for serenity,[29] for peace,[30] for unfailing joy,[31] for seeing one's Self as the self of all,[32] for union with Brahman,[33] for participation in divine being.[34]

This way of looking at human liberation is based on the assumption that what constitutes alienation is not a mode of human existence but the very *fact* of human existence. One can, therefore, speak only of liberation from history, not of the liberation *of* history. Nature and the product of labor are excluded from the realm of freedom. Such a view of the end can create an attitude of escape and act as a mental block to refashioning nature and society. There is, however, in the Indian tradition another view which seems the goal of life in the attainment of heaven (*svarga*) where man will enjoy the company of gods. Here cosmic existence is not left behind. For, even the gods are subject to the law of *karma* and *samsara*. Nonetheless, this view also fails to recognize the liberation of what humans create in history. Hence, the need for a new concept of liberation that is in tune with the demands of collective action for social change.

Here the Jesuan vision of the ultimate future becomes highly relevant. The reign of God he proclaimed is not a new creation in total discontinuity with past. Nor is it but the last phase in a unilinear evolution of history. It will be rooted in our earth and in our history. "Blessed are the meek, for they shall inherit the earth." In the humanized universe of the future, man will have land, houses, brothers, sisters, and mothers hundred-fold; those who mourn will have their tears wiped away; the hungry will be satisfied; and all will see right prevail and peace reign supreme. The "new heaven and the new earth" is none other than our heaven and earth suffused with love divine and human. While preserving whatever is good in human creation, it will leave behind everything tainted with sin. Only in this sense of dialectical transcension may we speak, from the Jesuan point of view, of mankind's liberation from nature and history.[35]

FROM COSMIC TO ETHICAL RELIGIOSITY

Orthodox Hindu religiosity tends to lack genuine humanizing power. True, Hinduism enjoins injunctions and taboos in regard to individual and social life. But the moral law (*dharma*) is generally assimilated to the cosmic law (*rita*). The performance of the duties inherent in one's caste (*jati-dharma*), clan (*kula-dharma*) and individual avocation (*svadharma*) is meant to ensure the harmonious functioning of the cosmos.[36] To be moral in this context means conforming to tradition. Even such conformity is, in the final analysis, no more than a means towards attaining liberation, which lies beyond good and evil.

Moreover, in the cosmic perspective of unending emanations and dissolutions, the individual person is divested of all absolute value. What constitutes personhood, the capacity for self-determination, is sacrificed to the determinism of cosmic evolution and involution. And where the abiding value of the person is not recognized, there can be no universal love, no all-embracing solidarity. Instead, one sees one's fellowman either as an element in a predetermined social structure (family, caste) or as an evanescent manifestation of the creative power (*maya*) of the Absolute, not as a being worth loving in his own right. Only as members of family or caste do individuals become subjects of rights and obligations. Within these institutions the average Indian knows how to relate to others; outside them he is at a loss, with neither norms nor guidelines to go by. That is why in the political sphere of bourgeois democracy, which recognizes the equality of all before the law, the Indian behaves as though he is above all law. Equipped with the particularistic morality of caste, he is unable to cope with the universal morality of citizenship. Here lies the root of the crisis of morality in contemporary India.

The rudiments, however, for a creative morality of universal love can be found in the Indian tradition itself: in the ethical teaching of the Buddha and the saints of the Bhakti movement. They need to be rediscovered and their hidden powers released. Here the Jesus tradition can act as a stimulant. For, the God whom Jesus encountered is one who reveals himself as love and calls upon human beings to love one another.[37] He is an angry God, angry with all those who trample upon their weaker brethren. Of course, the angry God is not unknown to the people of India. Indian art and the Puranas depict Siva, Kali and even Vishnu as emitting the fire of wrath and destruction.[38] But theirs is an anger directed not against unlove and injustice but against demonic, cosmic forces. It is not instinct with moral indignation but is a manifestation of the primal creative-destructive energy underlying the world process. The same holds true of most saints and ascetics of Indian mythology. Their wrath is not born of love; it is only a manifestation of the magical energy accumulated through asceticism. In contrast, the anger of Yahweh is the violence of love seeking to exterminate the love of violence on the part of the mighty. Hence, it is that the religious experience of Jesus is charged with the ethical power to uproot and to plant, to demolish and to build up. Only by appropriating this religiosity of creative love will India be able to overcome the divisiveness of caste and the inhumanity of existing social conditions.

FROM INDIVIDUAL TO COMMUNITARIAN SALVATION

The idea of collective salvation is foreign to the Indian religious tradition. Each individual is left to work out his liberation on his own. The reasons for this are both socio-historical and ideational. Historically, what India has succeeded in realizing is some form of organic social unity, not any real community. The nearest she came to a community was in tribal society when property was owned in common and all important decisions were taken on the basis of consensus among tribal chiefs and elders. But tribal society broke up, giving way to the divisive unity of caste. Within the system of caste, the lower castes were subordinated to the higher ones, and, within each caste, the individual to the collective centre of decision making. Nevertheless, within caste system and within each social group there was at least a semblance of community, some sense of collective responsibility. For, even the servile castes had some rights which their masters could not ignore. Today even this alienated unity is eroded by the disruptive power of capitalist exploitation. And the individual is exposed to the war of all against all. If any genuine sense of community remains it is only in those tribal societies which have successfully refused to be integrated into caste society and have managed to maintain their autonomy. For the mass of people historical experience provided no basis for the notion of communitarian salvation.

On the ideational plane, since history was viewed in cyclic terms, the community of men and women could not emerge as an ultimate value, destined as it is to be reabsorbed into the Absolute. The belief in karma and samsara also led to the devaluation of the community. How could one have a sense of human solidarity if in the life to come one might find oneself demoted to the level of an animal or raised to the status of a god?

The attempt to compensate for the loss of community resulted in the idea of the metaphysical unity of all. The Upanishadic equation, "Thou art That" (tat tvam asi) means that the ultimate ground of the individual self and the ultimate ground of the world are one and the same. Which, in turn, implied that, in their profoundest being, all men and women are the same Atman-Brahman. Such an understanding of the unity of mankind could easily be reconciled with actual social inequality. As Ram Manohar Lohia wrote, "Hinduism has given its votaries, the commonest among them, the faith of the metaphysical equality or oneness between man and man, as has never been the lot of man elsewhere. Alongside of this faith in metaphysical equality goes the most heinous conduct of social inequality."[39] For the abstract concept of the oneness of all humans not to become an ideology of legitimation, it must be transposed to historical categories and concretized in social relations. Neo-Hinduism, is, in fact, moving in that direction. Here is how a Marxist theoretician sums up the trend: "The self was no more abstracted from life. The self was the social self that could find its fullest being only in social life. Self-realization or the realization of the identity of the individual self with the universal self meant the identification of oneself with the whole community. Man could realize himself only in other men, in the totality of human existence, that of Brahman."[40]

The quest for a new societal humanism brings the Indian tradition closer to the Judaeo-Christian. The Hebrew idea of the collective destiny of mankind is rooted in the unity of tribal life, the collective experience of slavery in Egypt and in the organized march into the Promised Land. Jesus is heir to the same idea. The nodal point of his message is not the salvation of the isolated individual but the final reconciliation and reintegration of humanity as a whole. The project of the reign of God involves the emergence of a universal community, which will sacrifice neither the individual to the collectivity nor collectivity to the individual.[41]

FROM THE CULTURE OF FEAR TO THE CULTURE OF FREEDOM

If the West has developed a culture of craving for pleasure, profit and power, India, on her part, has perfected a culture of fear. Fear seems to pervade every aspect of life. There is the fear of being defiled by things, events, gestures, persons. Eating, drinking, sleeping, touching, mating, working, all become potential sources of pollution. Man fears woman as a threat to ritual purity and moral integrity. Woman, in turn, fears man's sexual violence and social dominance. And all, men and women, are afraid of the spirits, good and evil, hovering about and menacing illness, destruction and death. Under the grip of fear, the human spirit withers away and creativity dies. Neither literature nor art nor the sciences could develop in such a climate of fear. No wonder commodity production and artistic creation could flourish untrammelled only outside the pale of caste society as among the followers of Buddhism and Jainism. The ethos of fear, however, is much less in the lower rungs of caste hierarchy and is all but absent among the tribals.

Of this culture of fear Jesus' message is the antithesis. He repudiated the distinction between the pure and the impure, a distinction which is at the source of much fear in all religions. True, he believed in the existence of demons, but he showed through word and deed that anyone who surrenders himself to the divine is master over them. By proclaiming the primacy of man over the Sabbath, he set man free *from* the fear of guilt arising from the violation of man-made laws, and free *for* the enjoyment of sex, love, friendship and beauty. His message, therefore, is an antidote for that spirituality of self-castration—coupled with its own opposite of naked hedonism and debauchery—propagated by the Brahminic tradition.

LEARNING FROM THE INDIAN TRADITION

Every prophet is a product of his age, conditioned by a specific culture and conjuncture of history. This applies to Jesus as well. Though his life and message does set the pattern of authentic human existence for all times to come and for all peoples, they do not exhaust the plenitude of the divine. His religious experience has its own wealth and limitations just as similar experiences in other cultural and historical contexts have their own. The Jesus tradition can, therefore, be enriched by dialogue with other religions. I shall now proceed to indicate some aspects of the Indian religious tradition which the disciples of Jesus would do well to assimilate.

THE IMMANENCE OF THE ABSOLUTE OTHER

Jesus experienced God as *in* the world and yet beyond it. But he saw transcendence-immanence more in ethical than in ontic terms. That is, God transcends the world as the unconditional negation of injustice and unlove. He is the absolute Other to the evil than man begets. For the same reason, he is also immanent in the world as the One who affirms human fullness and freedom. To believe in divine transcendence, therefore, means translating into praxis the divine no to whatever degrades the human. Of course, ontic transcendence and immanence are not denied; rather, they are presupposed. This, essentially prophetic, experience of God is suited to founding and sustaining moral endeavor on the part of man. For, the believer cannot leave the scene of history. He has to seek the Unconditioned in the conditioned, the Absolute in the relative. The present is thus endowed with an ethical density and tragic finality.

But this way of encountering the divine has its limitations. It lends itself easily to an all too anthropomorphic conception of God as a person. Personhood evokes the idea of a centre of willing and loving, distinct from, and opposed to, both nature and other personal centres. Hence, the temptation to view God as standing outside man and nature, as though the universe were something added to the divine. Moreover, it is difficult to experience a personal God as the all-pervasive presence, as the One who is in everything and in whom everything is. So it is important for the Jesus tradition to dialogue with indigenous religiosity which stresses the ontic indwelling of the divine in nature and society. Both in the cosmic religion of the masses and the gnostic religion of the élite, the divine is one with the world of names and forms. In this perspective, God is neither personal nor impersonal but transpersonal, not only being but also becoming, reveals himself not only *in* but also as nature and history. Openness to this tradition will help Jesus' disciples to experience the ethical God of the Bible as the Absolute that becomes what he is in and through the world process.

DISCOVERING THE SELF WITHIN

While popular religion sought God in the world without, among the élite there was a search for him in the world within, in the inner recesses of the human spirit. The aim here was the discovery of the Self beneath the self, of the Atman that is identical with the Brahman. To this end was harnessed the technique of asceticism and integration called Yoga. Whether an experience of God can be engineered is a moot question. I personally do not think so. In any case, my concern is to highlight the type of humanism this kind of search for the divine promotes. The technique of Yoga involved withdrawal from the world of senses, from the world of action and passion, and the activating of the subliminal forces latent in the deeps of the human spirit. It sought to create the fully integrated man, self-possessed and serene amid the thousand strains and stresses of daily life. Here is how the Gita pictures the fully integrated man:

"That man I love from whom the people do not shrink and who does not shrink from them, who is free from exaltation, fear, impatience, and excitement. I love the man who has no expectation, is pure and skilled, indifferent, who has no worries and gives up all enterprise . . . I love the man who hates not nor exults, who mourns not nor desires, who puts away both pleasant and unpleasant things . . . I love the man who is the same to friend and foe, whether he be respected or despised, the same in heat and cold, in pleasure as in pain, who has put away attachment and remains unmoved by praise or blame, who is taciturn, contented with whatever comes his way, having no home, of steady mind."[42]

Admittedly, the spirituality enshrined here can breed cosmic pessimism, escapism, and even absolute unconcern for the welfare of one's fellowmen. It has, in fact, helped the upper castes to reconcile religion with ruthless exploitation. There is also the danger that one may mistake certain heightened experiences induced by *yogic* concentration for the self-unveiling of the divine. Nevertheless, the pursuit of the inner self has a positive value insofar as it serves as a means towards freedom from the tyranny of lust, acquisitiveness, hatred and violence. It can show the way to that mastery of the self so highly priced by the Buddha, who said, "If a man should conquer in battle a thousand and a thousand more, and another man should conquer himself, his would be the greater victory, because the greatest of victories is the victory over oneself."[43] The technique of Yoga can also help create the psychic prerequisites for the humanization of revolutionary praxis. The Jesus tradition must, therefore, incorporate the *yogic* ideal of detachment in the spirituality of commitment to the Kingdom and its justice.

THE MOTHERHOOD OF THE EARTH

Jesus saw nature as the object of divine action as is clear from his saying, "Consider how the lilies grow in the fields; they do not work, they do not spin; and yet, I tell you, even Solomon in all his splendor was not attired like one of these. But if that is how God clothes the grass in the fields, which is there today, and tomorrow is thrown on the stove, will he not all the more clothe you?"[44] Familiar with the book of Genesis, he must also have viewed nature as the object of human action in response to the divine call to fill the earth and subdue it. Yet one has the feeling that there is something wanting in this way of looking at nature characteristic of the Hebrew tradition. It is too male, too aggressive and too remote. There is no real sense of kinship with the earth, possibly because the Jews lived in desert regions inhospitable to man and beast alike.

How different is the traditional Indian attitude to the earth! To the Indian mind, nature is not something to be conquered or manipulated. She is the great mother, the womb of all creation, the source of all fertility. The same life force that courses through her veins also throbs in the human body. The Indian sees nature less from the pragmatic than from the religious, emotive point of view. The sense of kinship with the earth finds poignant expression in the great poetic work, Sakuntalam, where the heroine, on leaving the hermitage where she had been brought up, tenderly bids farewell to every plant she had nurtured and the deer she had lovingly fed from her own hands.

It was from nature too that man learned his first lessons in the art of living. So the Buddha could tell his followers: "Develop a state of mind like the earth Rahula. For on the earth men throw clean and unclean things, dung and urine, spittle, pus, and blood, and the earth is not troubled or repelled or disgusted. ... And similarly with fire, which burns all things, clean and unclean; and with air, which blows upon them all; and with space, which is nowhere established."[45] For our forebears, nature was also the self-revelation of the divine; the sound of Brahman could best be heard in the rustling of leaves and the chirping of birds and the music of the sea. So in times past the seekers after truth withdrew into the solitude of the forest to feel the divine in the heartbeat of Mother Earth. Even for the common people the things of nature had a symbolic value over and above their mere use-value.

Today, with the development of commodity production, nature is being reduced to a sum of exchange values. Man's umbilical bond with the earth is being severed and human existence impoverished. All the greater, therefore, is the need for us to recapture something of the traditional aesthetic, mystical approach to the earth.

Hindus who happen to read these pages might feel somewhat irked by the pre-eminence I attached to the Jewish tradition. True, I do affirm the unique position of Jesus as one who ushered in a new phase in the planetary evolution of the human spirit. He stands for the supersession of all religions including Christianity and heralds a future when human beings will worship God not in man-made temples but in spirit and truth. That future is also the future of India. But the higher phase he inaugurated had already dawned, however simply, in the message of the Buddha and later reasserted itself in the Bhakti movement. But these gropings towards an ethical, creative religiosity could not come to fruition in the face of opposition from Brahminic Hinduism. What I claim, therefore, is not the superiority of Christianity over the Indian religious tradition but the superiority of the humanizing religiosity of the Buddha, the radical Bhaktas and Jesus over the magico-ritualistic religiosity of orthodox Hinduism and the deprophe-ticized religiosity of tradition-bound Christianity.

If, on the other hand, Indian religiosity can enrich the Jesus tradition, it is because the former had developed for centuries in the immediacy of man's relationship with nature and society and has for that very reason been able to maintain the sense of oneness of the cosmic, the human, and the divine. Jesuan prophecy must appropriate this sense of oneness and wholeness, while India must make her own the Galilean's dream of the Total Man.

NOTES

1. *Gaudium et Spes*, 58.
2. *Decree on the Missionary Activity of the Church*, 22.
3. *Gaudium et Spes*, 58.
4. *Decree on the Missionary Activity of the Church*, 22.
5. See William Stewart, *Christian Presence and Modern Hinduism* (London: SCM Press, 1964), pp. 62-64.
6. Ibid., p. 84.
7. Quoted by M. M. Thomas, *The Secular Ideologies of India and the Secular Meaning of Christ* (Madras: CLS, 1976), p. 76.
8. Ibid., p. 79.
9. Ibid., p. 180.
10. Ibid., p. 151.
11. Ibid., p. 116.
12. An instance is *Magdalena Mariam* (Mary of Magdalene) by Vallathol, Poet-Laureate of Kerala. The new-wave poems in Malayalam by Satchidanandan, Kadammanitta, Chullikad and others abound in Christian symbols and motifs.
13. *Vishnu Purana*, 1.7.
14. Mircea Eliade, *Images and Symbols* (London: Harvill Press, 1952), pp. 62ff.
15. Is. 33:14.
16. *Brihadaranyaka Upanishad*, 3.1.5.
17. Ibid., 1.3.38.
18. *Svetasvatara Upanishad*, 3.2.5; also Gita, 13:24,26.
19. *Mundaka Upanishad*, 3.2.5.
20. *Brihadaranyaka Upanishad*, 1.3.28.
21. *Mundaka Upanishad*, 3.2.8.
22. Gita, 6:9.
23. *Brihadaranyaka Upanishad*, 1.3.28.
24. Gita, 13-34.
25. Ibid., 2:29; 2:28.
26. Ibid., 6:24.
27. Ibid., 6:23.
28. Ibid., 2:71.
29. Ibid., 2:64.
30. Ibid., 2:70; 4:39; 5:12.
31. Ibid., 5:21.
32. Ibid., 5:7.
33. Ibid., 5:24; 6:27; 14:26.
34. Ibid., 8:5; 13:18.
35. S. Kappen, *Jesus and Freedom* (Maryknoll, N.Y.: Orbis Books, 1977), pp. 53-67.

36. Heinrich Zimmer, *Myths and Symbols in Indian Art and Civilization* (New York: HarperTorch Books, 1962), pp. 13-16.

37. Kappen, pp. 60-64.

38. *Hindu Myths*, Penguin Classics, 1975, passim.

39. Thomas, p. 70.

40. K. Damodaran, *Man and Society in Indian Philosophy* (New Delhi: People's Publishing House, 1970), pp. 81-82.

41. Kappen, pp. 97-98.

42. *Gita*, 12:13-20.

43. *Dhammapada*, tr. Juan Mascaro (Penguin Classics, 1978), p. 50.

44. Mt. 6:30.

45. *Majjhima Nikaya*, see *Sources of Indian Tradition*, comp. William Theodore de Bary, et al. (Delhi: Motilal Banarsidass, 1988, reprint), pp. 111-112.

12

The Hope of Liberation
Lessens Man's Inhumanity:
A Contribution to Dialogue
at Village Level

MICHAEL RODRIGO

When old words die out on the tongue, new melodies break forth from the heart: and where the old tracks are lost, new country is revealed with its wonders. —Rabindranath Tagore, in *Gitanjali*, 37

To the Buddhist peasant of Uva-Wellassa in Sri Lanka, who for over a century bore the brunt of British colonialism from which he has never fully recovered nor ever will; to the Catholic seminary professor who after twenty years of Christian theology, ways of worship and philosophy suddenly went over to a contextual seminary program under a dynamic bishop; to two Salvatorian religious sisters who, trained in Rome, branched out, one to village health, the other into teaching theology and surveying village reality, the inner call, heard differently but firmly, must have been the same. The three Christians will say in faith that it is the imperious yet reassuring call of the Risen Christ hidden among the people, especially in the countryside ("I'll go before you into Galilee"). The peasant has already said with his life that he and his *embula*-carrying wife felt an urge to better the situation of all his people, and so, felt they had to be with those "who came to be with them."[1]

THE PRESENCE WITH THE PEOPLE

Accordingly, we—a Buddhist young man of thirty called Somadasa and I—came to an *illuk*-infested (*imperata cylindrica*), two-acre block. 140 miles east of Sri Lanka's capital city of Colombo, to an area in which *puranagam* (traditional villages) eked out an existence side by side with new colonizations by natural groups, mostly of Sinhala Buddhist peasants who formed over 95% of the people of the area. It was on July 11, 1980, the Feast of St. Benedict. The two Salvatorian sisters came on the 13th of June, the Feast of St. Anthony, 1931. Within a fortnight, a Buddhist monk asked us when we would be leaving the palace, for he thought for sure that we would be soon baptizing the people. A small-time businessman who detested us when we picked a few unlettered boys to teach them their own language, Sinhala, abused us in public, saying: "Why mix up religions? You see to your own religion; we'll see to ours." In 1982, after a particularly trying drought in this Dry Zone area of Sri Lanka, when we had listed 89 farmers for drought relief in a twenty-page report on how they incurred the losses and to what extent, the monks joined us and went for redress to the state officials. A puny official—the only one available at the time—refused to pay any drought relief. The peasant farmers, the monks and the two sisters and priest turned back, but by evening the local Member of Parliament had been informed that "two religious groups had got together for redress for the farmers," and on the morrow, the Buddhist monk of Alutwela visited us and said: "We must continue to work together for the rights of man. For whom did the Buddha work? For man. What did your founder, Christ, do? He lived and died for man. I was challenged yesterday by a state official because I went with you and the two sisters for drought relief."[2] We felt "together" in our distress. We hold, therefore, that there are not two histories but only one history of man's distress and of his salvation—liberation. Christians, within the Judeo-Christian tradition, believe that God, El-Shaddai, the Transcendent, became El Imanu (Emmanuel), the God who is *With* us. His power passed into people and the people became sovereign. Biblical covenantal language ever signifies: "I am in you and you are in Me," for God says through patriarch and prophet: "I will be your God and you will be my people" (Exodus 19: Jeremiah 31:31).

Then also the right composition of the Gospel according to Matthew, practically begins and ends with the word with, "They found the child *with* Mary his mother" (Mt. 1:23) and again: "Behold I am *with* you all days," (Matt. 28:19). But in the story of the anointing of Jesus' feet, the same word is used for the poor: "The poor you will always have *with* you." Some people brandish this text and flee responsibility for the poor by merely repeating these lines: "Christ said they will always be with us." But the story is quite other: Judas who held the purse strings did not care for the poor. Christ the poor Man defended Mary's action by quoting a text from the Book of Deuteronomy (15:11) which says: "The needy will never be lacking in the land. This is why I command you to open your hand to your brother, to him who is humiliated and poor in your land." The very text some take as argument against the poor is really an indictment of their reluctance to discover, and come to the aid of, the poor. It is our contention that our being present to the poor peasant here is also our being present to the Christ who identifies himself in some secret way with the poor.

We began this chapter with the Lord's call, and hence we feel it opportune to say that there is a subtle temptation to pride if we feel we are the only group "making the grade" and discerning Christ in the poor. It is easy to try to live like the poor and wag a finger at everyone else as the low grovelling lot, but that would be sinful, non-liberative and so unlike the real poor. It is he who calls. His is a humble, healing presence. He chooses whomsoever he wants to discover his varied presence: he is present in the assembly at the holy Eucharist; present in the minister, in the word proclaimed, present in the Sacrament reserved. The *Priestly Formation* decree, n.8 suggests that "the young cleric be taught to look for Christ in meditation, in the Eucharistic celebration, in the bishop who sends him, in his people, *and in the unbeliever.*" If all our life is an attempt to find his traces, his presence, in faith, then it is a humble task, not one that should fill us with pride.

Our desire is, however, to be more intensely branches in the Vine, so that our presence will show forth the Jesus praxis, our spirituality will be a following of Jesus who did not baptize but was baptized in his culture and proclaimed his suffering and death as the baptism of his preference: "I have a baptism which I must still receive and how great is my distress till it is over" (Lk 12:49-50). He said so to induce us all to a baptism, an illumination or enlightenment (what the Greeks call a *photismos*). Is it not into such a baptism that the suffering masses of rural Asia and the city-state broken-downs have been plunged? Does not this kind of baptism bring forth a peaceful, patient, long-suffering people whose life is often short-lived by the violent banding together of financially high, powerful leaders of elitist groups, and yet whose life is lived in newness and constant hope of betterment, collective and personal, arisen in their hearts?

The mystical union signified by the Vine and branches image is not laid aside when we say that Jesus is Word of God as doing-word, the Verb of God (*dabar* in Aramaic). It is the source of orthodoxy and orthopraxis, of Christian saying and doing, of promise and fulfillment. Our presence must speak to all, as an eloquent presence, to point to the eternal Word, just as the presence, word and activity of the Buddhist must deepen our belief and theirs in the *sanatana dhamma*, the eternal *dhamma* word, the firm word (*Dharma* = *firmus* = *firm*) of stability. Both groups wanting the fulfillment of an undying or a beyond-death truth (*satya*) is our exchange, our dialogy more than our theology.[3]

DIALOGICAL THEOLOGY OR DIALOGY

Out of the turbulence of the mid-sixties, dialogue came forth. Much under the influence of Bonhoeffer's theology, and worried about what the expected decline of traditional religion might do to the relevance of Christianity, Harvey Cox wrote *Secular City*, underlining the tirades of the prophets against mere cult, and Jesus' opposition to the priestly establishment of his own time.

Twenty years later, in 1984, the same author wrote *Religion in the Secular City*, underscoring religion as irrepressible. In no way rendering obsolete the earlier work, it furthers biblical faith as critical of all human religiousness. *Jesus was a subverter of evil.* He was and is seen as a dangerous threat to the bogus pseudo-peace, disorder and injustice that often passes for law and order, peace and national security.

The author introduces a study made by Carl Raschke, which outlines four ways in which students approach the truth question in religion. We need to outline the four ways here to see how Cox's own way may indicate future trends and even confirm our own.

1. A *judgment-less* approach about the validity of their truth; a sympathetic study of various expressions of faith; a watching without evaluating. But Cox suggests that the question Is it true? always arises as a matter of life and death.

2. Study the *faith in human.* It is not a question of comparing systems in dialogue, but of human beings within these systems. Here too, the question of truth is not answered, for one must ask: "What faith will guide my choice?" if the truth-question is personally posited after the description of the religions.

3. A single tradition lies behind various expressions of faith. All religions are variants of a larger whole: a *unity-behind-diversity approach.* Raschke calls it the Hindu solution. Cox suggests that while it can be true, it is not demonstrably true.

4. Panikkar's approach. One neither hides the differences nor trumpets the similarities but one has *awe and ecstasy* — a waiting and listening, a nonaggressive approach like Gandhi's *ahimsa.*

But perhaps it is in Raschke's suggestions and Cox's confirmation of a fifth way that truth indicators may be found. Raschke wishes to go "beyond theology," calling it "dialogy." Cox rightly refuses mere terms and asks: "By dialogy, does Raschke mean something close to what I am calling 'post modern' theology?"[4]

Religion is perhaps the only institution that has an inbuilt critique of itself and of society, but history has always shown that it has notoriously lent itself almost always to a defence of the status quo, thus blunting the liberative edge it has. It is very likely that Raschke castigates as theology what he thinks to be a monolith, but if theology is theologizing or "doing theology," and not the graven-in-stone image he seems to have, then it can also mean dialogy.

Cox repeats what we feel today to be the basic *locus theologicus*, namely, the poor on the march to freedom from all evil. In a first instance, the author says: "Christians meet their fellow human beings of the other great religious traditions, not in a detached or aggressive way but with a willingness to listen together to what the ancient runes say. It is important that this mutual listening take place not in some demarcated religious sphere but in the day-to-day combat and compromise of real life. The inner logic of the strictly academic approach to religious pluralism is leading it out of the academy and into the grimy world in which both fundamentalism and liberation theology are also trying to cope with the same cacophony."[5]

And soon. Cox repeats with emphasis, concluding his twentieth chapter, that the poor are systematically excluded in the inter-religious dialogue, that the favored format dialogue today "is one in which representatives of the various religions of the world—usually scholars or ecclesiastical leaders whose positions make them more attuned to confessional rather than class differences—meet and converse about what unites or separates them. But it is the hard reality of social conflict not the exchange of ideas that creates unity or foments division. Christians who have participated with Hindus and humanists and others in actual conflict against the powers that be 'do theology' in a different way. They do it as part of an emerging world-wide community made up of the despised and rejected of the modern world and their allies. In this new community, as in those tiny, first-century congregations of ex-slaves and day-workers in Colossae and Ephesus, where they had also begun to hear the same good news, the most intransigent of religious, traditional and cultural barriers no longer have the power to divide."[6]

Thus, if dialogue can gently and determinedly induce both parties, both religious groups (and in multi-religious dialogue areas), or all groups, to be prophetic at the service of the poor of God, by socio-political cooperation, then religion and dialogy would have done their obvious duty. Otherwise, dialogue will become only a frustrating task of aimlessly looking at each other and not transforming the world by the richness of a transforming presence.

GIVING WITNESS TO THE LIBERATIVE WORD

The Asian situation demands a clear-cut vision of a just society and of a new humanity which it purports to achieve. If development is truly *de-envelopment,* the removing of the envelope of bonds, then true development and liberation coincide in the release of the broken, and in transformation, not in mere reform of the oppressive and exploitative economic, social, political, cultural structures into a new society.

Then respect for human dignity becomes the creating of a society based on people's needs. If we are committed to them, involved with them and among them, rather than working for them, the very process of decision-making with them will become a transforming presence. We—the Jesus community—will not be mere catalysts, for in the process of a mutual presence, the people and we will be "doing the truth in love," and that transforms us both, when people become the architects of their own destiny.

The transforming presence of the Word in the world is the basis of our transforming presence among the people. The latter presence demands witness or confessing to its truth. To confess is to give witness to, to profess, to proclaim by life-witness: *Fiteor, prophetare*, being allied words. It also signifies today prophesying, correcting, rectifying, conscientizing, denouncing of evil and announcing of good.

The *logos* or word inherent in dialogue is accepted by us Christians as Jesus. In our process of dialogue, we hold this principle: the more Christians present in a Buddhist milieu learn of the Buddha praxis and of the depth-values of Buddhism's holiness (called *sara dharma*) operative among the Buddhists, the more they will come to a better understanding of their own faith in God, in Jesus, in the Jesus praxis, faith in men and women who reveal in their own way one single aim for all humanity, and that is total release from every type of bondage unto freedom.

THREE MOMENTS OF CONFESSING

We therefore present three moments or aspects, rather than phases, in our witness to the total Christ:

i. Confessing Jesus in a Christian context
ii. Confessing the Buddha-Dhamma in a Buddhist context
iii Confessing Jesus in a Buddhist context.

Confessing Jesus in a Christian context

We cannot proclaim Jesus today in the same old way. We must find new ways of living Him out in our life. And that will be a proclamation. The Christian context is accepted as the God-milieu; that is, Jesus is Word of the Father, Son of the Father, who opted for humankind, especially for the poor. Jesus never worked for himself but for the ongoing reign of God, the Kingdom. "The Bible and especially the New Testament presents Christ's work as one of liberation. God himself in the fullness of time sent his Incarnate Son into the world to free men from every form of slavery to which they were subject by reason of sin and of human egoism, from ignorance, destitution, hunger, oppression, hatred, injustice (Gal 4:4-5). Jesus' first preaching was to proclaim the liberation of the oppressed. Sin, the root of all injustice and oppression is in fact an egoistic turning back upon ourselves, a refusal to love God and others and therefore to love God himself. In continuing the prophetic mission of her founder, the Church must more forcefully preach and realize more effectively this liberation of the poor, the outcast and the worker working with others, building with others a world where every man, no matter what his race, religion or nationality can live a fully human life, freed from servitude imposed on him by other men or by natural forces over which he has not enough control."[7]

Jesus made a preferential option for the poor. Crowds (the *ochlos*) followed him, for they felt they were sheep without a shepherd. He loved them with compassion welling from his heart. The Greek verb *splagchni-*

zomai is from the noun *splachnon*, which means intestines, bowels, entrails or heart, those inward parts from which strong emotions arise, a "gut reaction," when Jesus was moved to pity. Those who follow must be like him, be on the side of the poor, *with* them, in all the circumstances of their life. This leads us to a spirit of detachment, release from the bonds of goods and consumerism; it will induce groups to live as did the first Jesus community, the original church of those called by him to go and sell what they had, give to the poor and then follow him.

This one, who opted for the poor to liberate them, loved them so much that he emptied himself to become this form of Eucharist, wherein he presents his body to us as sign and token of the kind of unity he wants all men to have eventually, starting from the now of life. The teaching of Jon Sobrino is relevant here, for he shows that Jesus' action and preaching and prophetic option indicated radical rupture with the synagogal type of religion. Jesus' prophetic option led to his death. So, we should take within the scope of the Eucharist not only the *how* of his life and death but also the *why* of it. Into this *why* comes his comparatively early death, because he stood for the human, fought for the poor. The following of Jesus (cf. Segundo Galilea) demands that we also defend what he defended, loving and preferring what he loved and preferred. In this we risk death ourselves.

It is this Jesus who asked that we preach to all nations—and nations are structures of society that today spew broken-down persons, oppressed, alienated caricatures of what the Father meant his children to be, and this, especially, in the Third World.

If, in third-world countries and elsewhere, the Synod of Justice (1971) is used for catechesis, instruction, education, prayer and reflection-action, we would avoid the senseless controversy on liberation theology and its allied tergiversations in high places. Why fear universal teaching?

The Good News of Jesus is, first of all, himself and his life as being the basis of all endeavour for the follower: "If you wish to be my disciple, you must deny yourself ... if you wish to follow me, sell what you have and give to the poor ... he who loves his life will lose it and he who despises his life in this world will keep it unto life everlasting ... go and do likewise ... love one another as I have loved you ... take up your cross and follow me ..."—these are imperious demands and yet coming from one who is very human and very understanding of our broken selves, one who would not quench the smoking flax nor crush the bruised reed. These demands have Jesus' example or self-emptying (*kenosis* in Philippians 2) as their basis. And yet, herein lies the challenge: It has been done, it can be done. No one who ever faced these challenges found himself discouraged. Jesus lived them out first in his life, showing himself free and forgetful of self.

In the small groups of Christians and religious who come here, we have much sharing of this message of Jesus Poor. We take it as a part of Education for Justice in the spirit of the Synod of Justice mentioned earlier.

The Church's presentation of this liberating Jesus—and his Name is translatable in any language as Saviour-Redeemer-Liberator — must continue in education: "Education demands a renewal of heart, a renewal based on the recognition of sin in its social and individual manifestations. Education will also include and inculcate a truly and entirely human way of life in justice, love, simplicity. Education will awaken a critical sense, which will lead us to reflect on the society in which we live and on its values. In the developing countries, the principal aim of education is for justice, and it consists in an attempt to awaken consciences to a knowledge of the concrete situation and in a call to secure a total improvement: by these means the transformation of the world has already begun."[8]

The open-hearted Jesus-community Christian after the Council (Vat. II) will see in Jesus the narrow way which is indeed the broad way of love for all. He will see in the Buddha the basis of the Buddhist's constant assertion: "*siyalu sattvayo nidukvethva*" (may all beings be happy). In it he would see a constant appeal for self-forgetfulness (*anatta*) in the life of the Buddha. Born of a princely, landowning family, he followed that inner urge of the higher self ("*atta hi attano natho*," self is the lord of self) to leave all things and go search for the truth; he never gave up the search, whether with his mentors Alara the Kalama or Udekka Ramaputta, or with himself, but looked beyond. He used the Dhamma, word, and changed the hearts of many a hearer, helped make the bad good and the good better by his example of selflessness. The four sublime states or *brahmaviharas* — metta, karuna, mudita, upekkha — are operative in Buddhism: they are loving, kindness, compassion, gladness at another's well-being, and equanimity. *Metta* or *maitri* is from *mejjati*, melting, a word so closely knit with the "bowels of compassion" in meaning. In these as in every one of the *pansil* (five precepts) and the *dasaparamita* (ten perfections), there is a radical turning away from self to the Other. When Bhikkhu Kassapa of Ampitiya took a copy of the New Testament to his Buddhist dhamma class on Sunday afternoons, he did so with red-ink markings on every sentence he found helpful to understand selflessness in the Christian way. When the Ven. Alutgama Dhammananda, in 1965, at the Malwatta Vihara, Kandy, wanted a Catholic priest to speak on "self-denial in the life of Christ and self-denial in the Dhammapada (of a Buddhist canon)," he too was looking for the common ground of a common urge to deny self so that others might grow.

Now, the Christian says that to believe in Jesus is to believe that he is divine. Some have money, ambition, power, profits, prestige, self and so forth as gods, as source of meaning and strength and drive. To believe that Jesus is divine is to choose him, to make a deliberate choice of him and what he stands for as our God. By his praxis, Jesus changed the content of the word *God*. If Jesus is our Lord and God, we must allow him to change our image of the unimaginable, transcendent God. Jesus is the Word of God, because he reveals God to us. God does not reveal Jesus to us. God is not the word of Jesus; that is, our ideas about God cannot cast any light on the life of Jesus.

God is the acme, the supreme source of selflessness, says the Christian. In Jesus we begin to see God's plan in its most human and incarnate expression as it reveals God's criteria: his mercy, his justice, his search for the lost sheep, his deep love for the little ones, the little flock, his demands, his love—a "contemplative Christology," as Segundo Galilea terms it.

Albert Nolan, in *Jesus Before Christianity*, holds that, "Our God does not want to be served by us, but wants to serve us; God does not want to be given the highest possible rank and status in our society, but wants to take the lowest place and to be without any rank and status; God does not want to be feared and obeyed, but wants to be recognized in the sufferings of the poor and the weak; God is not supremely indifferent and detached, but is irrevocably committed to the liberation of humankind, for God has chosen to be identified with all people in a spirit of solidarity and compassion. If this is not a true picture of God, then Jesus is not divine. If this is a true picture of God, then God is more truly human, more thoroughly humane, than any human being. God is, what Schillebeeckx has called, a *Deus humanissimus*, a supremely human God."[9]

For the man of faith, therefore, who begins reading the signs of the times as Jesus read them and answered with his life and death, the terminology of static nature of metaphysical realities may seem necessary, but may take second place. And who can blame him, for Christianity is not meant to be a following of Jesus only by academe. It is a real-life matter. Such a man of God, given faith, will say that Jesus' divinity is not an addition to his humanity. In Jesus, the human and the divine have been so united that Jesus' divinity is the transcendent depths of his humanity. Jesus was immeasurably more human than other men and that is what we value when we say he is divine, when he is acknowledged as our Lord and God.[10]

Jesus claimed to be the truth. In him the truth became flesh. (He felt to be a being at complete harmony with God.) Feeling and thinking with the mind and heart of God, he had no need to rely on any authority outside his own rich experience. He showed this all the way, with his life, compassion, passion-death-resurrection.

Confessing the Buddha-Dhamma in a Buddhist context

If we confess to a Total Christ, open on the reality of today's world through the Jesus community which he formed, then the very following of Jesus becomes a Jesus praxis.

It would inevitably lead us to "give honor to whom honor is due and to understand that renown, honor and peace come to all who do good" (Rom. 2:10). We could then proclaim to the world that Muhammad and the Buddha do not belong exclusively to these denominations or ways of life, but to the whole world and to all of mankind.

We in our village felt we had to give witness to the selflessness of the

Buddha, his renunciation, his praxis of detachment, his rejection of *lobha, dosa, moha,* the triple concupiscence, his *samanatma ta* (sense of equality and justice).

Without ever attempting to replace what or whom he "denied," if he did, the Buddha did not refer any glory to himself in his person, but only to the moment of the Enlightenment or its excellence. The manifest intent was: better to be enlightened than not to be; or in later language, it is better to be a *bodhisattva* (one who gives one's life for others) than not to be. There were and have been other Buddhas for other ages, but this Buddha is for this age. This is why the Enlightened One or the self-realized One is regarded as a refuge (a *sarana*). Even if mother or father were to disregard anyone, the *Buddhu-amme* (Buddha as mother) or the *Buddha-piye* (Buddha as father) will be near him/her . . . is an oft heard remark in the village.

Involving the people in decision-making, a week after our arrival here, we invited the people to see if it were opportune to start a clinic day every month. A lengthy discussion on the feasibility and mode of it, as a monthly exercise, proceeded and decision followed: "Plan it as you like; we will provide two nurses to be trained. You consulted us for permission. Go ahead also with our blessing." On the third monthly clinic day, October 1980, D. Karunapala, a youth leader, uttered these words at a *pilisandara* (causerie): "You always induce us to go to *bana* preaching in the temple. The monk's preaching of the *dhamma-word* should form our life. You always say: '*Vairayen, vairaya no samsindeth*' (Hatred is never appeased by hatred but by love alone: Dhammapada), but, tell me, what is the real meaning of 'Buddhuvenava' (becoming a Buddha)? I think it is to do what you are doing here: to see to the sick and distressed. Even the sick man is a Buddha if he leads you to live the Dhamma. If you help him to be cured, you too can become a Buddha. Why should I go to the temple and listen to *bana*? Religion cannot be relegated to the temple, nor life to ritual." A useful, healthy discussion ensued. Hence, our making available some religious space for getting to know the Buddha praxis more deeply made the Dhamma more firm (dharma) in the hearts of people.

Such dialogue is not a question of vogue, fashionableness or expediency. It is born of imminent need and human brotherhood to assert that religion is better than irreligion and that humanity's widest scope must take the cultural and religious, no less than the social and political, into account in the integral life of Man, of men and women, now.

Confessing Jesus in a Buddhist Context

We saw how the contemporary Jesus must be shown forth by today's Jesus community as witness to Jesus. We saw how good it is to give witness to the Truth in a Buddhist context, drawing principles and lines of action from the Buddhist. There seems really no need for a third, because embryonically the open-Jesus message and universal appeal is manifest in the first and second moments already. In other words, if we share our faith in the contemporary Jesus with all Christians, we will surely acknowledge the Buddha's role in liberation. And doing both these we will manifest the true Jesus to the world.

Montchemil is supposed to have said that no one is a proper missionary who having gone to a people, does not see that the Jesus spirit, the saving spirit of love, has been there at work already before him. That is the spirit of openness and kindliness and self-sacrifice best understood by the faithful Christian as much as by the faithful Buddhist.

"I was hungry and you gave me to eat," said Jesus. "I was thirsty and you gave me drink," or again: "I was a stranger and you took me in." So says Christian spirituality, drawing its lines from the Gospel according to Matthew. Going into the village of Illuklanda off Monaragala in 1976 for a survey, we saw a poor man who built a makeshift house and at the end of the day made a shelf of simple planks, placing thereon a pot of water (waterpot for merit, or *pinthaliya*) so that the "poor traveller might slake his thirst." We imitated him here in our hut too, since our first day in this place. Then again, the daily *dana* (midday offering of a meal as alms) and the annual *dansela* (food = gift meal hall for Vesak) are signs of giving the other something to eat and thus satisfying hunger, much as the *pindapatha* (the food placed in the monk's begging bowl) could be a sign of a farming people's prosperity or penury, depending on whether the food is higher or lower than the "equator" of the bowl. Then too, the *ambalama* (the way-farers' inn) was the Buddhist way of saying that he took in the traveller and the stranger. Names like Ambalantota, Ambalangoda in Sri Lanka are quite self-explanatory as wayside inns to welcome the stranger of yore.

Word hidden in the world, Jesus speaks in different ways and presences. But, the earliest presence of Christ, through a baptized group of British invaders, was harmful; the scar remains even if wounds are healed. We will have to let it be proven that ours is not a harmful presence but a presence for the good of the people.

Furthermore, Jesus did not invent the cross. One day I had forgotten to wear my cross-badge and Ran Banda, a small lad, said he would run into the house and get it before I started on my journey. To which the son of a mason replied: "There is really no need to rush to get the cross, because the cross is a sign of sorrow. We know it already. It is a *haras kepima*, an opposition to my will. I wish to do something and I'm called to do something else. See, every door has a lintel and two doorposts. Yesterday my father bought a wire mesh, and it has hundreds of crosses. That is why Jesus took a cross as a sign of his life." This incident took place in September 1980, when our hut was still a-building. The cross was a sign of contradiction, of juncture, of opposites, as universal as ever. Jesus accepted it as a political instrument of torture under the imperialist government of Rome. The cross has never been the same again for a Christian, whether he hangs it round his neck or is stretched on it as on a rack of torture both for himself and his fellow countrymen. St. Paul can still go on saying: "I preach Christ and

Christ crucified," and we feel he would be happy to see the cross emerging from the so-called uninitiated so far away from the Greek wisdom that failed to grasp the folly of the cross.

In March 1981 a *samghikadana* (almsgiving to the Sangha or monkhood) was given to six monks of the area. It had not occurred to us that this might have been the first time. At the *bana*-preaching following the meal, the chief monk announced: "This could well be the first time that a *dana* has been given to Buddhist monks in a Christian place. It is a historic action. I ask Father to come to the temple hall and teach Christianity to our teachers and relate it to other religions." A letter corroborated the invitation the next day.

Or take the Buddhist pilgrimage organized together with the farmers at their request in March 1982 to the ruined cities, to Anuradhapura and its eight holy places. The 48 farmers, and their wives and children, had visited the famed Polonnaruwa Gal Vihara, which had fascinated the Trappist Thomas Merton, and seen the Standing, Seated and Recumbent Buddha. What was their surprise on quietly entering a room to see an enormous, agonizing Christ. In the semi-darkness of the chapel — for it was the community chapel they had entered—the following dialogue took place:

Woman one: "... and who is this? I feel sorry for him. *Ane mata-dukkhai.*"
Woman two: "You see, this is their Christ, their God (*devio*)."
Woman three: "Yes, he also gave his life for others."
Woman one: "Yes, it's just like the Buddha. He also cut himself in pieces as the Jataka story says."
Woman two: "Yes, but that's only a story. It didn't happen."
Woman one: "That may be, but I'm very sorry about this man, Christ. Why did he die such a violent death?"

The priest who overheard was about to leave the chapel when they asked him: "Now tell us the whole story of his death." And they, who were looking for real freedom, listened, knowing full well that speaker and listeners had to be converted to the Truth of selflessness and sharing, justice and peace.

IS JESUS SHOWN FORTH HERE?

Wherever we are, we are the Jesus community and must act and express ourselves the way Jesus wants us to do, for Jesus and the Jesus community have to be one in all that is not sin. If, then, the Jesus community has the mind of Christ and acts like him and in him, those who see the Jesus community will somehow discover the Jesus praxis and be drawn to the living of Truth in *metta*, or a doing of the truth in love.

On August 25, 1984, Piyatilleke, a young peasant boy, said in conversation, "Some say that Muslims, by religious rule, help only Muslims, but here, I see that your rules allow help to be given to Buddhists. As Christians, you do not pretend riches but live united with us. You also educate our Buddhist children and drop-outs, without asking anything in return. That is *loku pinak* (a meritorious act)." His companion Ratnayake added, "You live like us and close to us without exploiting us (*sura kemen thoravan*). You are friendly and want our true good (*sebe yahapatha*). You are religious (*pevidi*) and observe it with kindness, prayer, ritual. Then also you honor the Buddha who we venerate as our teacher and master." To which Gunapala added: "Whatever you do, you do well and fully. You do good. In that way, you help the country. Yours is a good life without trouble to anyone. Some are good to their own people; you are good to all. I like that, and that is why I come here."

A youth leader said he wanted to write down, in his own tongue, what a lot he learnt from us. We place it here, *in toto*:

"I will accept Jesus as founder of a noble religion, one who showed a sincere love and affection for people (*janathava*). He had no 'high' and 'low' but loved all as equals, and equally lovable. His life shows this admirably. Owing to this I cannot empty him out of my mind. As for other religious leaders and founders, I revere them.

"Because the Church truly lays claims to much wealth and property, she cannot change the existing unjust system. It is difficult to think she will. Even though some, or even many, within its ranks are doing something for the true progress of human society, yet because the decision of many more is victorious, truth is sent underground and untruth seems to advance. But it is very clear that the *Suba Seth Gedera* group (your house and team) is untiring in its efforts to see that truth will win and that people will surely better themselves.

"Perhaps more than 99% Buddhists are found in this area, and for about five years, this little church-group has honored our traditional and time-honored customs and culture, and large numbers in this village area have already accepted the quiet effective good done by this group. We also like the friendly openness with which you work with our people.

"At the start, a few young people were watching you carefully: 'How will you act towards us?' 'Did you come to turn us to your ways somehow?' or 'Were you an international spy group or spy ring to eventually sell out our village?'—were questions which harassed us young people. But we went beyond mere observing and worked with you in your humble efforts as you worked with our people. There we discovered the true face of what you call *sabhava*, the Church.

"I now see after all these years and for the last year especially, that this little Christian group—all of you—have understood our sorrow, our plight (*dukvedana*) and are really very loving and compassionate towards our people, especially the poor. Despite objections of a few who dislike the poor, the work of three of you has gone on. It is a valuable service: to rescue and teach the drop-outs, to supply what is wanting in the school schemata as regards certain subjects, to help adults in non-formal education, in short, to give us a hand; by assuring continuity of a reasonable distribution of infant food (*triposha*) from the government, by helping in a clinic day program, seeing to primary health care with a team of barefoot nurses drawn from our own village, and now working with a wider field of 14 villages or so of this area; by helping self-sufficiency in agricultural inputs by training ten farmers to do research and have technical advice on local fertilizer (bio-fertilizer) according to traditional methods; thus showing you want our culture to advance, and so you honor our happy past. We also have had, due to you, training in culture and dance items for the less-skilled but eager, and we have had slide-shows, which really have helped us live. You helped us with a library of 400 books and now, a 3000 coconut-plant scheme. It is for the poor. All this proves the true meaning of *Suba Seth Gedara,* the name of your house, 'Good wishes house.' You wish us well and want our true good. There is a new awakening among us, a renewal.

"Were anyone to ask me, I could say: 'We know them as Christians, as a Christian group by the name of Jesus they possess and profess. But they haven't tried to foist their religion or religious beliefs on us.' Of course, to a Buddhist community, this presence of yours is a threat, a menace—some people may imagine. They are few who think so. Why do they think so and why are they disturbed? 'Although this small, Christian group does not parade its beliefs or have public cult, yet there is a very large crowd of people who like them and who realize the value of their service.' . . . I can say this to those who ask me. So, if anyone tries it, let them know that the villagers cannot be torn apart from this group. A very large number of young people, boys and girls and little children, honor and revere the Suba Seth Godara and Susith Bavana group and accept them.

"In former times, the Christian religion was preached and proclaimed with guns and bayonets. Many subtle methods were used, but this small Christian group, by helping the people in a real spirit of service, has sunk deep into the hearts of the people. Their presence has been accepted as up-building. It is a peaceful living together and is a great support for peace and reconciliation.

"The example of this Christian group will never be forgotten by the growing ones of the village. To the Christian churches at large and to other religions, this is an immense example and a challenge. If, in this way, and with this background, every village could have such a course of action, a new light will dawn. Of this I am certain. Only then will village peace spread throughout the land. Then, an intelligent, wise and exemplary people will arise in our country. The people will have a consoling, happy life.

"In the process of changing structures, this kind of activity might be termed 'reformist' by some, and yet what do we do with the sick, those who are bedridden, the destitute and illiterate and the weak? How shall we take them along with us in the onward march of the country? How can they go if they are not helped?

"This small Christian group works in such a situation, when other religious groups may be collecting money (*mudal garageniman*, literally, 'raking in the shekels'—ed.), when some are locked in a competitive cut-throat struggle. What the masses choose and the people opt for is right. That is the people's choice. This group is their choice. Let those who will, decry the choice or hurl insults. Truth will prevail. If their decisions are right, people will stand by this group. Their example will be the people's mainstay. It will be impossible to separate the people from such a group. Those who have a real love and show forth real love for the people, will never, ever leave the people.

"I say this to the group: 'Be with us and act with us in the future too. May you show the way. We wish you courage, strength and determination.' "[11]

A young peasant farmer, by thus wishing courage to a group to go ahead in collaboration, has honored the dignity of men and women. A deep chord may have been struck in relationships that spell holiness, in a spirituality that would take in the economic, social, political, cultural, and religious aspects of the human. Do not the Christian humanism and the Buddhist humanism point towards the total salvation or liberation of man from sin and all evil?

LIBERATION OF THE HUMAN FROM KLESAS (STAIN)

All reality: cosmos and man, world and nature are summed up in the Word.
Sometime in 1965, Horst Symanowski, a social worker of Berlin, said: "Today's question is 'How can I find a gracious neighbor?' We no longer ask the question: 'How can I find a gracious God?' or we label it antiquated. A different question haunts us today: 'How can I find a gracious neighbor? How can we still live at peace with one another?' "

God is not the first known. This is part of the depth of humility, the magnanimity of God. Even in His Word made flesh, or enfleshed (as Rahner would say), the Godhead is hidden. God sent his Word into the world which he loved so much as to bring into existence in Verbo, in the Word, with Word as model and example. Protology, then, is based on the Word; so is eschatology, the last reality, for consummation will also be in the Word. In between, the ongoing process of the Kingdom or reign of God is also under the guidance of the Word Incarnate. It comforts the Christian in his faith to realize that all religious aspirations and all history of past and present, and prognostique for the future is a *deroulement* of the Word and that all of reality is contained in the Word.

This Word is also word of protest: *pro-testis* (witness on behalf of ...) and of prophetism (to speak on behalf of the Truth), correcting deviations, judging malpractices. Judaism was a protest religion against the evil of oppression in rich "Egypt." Mahavina, founder of Jainism, and the Buddha, founder of Buddhism, both protested against (it was a protest for) wrong attitudes, of selfishness in the Hinduism of their day. Islam became a prophetic religion outside Israel defending the Word of God (*Kalima*) as also defending the orphan and the widow, for human reality is born of Allah's word: "Be and it is" (*kunfa yakunu*). Today, too, Islam stands at the gate of the Third World in vehement protest against evil.

What we see and know on the world level today and especially on an Asian level (not to say third-world level) is the human being's inhumanity to his fellow humans. In such a situation the Word in the world must be a corrective, reconciling, uniting word of truth which liberates. Why should the Church or the local Jesus community come and introduce the self-emptying Christ as if he were self-aggrandizing, accumulating, spreading the leaven all over the dough and making the food salty rather than salted? Why make the *incognite* Christ cognite as the Son of God, parading him as Son of God rather than son of man before they tested him as a man among men?

It must however be said that Buddhism is a soteriology, for it has a thrust of *moksha, vimukti* (from *munc-muncati*), which means liberation or release. Aloysius Pieris asserts that "soteriology is the foundation of theology" and that the universally valid starting point or basis of interreligious collaboration is Liberation rather than God.[12]

Nor should anyone write off Buddhism arrogantly by saying that it is atheistic. Let's hear their case. There is a Transcendent impersonal Absolute in Buddhism, termed Nibbana. But just as it is distasteful for the Muslim to hear that God is "Father," and that due to legitimate historical reasons of his own, so too it is unpleasant for the Buddhist to hear that the Transcendent impersonal Absolute is "three persons"—because "person" for him is a highly corruptible, disintegrating thing as *puggala*, individual. He hardly links up "person" with the *akalika buddhi* (timeless intelligence) or the *amat sacca* (truth that is beyond death). He feels that we say that the Transcendent is a threefold corruptible and terminable. Besides, the English and Anglo-Saxon "Gott" or "God," although translated in the Sinhala liturgy as *Devatide* (*Deum de Deo*, God of God), comes up against the same title given to the Buddha as *devatudeva* the one who has purified himself by his light (*dipa* or *div* or *dev*), carrying it to perfection, for he took eighteen thousand eons to purify himself or enlighten himself and thus went beyond all *devas* (gods) who can fall back from goodness and purity.

Dr. Gunapala Dharmasiri, speaking on the goal of morality, once said: "As forms of ethical cultures, Buddhism agrees with Christianity. As God is all good, it is necessary to perfect oneself morally in order to reach union with him. The Christian who thus becomes perfect morally invariably attains Nibbana. Similarly, the Buddhist who attains moral perfection, attains union with God."[13] Likewise, at a seminar held at Pilimatalawa, Kandy, in 1977, Dr. Lily de Silva ended with: "Now I know. It is not conversion, not converting me or my fellow Buddhists, that you are seeking. It is in seeing and appreciating my values, our Buddhist values, our spirituality, our effort at peace, sharing, justice, what you call Kingdom values. If you get the Kingdom and I am allowed to set my goal as the final peace of Nibbana, then you are not despairing about my future. Then I am glad. We can live together, we can get to know and have *metta* for each other."[14]

Buddhism thus focuses attention on man. Makhala Gosala had held that *samsara suddhi* (salvation through *gamenena* or wayfaring through rebirths) would suffice for man's salvation-liberation. The Buddha likened him to a fisherman casting his net at the mouth of a river for the destruction of many fish (AN.1.33). Reflecting him, the Buddha held *attakare* (free will) rather than *akiriyavada*, which is more akin to the popular use of *karma* as fate or non-use of will. Human initiative, enterprise, endeavour, courage, perseverance, human instrumentality were thus upheld by the Buddha. Buddhism thus extols man's humanness and greatness of free will, a point which amazed Vladimir Soloviev "that in a doctrine of no-self, so much stress is paid to the human."[15]

If the Buddhists are in touch with the Jesus community and if by his favor, the community presents the human face of Jesus, then by its mediation, the Buddhists are in touch with Jesus. They will follow Jesus from afar doing what he wants and what he did. They will be followers of Jesus and the Jesus praxis without even knowing it—Vesak light or the Light of Asia, or Sir Edwin Arnold's poem of that name, on the Buddha can never be against Christmas or Easter light. They will be touched by the Buddha, their immediate teacher, whose *aryas-tangika magga* they follow—the eightfold path. It is a human way and a righteous way, for "man is the way for the Church" said Pope John Paul II in his first encyclical on the Redeemer of Man. No one who knows both the righteous eightfold Path and the New Testament can fail to echo the words of John: "He who does right is righteous as he is righteous" (1 Jn. 3:7) ... "everyone who does right is born of him" (1 Jn. 2:29). The words used are *dikaiosune dikaios*, justice, quite redolent of the *samma* (right) in the eightfold path: right speech, right action, right livelihood (*sila*), right effort, right mindfulness, right concentration (*samadhi*), right understanding, and right thought (*prajna*). This is the only way to remove suffering, says the Buddha, for it is a path of righteousness.

The Word in the world expresses itself as *bana*, the corrective word of morality, which when lived to the full is capable of bringing men and women to the haven of peace through righteousness which is identical with the biblical peace through justice, so relevant even today. In Jesus, the Word of God showed us not only communication between God and men-women, but also the *logos* or the *mind of God*. We know God's will and mind by looking at the word of Jesus of Nazareth: he who fed the hungry, healed the sick, comforted the sad and lonely, preached the truth, who was a friend of outcasts and sinners, and who "stuck out his neck" for mankind, and man's rights.

INHUMANNESS IN ASIA

The Church's credibility is at stake in Asia today. How long will Asia be made to say that it likes Jesus but would withdraw from Christianity? We know what could well from within man: goodness, kindness, sympathy, compassion, the *saradharma*, but what we see is quite other.

The Word is in the world. So is Asia. And has the Word nothing to say to an Asia that is slowly being crucified on the rack of pain? This nailing and crucifixion are carried out right into the villages of rural Asia—*pagans* (from *pagus*, village) and *paysans* (French for peasant) being gaily mixed in favor of the semanticists and anthropologists, and the shopping complex, supermarket, agribusiness cartel, law of the sea are all turned against the poor.

How can quiet, peaceful Asia, cradle of many religions of the world, live peacefully when she is told: "Let Asians fight Asians" and when her people are decimated by indiscriminate family planning? Where the quantity of the poor in the world is reduced so that the standard of life of the white Western world may be raised—a terrible indictment on Christianity which should have shown the Jesus praxis of opting for life and having it more abundantly. More than that, while larger nations are banding together or at the other end of the scale, we see small countries cut up in a vicious neo-colonialism on the principle of "divide and rule": Vietnam was cut up into north and south, Korea is still divided into north and south, majestic India is now cut up into Pakistan and Bangladesh. And foreign backers, for their own ends, adore the plan of a Khalistan and Tamilnadu. While peace prizes reach some, others get only the bullet, depending on whether remote causes of exploitation and oppression are left aside or raked up.

Then again, while most colonizers condescended to grant flag-independence and apparently pull away, some returned in a more voracious, yet subtle, manner to deplete villages through the transnational corporations, to commandeer large tracts of land in the name of benign development projects (whose development, really?). Trees of great girth and value—satinwood, teak, ironwood, whole forests of them, are raped, wantonly felled with razor-edge machines, then heaped up and burnt with the flames of a people's aspirations; birds' nests, generations of birds are lopped off; beehives and honey (so needed for the poor) are wrecked forever; deer, sambhur, elephants are lunged at and killed, the prime resources of poor countries, the jungle habitats, gone forever in the name of a nebulous development that spells bondage.

And the irony of it is in a possible desertification. The operation of destruction in one area known to us left dry seven once-gurgling streams which first drew the multinational companies to that area. Today the streams are dry because of the clearing. The Buddhist peasants have no Rutilio Grande or Oscar Romero to fight for them, only a few Buddhist monks and some of their own farmers. The whole process brings the institutional religions to disrepute and results in the sullen silencing of the people rendered voiceless because landless, but a hidden power, hopeful and renewed all the while, rests with them.

Does the Jesus community in the world show anxiety that the developing countries have fallen into a debt trap engineered by the big blocs of the world? Hasn't the World Bank admitted that it cannot reach the Third World's poorest people?

Pascal's words are still verified: "Jesus is in agony till the end of time. We must not sleep till then. This agony (struggle) well describes the tragedy of rural Asia. Jesus suffers in the suffering poor. Every time we learn of the failure of an UNCTAD, Jesus suffers in the poor; their hopes raised high and dashed low when proper prices for raw materials are not paid, low salaries given, buffer stocks not raised, when pesticides rejected in other countries are dumped in the poorer and more voiceless ones, when poisonous inputs are so easily available to the illiterate that they die an early death. In rural areas Jesus suffers each time the poor man's *chena* is sold off or grabbed when the aforementioned multinational companies hold sway; when rain holds off or a flood comes at the wrong time, sometimes with neighboring seas disturbed with submarine nuclear tests, Jesus suffers in the poor man. After a hard day's work, he sits up all night in the *pela* (watch-hut made of poles and sticks) listening to marauding wild boar and elephant. Sleepless nights follow as he goes about wanting to feed his wife and children, till the harvest comes and indebtedness stares him in the face. Strong market forces are pitted against him and his soul is sorrowful even unto death" (*mata marenda tharam dukkhai*). "All sufferers in history appear as special servants of Jesus, the Suffering Servant." In them, there is a deeper and profound presence of Christ, says Leonardo Boff.

CONCLUSION

Jesus' suffering among the people is the Passion. It needed a courageous man to tell the world by his praxis that "profound religion leads to political commitment and in a country such as ours where injustice reigns, conflict is inevitable." So said El Salvador's late Archbishop Romero, who died defending the Word and his peasants against a repressive military regime. When a dictatorship seriously threatens human rights and the common good of the nation, when they become insupportable and close themselves to all channels of dialogue, understanding and rationality, then the church speaks of the legitimate right to insurrectional violence. It is such religious, faithful forthrightness that is prophecy.

Jesus was accused of being a political man, disturbing the false peace of Israel under imperialist Rome. One of the charges against him was that he forbade the paying of tribute to Caesar, when the real praise should have been that he upheld the "things that are of God"—namely, what all his bystanders must surely have known: the land, the resources and the people, Yahweh's own possession which through the Covenant had passed to the people.

We situate our conclusion under six aspects of challenge:

Biblically: *Dharmayano* or the Dhamma word personified is the new term used in the Sinhala Bible. The *dharma,* stable norm of all life, is the still point in the turning world of *samsara.* The *dharma* is also the norm of relational holiness: "Be holy as I am holy" (Lev. 20:7). If the Spirit blows where he will, he can inspire truths in other moral codes. If we distinguish static truths (like two and two equals four) and operative truths, these that men and women live by, we can see that the Spirit who can never contradict himself has been in the scriptures of many a code.

Theologically: To emphasize the need for presenting the deeply human side of Christ in no way means the denial of the sonship of God. One could meet him as the Word of life, enfleshed as the Word of life in the world of every-day reality, where depth of relationship becomes holiness. The conclusions of Chalcedon or Ephesus are not rejected or abandoned but absorbed into the main-stream of history. Jesus takes us to greater truths as orthopraxis rather than mere orthodoxy.

The uniqueness of Christ and Christ crucified: This is an appeal of Paul and an inner demand of the Christian faithful according to the Christian scriptures. Christ is being re-crucified today as a corporate community, especially among the poor who manifest him. His passover from sin to holiness (Jn. 13:1) is seen in the passion and death of the people, and his resurrection is seen every time they band together in the hope of new life and community building, this last belonging to his kingship. The Word builds community.

Founder (Buddha)—presented the Word, and that word built the Samgha (*sam*)	God presented the Word, the Word built the Community (*com*)

The Messiah emerges from the suffering people and identifies with the people. One of the key points of *minjung* theology is that the Crucifixion of Jesus took place as a historical event in the political arena.

In the missionary sense: The great Mission mandate: "Go ye and teach all nations," is not primarily a mandate to proselytize and convert the individual or turn him away from his faith in goodness. Biblical conversion has no object. "Making converts" and "conversion" make no sense. Conversion is the turning away from oneself to God who is always turned to us. This is the goal of our missionary action. The evangelizer must now get evangelized and turn to the Truth. The mandate is primarily a message to "make disciples of all nations" (structures of society). There is no opposition but continuity between Lk. 4:13: "He has sent me to preach the Gospel to the poor . . ." and the last message: "Go ye and teach all nations," for they are held together by Mt. 25: "I was hungry and you gave me to eat . . . thirsty and you gave me to drink." This last might mean today to make political action (to agitate) to set up a water works.

The social and liberative aspects: The Buddhist schema allows not only the token of *samgha* (community) through the Theravada (Sri Lankan basic) Buddhism, but also through the Mahayana Buddhism which induces the salvation of all beings as salvation or liberation for all. Christ is the Healer: I am the Life. So dialogical collaboration takes place in matters of food, health and ill-health as reference to the Deed of Logos, the Word. The Buddha is also known as the Maha-ausadha pandita, the great wise healer. Christ is also the *Truth*: I am the Truth. The Buddha said: Truth is beyond death. Here collaboration should take place in works of education for justice, formal and non-formal ways of education and conscientization.

Eschatologically: The Exodus-Resurrection-Passover paradigm is verified in Buddhism in the Buddha's renunciation (*nekkhama, naiskramya*) each time he made a passage from evil to goodness, from selfishness to selflessness—a pattern found in Buddhist morality. The Buddha is also called a Jina or victor over evil, of *tanha, lobha, dosa, moha*. Theologically too, the messianic expectation of the people is based upon theodicy, the victory or vindication of God's justice over evil in history. The Messiah and the people actualize the justice of God in history. In that sense, true messianism, which coincides with the true role of the Maitreya Buddha or Buddha Amitabha (*amitayus, amida*), is an eschatologcial phenomenon closely linked to an apocalyptic understanding of history.

The liberation of men and women, rather than a direct search for God, will let us all meet in the arena of Asia, even the Third World or Sri Lanka, today. The Jesus community, born of the Word in the world, would like the Buddhist to live the truth in love (*metta*), inspired by the Buddha teaching. The upholding of human compassion does in no way mean a denial of what Christians term the Divinity. "Break captive chains . . . give sight to the blind . . . Go teach all nations . . . feed the hungry . . . take in the stranger . . ."—are all injunctions born of compassion. Jesus the healer, Jesus the teacher loves the masses—the *minjung*—now as then, for they are like sheep without a shepherd, and he takes them as they are, unconditionally. So too, the Buddha praxis reflects compassion for all creatures. From the Buddha's life we can deduce that he would have been serenely joyful to see One such as Jesus so profoundly human, so intensely divine.

There is no need to ask which is first: human or divine, or is it human and divine or divine and human?

In the tragic vortex of today, there is not even a question of how these two natures co-exist in Christ. While holding on to what it signifies, let us push on to the truth of Christ: *actus fidei terminatur non ad enuntiabile sed ad rem*; the act of faith is not in the statement, but in the reality of it. The Jesus reality for all ages cannot be domesticated by decree but accepted and formulated, however feebly, in faith.

If we but knew with Sobrino that Jesus is the way to liberation, then we would know that he is not an obstacle to anyone on the Way with him, nor is that person a stumbling block when he too is on the right way.

NOTES

1. The team is made up of an Oblate missionary, Fr. Michael Rodrigo OMI, and two Salvatorian missionaries, Sr. Benedict Fernando-pulle and Sr. Milburga Fernando.

2. The date in our house diary is one in March 1992. The monk is Venerable Alutwela Upananda of Alutwela temple. Several other areas received drought relief, but this area was ignored.

3. Harvey Cox, *Religion in the Secular City: Towards a Post-Modern Theology* (New York: Simon and Schuster, 1984) p. 304. We have borrowed the word "Dialogy" from Cox's quotation of Raschke's paper, p. 228: "Dialogue must cease to be a secondary quest or reflection about religion, but must become itself a religious quest. This kind of Dialogy will bring about an 'interpretive tension' says Raschke."

4. Cox, p. 228.

5. Cox, p. 229.

6. Cox, p. 239.

7. "The Church and Human Rights," Work Paper 1, Pont. Com. Justitia et Pax, Vatican, no. 56, p. 23.

8. Synod of Justice, "Justice in the World," TPV, 1971, pp. 12-13.

9. Albert Nolan, *Jesus Before Christianity* (Maryknoll, N.Y.: Orbis Books, 1992; London: Darton, Longman, Todd, 1992), p. 167.

10. Ibid.

11. A youth leader called HMJ, a young and knowledgeable farmer gave this piece in writing, in Sinhala.

12. Aloysius Pieris, *An Asian Theology of Liberation* (Maryknoll, N.Y.: Orbis Books, 1988; and Edinburgh: T & T Clark, 1988), p. 107.

13. Gunapala Dharmasiri, "The Meaning of Religion in Sri Lanka Today," *Dialogue* 2 (1975): 7-14.

14. Lily de Silva, quoted in Michael Rodrigo, "Moral Goodness: Doorway to Final Peace," *Sevaka Sevana bulletin* (December 1978): 262.

15. Vladimir Soloviev, *La justification du bien* (Paris: Aubier), p. 237.

13

Christology from an Asian Woman's Perspective

VIRGINIA FABELLA

Asian women are beginning to articulate their own christologies. For too long, what we are to believe about Jesus Christ and what he is to mean for us have been imposed on us by our colonizers, by the Western world, by a patriarchal church, and by male scholars and spiritual advisers. But now we are discovering Jesus Christ for ourselves. What we say may not be anything new; what is important is now we are saying it ourselves. To the question posed by Jesus "Who do people say that I am?" we are giving answers that reflect not only what we encounter in Scriptures, but also our reality and experience as Asian women. Thus our christologies are not only interpretations of Jesus, but confessions of our faith in this Jesus who has made a difference in our lives, and not only as a speculative activity, but as active engagement in striving towards the full humanity Jesus came to bring.

Although women doing theology and constructing christologies have experienced discrimination and "tokenism" in both church and society, ours is a life of privilege compared to that of other women in Asia. The reality, backed by cases and statistics, is that "in all spheres of Asian society, women are dominated, dehumanized and dewomanized ... viewed as inferior beings who must always subordinate themselves to the so-called male supremacy ... treated with bias and condescension. In Asia and all over the world, the myth of the subservient, servile Asian women is blatantly peddled to reinforce the dominant male stereotype image."[1] Thus, even if this is an attempt to express "my" christology, I need to take into account these countless women, whether they believe in Jesus Christ or not. Jesus' liberating and human message has meaning for all women struggling for full humanity and their rightful place in history, for Jesus' message not only liberates but also empowers.

I

Christology is at the heart of all theology for it is Jesus who has revealed to us the deepest truths about God. In his humanity, Jesus revealed God as a loving God who cares for the weakest and lowliest and wills the full humanity and salvation of all, men and women alike. In his humanity, Jesus has shown us what it means to be truly human, to have life abundantly, to be saved. This christology is central and integral to any talk about God, human-God relationship and all right relationships and of any discussion about salvation and liberation.

There are important issues which any christology must deal with. However, here I will only touch on those that have a bearing on my being Asian and woman, those that are more pertinent to the Asian context and the issue of gender. Feminist theologians in the U.S. have raised the question of the maleness of Jesus. Among Asian women, the maleness of Jesus has not been a problem for we see it as "accidental" to the salvific process. His maleness was not essential but functional. By being male, Jesus could repudiate more effectively the male definition of humanity and show the way to a right and just male-female relationship, challenging both men and women to change their life patterns. Historically, however, christology has been patriarchalized and has been the doctrine of the Christian tradition most used against women.[2] Thus the feminists' question stands.

An issue facing christology pertinent to our Asian context is the new understandings of salvation in different cultures. Salvation/liberation takes on different meanings within a reality of massive poverty and multiple oppression on the one hand, and of religious, cultural and ideological plurality on the other. In a continent where 97 percent of the people are not Christian, can we claim Jesus Christ as the savior of the whole world? How is he the unique and universal savior when the majority in Asia alone have never heard of him or have even ignored him in their quest for a better world? Some of the Asian faiths offer salvation which relates more closely than Christianity to the soteriological depths of our cultures, to the desire for liberation from both individual and organized greed.[3] Have we listened to what other major faiths have had to say about Jesus, especially those who have seriously grappled with his mystery, or have we as Christians tended to be "protective" and exclusive about Jesus?

These and other pertinent issues need to be addressed in the process of constructing an Asian christology, a process which is just beginning. Theologians like Aloysius Pieris have indicated guidelines for this effort,[4] but these have not included anything that speaks directly to women's reality. Though the christology be educed from the depths of our cultures and expressed in Asia's soteriological idiom, the result will not be relevant unless it takes into account the women's experience, perspective and contribution. Only then can we agree with Indian theologian George Soares that spelling out the place of Jesus in Asia is "Asia's ultimate challenge to Christian theology."[5]

II

In formulating my christology, I shall reflect on some of the important christological themes and consequent implications. Every christology focuses on the life and significance of Jesus Christ; therefore, the historical Jesus plays a central role. It is necessary to return to the Jesus of history, to the man Jesus who was born and who lived on our continent, whose life was rooted in Jewish culture and religious tradition. By his life, words, and actions, Jesus of Nazareth has shown us the meaning of humanity and divinity. To bypass history is to make an abstraction of Jesus and thus to distort his person, mission and message of love and salvation. Moreover, it is only in reference to the historical Jesus that we can test the authenticity of our Jesus images and see how closely they relate to the reality.

Jesus' core message centered on the kingdom of God: The reign of God is near; repent and believe in the good news (Mk 1:15). His central message focused not on himself but on God and our response to God's gift of the kingdom. Seeing God's reign as imminent and becoming conscious of a special call, Jesus proclaimed its coming and urged the people to reform their lives, believe the good news, and be saved. To enter the kingdom meant to change one's ways of behaving and relating. The notion of God's kingdom was a familiar one to the people for it is contained in Hebrew Scriptures and intertestamental literature, although by Jesus' time it had acquired a variety of interpretations. For this reason, Jesus aligned himself with John the Baptist and accepted John's baptism, for John preached the same message to the "crowds," the ordinary men and women, demanding repentance. This was so unlike the stance of the other groups: the Essenes, with their passive, elitist interpretation of the Kingdom, or the legalistic Pharisees or aristocratic Sadducees.

As an itinerant preacher/healer, Jesus drew a following for he performed signs and spoke with authority, and what he taught he practiced. He chose twelve apostles whom he instructed in the way of the kingdom. Although his message was for all, the people he attracted most were those on the fringes of society, those who were in "most need of salvation." However, not everything Jesus taught and practiced in terms of the kingdom was familiar or easy to understand, accept or follow. His message included what others have never taught: the inclusive character of God's reign. Jesus lived out his teaching by freely associating with, and showing preference for, the poor and marginalized—sinners, outcasts, women. They were the last who had become first; the humble who had become exalted.

Jesus' attitude towards women and treatment of them was most uncommon even for a "good" Jew of his day, for he was not only considerate of them and treated them with deep respect, but even acted contrary to the prevailing customs and practices. Women were among the non-persons in society, mere chattel. But Jesus never ignored them when they approached him for healing; they were human beings worth making whole again. They were entitled to the "life in abundance"; they were worthy of learning the Torah. He not only valued them as friends but affirmed their trustworthiness and capability to be disciples, witnesses, missionaries, and apostles.[6]

Jesus taught something else that was new and more difficult still: that love of God and neighbor must include love of enemies. From the time of Ezra, Jews and Samaritans had become irrevocable enemies. Yet by parable and example, Jesus made his point to "love your enemies; do good to those who hate you" (Lk 6:27). The good Samaritan's concern for his neighbor made a model to follow; the Samaritan woman who gives him to drink becomes his missionary to her people. Jesus likewise showed compassion on the foreigner, being touched by a Roman centurion's "faith" and concern for his servant, and allowing himself to be challenged by the entreaties and confidence of a Syrophoenician woman. Thus Jesus showed that to live a truly human life, one lives a life-in-relation, demonstrated by care and service even to the least: the women, the enemy, the outsider. But this was not all. Jesus spelled out what right human relationship is in practice, what it means to "love one another": there is no lording it over others; even masters shall serve; right relation to one's neighbor has priority over temple worship; discipleship is above blood relationship; only by losing one's life shall one find it. What a liberating message for the women; they were the dominated, the taken-for-granted, the one-sided servers, the "mother of" or "daughter of." Jesus made clear what being human means; only thus can one enter the kingdom of God. And the invitation is open to all.

Jesus' words and deeds brought him into conflict not only with the Jewish religious authorities but also with the Roman leadership. Even as he announced the kingdom, he denounced hypocrisy, oppression and misuse of power. The Romans were threatened by the former, the religious leaders by the latter. Seeing that his end was near, Jesus "bequeathed" to his apostles the basic meaning of his message and ministry at a last meal together. That very night, Jesus was arrested, tried in two courts, found guilty of sedition by the Romans and sentenced to death by crucifixion. Jesus did not resist; he understood the consequences of his word and works in fidelity to God's call.

III

For the apostles, Jesus' death was a shame and a scandal which shook their faith and shattered their hopes. In fact, afraid of Roman reprisals, they dispersed, and only a few disciples, mostly women, remained with Jesus as he died on the cross, to all semblances a failure. But then, the unexpected happened. The disciples, beginning with the women, started to report appearances which they gradually began to identify with Jesus as they experienced peace and forgiveness. He had "risen from the dead!" The apostles reassembled and recalled all that Jesus taught and did, and recognized God's confirmation of his words and deeds in raising him from the dead. Their new experience of Jesus radically transformed them into people of courage and faith, impelling them to continue Jesus' ministry and spread his message of salvation as they witnessed to him as their Lord and God. The small Jesus movement/community began to grow and extend to the four corners of the earth. All this "unexpected" is the reality of the resurrection. By his rising, Jesus has conquered death, the "first fruits of those who sleep" (1 Cor 15:20), embodying the advent of God's promise of salvation, signaling the dawning of God's kingdom. By his rising, Jesus is confirmed as the Christ and God's true son, the model of redeemed humanity, the incarnation of true divinity, no longer limited to the particularities of his maleness and Jewishness. Jesus Christ lives and continues to affect, renew, and give hope to the millions all over the globe who would believe and follow him. Jesus Christ is alive and we encounter him in our sisters and brothers.

The apostles' resurrection faith enabled them not only to understand God as Jesus revealed God in his life, death and rising, but also to interpret Jesus' death differently. The apostles and other disciples had taken Jesus' death as a disappointing, shameful end of an eschatological prophet whose life failed to bring about the kingdom he preached. Their Easter faith, however, told them that Jesus' death was not a failure but a fulfillment. This later gave rise to varied explanations, but the one that perdured defined Jesus' death as an offering to God as sacrifice and reconciliation. Jesus is the suffering servant who died for our sakes. The cross acquires a religious cultic significance and Jesus' death becomes an act of communication with God, "to bring repentance to Israel and forgiveness of sins." Jesus died as "a ransom for many, whose shedding of blood expiates sins." Jesus gave himself for a purpose. His death was an outpouring of love. From a negative event, the cross acquires a positive meaning.

In the course of time and movement across cultures, the positive meanings of Jesus' death became lost or distorted. In the Philippines, we have developed (or inherited) a dead-end theology of the cross with no resurrection or salvation in sight. Most of the women who sing the "pasyon" during Holy Week look upon the passion and death of Jesus as ends in themselves and actually relish being victims. This attitude is not uncommon among other women outside the "pasyon" singers, and it is not helped when priests reinforce the attitude through their homilies. One of them said not long ago that he does not preach the resurrection as "the people are not prepared for it."

In India, the theology of sacrifice thrust upon women is of no purpose. Indian women theologians[7] tell us that their women silently bear taunts, abuse, and even battering; they sacrifice their self-esteem for the sake of family honor, subject themselves to sex determination tests, and endure the oppressive and even fatal effects of the dowry system. A woman who is raped will invariably commit suicide rather than allow her husband and family to suffer the ignominy of living with a raped woman. While we seek in Jesus' passion, death and resurrection a meaning for our own suffering, we cannot passively submit ourselves as women to practices that are ultimately anti-life. Only that suffering endured for the sake of one's neighbor, for the sake of the kingdom, for the sake of greater life, can be redeeming and rooted in the Paschal mystery.

The death of Jesus was not only a redeeming event; it was also revelatory. In Jesus' death, God revealed the deepest meaning and extent of divine love for humankind as well as the true nature of God. Jesus' whole life was a disclosure of God and God's will for humankind. He always felt a deep communion and intimate relationship with God which was manifested in his being and in his prayer. It was only on the cross that he felt abandoned by this very God whom he called Abba—"Father." But God was both absent and present on the cross. "On the cross of Jesus God himself is crucified ... In this ultimate solidarity with humanity, he reveals himself as the God of love, who opens up a hope and a future through the most negative side of history."[8]

IV

The nature of Jesus' relationship to God was only reflected upon and gradually formulated after the resurrection. At first it was simply the application of the biblical titles to Jesus in the light of the resurrection experience: the Christ, Son of Man, Suffering Servant, Son of God, Lord, Son of David. Initially functional, the designations gradually took on a confessional dimension. Eventually, with increasing association with the Hellenistic world, ontological implications were drawn out. Thus through a process of historical growth and theological development, the identity of Jesus in terms of divinity was recognized and accepted by the early church, paving the way for the doctrine of the incarnation, the doctrine of the Word made flesh.

Whether Jesus is true God and true man, or only seemingly God or only seemingly man, became the subject of intensive debates that were dogmatically put to a halt by the authoritative formulations of the Council of Nice (325 C.E.) and later the Council of Chalcedon (451 C.E.), asserting that Jesus Christ is fully divine of one substance with God the Father (Nicea), the same perfect in his divinity and the same perfect in his humanity, one and the same Christ, Lord, only begotten, in two natures (Chalcedon).[9] The language and substance of these christological doctrines betray their historical and cultural conditionings, addressing as they did the disputes of another time and place which do not relate to the vital problems of present-day Asia. These doctrines are no longer of the greatest importance for many Asian theologians, for, taken as they are, they close off any authentic dialogue with people of other faiths, who are the vast majority in Asia. In fact, in one Asian theologian's view,[10] christology has become passé in Asia, because we are still depending on Nicea and Chalcedon whose formulations are largely unintelligible to the Asian mind. Thus the true significance of these councils is not so much their content, but the underlying challenge they pose to us to have our own contemporary culturally based christological formulations. And that is what small groups of Asian theologians, both men and women, are doing—having their own mini and informal Niceas and Chalcedons to determine, based on their context and concerns, who Jesus Christ is for them.

Just as the formulations of Nicea and Chalcedon have placed barriers in our efforts to have an honest dialogue with people of other faiths, so have our claims about Jesus as the universal savior. In Asia we experience dialogue on two levels, a more formal one commonly referred to as "interreligious dialogue" and a less formal one we refer to as "dialogue of life." Our experience in the latter where we share the life conditions, pain, risks, struggles, and aspirations of the Asian poor (the majority of whom are of other faiths or even of "no faith") has made us aware of our common search for a truly human life, our common desire for liberation from whatever shackles us internally and externally, and our common thrust towards a just society reflective of what we Christians term "the kingdom." In the struggle that binds us, there is an implicit acknowledgment and acceptance of our religious differences and our different paths to "salvation."

On the more formal level, Asian theologians engaged in authentic interreligious dialogue (which has mature enlightenment and not conversion as goal) are explicitly questioning our traditional claims about the uniqueness and centrality of Jesus and the universality of Jesus as savior ... for all religions. Biblical and historical research and in-depth study of other religions have raised serious questions about our Christian claims. Admitting God's universal love and desire to save, the Catholic position recognizes both revelation and salvation outside Christ and Christianity, but insists that Christ be proclaimed as "the unique mediator of salvation" and God's "unique historical revelation."[11] But is it not possible to claim Jesus Christ as "our" unique savior without claiming the same for all other people? The present direction toward theocentric or soteriocentric christologies seem to be where some Asian theologians are tending as a result of their experience of dialogue, encounter, study and reflection. Jesus himself centered on God and the kingdom and not on himself. As an old saying goes: let us not take the finger pointing at the moon to be the moon itself.

Theologians proclaiming that Jesus is wholly God but not the whole of God, or that Jesus is the Christ but the Christ is not Jesus,[12] should in no way lessen our own personal commitment to Jesus whom we Christians have personally known and experienced as revealer, savior, truth, way, and life. It should in no way disaffirm for us that the "vision and power of Jesus

of Nazareth is an effective, hope-filled, universally meaningful way of bringing about God's kingdom."[13] We believe and confess that Jesus has brought
us total salvation; others, however, are making similar claims about their
own mediators with the same Ultimate Source of life's meaning whom we
call God.

V

I shall now examine some implications of my christology for certain
aspects of Christian practice, including the use of Jesus images. In particular, I shall reflect on its implications for mission ministry.

From the start, though I set out to write a christology I can claim as
mine, I have tried to keep in mind the plight, concerns, and aspirations of
my Asian sisters. In the light of Asian women's reality in general, a liber-
ational, hope-filled, love-inspired, and praxis-oriented christology is what
holds meaning for me. In the person and praxis of Jesus are found the
grounds of our liberation from all oppression and discrimination: whether
political or economic, religious or cultural, or based on gender, race or
ethnicity. Therefore the image of Jesus as liberator is consistent with my
christology. On the other hand, in view of what I have written, it would be
inconsistent to hold on to the title and image of "lord" in reference to
Jesus, because of the overtones of the word as used today. In Asia, the
word "lord" is connected with the feudal system which in my own country
is one of the root causes of the poverty, injustices, inequalities, and violent
conflicts that exist there today, many of the victims being women. It is also
a colonial term for the British masters which is still used in countries like
Pakistan for those who have taken their place. "Lord" connotes a relationship of domination, which is opposite to what Jesus taught and exemplified.
"The rulers of the gentiles exercise lordship over them . . . but not so with
you" (Lk 22:24). His apostles called him "teacher" and "lord," yet Jesus
preferred to be remembered as one who serves (cf Jn 14:13-16). Asian
women have been "lorded over" for centuries and all the major religions
including Christianity have contributed to this sinful situation. The title
"lord" would not be in keeping with a liberating Jesus.

In my own culture, however, not many women would be familiar with
the figure of a liberating or liberated Jesus. They know him as the suffering
or crucified Jesus who understands their own suffering which they passively
or resignedly endure. Many remain unaware of their class and gender
oppression and simply live on with a "status quo" christology. Nevertheless,
an increasing number of women are becoming aware of our subordinate
place and exploited state in a patriarchal church and society, and see this
as contrary to the will of a just and loving God, who created both men and
women in God's own image. As these women strive to change this ineq-
uitable situation within the overall struggle against economic, political and
social injustices, they, too, see Jesus as their hope and liberator.

In our quest for a world of right human relationships, Jesus has shown us the way, and therefore Jesus is the norm for our action in reforming our lives and renewing society. Jesus never spoke of human rights or the common good or liberation from oppressive structures, yet his whole life, teachings and actions embodied all of them, manifesting what it meant to be human and to act humanly. He showed us that we cannot work toward our true humanity, our true liberation, unless we seek the true humanity, the true liberation, of all. Thus, efforts to transform the existing structures and patterns of domination that prevent the least of our sisters and brothers from living truly human lives and enjoying just, reciprocal relationships, are moral actions.

Just as my christology has implications for ethics, so it has implications for ecclesiology and my sense of anthropology and culture. In relation to ecclesiology, I have already mentioned that the present Catholic model admits the possibility of salvation beyond the borders of Christianity. God loves and wills the salvation of all humankind. Thus the church can claim to be *a* sign but not, as Vatican II put it, "*the* sign of salvation for the entire world" (*italics mine*).[14] There are other fingers pointing at the same moon. The Church needs to reexamine its sense of "uniqueness" and "universality." Also, if its dialogue with other religions is to be serious and sincere, then it must reexamine its meaning and use of "definitiveness" and "normativeness."

To be a credible sign of salvation and to witness to Jesus' universal love, the Church as institution has to rid itself of its non-liberating structures and non-loving practices, its exclusive, hierarchical mode of operation. It would do well to retrieve the egalitarian spirit of the early Christian communities. Unfortunately some of today's new experiences of being community are construed as a threat by the institutional Church, instead of as an attempt to live out that spirit which grew from a faithful following of Jesus. If the Church is indeed following in the steps of Jesus, then it should focus, as Jesus did, on preaching and living out the truths of the kingdom rather than in maintaining itself. If the Church is serious in following Jesus, then it should encourage and support all efforts towards inclusiveness and full humanity.

Jesus intended this full humanity for all, not just for men, or less for women. Men and women have the same human nature and are endowed with the same potentials for "fullness." Men do not image God more than women do. Yet patriarchy has distorted these truths to promote a hierarchical and complementary model of humanity, which puts women in second place. Women's inferior status has become part of the working definition of being human in Asia, buttressed by the doctrines and practices of the major religions. This has had degrading and dehumanizing consequences for women in all areas of life down the ages, stark evidences of which are still present on our continent today. One of the deplorable consequences is the very internalization of this "ideology" of women's inferiority by women themselves as part and parcel of our cultures. Part of the work of an Asian christology would be to determine the emancipating and enslaving elements of cultures and religions, to discern which ones foster and which ones impede the creation of a more human and humane life and a more just society.

VI

Lastly, there are certain implications of my christology for mission ministry. The understanding of mission has undergone changes over the years and especially of late when the church has been present in almost all parts of the world. Transmission of the message in a transcultural milieu has acquired new modalities.[15] Besides direct evangelization, missionaries are engaged in other activities: "witness" on behalf of the Gospel, "prophetic" communication in word and sign, and involvement in personal and social transformation.

Throughout the past centuries, there has been such an urgency about planting the Church that in preaching Jesus Christ, the stress has been given to the Church he "founded" and its doctrine rather than the reign of God he proclaimed. Indeed, if our mission is an extension of Jesus' own mission, then we need to refocus on preaching the good news of God (Mk 1:14) and God's reign which Jesus has already inaugurated and will come in its fullness in the future as God's gift. Jesus' message of salvation was not only preached, but also actualized as something to be experienced in this life. To make Jesus' message comprehensible to Asians (its core and not its cultural overlays), we Christians need to engage in sincere and humble dialogue with people of other faiths, a dialogue which is as open to receive as to give, that in so doing we ourselves may come to grasp a fuller meaning of God's revelation. To make Jesus' message credible to Asian women, it must directly touch their everyday lives. Interreligious dialogue that is silent on women's oppression and thus simply perpetuating their subordinate status in religion and society is contrary to Jesus' saving word.

Our witness is for the sake of the good news of God's reign; the good news is not just to be preached but lived. Thus our life and work style must conform to the kingdom norms and values. We cannot proclaim a reign of justice, love and peace, while at the same time contradicting its inclusive, non-dominating character in our mission practice and structures. If the kingdom is our focus, then a more collaborative, egalitarian, ecumenical effort in mission will be a more compelling witness.

Some missionaries will be called to prophetic witness, which is not only to announce the liberating message of Jesus but, in solidarity with the people, to denounce what is incompatible with it. This requires both prayerful discernment and courage. New styles of mission presence will indeed create misunderstanding and provoke resistance, not only from outside but within the church itself. But suffering and even persecution are to be expected in a missionary's life if indeed it follows the path of Jesus. Suffering for the sake of God's reign is a way of being in mission.

While many mission societies still insist on the primacy of first evangelization in mission, others have moved on to works of inculturation and liberation, both urgent tasks in Asia. While these are primarily the tasks of Asians themselves, they invite the support and collaboration of others, and missionaries have responded to this invitation. Missionaries are taking seriously what the Synod of Bishops said in 1971, that the mission of preaching the gospel demands our participation in the transformation of the world.[16] Thus active solidarity with the people against sexism, racism, ethnic discrimination and economic injustice is truly missionary. For women missionaries all over the world, there is need to explore new mission ministries among, and on behalf of, women who need other women's support, presence, defense, sisterly help, friendship and active solidarity as they awaken to their reality and struggle for their full humanity. In Asia these women are numberless.

I have reflected on the significance of Jesus' life, death, and resurrection from a specific horizon. It was my concern, however, that my christology not only express who Jesus is for me, but also recapture Jesus' life and message in such a way that it can be liberating and empowering for other women. Hopefully my christology will form part of the collective effort of Asian Christian women in search of a christology that is meaningful not only to us but to our Asian sisters whose life's struggles we have made our own. For now this is what I submit as my christology as an Asian woman, knowing that it is subject to additions and revisions, and aware of the fact that the task of christology is ongoing and never really finished.

NOTES

1. "Proceedings of the Asian Women's Consultation," Manila, Philippines, November 21-30, 1985. Mimeographed.

2. Rosemary Radford Ruether, "Feminist Theology and Spirituality," in *Christian Feminism: Vision of a New Humanity,* ed. Judith L. Weidman (San Francisco: Harper & Row Publishers, 1984), p. 20.

3. Some Asian women question this claim as coming from a male perspective. What Asian women need liberation from is not inordinate greed but excessive self-effacement.

4. Cf. Aloysius Pieris, "Speaking of the Son of God in Non-Christian Cultures, e.g. in Asia," in *Jesus, Son of God, Concilium* 153, eds. E. Schillebeeckx and J. B. Metz (New York: Seabury Press, 1982), pp. 65-70; "To Be Poor As Jesus Was Poor," *The Way* 24, no. 3 (July 1984): 186-97; and "Spirit Dimension of Change," *The Way* 28/1 (January 1988): 36-37.

5. George M. Soares, interview by author, 5 December 1987, New Delhi, India.

6. Paul's claim to be an apostle because he had seen the risen Jesus and received a direct commission to preach the good news applies equally to Mary Magdalene (cf. John 20:16-18).

7. "Proceedings of the Asian Women's Consultation," pp. 54-55.

8. Jon Sobrino, *Christology at the Crossroads* (Maryknoll, N.Y.: Orbis Books, 1978), p. 224.

9. Dermot A. Lane, *The Reality of Jesus* (New York: Paulist Press, 1975), pp. 99, 105.

10. Francis D'Sa, interview by author, 5 December 1987, New Delhi, India.

11. R. Hardawiryana, "Towards a 'Theology in Asia': The Struggle for Identity," *Inter-Religio* 12 (Fall 1987): 52-53.

12. Paul F. Knitter, *No Other Name?* (Maryknoll, N.Y.: Orbis Books, 1986), pp. 152, 156.

13. Ibid., p. 196.

14. Cited in ibid., p. 130.

15. Donald Senior and Carroll Stuhlmueller, *The Biblical Foundations for Mission* (Maryknoll, N.Y.: Orbis Books, 1983), pp. 332-39, passim.

16. Synod of Bishops 1971, "Justice in the World," in *Renewing the Earth,* eds. David J. O'Brien and Thomas A. Shannon (Garden City, N.Y.: Image Books, 1977), p. 391.

14

Who Is Jesus for Asian Women?

CHUNG HYUN KYUNG

TRADITIONAL IMAGES

In order to express their experiences of Jesus, the majority of Asian women use the traditional titles that they received from missionaries. Since many Christian churches in Asia are still dominated by Western missionary theologies and androcentric interpretations of the Bible, some Asian women's theologies on the surface look similar to Western missionary or Asian male theologies. However, when we look closely at the Asian women's usage of the traditional titles of Jesus, we can find the emergence of new meaning out of the old language. The following are examples of traditional images of Jesus which have gone through the welding of meaning by the experiences of Asian women.

JESUS AS SUFFERING SERVANT

The most prevailing image of Jesus among Asian women's theological expressions is the image of the suffering servant. Asian Christian women seem to feel most comfortable with this image of Jesus whether they are theologically conservative or progressive.

According to the "Summary Statement from the Theological Study Group of Christology,"[1] developed by the Asian Women's Theological Conference, Singapore, Asian Christian women from many different countries defined Jesus as "the prophetic messiah whose role is that of the suffering servant," the one who "offers himself as ransom for many." They claimed that "through his suffering messiahship, he creates a new humanity."[2]

Asian Christian women at the Singapore conference rejected such images of Jesus as "triumphal King" and "authoritative high priest."[3] They contended that these images of Jesus have "served to support a patriarchal

religious consciousness in the Church and in theology."⁴ Jesus became the
Messiah through his suffering in service to others, not by his domination
over others. Like Korean theologian Choi Man Ja, many Asian Christian
women make connections between their humanity and Jesus' humanity
through "suffering and obedience."⁵ Because Asian women's life experience is filled with "suffering and obedience," it seems natural for Asian
women to meet Jesus through the experience that is most familiar to them.

When Asian women live through the hardship of suffering and obedience
their family, society, and culture inflict upon them, they need a language
that can define the meaning of their experience. The image of a suffering
Jesus enables Asian women to see meaning in their own suffering. Jesus
suffered for others as Asian women suffer for their families and other
community members. As Jesus' suffering was salvific, Asian women are
beginning to view their own suffering as redemptive. They are making
meaning out of their suffering through the stories of Jesus' life and death.
As Jesus' suffering for others was life-giving, so Asian women's suffering is
being viewed as a source of empowerment for themselves and for others
whose experience is defined by oppression.

However, making meaning out of suffering is a dangerous business. It
can be both a seed for liberation and an opium for the oppression of Asian
women. These two conflicting possibilities shape Asian women's experience
of encounter with Jesus.

Asian women have believed in Jesus *in spite of* many contradictory experiences they receive from their families, churches, and societies. Believing
in spite of great contradictions is the only option for many Asian women
who are seeking to be Christian. For example, their fathers are supposed
to be the protectors, the ones who give Asian women safety in an oppressive
world, providing food, shelter, and clothing. But too often Asian women
are beaten by their fathers or sold into child marriage or prostitution. Asian
women's husbands are supposed to love them, but frequently they batter
their wives in the name of love and family harmony. Asian women's brothers
are supposed to support and encourage them, but they instead often further
their own higher educations by tacitly using their Asian sisters, ignoring the
reality that their sisters are selling their bodies to pay for tuition. The
promises of safety, love, and nurturing have not been fulfilled. Asian women
have trusted their beloved men, but their men have often betrayed them.
Yet Asian women still hope, still believe that, "Maybe someday, somewhere, somebody will love me and nurture me as I am." Is Jesus that
somebody?

Some Asian women have found Jesus as the one who really loves and
respects them as human beings with dignity, while the other men in their
lives have betrayed them. At the Singapore conference, Komol Arayapraatep, a Christian woman from Thailand, shared her appreciation of Jesus:

We women are always very grateful to Jesus the Christ. It is because
of him that we can see God's grace for women. God saw to it that

women had a vital part in the life of Jesus the Christ from his birth to his death and resurrection.[6]

Yet the church's teachings about Jesus are very similar to what their fathers, husbands, and brothers say to Asian women, rather than what Jesus actually says to them in the gospels. The church tells Asian women:

Be obedient and patient as Jesus was to his heavenly father. He endured suffering and death on the cross. That is what good Christian women are supposed to do. When you go through all the suffering, you too, like Jesus, will have a resurrection someday in heaven. Remember, without the cross, there will be no resurrection; no pain, no gain. You must die first in order to live.[7]

This is a hard and confusing teaching for Asian women. They are asking, "Why should we die in order to gain Jesus' love? Can't we love Jesus while being fully alive?" For Asian women self-denial and love are always applied to women in the church as they are in the family. But why isn't this teaching applied to men?

Western colonialism and neo-colonialism have created an added burden to Asian women's belief in Jesus. When Western Christians brought Jesus to Asia, many also brought with them opium and guns.[8] They taught Asians the love of Jesus while they gave Asians the slow death of opium or the fast death of a bullet. When the soldiers of the United States of America raped Vietnamese women and children and killed many Vietnamese people with Agent Orange, guns, and bombs in the name of democracy, the people of the United States still sang, "God Bless America." Death and love are connected in missionary acts whether they are religious or secular.[9]

Some Asian women still choose Jesus in spite of these contradictory personal and political experiences. Why have they continued to choose Jesus over and over again? Where was Jesus when Asian women's bodies were battered, raped, and burned? What has he done to protect them from suffering? Who is Jesus for Asian women? Is he like his own father, who allowed his son to be killed by Roman colonial power and religious hierarchies even though he cried out for help? ("My God, my God, why have you forsaken me?") Is Jesus like one of those irresponsible, frustrated Asian men who promise their lover and wife love and "the good life" but then, after stealing the woman's heart and body, say: "I will come back soon with money and gifts. While I am away, take care of *my* children and old parents. Be loyal to me." Of course such men almost never come back to their hopelessly waiting lover and wife, leaving all the burdens of survival on her shoulders. Are Asian women stuck in the battered women's vicious cycle of passive dependency? In Jesus are they again choosing a male whom they again try to love in spite of his neglect and abandonment simply because they know of no other type of relationship with men?

Some brave Asian women proclaim a resounding no to this endlessly confusing love game defined by "in spite of." They say they love Jesus *because of* and not *in spite of* who he is. They refuse to accept old, familiar ways of relating to their loved ones, which were based on forced sacrifice by women. Rather, they choose the *respect* of self. Jesus is only good for these Asian women when he affirms, respects, and is actively present with them in their long and hard journey for liberation and wholeness. Asian women are discovering with much passion and compassion that Jesus takes sides with the silenced Asian women in his solidarity with all oppressed people. This Jesus is Asian women's new lover, comrade, and suffering servant.

One example of choosing Jesus *because of* is witnessed by a Filipino, Lydia Lascano, a community organizer for slum dwellers for more than ten years, who presented her experience of Jesus as a suffering servant actively present with Filipino women in their suffering and resistance.[10] She believes Jesus' suffering has two different moments. One is "passive" and the other is "active." She identifies poor Filipino women's suffering under colonialism, military dictatorship, and male domination with the suffering of Jesus. She quotes from Isaiah as an example of the passive moment of Jesus' suffering:

He had no beauty, no majesty to draw our eyes, no grace to make us delight in him; his form, disfigured, lost all the likeness of a man. Without beauty, without majesty . . . a thing despised and rejected by men, a man of sorrows familiar with suffering (Is. 53:2-3 NEB).

Lascano sees that the humiliation and dehumanization of the suffering servant are the same as the core experience of Filipino women. Many Filipino women are "suffering passively without hope of freeing themselves" due to the overwhelming hardship of their day-to-day survival and the unawareness of the root causes of their oppression.[11] The suffering servant image of Jesus expresses well the reality that Filipino women are undergoing.[12] Jesus' passive moment of undergoing suffering is very important for poor Filipino women because they then can trust Jesus for his *lived* suffering. Jesus does not lecture or preach about suffering in the way the institutional church does. He knows women's suffering because he was the one who once suffered helplessly like them.

Lydia Lascano also identifies an active moment of Jesus' suffering which contrasts to the passive moment. The active moment of Jesus' suffering is "doing" and "accompanying" as acts of solidarity. For her, to accompany is to be beside and walk with someone.[13] Jesus is actively present in the Filipino women's struggle for liberation, accompanying them in their doing justice. For Filipino women Jesus is not a dispassionate observer of their struggle. Rather, Jesus is an active participant in their fight for justice. Another Filipino woman, Virginia Fabella, explains this accompanying and doing aspect of Jesus' suffering in this way: "Because he stood for all he taught and did, he consequently endured suffering at the hands of his captors as a continuation and overflow of his act of identification with his people who saw no clear end to their misery at the hand of the system."[14]

For Filipino women Jesus is neither a masochist who enjoys suffering, nor a father's boy who blindly does what he is told to do. On the contrary, Jesus is a compassionate man of integrity who identified himself with the oppressed. He "stood for all he taught and did" and took responsibility for the consequences of his choice even at the price of his life. This image of Jesus' suffering gives Asian women the wisdom to differentiate between the suffering imposed by an oppressor and the suffering that is the consequence of one's stand for justice and human dignity.

Korean theologian Choi Man Ja makes this liberative aspect of Jesus' suffering clear in her presentation on feminist Christology. She asks this question: "How do women, who are in the situation of suffering under and obeying oppressive power, take on significance as suffering and obeying servants?"[15] Her answer is:

Suffering is not an end in itself . . . it has definite social references of divine redemptive activity. Suffering exposes patriarchal evil. Jesus endures the yoke of the cross against the evil powers of this patriarchal world. This obedience is different from simple submission to the worldly authority.[16]

Another Korean woman theologian, Park Soon Kyung, developed further the meaning of Jesus' servanthood. According to her, Jesus' servanthood changed the meaning of being a slave among the oppressed people. The yoke of slaves is proof of the world's injustice and witness to the desire for God's righteousness.[17] Therefore, servanthood is not mere submission or obedience. It is instead a powerful witness to evil and a challenge to the powers and the principalities of the world, especially male domination over women. This suffering servant who is undergoing passive suffering with powerless Asian women and who is also accompanying them in their struggle for liberation by doing liberation is the prophetic Messiah who creates a new humanity for oppressed Asian women. Through Jesus Christ, Asian women see new meaning in their suffering and service. They see life-giving aspects in their suffering and service that create a new humanity for the people they serve.

JESUS AS LORD

If the liberative dimension of the suffering servant image frees Asian women from imposed suffering and empowers them to accept suffering as a consequence of their own choice for liberation, the liberative dimension of the Lord image of Jesus frees Asian women from the false authority of the world over them and empowers them to claim true authority which springs from life-giving experiences.

Yet like the image of the suffering servant, the image of Lord also has been used against Asian women, perpetuating their submissive and oppressed status in Asian society and the church. Traditionally Asian women have not been the owners of themselves under mainline patriarchal culture. In the East Asian context where Confucianism was the dominant social and religious ideology, women have had to obey the men in their lives: fathers before marriage, husbands in marriage, and sons in widowhood. The Asian woman's man was her lord. In addition to Confucianism, feudalism and the emperor system did not give much space for the self-determination of women. Even though women could not actively participate in any public or political affairs, they did, of course, suffer from the results of the hierarchical social system (in such concrete ways as lack of food due to oppressive taxes).

Western colonialism used Jesus' image as Lord to justify political and economic domination over many Asian countries. Western missionaries tried to brainwash Asian people by identifying the Western colonizer's Lord Jesus with the Lord for Asians, claiming that the colonizer's Lord Jesus was ruler of the whole universe. Therefore to become a Christian meant obeying the Lord Jesus and the colonial power which brought him to Asia.

This ruler image of Lord Jesus became especially strong in countries like the Philippines which were colonized by Spain. The Spanish conquistadores put Lord Jesus over all the indigenous spirits in the Philippines and put their king over the tribal leadership of the Filipino people. In their recent research many Filipino women theologians have begun to name this lordship ideology of colonial Christianity and its impact on Filipino women's lives.[18] They demonstrate that the lordship ideology of colonial Christianity domesticated the vibrant pre-colonial Filipino women's self-understanding and power in the community.[19] Filipino women shared equally or with even more power than men in domestic and public life before Spanish colonialism. Filipino women were active members in local politics and economics. According to Mary John Mananzan's research, even some male scholars believe that Filipino society was based on a matriarchal culture before colonization.[20] This active image of the power of Filipino women was diminished as Christianity was spread along with the feudal ideology of the colonial power. The ideal image of the Filipino woman became one of passivity, submissiveness, obedience, and chastity.

Under this historical reality many Asian women who were seeking women's liberation and self-determination have become suspicious of the Lord image of Jesus. Yet they also see the liberative power of the image of Jesus as Lord of the poor and oppressed women in Asia. One of the most articulate voices who illustrate this point is Park Soon Kyung from Korea. She is fully aware of ruler ideology (*Herren–Ideologie*) of the image of Jesus as Lord, but she asserts that the lordship of Jesus is "the exact opposite" of patriarchal lordship.[21] For her, the lordship of Jesus means the lordship of justice, which "judges the evil power of rulers in this world."[22] While patriarchal lordship of this world means the ruling power that oppresses people, lordship of Jesus means the power that liberates people. The concept of power and authority in Jesus' lordship is completely different from that in patriarchal lordship. Jesus' lordship is the lordship of the "creator and savior of human and nature."[23] The title *Kyrios* (Lord), which was the word for ruler in Hellenistic culture, transformed its meaning radically when it was used to name the power of Jesus. According to Park Soon Kyung, the lordship of Jesus which comes from God limits the lordship of the rulers in this world by showing the real meaning of lordship through Jesus' deeds and his eschatological vision. All lordship in this world "should return to its origin," which is God.[24] Therefore, all lordship in this world becomes "relativized" under the eschatological vision of Jesus. The lordship in this world should be "the means which serves the salvation of humankind" and "the righteousness and providence of God."[25] Park says:

The Lordship of Christ means that his Lordship is exact opposite of patriarchal Lordship and he eschatologically places the rule of the evil powers in this world under God's judgement. Jesus put a period to the power of patriarchal history by obeying to the righteousness of God as a male even to his death. His Lordship is the Lordship of the righteousness of God which is established by his suffering and death. This Lordship destroys the principality and power of the world and returns all the power and authority to God.[26]

Jesus' lordship, then, says no to patriarchal domination, freeing Asian women from false authority and empowering them to obey only God and not men.

JESUS AS IMMANUEL (GOD-WITH-US)

Jesus, who became the Lord of the universe through his suffering and service for humanity, also shows Asian women God's presence among them. Many Asian women cherish the mystery of the incarnation through Jesus' person and work. "Both the human and divine nature of Jesus are important" for Asian women's identity and mission.[27] Their understanding of Jesus' humanity and divinity, however, is very different from that of Nicene-Chalcedonian theological definitions stressing the Son's relationship to the Father and the two natures of his person. Asian women's concern for the humanity and divinity of Jesus derives from their resistance to colonial, male domination in their churches and cultures. Two distinguished voices which articulate the meaning of incarnation (Logos becoming flesh in Jesus) come from India and Korea. Indian theologian Monica Melanchthon and Korean theologian Lee Oo Chung express the meaning of incarnation and

Immanuel from their specific socio-political and religio-cultural contexts.

Monica Melanchthon locates Jesus' divinity in his sinlessness, virgin birth, resurrection, and "the tremendous authority Jesus claimed and exercised."[28] She explains Jesus' divine power further:

> The thing that impressed the masses was that the teaching of Jesus was differentiated from that of the Scribes by its innate sense of authority. It was with this power vested in him that he performed exorcism, forgave sins, healed the sick and preached with authority. That any mere human could claim such authority and back it up with his actions is beyond the remotest possibility. Hence every New Testament book attributes deity/divinity to Jesus either by direct statement or by inference.[29]

But this Jesus also shares human finitude with us by "lying in the cradle, growing, learning, feeling the pangs of hunger, thirst, anxiety, doubt, grief, and finally death and burial."[30] For Melanchthon, Jesus is a "representative"[31] of the reality of "God-with-us"(Immanuel). She claims, however, that the institutional church distorted Jesus' image by emphasizing his maleness rather than his humanity. Jesus' maleness became "a constitutive factor in deciding the place and role of women."[32] Jesus' maleness excluded women from full participation in the church. She emphasizes that through his incarnation Jesus becomes the representative of a new humanity, not only of men, who are just one-half of the human race, but of women too. Melanchthon warns that emphasizing the maleness of Jesus is a pagan act.

> If we ascribe maleness to Jesus Christ, we are also committing the mistake of ascribing the pagan/Hindu notions of sexuality to our God who transcends this. The Church in India needs to recognize the personhood of Jesus Christ and the fact that Christ is the representative human being for all people including Indian women.[33]

For her, Jesus' humanity embraces all people. The Christian God transcends sexuality and therefore frees Indian women from the stereotypical role assignments in Indian culture. Jesus as the Immanuel (God-with-us) transforms Hindu culture.

In contrast to Melanchthon, Lee Oo Chung shows how Korean culture transforms the meaning of Immanuel, incarnation, and the divinity and humanity of Jesus. Lee Oo Chung advocates a Christology from below in a Korean context. According to her the traditional concept of Korean gods in general is that "special persons having done special things in a lifetime, become gods after death."[34] There is a popular format for these special persons becoming gods:

1) The issue of noble family
2) Extraordinary birth

3) Extraordinary childhood

4) Becoming an orphan at an early age or facing other kinds of suffering

5) Being rescued from the situation or surviving by encountering foster parents

6) Facing a crisis again

7) Winning a victory by fighting and obtaining glory.[35]

The above format is often seen in the stories of heroes who became gods. However, interestingly enough, when the story is about heroines, it has similar steps up to the sixth stage but "in the end she wins victory to become a god by suffering, loving, being patient, and sacrificing instead of fighting."[36] There are many gods in Korea who ascended to the position of god from being human through his or her love, suffering, and sacrifice. Among them, the majority are female.[37]

In this cultural framework Christology from above (God become human) is difficult to understand for the ordinary masses of people (minjung), especially laborers. Conceptual and abstract images of God in Christian theology, such as "totally other," "unmovable mover," and "immutable, impassable, unchangeable God," do not make much sense to Korean people. Lee Oo Chung observes Korean people's understanding of Jesus:

> The doctrine of God's becoming a man is a hard proposition for them [Korean Minjung] to accept. However "A man becomes a god" is easy for them to understand. Jesus Christ as Messiah can be better understood in the image of historical Jesus who has loved his neighbors more than himself and for this great love he went through surmounting suffering and sacrifice to become the Messiah, the Savior of humankind. Whereas the theory which says that because Jesus was God he was Messiah does not appeal too much.[38]

Lee proposes a radical task of liberation for Korean Christian women: In order to fully "experience the mystery of doctrine of incarnation by choice," Korean women must get out of the imposed service role in the church and society. This is possible when Korean women "elevate our self-consciousness as high as in the realm of the divine."[39] This elevation of women's self-consciousness will be generated from women's "experience of real love of God, for our totality of being the body, mind, and soul, as an individual and as a social being."[40]

Korean women experience the mystery of incarnation and "God-with-us" by becoming like Jesus. Many Korean Christians in the movement claim that we should become "little Jesuses" in order to become true Christians. For many Korean women, Jesus is not the objectified divine being whom people must worship. Rather, Jesus is the one we relive through our lives. The meaning of Immanuel, then, has been changed through Korean mythological symbols and language from God-*with*-us to God-*among*-us, and finally to God-*is*-us in our struggle to reclaim our full humanity.

NEW EMERGING IMAGES

New images of Jesus have emerged from Asian women's movements for self-determination and liberation. The freer Asian women become from the patriarchal authorities of their family, church, and society, the more creative they become in naming their experience of Jesus Christ. Sometimes the images of Jesus are transformed to the degree that they show the radical discontinuity between the ones found in the Jewish and Christian culture and those from the Asian women's movement. Some Asian women have become confident enough in themselves to name the presence of Jesus Christ in their own culture, indigenous religions, and secular political movements, a Christological identity that is not directly connected in the traditional sense with Christianity. They use religio-political symbols and motifs from their movement in order to describe what Jesus means for them in today's Asia. This is a *Christological transformation* created out of Asian women's experiences as they struggle for full humanity. The old Christological paradigms are transformed, new meanings are achieved, and diverse images of Jesus Christ emerge. Asian women as meaning-makers jump into an unknown open future shaping a new Christianity out of their own experience that never before existed in history. The following are examples of new, emerging images of Jesus Christ derived from Asian women who believe in their historical lived experience more than imposed authority.

JESUS AS LIBERATOR, REVOLUTIONARY, AND POLITICAL MARTYR

Jesus Christ is portrayed as liberator in many writings of women from various Asian countries such as India, Indonesia, Korea, the Philippines, and Sri Lanka. The reason why Jesus as liberator is the most prominent new image among Asian women is a consequence of their historical situation. The liberation from colonialism, neo-colonialism, poverty, and military dictatorship, as well as from overarching patriarchy, has been the major aspiration of twentieth-century Asian women.

In the composite paper of the EATWOT Asian Women's Consultation, entitled "Women and the Christ Event," Jesus is defined as "the prototype of the real liberator."[41] They also claim that Jesus as liberator is evident "in the image of liberators in other non-Christian religions and movements."[42] A participant at the consultation, Pauline Hensman, a woman theologian from Sri Lanka, described Jesus Christ as the one who "came with good news to the poor, oppressed and downtrodden" and through whom "humankind was released from servitude and alienation by those who dominated and oppressed them."[43] This image of Jesus Christ as liberator is made concrete as revolutionary or political martyr in the Filipino women's reflection on the Christ event presented at the same consultation. According to Lydia Lascano from the Philippines, Filipino women who participate in the people's struggle for liberation "live out with their lives the Christ event — Jesus' life, passion, death and resurrection — leaving the mark of their womenhood in the Philippine liberation project, the project of God."[44]

Filipino women have suffered (under more than three hundred years of Spanish and American colonialism and military dictatorships) and have resisted in order to survive and reclaim their human dignity as a people. Filipino women find Christ's suffering, death and resurrection *in* the suffering, death, and resurrection of Filipino women themselves. They see revolutionary acts of Christ among "the militant protesting Filipino women who have taken up the struggle for themselves and for the rest of the Filipino nation."[45] In their organized action for liberation, Filipino women have been arrested, raped, tortured, imprisoned, and displaced from their homes. Many have even been killed in their struggle toward self-determination for their people. Their names are today remembered by women in protest movements. Some names include:

> Lorena Barros, a freedom fighter; Filomena Asuncion, a deaconess who offered her life for the conscientization of peasants; Leticia Celestino, a factory worker shot in the picketlines while demanding for a just wage; Angelina Sayat, a freedom fighter who died while in the custody of the military; Puri Pedro, a catechist who served the farmers, was tortured and killed while being treated in a hospital.[46]

In the death of those political martyrs for freedom is the death of Jesus. Unlike the women of Jerusalem in Jesus' time, women are not just comforting or shedding tears for Jesus on his way to the cross. Filipino women shed blood for their people. Sister Lascano explains the political martyrdom among Filipino women:

> Today, the passion of Christ in the Filipino people is fashioning women disciples who would accompany the suffering Christ alive among the people, not merely to comfort and support but even to die with them. In the passion for social transformation, death takes on a new level of meaningfulness. . . . Today many Filipino women do not merely accompany Christ to Calvary as spectators. They carry the cross with him and undergo his passion in an act of identification with his suffering.[47]

The resurrection of Jesus comes alive in the resurrection of these martyrs. The Filipino women's resistance movement makes the spirit and vision of these martyrs come alive by persistent "organized action" and "active waiting and watching" for the future victory of the struggle.[48] When poor Filipino women are awakened to see the root cause of their suffering in structural evils, they begin to claim for themselves land and rights as human beings. They utter in discovery, "We will also have our Exodus!"[49] And they take political action. This discovery has stirred hope in their hearts, believing that "the liberating God of the Exodus has become alive in the resurrected Christ, now alive among them as the *Bagong Kristo* (the New Christ)."[50]

JESUS AS MOTHER, WOMAN, AND SHAMAN

Many Asian women portray Jesus with the image of mother. They see Jesus as a compassionate one who feels the suffering of humanity deeply, suffers and weeps with them. Since Jesus' compassion is so deep, the mother image is the most appropriate one for Asian women to express their experience of Jesus' compassion. Hong Kong theologian Kwok Pui-lan explains this point in her essay "God Weeps with Our Pain":

> Jesus cried out for Jerusalem. His sorrow was so deep Matthew had to use a "feminine metaphor" to describe what he actually felt: How often would I have gathered your children together as a hen gathers her brood under her wings (Matt. 23:37).[51]

Like a mother who laments over her dead son who died in the wars in Indochina, like many weeping Korean mothers whose sons and daughters were taken by the secret police, Jesus cried out for the pain of suffering humanity. Korean theologian Lee Oo Chung questions why Jesus suffered so keenly before his death.[52] Even Jesus says to the disciples: "The sorrow in my heart is so great that it almost crushes me. Stay here and keep watch." Jesus was not like one of those saints and heroes who died calmly and serenely. According to Lee, Jesus was different from those saints and heroes because they "bore only their own suffering while Jesus took on himself the pain and suffering of all his neighbors, even of all humankind."[53]

Like some of Jesus' disciples, people who were only interested in the expansion of their personal glory, honor, and power ("When you sit on your throne in your glorious kingdom, we want you to let us sit with you, one at your right and one at your left" — Mark 10:37) could not feel the pain of the suffering poor nor see the violence and evil of the oppressors.[54] Jesus was different from them in that he felt the pain of all humanity like a compassionate mother. Lee discovers the image of Jesus as a compassionate mother who really feels the hurt and pain of her child in Korean folklore:

> In the National Museum in Kyungju, Korea, capital of the ancient Silla Kingdom, is a beautiful bell. The Silla Kingdom at the time enjoyed peace, but the King, a devout Buddhist, wanted to protect his people from foreign invasion. His advisors suggested that he build a huge temple bell to show the people's devotion to the Buddha.

A specialist in the art of bellmaking was commissioned. But despite his skill and care, he failed time and again to produce a bell with a beautiful sound. Finally, he went back to the council of religious leaders. After a long discussion, they concluded that the best way to give a beautiful tone to the bell was to sacrifice a pure young maiden.

Soldiers were sent to find and fetch such a young girl. Coming upon a poor mother in a farm village with her small daughter, they took the child away, while she cried out piteously: "Emille, Emille!" — "Mother! O Mother!" When the molten lead and iron were prepared, the little girl was thrown in. At last the bellmaker succeeded. The bell, called the Emille Bell, made a sound more beautiful than any other.

When it rang, most people praised the art that had produced such a beautiful sound. But whenever the mother whose child had been sacrificed heard it, her heart broke anew.[55]

For Lee, Jesus is like the little girl's mother. Jesus' heart breaks anew when he hears the cry of humanity. People who do not know the meaning of sacrifice enjoy the achievement based on other people's sacrifice. But people "who understand the sacrifice can feel the pain."[56] This image of Jesus shows Asian women that the redemption of humankind "has not come through those who are comfortable and unconcerned, but only through the One who shared the suffering of all humankind."[57]

This compassionate, sensitive mother image of Jesus was shared by the Indonesian theologian Marianne Katoppo. She illustrates her point by quoting a prayer of Anselm and a poem from the Indian poet Narayan Vaman Tilak:

And thou, Jesus, sweet Lord, art Thou not also a mother?
Truly, Thou art a mother, the mother of all mothers
Who tasted death, in Thy desire to give life to Thy children
— Anselm[58]

Tenderest Mother-Guru mine,
Saviour, where is love like thine?
— Narayan Vaman Tilak[59]

This mother image of Jesus demolishes "the paternalistic, authoritarian and hierarchical patterns" in our life and builds the "maternal, compassionate, sensitive, bearing and upbearing" relationship among people.[60]

Some Asian women see Jesus Christ as a female figure in their specific historical situation. Two articulate voices on this position are found in Korea. Park Soon Kyung concluded her Christology at the gathering of the Korean Association of Women Theologians by saying that even though Jesus has a male physical form, he is "a symbol of females and the oppressed" due to his identification with the one who hurts the most. Therefore, on a symbolic level, we may call Jesus the *"woman Messiah"* who is the liberator of the oppressed.[61] She claims justification for naming Jesus' humanity as female in the current historical situation because Christology needs to be liberated from the patriarchal church structure.

Choi Man Ja goes one step further by identifying Korean women's historical struggle for liberation with "the praxis of messiahship."[62] She says, "Even though women are excluded from the ordained ministry, in fact women are the true praxis of messiah-Jesus, in Korea."[63] For her, Jesus' messiahship comes from his suffering servantship. Therefore, she can recognize the praxis of new humanity most clearly through a female messiah who is in the suffering and struggle of Asian women. This female Christ is "the new humanity, siding with the oppressed, and liberating women from their suffering."[64]

Another female image of Jesus comes from the image of the shaman. Virginia Fabella shares her learning from Korean women in her article "Asian Women and Christology."[65] Under oppressive political and economic oppression, and under the added burden of the Confucian system of ethics which inculcates male domination, Korean women's life experience is *han* itself. The resentment, indignation, sense of defeat, resignation, and nothingness in *han* make many Korean women brokenhearted and physically sick. In this situation, what would be the significance of Jesus Christ for them? Fabella cites an answer from a Korean woman: "If Jesus Christ is to make sense to us, then Jesus Christ must be a priest of Han" for minjung women.[66] For the minjung women, salvation and redemption means being exorcised from their accumulated *han,* untangling of their many-layered *han.* Since Korean indigenous religion is shamanism, Korean women easily accept the Jesus of the synoptic gospels, who exorcised and healed the sick and possessed like a Korean shaman. As the Korean shaman has been a healer, comforter, and counselor for Korean women, Jesus Christ healed and comforted women in his ministry.

In Korea the majority of shamans are women. Shamanism is the only religion among the various Korean religious traditions where women have been the center all through its development. Women shamans have been "big sisters" to many deprived minjung women, untangling their *han* and helping them cope with life's tribulations.[67] When Korean women, therefore, see Jesus Christ as the priest of *han,* they connect with the female image of Jesus more than the male image of Jesus. They take Jesus as a big sister just as they take the shaman as a big sister in their community.

The female image of Jesus Christ is expressed most vividly by a theologian in India, Gabriele Dietrich,[68] who makes a connection between women's menstruation and Jesus' shedding of blood on the cross. She sees the meaning of the Eucharist in women's monthly bloodshed. She expresses her point powerfully through her poem:

I am a woman
and my blood
cries out:
Who are you
to deny life
to the life-givers?
Each one of you
has come from the womb
but none of you
can bear woman
when she is strong
and joyful and competent.
You want our tears
to clamour for protection.
Who are you
to protect us
from yourselves?

I am a woman
and my monthly bloodshed
makes me aware
that blood
is meant for life.
It is you
who have invented
those lethal machines
spreading death:
Three kilotonnes of explosives
for every human being
on earth.

I am a woman
and the blood
of my abortions
is crying out.
I had to kill
my child
because of you
who deny work to me
so that i cannot feed it.
I had to kill my child
because i am unmarried
and you would harass me
to death

if i defy
your norms.

I am a woman
and the blood
of being raped
is crying out.
This is how you keep
your power intact,
how you make me tremble
when i go out at night.
This is how you keep
me in place
in my house where
you rape me again.
I am not taking this
any longer.

I am a woman
and the blood
of my operation
is crying out.
Even if i am a nun
you still use my body
to make money
by giving me a hysterectomy
when i don't need it.
My body is in the clutches
of husbands, policemen,
doctors, pimps.
There is no end
to my alienation.

I am a woman
and the blood
of my struggles
is crying out.
Yes, my comrades,
you want us
in the forefront
because you have learnt
you cannot do without us.
You need us
in the class struggle
as you need us

in bed and to cook
your grub
to bear
your children to dress
your wounds.
You will celebrate
women's day
like mother's day
garlands
for our great supporters.
Where would we be
without our women?

I am a woman
and the blood
of my sacrifices
cries out to the sky
which you call heaven.
I am sick of you priests
who have never bled
and yet say:
This is my body
given up for you
and my blood
shed for you
drink it.
Whose blood
has been shed
for life
since eternity?
I am sick of you priests
who rule the *garbagriha,*
who adore the womb
as a source for life
and keep me shut out
because my blood
is polluting.

I am a woman
and i keep bleeding
from my womb
but also from my heart
because it is difficult
to learn to hate

and it might not help
if i hate you.

I still love
my little son
who bullies his sister.
He has learnt it outside,
how do i stop him?
I still love
my children's father
because he was there
when i gave birth.
I still long
for my lover's touch
to break the spell
of perversion
which has grown
like a wall
between women and men.
I still love
my comrades in arms
because they care
for others who suffer
and there is hope
that they give their bodies
in the struggle for life
and not just for power.
But i have learned
to love my sisters.
We have learned
to love one another.
We have learned
even to respect
ourselves.

I am a woman
and my blood
cries out.
We are millions
and strong together.
You better hear us
or you may be doomed.

Dietrich questions the hypocrisy of the patriarchal church and society
which "deny life to the life-givers." They "adore the womb as a source"

but shut out women from full participation in life. The womb is praised but not those who have wombs. Most of the so-called higher world religions condemn women's menstruation as dirty or polluting. Women cannot preside in the ritual of many religions because their monthly flow will "corrupt" holy altars. Dietrich asks Christian priests who worship the holy blood-shedding of Jesus: "Whose blood has been shed for life since eternity?" Then she claims priests, not women, "have never bled and yet say: this is my body given up for you and my blood shed for you, drink it." Jesus shed blood on the cross due to his solidarity with the poor, oppressed, and alienated. He bled so as to give others everlasting life. Like Jesus, women's blood has been shed from eternity. Women's menstruation is a holy Eucharist through which the renewal of life becomes possible. Jesus joins women in his life-giving bleeding.[69]

JESUS AS WORKER AND GRAIN

Female images of Jesus Christ enable Asian women to image Jesus on the earth. The revelation of God they have heard from the church is usually the revelation from above. Theology based on the revelation from above can easily be distorted into a theology of domination because this theology is based on the abstract thinking of the head and not on the concrete experience of the body. It is based on distant (and largely male) intellectualism and not on the everyday, experiential reality of Asian women. Some Asian women find Jesus in the most ordinary, everyday experience. They see the revelation of God from below, the bottom, the earth. They refuse any kind of heroism. They are not looking for great men and women to worship. Rather, they want to find God, the saving presence within their daily lives.

A witness of faith from a Korean factory worker shows the meaning of Jesus Christ among the ordinary poor people:

I don't know how to live a Christ-like life. But I am discovering and awakening to the meaning of it little by little in my daily life. This is a cautious and mysterious process. [In order to explain this point,] I would like to talk about my mother. She is a woman full of "Han." She describes herself like that. She was married when she was seventeen. She gave birth to three children. Then her husband died even before she became thirty. Now my mother gets up 4:30 a.m. every morning and goes to marketplace for banding. There are too many people in the marketplace. It is hard to walk there. I think that marketplace is truly our context of life.

From early morning my mother carries heavy bundles and walks around the marketplace distributing the vinyl bags used for wrapping to banders and stores. She gathers the money from them later. That work is too strenuous for a woman of my mother's age and physical strength. Therefore, whenever she happens to have a holiday (like a full moon festival), she becomes sick and has to stay in bed. Her shoulder becomes unbalanced and her back is bent. Her cheek becomes red with ice since she has to work outside in the cold winter. Her life seems like a tired, hard, and insignificant one.

Whenever I see my mother, her face reminds me of the tired faces of my friends in the factory who are working eighteen to twenty-four hours a day without even any facial expression. Workers do not stop their work even when they are overwhelmed by despair and disgust. And workers really know how to love other people. Since they experience despair, are humiliated by the rich and endure miserable situations, they know how to love the people in despair under every circumstance—even though we are in despair all the time. The world is constructed out of these hearts.

When I see workers, I feel the breath and heart-beat of history and the meaning of humanity and Christ in them. I think we will not be saved without workers because workers truly have the loving power and unbeatable endurance. I wonder how Jesus the Christ will look when he comes back again. When I was young, I dreamt about Jesus wearing silvery white clothing, accompanying many angels with bright light and great sounds of music. But now I wonder. If Jesus comes again, he may come to us wearing ragged clothing and give my tired mother, who even dozes off while she is standing, a bottle of *Bakas*[70] or he may come to me, working mindlessly in the noisy factory, and quietly help my work while wearing an oily worker's uniform. I think *our Christ is the ground of life, and my faith is in the midst of this working life and workers.*[71]

This factory worker sees her Christ in workers and their hard struggle for survival. She does not believe any longer in the image of a flamboyant Jesus who looks like one of the rich and famous people in her childhood. She finds Jesus in her fellow workers who endure despair, humiliation, and back-breaking hard work, yet share their love and resources with other workers. Jesus Christ does not descend from glorious-looking heaven; Christ emerges from the broken-body experience of workers when they affirm life and dare to love other human beings in spite of their brokenness. Workers become Christ to each other when they touch each other's wounds and heal each other through sharing food, work, and hope.

Another image of Jesus Christ which emerges from the earth is found in a poem from an Indian woman. She meets her Jesus Christ when she receives two hundred grams of gruel in a famine-stricken area. For her, Christ, God's beloved Son, is food for hungry people.

> Every noon at twelve
> In the blazing heat

God comes to me
in the form of
Two hundred grams of gruel.

I know Him in every grain
I taste Him in every lick.
I commune with Him as I gulp
For He keeps me alive, with
Two hundred grams of gruel.

I wait till next noon
and now know He'd come:
I can hope to live one day more
For you made God to come to me as
Two hundreds grams of gruel.

I know now that God loves me —
Not until you made it possible.
Now I know what you're speaking about
For God so loves this world
That He gives His beloved Son
Every noon through You.[72]

Without food, there is no life. When starving people eat the food, they experience God "in every grain." They "know" and "taste" God when they chew each grain. Food makes them alive. The greatest love of God for the starving people is food. When the grain from the earth sustains their life, they discover the meaning of the phrase, "For God so loves this world that He gives His beloved Son." When God gives them food through other concerned human beings, God gives them God's "beloved Son," Jesus Christ.

In conclusion, we have observed that there are *traditional* images of Jesus, which are being interpreted in fresh, creative ways by Asian women, largely based on their experiences of survival in the midst of oppression and on their efforts to liberate themselves. We also have observed *new* images of Jesus that offer a direct challenge to traditional Christologies. These new images of Jesus are also based on Asian women's experiences of survival and liberation. Because Jesus was a male, however, some Asian women think there is a limit to how much he can be transformed to meet the needs of Asian women. This is the main reason why Asian women theologians have emphasized the importance of Mary in their recent writings.

NOTES

1. "Summary Statement from the Theological Study Group," paper presented at the Consultation on Asian Women's Theology on Christology, Singapore, Novem-

ber 20-29, 1987. This consultation was sponsored by *In God's Image*. For more information on the conference, see *IGI* (December 1987-March 1988). The documents from the consultation were published in *IGI* during 1988-1989. (Hereafter referred to as Consultation on Asian Women's Theology–1987.)

2. Ibid., p. 1.

3. Ibid., p. 2.

4. Ibid.

5. Choi Man Ja, "Feminist Christology," Consultation on Asian Women's Theology – 1987, p. 3.

6. Komol Arayapraatep, "Christology," Consultation on Asian Women's Theology – 1987, p. 6.

7. This is the common teaching Asian women receive from the institutional, male-dominated churches in Asia. When I was a Sunday school teacher at a Korean church in Orange County, California, in 1983, I witnessed a Korean woman, who was a bible teacher for a college student group, share her experience of death and resurrection of self in front of the entire congregation. She confessed how sinful she was in relation to her husband. She said that she was not able to obey her husband because she thought he was not reasonable and fair. So she argued with him a lot. One day her husband, who was a medical doctor, threw a kitchen knife at her out of anger during an argument. Fortunately the knife missed her and stuck into the wall behind her. At that point, she said, she experienced the love of God through the judgment of her husband. She believed then that as a wife she had to obey her husband as God's will. She witnessed to the congregation that her old self was *dead* and her new self was born through her husband's *love*. This woman concluded her statement with: "There have been no arguments and only peace in my family after I nailed myself on the cross and followed God's will." After her talk, the entire congregation responded to her with a very loud "Hallelujah!" This is only one example of "woman hate" in Asian churches. I have heard countless examples of women's oppression in the church from other Asian women through various church women's gatherings.

8. For more information on the missionary history of China, see Kwok Pui-lan, "The Emergence of Asian Feminist Consciousness on Culture and Theology" (Hong Kong: unpublished paper, 1988).

9. I know that there are conflicting views on the role of the missionaries in Asia. Some people think that their role was destructive and others believe it was positive. My view is that their role was primarily, though not exclusively, negative.

10. Lydia Lascano, "Women and the Christ Event," in *Proceedings: Asian Women's Consultation* (Manila: EATWOT, 1985), pp. 121-29.

11. Ibid., p. 123.

12. Ibid., p. 125.

13. Ibid.

14. Virginia Fabella, "Asian Women and Christology," *IGI* (September 1987), p. 15.

15. Choi, p. 6.

16. Ibid.

17. Park Soon Kyung, *Hankook Minjok Kwa Yeosung shinhak eu Kwajae* [*The Korean Nation and the Task of Women's Theology*], p. 50.

18. See Honclada, pp. 13-19.

19. See Mary John Mananzan, "The Philipino Woman: Before and After the

Spanish Conquest of the Philippines," in *Essays on Women* (Manila: Woman's Studies Program, Saint Scholastica's College), pp. 7-36.

20. Ibid.

21. Park Soon Kyung, *Hankook Minjok Kwa Yeosung Shinhak eu Kwajae* [*The Korean Nation and the Task of Women's Theology*], p. 47.

22. Ibid.

23. Ibid., p. 48.

24. Ibid.

25. Ibid., p. 49.

26. Ibid., p. 47.

27. Consultation on Asian Women's Theology—1987, p. 2.

28. Monica Melanchthon, "Christology and Women," Consultation on Asian Women's Theology—1987.

29. Ibid., p. 1.

30. Ibid.

31. Ibid., p. 2.

32. Ibid., p. 4.

33. Ibid., p. 6. Note the contradictory theological position on the appropriation of the Hindu notion of God in Christian theology (cf. Gallup).

34. Lee Oo Chung, "Korean Cultural and Feminist Theology," *IGI* (September 1987), p. 36.

35. Ibid.

36. Ibid., p. 37.

37. Ibid.

38. Ibid.

39. Ibid., p. 38.

40. Ibid.

41. "Women and the Christ Event," in *Proceedings: Asian Women's Consultation* (Manila: EATWOT, 1985), p. 131.

42. Ibid.

43. Pauline Hensman, "Women and the Christ Event," in *Proceedings: Asian Women's Consultation* (Manila: EATWOT, 1985), p. 116.

44. Lascano, p. 121.

45. Ibid., p. 125.

46. Ibid., p. 127.

47. Ibid.

48. Ibid., p. 128.

49. Ibid.

50. Ibid.

51. Kwok, "God Weeps with Our Pain," in *New Eyes for Reading: Biblical and Theological Reflections by Women from the Third World,* ed. J. Pobee and B. von Wartenberg-Potter (Oak Park, Ill.: Meyer Stone Books, 1986), p. 92.

52. Lee Oo Chung, "One Woman's Confession of Faith," in Pobee and von Wartenberg-Potter, p. 19.

53. Ibid.

54. Ibid.

55. Ibid., pp. 19-20.

56. Ibid., p. 20.

57. Ibid.

58. Marianne Katoppo, "Mother Jesus," in *Voices of Women: An Asian Anthology*, ed. Alison O'Grady (Singapore: Asian Christian Women's Conference, 1978), p. 12.

59. Katoppo, *Compassionate and Free*, p. 79.

60. Katoppo, "Mother Jesus," in O'Grady, p. 12.

61. Park Soon Kyung, *The Korean Nation and the Task of Women's Theology*, p. 51. See also James Cone, *God of the Oppressed* (New York: Harper and Row, 1975). Cone makes a similar argument. For Cone, Jesus is black because if Jesus represents oppressed humanity, Jesus must be black in our historical situation where black people are constantly crucified.

62. Choi, p. 8.

63. Ibid., p. 7.

64. Ibid., p. 6.

65. See Virginia Fabella, "Asian Women and Christology."

66. Ibid.

67. Ibid.

68. Gabriele Dietrich is of German origin. Since 1972 she has been working in South India, first in Bangalore, and for the last ten years in Madurai, teaching in a Tamil-medium college. She is committed to the women's movement. I include her as a theologian in India due to her commitment and her identification with Indian women and her acceptance by other Indian women in the movement.

69. Gabriele Dietrich, *One day i shall be like a banyan tree* (Belgium: Dileep S. Kamat, 1985).

70. Popular Korean drink.

71. Suh Nam Dong, *In Search of Minjung Theology* (Seoul, Korea: Kankil Sa, 1983), pp. 355-56. Translation and emphasis mine.

72. Anonymous, "From Jaini Bi—With Love," in O'Grady, p. 11. The editor explains that the Jaini Bi stands for all people who suffer extreme deprivation in a seemingly uncaring world but who receive a spark of hope from humanitarian concerns and actions.

15

Jesus Christ in Popular Piety in the Philippines

SALVADOR T. MARTINEZ

Andres Cruz is in his fifties. He drives a jeepney fourteen hours a day, seven days a week, to support his wife and five children. His daily earnings of twenty-five pesos are hardly sufficient to buy food for his hungry family. But he has a *panata* (vow) to buy a garland of *sampaguitas* (jasmine) every day to decorate the image of the Black Nazarene which hangs on the wind-shield of his vehicle. He fulfills his promise unfailingly. Also, every Friday afternoon he goes to Quiapo Church, lights a few candles, recites the rosary, wipes the feet of the image of the Black Nazarene with a towel which he wraps around his neck all day. He believes that some power is transferred from the image to the towel and carrying it on his body will bring him luck and protect him from harm. He keeps another towel in his house, one that has touched the sacred image on its special feast day in January, to guar-antee the good health and happiness of his family.

My primary task here is to describe how the majority of Filipinos think of Christ. Andres Cruz belongs to that majority. "Majority" here refers to Filipinos, usually Roman Catholics,[1] who are poor, rural, and have had minimal or no education They practice folk Catholicism. Their religious observances, from the ordinary Sunday mass to the elaborate town fiesta, which in the first place were of Spanish folk origin, are embellished with local customs and traditions.

Jaime Bulatao, a Jesuit psychologist, describes Philippine Christianity as "split-level," which he defines "as the co-existence within the same person of two or more thought-and-behavior systems which are inconsistent with each other."[2] The inconsistency may not be perceived by the person or it is pushed "into the rear portions of consciousness." It is taken for granted and forgotten. Hence, neither the feeling of inconsistency nor of hypocrisy arises.

BEGINNINGS OF CHRISTIANITY

Christianity came to the Philippines with Ferdinand Magellan in 1521. On an Easter Sunday, March 31st of that year, the first mass was celebrated on the island of Limasawa. Many became followers of Magellan's faith. They were convinced that the "thunder and lightning" from his ships' cannons were a display of the power of his gods.

In the island of Cebu, Magellan made further advancement for Christianity. Christianization, he felt, was the perfect way to strengthen the link between Spain and the newly conquered islands. The process was facilitated by three factors: fear, materialism and sex. First, the people were afraid that they would be destroyed if they refused to embrace the faith of their conquerors. Indeed, Pigafetta, Magellan's chronicler, wrote: "As handkerchiefs wipe off the sweat, so did our arms overthrow and destroy our adversaries and those who hate our faith." Secondly, they believed that the religion of the foreigners was the source of their power and might. Magellan in fact promised Rajah Humabon, the island chief, that if he became a Christian he would become more powerful and would be invulnerable. Thirdly, Magellan tried to control the sexual activities of his crew by denouncing as mortal sin any sexual affair with pagan women. Hence, to appease God's wrath, Magellan's men zealously made it their mission to convert the native women and artlessly baptized those whom they fancied. In a week's time, King Humabon, his whole household and 800 of his subjects were baptized by the fleet's chaplain. As a baptismal gift, the Queen was given a wooden statue of the Child Jesus. Pigafetta wrote that upon seeing the statue, "she was overcome with contrition and asked for baptism amid her tears ... (later) she asked to give her the little Child Jesus to keep in place of her idols."[3]

RELIGIOUS PRACTICES OF PRE-SPANISH FILIPINOS

Before going any further, a brief look at the religious beliefs and practices of the early Filipinos would be helpful.

Four hundred years is a very long time. It would seem that the beliefs and practices of the early Filipinos, indeed, their native identity, would have been removed and erased by colonization and "Christianization," first by Spain and then by America. Yet, they persist. They were woven into the religion imposed on them by their colonizers. As one historian argued:

The Filipinos were no mere passive recipients of the cultural stimulus created by the Spanish conquest. Circumstances gave them considerable freedom in selecting their responses to Hispanisation. Their response varied all the way from acceptance to indifference and rejection. The capacity of Filipinos for creative social adjustment is attested by the manner in which they adapted many Hispanic features to their own indigenous culture.[4]

The pre-Spanish Filipinos believed in a Supreme Being, *Bathala*,[5] who is Lord of all, the all-powerful *maykapal* (creator or maker of all things). Bathala lives up in the sky. He is represented on earth by *anitos*. There are varieties of *anitos* and they are assigned to specific offices: there are *anitos* who are assigned to help the farmers and protect their fields; there are *anitos* of fishing and navigation; there are *anitos* of the battlefield, of diseases, of the sucking child, of nursing mothers and *anitos* of lovers and of generations.

Like their Asian neighbors, the early Filipinos also practiced ancestor worship. They deified their dead ancestors, gave them *anito* stature and attributed divine powers to them. They called upon them to intercede on their behalf with Bathala. They preserved their memory in *larawan* or *likha*, images made of wood, bone, ivory or gold and they offered food, wine, gold ornaments and invocations before them.

The rites and rituals of sacrifices and thanksgiving were performed by priests and priestesses (*katalona*). They were actually witches and sorcerers. In addition, there were lesser priests or quasi-priests who performed various incantations and witchcrafts.

Some of these beliefs and practices are still held by many Catholic, especially rural, Christians. This leads to the question by some scholars as to whether there is Christianity (or Catholicism) as such in the Philippines. Comments Juan Francisco,

> For we can say without being accused of partiality that much if not all of the indigenous religious practices were unclothed of their native garments, and then garbed with the accepted Christian (or Catholic) habiliments, which made it possible for the *Indios* to be converted easily. But the conversion was not substantial, for it was only a change of garments.

The first Filipino converts to Catholicism substituted veneration of saints for the *magaanito* rituals and replaced their *anitos* with images of the Christian saints. So, as there were *anitos* for every human activity, there are now saints for specific favors: a saint for sterile mothers to pray to, one for finding a good husband, another for finding lost objects, and so on.

DEVOTION TO THE INFANT JESUS

Historians speculate that the Santo Nino image given to the Queen of Cebu on the occasion of her baptism and which she kept "in place of her idols" was the very image that was found by one of the soldiers of Legaspi in an unburned house of a fleeing Cebuano native in 1565. Legaspi considered the discovery a good omen, a sure sign that his mission to spread Christianity and establish a Spanish colony in the Far East would succeed. On the spot where the image was found he ordered a chapel and the first Spanish settlement in the Philippines to be built. The image was enshrined in the main altar, and the settlement was dedicated to the blessed name of Jesus. When the natives returned to the city and saw that their *Balahala,* as they called the image, was equally revered by the Spaniards, they became friendly with them. The *Balahala,* they testified, had been their protector for many years.

Since then the Santo Nino has been venerated by the people of Cebu. It has become the symbol of protection in times of hardship: drought, disease, hunger, fire and war.

Through the years many tales have been told about the numerous miracles of the Santo Nino. It is said to have checked an epidemic in 1572 and in the succeeding years brought an end to a drought, helped to win a battle, saved a ship and her passengers from sinking, spared the city from burning. Practical jokes have also been attributed to it: that it has come down from its pedestal to take a walk, to buy fish in the market, and at one time, to enlist in the army.

On every second Sunday after Epiphany, the feast of the Santo Nino has been celebrated since Legaspi's time. The main feature of the feast is the *sinulog.* It is a dance patterned after Muslim ceremonial dances and performed by the pilgrims purportedly to offer praise and supplications to the Santo Nino. The origin of the practice is unclear. The legend is that it was first performed after a Muslim raid of the Visayas. In the attack, it is believed that the Santo Nino made the island of Cebu invisible to the enemies.

The *sinulog* is danced following the high mass. With blaring drum music in the background, pilgrims from all walks of life begin dancing at the courtyard into the sanctuary, inching their way to the altar with shouts of thanksgiving and petition to "Pit Senor," as the image is popularly called. The dancing goes on for several hours, from mid-morning till late in the afternoon. When the dancers reach the altar, they kiss the image and touch it with their handkerchiefs, rosaries and other articles, which they believe acquire healing powers.

Devotion to the Holy Child is not limited to the people of Cebu. It has spread throughout the archipelago in the same way that the Infant of Prague has gained devotees in Europe in the 17th century. Santo Nino is the patron saint of the cities of Tacloban, Iloilo, Cadiz, two districts of Manila (Pandacan and Tondo), and many towns all over the Philippines. The towns of Kalibo, Kabankalan, Cadiz, Iloilo, and Bacolod have their own versions of the *sinulog.* In these places, the Mardi Gras-like festivals have become a tourist attraction. The preparation for them is long, elaborate and expensive. "Tribes" (actually composed of peasant workers of the big sugar haciendas) compete with each other for prizes for the best or the most original float, costume, dance steps, cheers, beat, etc.

The *sinulog*, or *ati-atihan*, or *dinagyang*, may have lost some of its original religious significance. But to many pilgrims it remains more than just a dance or just a simulation of the battles between the Christians and the Muslims. As one psychologist puts it: "It is the creative expression, the serious enactment of a true-to-life situation: a cry of need, an appeal for help, a shout of joy, a thanksgiving, an act of faith and worship, a total religious experience felt and expressed by the whole person, hands and feet, head and face, limb, nerve, and sinew, body and soul."

CULT OF THE BLACK NAZARENE

Another example of folk religious devotion is centered in Quiapo Church in Manila, where since the 17th century people pay homage to the image of the Black Nazarene, a larger than life-size image of Christ carrying a heavy cross on bended knee. The image is believed to have been sculpted by a Mexican artist and brought to Manila by Recollect fathers in the late 16th century. On every 9th of January, the feast of the Black Nazarene is celebrated. Devotees carry the huge image on their shoulders and thousands of others follow, jamming their way through the crowded, narrow streets of Quiapo and squeezing their way to touch the image. A similar procession is staged on Mondays of every Holy Week.

Like the Santo Nino devotees, the Black Nazarene followers believe that their patron saint can effect healing to the sick, bring about success and help in times of need and distress. On any ordinary Friday afternoon, Quiapo Church spills over with worshippers who come to kiss, to touch, to wipe, or to offer a prayer to *Nuestro Padre Jesus Nazareno*. Most of the devotees are in their late 40s and early 50s, married, and from different economic and social levels. They are motivated by spiritual and material needs. They come to bring petitions on behalf of their families and friends. They look to Christ as Saviour and Redeemer, as Father and Provider, as one who can satisfy their spiritual and material needs. They make a *panata* (vow) to do something meritorious and sacrificial in return for answered prayers and blessings received. It may be a simple pledge to hear mass on Fridays, or to give money to charity, or to give up vices and live a good Christian life. Whatever it be, the devotees claim that through their *panata* they have a genuine religious experience; they feel the divine power working in their lives.

The Filipino concept of Christ was heavily influenced by the traditional Spanish image which places importance on the suffering and death of Christ. The concept grew out of the oppression and suffering which they experienced under the Moors. The Filipinos also knew suffering and oppression from the hands of the Spaniards. It is, therefore, not surprising that the suffering Christ also has become a predominant figure in their religion and that many Filipinos identify with the Christ of the cross. In a recent article in *Image* Gabriel Casal remarks that "Perhaps the Filipinos recognized in the tortured *Via Dolorosa* of the agonizing Christ much of their silent sufferings under the frequently stifling and abusive rule of the Spaniards."[6] In many towns in Central Luzon flagellation is still practiced.

The cult of the Black Nazarene reinforces this tradition. The novena-prayers used by the devotees hardly mention the resurrection. Consequently an attitude of passive resignation and complacency is fostered among the devotees. They have no vision beyond the satisfaction of their immediate personal needs. Their devotion lacks a social dimension. Jacob complains that it lacks "the hope which longs for true divine life—a longing that ultimately proclaims the victory of the resurrection over death, inhumanity and selfishness."[7]

The same criticism can be said of devotions to other saints, for example, to St. Jude, St. Anthony, the Sacred Heart, the Virgin Mary, and others. In fact, in 1975, the Catholic bishops deplored the lack of social dimension and the tendency of devotion to Mary to become pious individualism. They pointed out that the Magnificat, though it cannot be interpreted in terms of contemporary class struggle, certainly points "to a reversal of the social order in the kingdom of God." It echoes the prophets' condemnation of the wealthy for their injustice, greed and deceit. Their letter concludes thus:

> Our devotion to Mary should never lose sight of the present plight of the vast majority of our Filipino brethren who live lives unworthy of human beings. These poor and oppressed brethren of ours are devotees of Mary too, and they call out to her, their Mother, to ease their sufferings and free them from their chains. Surely her maternal heart goes to them. Her appeal comes to those of us who can help the helpless. Mary is the model of the perfect disciple of the Lord: the disciple who builds up the earthly and temporal city while being a diligent pilgrim towards the heavenly and eternal city, the disciple who works for that justice which sets free the oppressed and for that charity which assists the needy. Devotion to Mary shows itself in works, and the works which are needed in the Philippines today are the works of justice and freedom from oppression. As the Church points out to us, our mission is to be present in the heart of the world proclaiming the Good News to the poor, freedom to the oppressed, and joy to the afflicted (Bishops Conference, 1975).

CHRIST OF THE *PASYON*

As part of the Lenten season celebrations in the Philippines, the life and death of Christ are dramatized and relived through passion plays and readings. The practice is prevalent in the Tagalog region, where the *sinakulo* (passion play) and the *pabasa* (passion reading) have had a long history.

Apart from a purely religious purpose the *sinakulo* was used by the friars during the Spanish regime to make the *Indios,* as the Filipinos were referred to at that time, loyal to the feudalistic church and subservient to the colonial government. A "lowly and meek Christ" was exhibited as a model for everyone to follow. Anyone who refused to obey the church and the colonial government was branded as a "Jew."[8]

However, unintended though it may be, the passion plays and readings became the avenue for the articulation of the values, ideals and even the hopes toward liberation of the lowland Filipinos. In his book *Pasyon and the Revolution* Reynaldo Ileto claims that the Pasyon became "the social epic of the 19th century Tagalogs and probably other lowland groups as well."[9]

Commenting on the *Pasyon Pilapil,* the most popular of the church-approved texts, he argues that its narration of the suffering, death and resurrection of Christ and of the Day of Judgement provided powerful images that "nurtured an undercurrent of millennial beliefs which, in times of economic and political crisis, enabled the peasantry to take action under the leadership of individuals or groups promising deliverance from oppression."[10]

The *pasyon* portrayed Christ as one who was born poor and lowly:[11]

> ... his father
> is just a simple carpenter
> devoid of fame and wealth
> living in poverty
> without property of his own (116:5).

In spite of his humble background, however, he dared to go against the conventions and defy the authorities of his day.

It was unthinkable for a Filipino son to leave his mother. Because of *utang na loob* (debt of gratitude), he was bound to love, respect and support his parents in their old age. But the example of Jesus to leave his mother,

> The longed-for hour
> when I shall serve mankind
> has now arrived.
> Mother, from this day on
> each other we shall not see (78:7)

opened his mind and challenged him to the possibility of separating from his family to pursue noble aims such as joining a movement to free his country from its oppressors.

The followers of Christ were "the poor and the ignorant," the description given by the Spaniards to the Filipino masses:

> poor and lowly people
> without worth on earth
> ignorant people
> without any education.
> These were the ones selected
> by Jesus the beloved master
> to popularize his teachings
> to perform astonishing feats
> here in the universe (49:7-8).

The *pasyon* abounded with similar passages, Ileto notes, "suggesting the potential power" of the poor and the ignorant. Furthermore, Christ was depicted as a troublemaker who advocated civil disobedience:

> Another treacherous act
> of this troublemaker
> is his plot with the people
> not to pay taxes to Caesar,
> such great arrogance! (115:14)

He was a subversive who attracted the poor, the common people, drawing them away from their families and their colonial masters and founded a brotherhood to proclaim a new age for mankind.

Whether the *pasyon* directly encouraged the peasants to rise against the Spanish government is still an open question. It is difficult not to think, however, that Christ, as they encountered him in the *pasyon*, became their model and their hope. As a matter of fact, they identified some of the revolutionary leaders with the Christ figure: Apolinario de la Cruz (1814-1841), Felipe Salvador (1899-1906) and Jose Rizal (1861-1896).[12] The leaders themselves exploited the people's familiarity with the *pasyon* to win sympathy and converts to their cause.

CHRIST OF THE INDIGENOUS RELIGIOUS MOVEMENTS

There are autochthonous "messianic" religious movements that proliferate in the Philippines. They are usually syncretistic. Their beliefs and practices are a mixture of Catholic, Protestant and animistic traditions. Some are esoteric, and they practice faith-healing and spiritism. Their church organizations are patterned after either the Roman Catholic hierarchy or the Protestant structures or a mixture of both.

One such movement is known as the *Iglesia Watawat ny Lahi* (Flag of the Race Church). Founded in 1936, its central tenet is that Jose Rizal, the Philippine national hero, is the saviour of the Filipinos as Jesus was the Saviour of the Jews:

But by treacherous men you were executed
When we, truly slaves, you redeemed;
Jose Rizal, Saviour of the oppressed,
Christ of the Tagalogs, perfect martyr.[13]

Jose Rizal, latinised as *Jove Rex Al* (God King of All), they proclaim, is the reincarnation of Christ. They believe in an anthropomorphic trinity consisting of Jehovah (God the Father), Jesus (God the Son) and Jose Rizal (God the Holy Spirit) — three "J's." They await the second coming of Jose Rizal, who will bring the final deliverance to the Filipinos.

The Watawat and other similar nativistic movements flourish among the impoverished and exploited rural folks. Their religion is sort of a social protest against agrarian injustice and other socio-economic inequalities. They try to do away with imported values and to revive traditional beliefs and practices. They advocate a non-violent nationalism in their fight against poverty, injustice and human exploitation.

Another organization that needs to be mentioned is the *Iglesia Ni Cristo*. It is the largest, the richest, the fastest growing and the most politically influential indigenous church body in the Philippines. It was founded in 1914 by Felix Manalo who claimed to be the "angel from the east" prophesied in Revelation 7:2-3. The doctrine of Christ Manalo taught is similar to Arian Christology: Christ is only a man. Since he pointed to the Father as the true and only God, hence, he himself is not God. Manalo also preached that outside of the Iglesia ni Cristo (Church of Christ) salvation is not possible. Only the members of the Iglesia are saved from God's wrath having been justified by the blood of Christ. Writes one of his ministers:

If this exclusivism is detested by other preachers and professing Christians then they detest our Lord Jesus Christ and God. It is an act of God, His will, that man be gathered together in Christ, and to fulfil this will of God, Christ laid down his law and established his Church, the *Iglesia ni Cristo* (Church of Christ). Anyone then who wants salvation should enter it.[14]

The Iglesia has had its greatest influence among the lower-income and less-educated sector of the society. However, many professionals can now be counted among its ranks. In just a few decades the Iglesia has grown into a national organization noted for its imposing and ornate church buildings and headquarters and its close-knit and well-disciplined members who live simply and honestly and loyal to their church and supreme head, Erano Manalo. Manalo, who took over the leadership of the Iglesia after his father died, exercises absolute spiritual and political authority over its members. The INC claims to have more than three million members world-wide.

The success of the INC has been attributed to, for one, its strong organization and dynamic and aggressive leadership. Another is its reliance solely

on the Bible and the "teachings of Christ" interpreted by its church hierarchy, which goes very well with the Filipino respect for authority. Another
factor in common with other religious movements in the country is its
emphasis on nationalism (e.g., only the dialect is used in its liturgy) and
social justice, fostering a sense of belonging and community among its members.

CONCLUSION

It is apparent from the foregoing survey of popular piety in the Philippines that a great gap exists between what the ordinary church member
believes and practices and what the church and its theologians teach. The
great majority of the Filipino people have yet to understand what Christianity really is much less live up to its demands. Thus, we have a split-level
Christianity. Many of the so-called Christians still live in a world peopled
with spirits, whose permission and advice they often seek before embarking
on any activity. They venerate saints, ascribing to them divine powers,
expecting them to perform miracles and to satisfy their daily need like their
anitos of old. For many, the church is a refuge from the harsh realities of
life. Small wonder the indigenous messianic movements that promise the
advent of a golden age and, more recently, the charismatic movements that
proclaim "Christ is the answer," have such a wide appeal.

To a nation, 70 percent of whose people live in absolute poverty, constantly menaced by hunger and disease, by ignorance and fear, deprived of
education and other basic rights, where the gap between the poor and the
rich is ever widening, who do we say Christ is?

The new breed of Filipino theologians has opted to speak of Christ from
the point of view of liberation theology or theology of struggle: Jesus as
the Messiah proclaims his solidarity with the poor, the outcasts, the powerless, the dregs of the society. His mission, as he himself understood it, is
to liberate the "least of his brethren" from the chains of oppression and
suffering. The incarnation is God's initiative to identify himself with the
poor and oppressed humanity. The crucifixion is his ultimate act of liberating the oppressed by obediently accepting an ignominious death on the
cross. The resurrection is his final victory over evil and death, over the
dehumanizing and oppressive forces in the universe. To have faith in the
incarnate, crucified and resurrected Christ means to be a part of his revolutionary task to liberate man. As Levi Oracion says: "Christian hope does
not engender a passive, non-involved waiting for the breaking in of God's
action in history but fosters a willingness to be drawn into the vortex of
God's liberating activity which seeks solidarity with the poor, the oppressed,
the powerless, and takes up their cause and struggles with them, even unto
death."[15]

This kind of faith is now being lived by some Filipino Christians who
have come to understand who Christ really is and to discover their true

worth and that of their fellow human beings as they experience "captivity" and engage in the struggle for liberation. Through the basic Christian communities and parallel movements in the Protestant churches, the people are being helped to reflect on their situation in the light of their faith. More are being convinced that liberation theology or the theology of struggle as it emerges from the people's life situation, their struggles to transform those structures and situations which oppress and deprive them, is valid in the present Philippine context.

But even as theologies have been criticized as irrelevant because they do not originate from actual realities of life, some have expressed concern that the theology of liberation, purportedly evolving from the grassroots, actually arises out of concern for the suffering and oppressed masses but does not really reflect the beliefs and aspirations of the people. As Bishop Julio Labayen cautions: "We must make sure that the theology we are practicing is not just imposed on the base or just manipulating people to realize somebody's ideas without drawing them out from the people."

NOTES

1. Of an estimated population of fifty-three million, 94% are professing Christians. Of these, 84.1% are Roman Catholics, 6.2% belong to indigenous churches (Aglipayans, Iglesia ni Kristo, etc.), and 3.9% are Protestants. 4.3% of the population are Muslims, .7% are animists, and the rest are Buddhists, Bahais, Hindus, and non-religionists.

2. Jaime Bulatao, *Spirit-level Christianity* (Quezon City: Ateneo University Press, 1966), p. 2.

3. Pigafetta cited in Rosa Tenazas, *Santo Nino of Cebu* (Manila: The Catholic Trade School, 1965), p. 22.

4. John L. Phelan, *The Hispanization of the Philippines* (Madison: University of Wisconsin, 1959), p. viii.

5. *Bathala* is a development of the word *"Bhatara"* (Javanese for "god" or *"Batara"* (Malay term for the Hindu gods, e.g., *Betara Berhama, Betara Bisnu,* and *Betara Indera*). Both terms were a development from the Sanskrit word, *"bhattara"* ("noble Lord, great Lord").

6. Gabriel Casal, "Images of Christ in the Philippines," *Image* 21 (1984): 6, 7.

7. See Leonardo N. Mercado, ed., *Filipino Religious Psychology* (Tacloban City: Divine Word Press, 1972), p. 88.

8. Niacanor G. Tiongson, *Kasaysayan ng Estetika ng Sinakulo at Ibang Dulang Panrelihiyon* (Quezon City: Ateneo de Manila University Press, 1975), p. 195.

9. Reynaldo C. Ileto, *Pasyon and Revolution* (Quezon City: Ateneo de Manila University Press, 1979), p. 18.

10. Ibid., p. 19.

11. Verses quoted from Ileto.

12. Miguel de Unamuno, the Spanish philosopher, referred to Rizal as "the Tagalog Christ" because of his life-giving sacrifice to purify his people's religion.

13. Author's translation from "Jose, Jesus and Jehova," *Tugon* 2 (1982): 16.

14. Randy L. Wier, "Is the Church of Christ Exclusivist?," *Pasugo* 35 (1983): 18.

15. Levi Oracion, "Christology: An Urban Rural Mission Perspective," unpublished paper.

Epilogue

Reconceiving Jesus: Some Continuing Concerns

R. S. SUGIRTHARAJAH

Briefly, then, the following would be some of the christological concerns of Asian Christians as they continue to make sense of their lives and, in that process, make sense of Jesus.

THE ONE AND THE MANY

The first is a practical concern, and not one confronted only by Asian Christians but by Christians all over the world. How does one deal with the proliferation of images of Jesus? The spate of christological profiles, ranging from Jesus as pure consciousness to Jesus as a social activist, causes confusion and bewilderment among ordinary Christians as well as among trained theological practitioners. The temptation under this hermeneutical onslaught is to long for a wholesome, total and fixed portrayal of Jesus. The likelihood is that those who look for such christological comfort will be disappointed. The christological enterprise is an ongoing task. Cultures and contexts are not static entities; they constantly change and throw up warp and woof of political, social and religious strands in an ever-new fabric. As cultures evolve, as new contexts and experiences emerge, as new questions surface, so features and aspects of Jesus will continue to be discovered.

The multiplicity of new images of Jesus is often attributed to and blamed upon the overly enthusiastic response of Asian and Latin American and African theologians. But what is overlooked is that this proliferation of images is not due only to the vigorous and passionate response of Asian Christians and others engaged in contextual christologies, but is due also to the nature of the gospel narratives themselves, which lend themselves to a variety of expositions. It is possible from gospel records, depending on what text one chooses, to construct almost any picture of Jesus one wishes. For instance, a brewer can show Jesus supporting distilleries by citing Luke 7:33-34, or a social worker who wants to plan additional shelters for the homeless and outcasts of society can, from the same gospel, show Jesus as a homeless drifter (Luke 9:57-58).

The hermeneutical task then is to address the issue of a profusion of images of Jesus. The simplest and theologically safest option would be to echo the words of Thomas, "My mouth is utterly unable to say what you are like" (*Logion* 13), and to refuse to add to the existing accumulation of images. Another would be to choose one from among the many renderings and project this as the normative center from which to judge and evaluate other christological constructs. In other words, for the sake of maintaining theological law and order, choose one and help to establish some semblance of orthodoxy. The trouble with this method is that no image that is chosen will commend itself to all. Such a choice would be construed as one group of people trying to impose their own particular understanding of Jesus on others. More specifically, it would not only deny plural historical mediations of the Divine but would also deny that creative interaction of story, myth and legend which holds such promise of human enrichment.

But the most challenging approach would be to accept these multiple images as a gift, scrutinizing their diversity and probing their meaning, purpose and function, and above all, celebrating the gift. Rather, this approach would intensely analyze the current contexts in which the images are embodied. It would address contemporary situations, which constantly provide the raw material for Asians to shape their profiles. From among these accumulating images the task is not to identify those that represent correct christological formulations, as the old church councils used to do, but to look afresh at the contexts that bring forth these sketches of Jesus and to find appropriate ways to transform them.

COMMUNITIES AND COUNTER-COMMUNITY

Second, it has been fashionable among recent biblical scholars to project Jesus as the founder of a movement, a movement designed as a counter-community with its own identity and distinction. Gerd Theissen popularized this notion, and since then some Asian Christian thinkers have adopted the idea to illustrate the new identity of Christians. Such a notion of a counter-cultural community, although it has its value, may, if it is stretched too far, cause tension in Asian communities. On the one hand, it may provide a sense of liberation from conventional constraints imposed on people by some aspects of Asian culture. On the other, it has oppressive connotations, for it tacitly encourages Asian Christians to leave their own cultural heritage and join Christian communities whose lifestyle, organizational structure and worship largely imitate Western patterns. Thus, any christological formulations that tend to alienate people from their own cultural heritage should be discouraged; however, christologies that adduce mutual criticism, mutual learning and mutual well-being, both of humankind and of the ecological order, should be encouraged.

PURE GOSPEL AND PAGAN CULTURE

This leads to a third concern: the knotty problem of syncretism. Put simply, the issue is where to draw the line in using and applying local resources to fashion images of Jesus. The question is not new. It has plagued Christian interpreters ever since the gospel moved out of the village confines of Palestine and entered the urban environs of the Roman world and thence to other parts of the globe. There is no need to rehearse the arguments for and against syncretism. The anti-syncretistic lobby is based on two ideas. One is that there is a pure, unalloyed and unvarnished gospel that can be planted in any situation. The second is the notion that culture, especially the receiving one, is a static, finished product that is usually evil, and waiting to be purified. Both are based on false premises. First, the gospel narratives indicate that the gospel never existed in a pure state and its power is evident only when it is couched in the historical and cultural experience of a people. Second, cultures are constantly in a process of radical renewal and enrichment.

The whole debate about syncretism is a prime example of the hermeneutics of suspicion. When the bogey of syncretism is raised, by whom is it raised? Sometimes by Euro-American interpreters who are uneasy when Asians attempt anything. Sometimes it is raised by the Asian church hierarchy when ordinary people imaginatively mold a rich variety of local symbols to express their understanding of Jesus. Sometimes these ordinary people themselves resist the proposals of Asian theologians to use indigenous components which Asians feel they have left behind. Ultimately it boils down to questions like Who has the power to interpret? Who possesses the truth? What makes the gospel Christian?

What one needs to keep in mind is that Christian faith ultimately triumphed in its own environment, and not only because it had something special to offer or because it had superior answers to ultimate questions. It basically triumphed because of its ability to assimilate, accommodate, reshape and remold the elements that were prevalent in the surrounding culture. Its uniqueness was the new amalgam it created out of borrowings from adjacent cultures. Future understandings of Jesus should be bold enough to incorporate life-enhancing and affirming elements from within the culture that will make the face of Jesus more Asian than hitherto.

MESSAGE AND IMAGE

Fourth, one cannot talk about Jesus without invariably talking at the same time about his followers, or, more precisely, the Christian church. In other words, any Christ-talk is linked to Christian identity, and this identity is mediated through the prevailing patterns of the Christian church. Often within the church the figure of a Jesus who distanced himself from social realities and human problems and spoke condescendingly of the poor as objects of his mercy and compassion has replaced the Jesus who takes the side of the poor and champions their cause. It was this cause that led to his rejection, humiliation and, even more revealingly, to the scars and wounds on his body. Following Jesus inevitably involves a lifestyle that reflects his identification with people, his weakness and vulnerability. The real question then is if the structures and the hierarchies of Asian churches do reflect this vulnerability. No christological construct, however clever, will make any sense unless the church as Christ's body is willing to demonstrate this powerlessness. Any proclamation of Jesus' powerlessness will be met with suspicion unless the Christian church in Asia is willing to exhibit the wounds and scars in her body. The true nature of Jesus will shine forth only when churches in Asia make the marks visible. Like Thomas of old, Asians would like to see the scars before they accept the presence of Jesus in their midst.

WHAT'S IN THE NAME?

At present there is a resurgence of religious fundamentalism, and its virulent impact is very much felt in Asia. This revivalism is not confined to one religion alone. It is prevalent among Hindus, Muslims, Sikhs, Buddhists and, of course, among Christians as well. The whole phenomenon is a curious mixture of religion, politics and culture. It uses the language of faith to legitimize radical reformist programs and appeals to a selective and arbitrarily interpreted past tradition and text to ground its vision of humanity and the future. The result of such revivalism is that the more one faith tradition asserts its distinctiveness, the more it alienates other faith communities. This leads to communal tension and disunity. In this increasingly tension-filled situation what sort of Jesus should the Christian church project? Should one respond to one fundamentalism with another and create even greater tension and disharmony? Or should one look for alternative images of human solidarity that would mediate hope in the midst of communal tensions, religious bigotry and social disruption? Does the power of Jesus' name become less effective if Christians refrain from commending it competitively among the other divers names?

THE QUESTION OF UNIQUENESS—A RE-LOOK

This leads us to the next issue, the question of Christian claims for finality and uniqueness of Jesus. In the light of changed circumstances, hitherto held christological presuppositions have to be rethought. At a time when Asian Christians are involved in vigorous dialogue with people of other religions, consciously trying to be less arrogant in their theological appraisal of other faiths, and earnestly engaged in building up an equitable society in conjunction with peoples of other faiths or none, how do Asian Christians redefine these terms? How and who determines this finality and uniqueness of Jesus? Are these claims made by Jesus or are they made on his behalf by faith communities? How does one perceive the finality of Jesus after historical-critical methods have modified some of the excessive claims made for Jesus in the gospels? In other words, are the assertions made on behalf of Jesus truth claims or the confessional statements of a community? Are they objective claims or the subjective reading of a faith community? How does a person or a text come to generate extraordinary power and influence within a group of people? Is it because communities of faith tend to invest certain persons with authority and aura?

Whatever may have been the usefulness of some theological terms in the past, can Asian Christians go on making claims of uniqueness and finality? Even the recent distinction made by some Christian thinkers between Logos/Word of God as the historical Jesus and Logos/Word of God as the universal bond between humanity and the divine is paternalistic and condescending. Is it not time for Christians to have another look at such basic tenets as the figure of Jesus, the place of scriptural authority, and the function of Christian traditions which were all formulated in Europe of a bygone era? At that time and place they may have looked inoffensive, yet they may look harmful today in a multiple religious and social context. Basically, what Asian Christians need is to look again at the relation between God's self-disclosure in the person and work of Jesus and God's relation toward all human beings. How special is this revelation in comparison to the experiences of Buddha, Mohammed and Confucius? Does the Christian claim to uniqueness limit God's freedom to be present to people in other religious histories?

THE SEARCH FOR THE ACTUAL JESUS

Following from this last concern, the hermeneutical assignment that awaits Asian Christian theologians is to construct a new image of Jesus, one which is faithful to the actual, earthly Jesus. So far, there have been few serious attempts by Asian Christians to produce a scholarly picture of the historical Jesus. It is not as if this quest has had its day. Among North American scholars especially, after a lull and hesitancy, there has been a renewed interest in the question of the historical Jesus.[1] This is made increasingly significant by the increased access to extra-canonical data, new archaeological discoveries and the use of new methods from disciplines such as anthropology and the social sciences. Asians need to take advantage of this and study the past, not for the sake of the past as many of the present questers seem to do, but to glean christological and theological insights that may have significant implications for the Asian context.

Asians inherited images of Jesus which could be broadly classified under two headings: Confessional Christ and Ideological Christ. The first was shaped by the debates of the great ecumenical councils, especially Chalcedon; the second was influenced by the ideological and expansionist needs of the early modern missionary era. Neither of these constructs of Jesus was concerned with retrieving the actual Jesus. The challenge present-day Asian Christians face is to refashion in a fresh way the claim that Christianity would make for Jesus without being unfaithful to his Jewish milieu, and at the same time making accessible the mystery of Jesus to different faith communities without sounding superior. The latter is an important task repeatedly expressed in these pages. But the former is equally imperative because some of the Asian christological constructions border on the anti-Semitic. Historically, Western exegesis contributed significantly to fomenting anti-Jewish feeling. Hermeneutically Asians did not play any direct part in such an exercise, but anti-Semitism was bequeathed to them, and the uncritical use of it is evident in some Asian writers. To look for the historical Jesus and place him, as far as one is able, in his own social, economic and political context is to overcome such pitfalls. Such a placement of Jesus in his cultural ambience will also enable Asian Christians to go beyond the initial, ideal and predominantly dogmatic images.

JESUS: WISDOM TEACHER

One aspect of the actuality of Jesus which is under-exploited by Asian Christian thinkers is that of Jesus as a sage. Jesus as a Wisdom figure may be a means to appropriate him in a religiously pluralistic milieu. The strength of the Wisdom tradition is that it is universal. It belongs to all cultures and finds expression in all lands. Wisdom acknowledges that if Wisdom is spirit, it is not restricted to Israel alone (Wis. 1:17). The potency of the Wisdom tradition is its ability to borrow from other cultures, and Israel's Wisdom is no exception.

One of the fruits of the recent Jesus research is the emergence of Jesus as a sage and the increasing attention being paid to his Wisdom sayings. This provides an opportunity for Asian interpreters to engage in fruitful dialogue with their Euro-American counterparts. Present researchers are not sure whether to place Jesus within the context of conventional Jewish Wisdom of his day or to depict him within the hellenistic culture and portray him as a Cynic teacher.[2] Irrespective of these questions, what emerges is the figure of a sage who uses material not only from rural Palestine but also from the wider Hellenistic culture and who offers a critique of the oppressive values of those institutions and issues that matter most to Asians—family, honor, purity, marriage and poverty.

The undue concentration on the distinctive features of Jesus' teaching has not only tended to obscure the aphoristic elements in his sayings but has also led to a low view of other cultures and faiths. Bracketing Jesus with other sages does not minimize his importance. Rather, it points to the creative possibilities of the universally held elements in the teachings of Jesus. The common elements should provide a starting point to engage in dialogue with people of other faiths, rather than the distinctive features which have been used to sustain the traditional claim to a superior knowledge of the truth. In the new figure of Jesus as a sage, Asian Christians may discover a person who helps them to find a way to respond to religious pluralism and the greater problems of human injustice. Jesus as sage is open and less imperialistic than some alternative portraits, and at the same time committed to the uplifting of the poor, women, children and the dispossessed.

A HERMENEUTICAL CONUNDRUM

Finally, I would like to end with an exegetical poser. I invite you to look at the Caesarea Philippi incident again. Not the one recorded in Mark's gospel but the one found in the Gospel of Thomas, the apostle of Asia. As in Mark's gospel, Jesus conducts an in-house survey among his disciples, but the wording of his question is different—"Compare me to something and tell me what I am like." The disciples' responses are also different from those of the synoptic accounts. Simon Peter answers, "You are like a just angel." Matthew responds, "You are like a wise philosopher." Thomas' answer is "Teacher, my mouth is utterly unable to say what you are like," to which Jesus answers, "I am not your teacher," and accuses him of being intoxicated. Jesus takes Thomas aside, and the text says that Jesus then spoke three sayings to him. When Thomas joins the others, naturally they are keen to know what Jesus has told him and not told them. Thomas says to them, "If I tell you one of the sayings that he spoke to me, you will pick up rocks and stone me, and fire will come from the rocks and devour you."

The question then is what did Jesus say to the apostle of Asia that would cause dissension and disruption among his own friends? Perhaps these Asian attempts to discern the lineaments of Jesus begin to provide us with an answer.

NOTES

1. See Marcus J. Borg, "Portraits of Jesus in Contemporary North American Scholarship," *Harvard Theological Review* 84:1 (1991):1-22; "A Renaissance in Jesus Studies," *Theology Today* 45 (1988):280-92. For implications of such research for third-world theologies, see R. S. Sugirtharajah, "What do Men Say Remains of Me?: Current Jesus Research and Third World Christologies," *Asia Journal of Theology* 5 (1991):331-37.

2. See Burton L. Mack, *A Myth of Innocence: Mark and Christian Origins* (Philadelphia: Fortress Press, 1988); F. G. Downing, *Jesus and the Threat of Freedom* (London: SCM Press, 1987) and *Christ and the Cynics: Jesus and Other Radical Preachers in the First-Century Tradition* (Sheffield: JSOT Press, 1988).

Contributors

Michael Amaladoss, an Indian Jesuit, is currently a member of the Jesuit General Council in Rome. Previously he has taught systematic theology at Vidyajyoti Institute of Religious Studies, Delhi, India. He has published several articles on theology of mission, Indian theology and hermeneutics. He is the author of *Mission Today: Reflections From an Ignatian Perspective* (Rome: Centrum Ignatianum Spiritualitatis, 1988) and *Making All Things New: Dialogue, Pluralism and Evangelization in Asia* (Maryknoll, N.Y.: Orbis Books, 1990).

Byung Mu Ahn, Korean New Testament professor and activist, is a pioneer of Korean *minjung* theology. He has published several articles explicating the nuances of *minjung* theology and biblical interpretation in international journals. His primary and ground-breaking expositions have been in reading St. Mark's gospel from the perspective of *minjung*. His rereading of *ochlos* (crowd) from the perspective of *minjung* has been widely referred to in various theological writings.

Chung Hyun Kyung is Korean and teaches systematic theology at Ewha University, Seoul. She is one of the second generation of *minjung* theologians. She attracted the attention of the ecumenical world at the 1991 Canberra Assembly of the World Council of Churches with her bold and innovative rereading of the assembly theme. She is actively involved with many women's groups and has written extensively about their issues. Her recent publications include *Struggle To Be the Sun Again: Introducing Asian Women's Theology* (Maryknoll, N.Y.: Orbis Books, 1990; and London: SCM Press, 1992). Her autobiographical-theological piece, "Following Naked Dancing and Long Dreaming," in *Inheriting Our Mother's Gardens: Feminist Theology in Third World Perspective*, ed. Letty M. Russell, et al. (Philadelphia: Westminster Press, 1988) is one of the bravest and most imaginative of theological writings by an Asian woman.

Virginia Fabella is from the Philippines and belongs to the order of Maryknoll Sisters. She is the Asia Co-ordinator for the Ecumenical Association of Third World Theologians (EATWOT). Besides editing a number of their collections of conference papers, she herself has contributed significantly toward Asian ways of doing theology. *In God's Image,* a quarterly published by the Women's Resource Centre for Culture and Theology, Hong Kong, carries many of her articles.

Jung Young Lee comes from Korea and is currently chairperson of the

Department of Religious Studies at the University of North Dakota. He sees one of his prime tasks as interpreting Eastern thinking to the West. Two of his books, *The Theology of Change* (Maryknoll, N.Y.: Orbis Books, 1979) and a volume he edited with José Míguez Bonino, et al., *An Emerging Theology in Western Perspective: Commentary on Korean Minjung Theology* (Mystic, Conn.: Twenty-Third Publications, 1988), are demonstrations of his efforts.

Sebastian Kappen is closely associated with activist groups throughout India and is at present deeply involved in ecological issues. His significant contributions toward Christianity in relation to Marxism and to social praxis through his publications, lectures and personal involvement have influenced many. Currently he is working on a theology of liberation from the perspective of Indian subaltern religious traditions. Among his many books are: *Jesus and Freedom* (Maryknoll, N.Y.: Orbis Books, 1977), *Marxism and Atheism, Liberation Theology and Marxism* (Puntamba, India: Asha Kendra, 1986). Kappen belongs to the Society of Jesus.

Kosuke Koyama is Professor of Ecumenics and World Christianity at Union Theological Seminary, New York. His experience of working as a Japanese missionary in Thailand prompted in him the need to work out a contextual theology that would avoid using abstract ideas and speak to the everyday experience of the people with whom he was working, with their stomach aches and leaking roofs. The result was the highly entertaining yet eminently profound *Waterbuffalo Theology*. Since then he has published a number of articles and books on Asian Christian theology. Among his most recent books is *Mount Fuji and Mount Sinai*, an absorbing investigation of the relationship between East and West, leading to a theology of the cross against the menace of the nuclear threat.

Alexander Malik is Bishop of the Lahore Diocese of the Church of Pakistan and is considered one of the eminent leaders of his community.

Ovey N. Mohammed, a Jesuit, is the Vice-President of Regis College of the Toronto School of Theology. His field of research and publication is theology of religions and interfaith hermeneutics. Two recent examples of his work are "Ignatian Spirituality and the *Bhagavad Gita,*" *Thought* (December 1987) and "Hinduism and Spirituality," *The Way Supplement* (Summer 1990).

Salvador T. Martinez is Secretary for Theological Concerns for the Christian Conference of Asia. Formerly he was Dean of the College of Arts and Sciences, Silliman University, Dumaguete City, Philippines. His major theological interests are in the areas of Asian popular religiosity and Filipino theologies.

Aloysius Pieris, a Sri Lankan Jesuit, is Director of the Tulana Research Center, Kelaniya, Sri Lanka, which promotes Christian-Buddhist dialogue. He was the first among the Asian theologians to argue that Asian Christians should not only address the double reality of Asia—poverty and religious pluralism—but should respond to them together. This he describes as baptismal immersion in the Jordan of Asian religiosity and the cross of Asian poverty. He has written a number of articles explicating his thesis. His books include *An Asian Theology of Liberation* (Maryknoll, N.Y.: Orbis Books, 1988; and Edinburgh: T & T Clark, 1988) and *Love Meets Wisdom: A Christian Experience of Buddhism* (Maryknoll, N.Y.: Orbis Books, 1988).

Michael Rodrigo was murdered by gunmen on October 11, 1987, when he was celebrating Mass at Suba Seth Gedera—a grassroots Christian-Buddhist dialogue center he started. His work with the villagers had made him unpopular among the rich and privileged, and he and his center were often severely threatened. The question Michael Rodrigo and his co-workers agonized over was whether to stay on or to leave the people at the mercy of the exploiters. It was at this Mass, when Michael and his co-workers, weighing the pros and cons, eventually decided to carry on with their work, that he was felled by an assassin's bullet. In his death the inarticulate and the powerless lost an effective voice. For a selection of his writings, see *Logos* 27, 3 and 4 (1988), a journal published by the Center for Society and Religion, 281 Dean's Road, Colombo 10, Sri Lanka.

Stanley Samartha was the first Director of the Dialogue Programme of the World Council of Churches, Geneva. He is currently Visiting Professor at the United Theological College, Bangalore, India. He was influential in helping ecumenical circles to rethink Christian attitudes toward people of other faiths. He has published extensively on interfaith issues. The title of his latest book is *One Christ—Many Religions: Toward a Revised Christology* (Maryknoll, N.Y.: Orbis Books, 1991).

Choan-Seng Song is Professor of Theology and Asian Cultures at the Pacific School of Religion, Berkeley, California. He has been a pioneer in advocating Asian ways of doing theology using Asian resources and insights. His booklet *The Tears of Lady Meng: A Parable of People's Political Theology* (Geneva: WCC, 1981) is required reading for those who are interested in such hermeneutical enterprises. His Orbis publications include *The Compassionate God* (1982), *Tell Us Our Names* (1984) and *Third-Eye Theology* (1979). His most recent book is *Jesus, the Crucified People* (New York: Crossroad Publishing Company, 1990). He is currently Dean of the Programme for the Theology and Cultures in Asia (PTCA)—a program set up to encourage Asians to use their histories, cultures, religions, social and political struggles as the data for doing theology.

Seiichi Yagi is Professor of Philosophical and Religious Thought at the University of Yokohama, Japan. He is also a New Testament scholar. In his teachings and publications he combines his primary interest in Christian-Buddhist dialogue with biblical theology. He has published extensively in Japanese on Christian-Buddhist dialogue issues. His open approach to Buddhism has made him popular among the adherents of that tradition.